SECURITY INTERESTS UNDER THE CAPE TOWN CONVENTION ON INTERNATIONAL INTERESTS IN MOBILE EQUIPMENT

This book provides an extensive analytical examination of the Cape Town Convention and its Protocols. The Convention aims to facilitate asset-based financing and leasing of aircraft, railway and space objects by establishing a uniform legal regime for the creation and protection of security and related interests in these types of equipment. The book provides a detailed treatment of issues arising from the creation of security and other international interests under the Convention, from the need to ensure their priority among competing interests to the enforcement of remedies in the case of the debtor's default or insolvency. Security interests in aircraft, railway and space objects are among the most frequently invoked mechanisms used to ensure repayment of the debt. It is their significance, effectiveness and frequency of use that explains this work's focus and scope.

Security Interests under the Cape Town Convention on International Interests in Mobile Equipment

Sanam Saidova

•HART•

OXFORD • LONDON • NEW YORK • NEW DELHI • SYDNEY

HART PUBLISHING
Bloomsbury Publishing Plc
Kemp House, Chawley Park, Cumnor Hill, Oxford, OX2 9PH, UK

HART PUBLISHING, the Hart/Stag logo, BLOOMSBURY and the Diana logo are trademarks of Bloomsbury Publishing Plc
First published in Great Britain 2018

First published in hardback, 2018
Paperback edition, 2020

A catalogue record for this book is available from the British Library.

Library of Congress Cataloging-in-Publication Data

Names: Saidova, Sanam, author.

Title: Security interests under the Cape Town Convention on International Interests in Mobile Equipment / Sanam Saidova.

Description: Oxford [UK] ; Hartland, Oregon : Hart Publishing, an imprint of Bloomsbury, 2018. | Includes bibliographical references and index.

Identifiers: LCCN 2018005590 (print) | LCCN 2018005871 (ebook) | ISBN 9781782258209 (Epub) | ISBN 9781782258216 (hardback)

Subjects: LCSH: Convention on International Interests in Mobile Equipment (2001 November 16) | Convention on International Interests in Mobile Equipment (2001 November 16). Protocols, etc. (2001 November 16) | Security (Law) | Contracts (International law) | Aeronautics—Equipment and supplies—Purchasing. | Aeronautics, Commercial—Finance—Law and legislation. | Convention on International Interests in Mobile Equipment (2001 November 16). Protocols, etc. (2007 February 23)

Classification: LCC K4093.32001 (ebook) | LCC K4093.32001 .S25 2018 (print) | DDC 346.07/4—dc23

LC record available at https://lccn.loc.gov/2018005590

ISBN: HB: 978-1-78225-821-6
PB: 978-1-50994-364-7
ePDF: 978-1-78225-819-3
ePub: 978-1-78225-820-9

Typeset by Compuscript Ltd, Shannon

To Djakhongir, Malika, Amina and my parents

Preface

The Cape Town Convention on International Interests in Mobile Equipment is a major development in the field of international commercial law. Its aim is to provide the uniform legal regime for the creation, protection and enforcement of interests of secured creditors, conditional sellers and lessors in aircraft objects, railway rolling stock and space assets. The Convention sets an unprecedented example of innovative treaty-making. It is a framework document, providing general rules on the creation, priority, registration and enforcement of the interests governed by it. It is supported by the equipment-specific Protocols, which can modify the Convention's provisions. The drafting of the Convention and its Protocols was also special in that it involved extensive collaboration of representatives of different organisations and interest groups, including legal scholars from various jurisdictions, legal and industry practitioners. This approach helped ensure that the Convention and its Protocols reflected the needs of the relevant industries and gained their support. The Convention is unique in creating a novel legal concept of an 'international interest'. Another creation of the Convention is a fully electronic asset-based International Registry, in which interests held in the objects governed by the Convention can be registered. The interests governed by the Convention are protected by an elaborate set of remedial rules exercisable in the case of the debtor's default or insolvency. This book assesses the effectiveness of the Convention's regime and tests whether it can help facilitate financing and leasing of aircraft, railway rolling stock and space assets. The strengths and weaknesses of its various provisions are evaluated by drawing on the experience of some major legal systems.

This book is a result of several years of research conducted in the School of Law, University of Nottingham. During that period, I have benefited from the help and comments of many people. I owe a debt of gratitude to Dr Sandra Frisby and Professors Michael Bridge, Djakhongir Saidov, Irit Mevorach, Howard Bennett and Sarah Dromgoole for reading and commenting on draft chapters of this book. I would also like to thank Hart Publishing for supporting this project. Finally, I am grateful to my family for their patience, support and encouragement.

The book is based on the materials that were available to me as at 31 October 2017.

Sanam Saidova
11 April 2018

Contents

List of Abbreviations

ASU	Aircraft Sector Understanding
AWG	Aircraft Working Group
CTC	Cape Town Convention
D	debtor/lessee
DEP	direct entry point
DPEU	direct point entity user
HS	Harmonised System
IATA	International Air Transport Association
ICAO	International Civil Aviation Organization
IDERA	de-registration and export request authorisation
IR	International Registry
L	manufacturer/lessor
MAC	mining, agriculture and construction
MSN	manufacturer's serial number
NCRI	non-consensual right or interest
OC	Official Commentary
OECD	Organisation for Economic Co-operation and Development
OTIF	Intergovernmental Organisation for International Carriage by Rail
PERI	pre-existing right or interest
PKI	public key infrastructure
PMSI	purchase money security interest
PU	professional user
PUE	professional user entity
RoT	Retention of title
RU	registry user
RUE	registry user entity
RWG	Restricted Working Group
SC	secured creditor
TT&C	telemetry, tracking and command
TU	transacting user
TUE	transacting user entity
UCC	Uniform Commercial Code
UNIDROIT	International Institute for the Unification of Private Law
URVIS	Unique Rail Vehicle Identification System

1

The Cape Town Convention and the Concept of the International Interest

I. INTRODUCTION

A. The Need for Credit

CREDIT HAS BEEN described as the oil of a market economy,[1] something on which an enterprise's lifecycle depends.[2] Regardless of whether the enterprise in question is a small business or a large aircraft manufacturer, it will need to invest funds in hiring staff, renting premises, acquiring equipment and other costs of running the business before receiving any benefits of the trade. To make ends meet between the outlay of funds and the receipt of profit, the enterprise will often need to rely on the creditor to provide funding. However, the debtor's financial circumstances may change, and even highly reputed enterprises may be struck by insolvency.

When the debtor is faced with financial difficulties, the creditor may learn that the assets of the troubled enterprise are not sufficient to satisfy the claims of its creditors. The debtor's employees may demand their wages, rent for the premises and the equipment may need to be paid, the debtor's trade creditors may demand payment for materials supplied, and some of the creditors may have even obtained a court order for the repayment. The prospects of repayment can be even bleaker if some of the debtor's key assets have been moved and are now in a different country under a different legal system. In some cases, the circumstances may have changed so much that the property is no longer even located on Earth at all. For instance, a creditor financing the construction of a satellite, may learn that

[1] U Drobnig, 'Secured Credit in International Insolvency Proceedings' (1998) 33 *Tex Int'l LJ* 53, 54.

[2] E McKendrick (ed), *Goode on Commercial Law*, 5th edn (London, Penguin Books 2016) 623–24.

the object will be difficult if not impossible to seize on the debtor's default or insolvency once it has been successfully launched into outer space.[3]

How is a creditor to ensure that it can obtain the repayment of the borrowed funds and the agreed interest? According to a principle of insolvency law well known to many legal systems, the debtor's assets should be distributed between the creditors on an equal or a *pari passu* basis.[4] In effect, the creditors should share the assets of the insolvent debtor in proportion to their pre-insolvency entitlements.[5] If the value of the debtor's assets is less than that of its liabilities, some creditors may receive less than expected or nothing at all.

Security interests are taken by the creditors precisely to avoid the consequences of the *pari passu* principle.[6] By taking a security interest in the debtor's property, a secured creditor can ensure that in the case of the debtor's default or insolvency, it can apply this property to the discharge of the debt prior to the distribution of the remaining assets between the debtor's unsecured and junior secured creditors.[7] Effectively, the insolvent debtor's estate available for equal distribution between its creditors is said to be comprised of whatever remains after the secured creditors have enforced their claims.[8] Another reason for taking a security interest is to ensure that the secured obligation is performed. In many cases, the value of the object used as a security or 'collateral' for the performance of an obligation is significantly larger than the amount of the debt.[9] Because a secured creditor can enforce its security on the debtor's default, the debtor may prefer to repay the debt rather than lose the collateral.[10] Finally, from the debtor's perspective,

[3] S Davis, 'Unifying the Final Frontier: Space Industry Financing Reform' (2001) 106 *Com LJ* 455, 459; P Larsen and J Heilbock, 'UNIDROIT Project on Security Interests: How the Project Affects Space Objects' (1998–99) 64 *J Air L Com* 703.

[4] For an explanation of the *pari passu* principle, see R Calnan, *Proprietary Rights and Insolvency*, 2nd edn (Oxford, OUP 2016) Part 1; D Cunningham and T Werlen, 'Cross-Border Insolvencies in Search of a Global Remedy' (1996) 15 *Int'l Fin LR* 51, 52. For the manifestation of the *pari passu* principle under English law, see s 107 of the Insolvency Act 1986, r 4.218 of the Insolvency Rules 1986.

[5] G McCormack, *Secured Credit under English and American Law* (Cambridge, CUP 2004) 11.

[6] McKendrick (n 2) 623–24.

[7] This principle is not without exceptions. For a brief overview of various legal systems allowing preferential creditors priority over secured creditors, see P Wood, *The Law and Practice of International Finance Series, Volume 2: Comparative Law of Security Interests and Title Finance*, 2nd edn *(London, Sweet & Maxwell 2007)* 231–33.

[8] H Beale, M Bridge, L Gullifer and E Lomnicka, *The Law of Security and Title-Based Financing*, 2nd edn (Oxford, OUP 2012) 7.

[9] See L Gullifer (ed), *Goode on Legal Problems of Credit and Security*, 5th edn (London, Sweet & Maxwell 2013) 1–2.

[10] As, for instance, was the case in *In re Panama, New Zealand and Australian Royal Mail Company* (1869–70) LR 5 Ch App 318, 319, where the company was able to grant its undertaking worth more than £600,000 as a security for two loans totalling £150,000.

an ability to grant a security interest in an object held by the debtor may present the possibility of obtaining finance which would otherwise be unavailable to it or only able to be procured at a great price.[11]

Performance of an obligation can be also secured by utilising various forms of transactions involving the retention or reservation of the creditor's interest in the object until certain conditions are satisfied. These transactions can be structured in many ways. A conditional sale contract, whereby the seller transfers possession of the goods to the buyer but retains title in them until the purchase price is paid, is one example. Should the buyer default, the seller can exercise its rights as the owner. This way, the seller's retained title serves the same function as a security interest.[12] A lease, involving the retention of title and transfer of possession of the object in return for the rentals, is another example. A lease can take the form of an 'operating' lease, whereby the goods are hired out to different lessees for short periods of time and a 'finance' lease, whereby the lessor hires the object out for the duration of its economic life and receives by way of the rentals its expenses in acquiring the object and the profit. Since the lessee under the finance lease enjoys the possession and use of the object for the duration of its useful life, the lessor's retained title performs the same function as that of the security interest, in that it ensures that the lessee's obligations under the lease are fulfilled.[13] Due to this functional similarity, some jurisdictions treat these retention of title (RoT) devices as forms of security interests and others, while refusing to recognise them as such, often refer to them as *quasi* security interests.[14]

Security interests can be *real*, that is proprietary, or *personal*, whereby the performance of the debtor's obligation is supported by the personal undertaking of the debtor itself or, more frequently, by a third party. The latter can take the form of a suretyship guarantee, a demand guarantee or a grant of a negotiable instrument as a security of performance.[15] Security interests can be taken over tangible and intangible objects, and existing and future assets, and take possessory (that is, requiring the transfer of possession of the collateral to the creditor) forms or non-possessory forms which do not depend on the transfer of possession. This book focuses on *real* security interests in tangible and existing objects held by the debtor, such as aircraft, railway and space objects.

[11] Gullifer (n 9) 2.

[12] Beale, Bridge, Gullifer and Lomnicka (n 8) 249.

[13] See *Celestial Aviation Trading 71 Ltd v Paramount Airways Private Ltd* [2010] EWHC 185 (Comm), [2010] 1 CLC 165; *On Demand Information plc v Michael Gerson (Finance) Ltd plc* [2000] 4 All ER 734, 737.

[14] Gullifer (n 9) 3–4.

[15] *Ibid* 5.

B. A Brief Introduction to the Cape Town Convention

This book focuses on the security interests that can be created as international interests under the UNIDROIT Convention on International Interests in Mobile Equipment ('the Convention'). The Convention provides a uniform legal regime for the creation, perfection, priority and enforcement of the international interests in objects such as aircraft, railway and space objects. The financing and leasing of these types of equipment, which can be accomplished by means of a secured loan, a conditional sale or a lease, can be a risky and highly unstable investment. Their nature is such that they are likely to constantly physically cross national borders, rendering a creditor's interest in them unprotected.

The advantages of a validly created and perfected security interest granted to a secured creditor in one legal system can be subverted if it has to be enforced in a different legal system. Among the problems which the secured creditor may encounter are, for instance, varied attitudes towards security interests in different jurisdictions. Some jurisdictions are supportive of secured creditors' rights, in that they recognise non-possessory security interests created with little formality and protected with readily available and adequate remedies that, in many cases, can be exercised extra-judicially; however, other jurisdictions can be more restrictive.[16] In addition, although some jurisdictions recognise foreign security interests, provided that they are similar to the ones existent in the country of enforcement and in line with that country's formal requirements, some jurisdictions do not recognise foreign security interests.[17] Some forms of security interests may be unfamiliar to a jurisdiction where a secured creditor hopes to enforce it. The concern of the secured creditor in this case will be that its security will not receive the same treatment as it would have received in the country of origin.[18] Furthermore, the high mobility of aircraft and railway objects and the fact that space assets, such as satellites, are often intended to be launched into space, mean that the conflict of laws rules pointing to, for example, the law of the object's location (*lex rei sitae)* to govern the interests of a secured creditor, conditional seller and lessor in these objects are not well suited. Reliance on the conflict of laws rules also means

[16] Wood (n 7) 18–19.

[17] See G Ferrarini, 'Foreign Law Mortgages, Hypotheques and Charges in Italy' (1991) 6 *JIBL* 191, 192; H Waasgren, 'Rights of Financiers in Aircraft: a Finnish Perspective on the 2001 Cape Town Instruments' (2004) 9 *Unif LR* 557, 562.

[18] R Goode, 'Security in Cross-Border Transactions' (1998) 33 *Tex Int'l LJ* 47, 48; G Kajtar, 'Hungary—Foreign Investment: Security for the Interests of Foreign Lenders' (1993) 8 *JIBL* 162, 163.

dependence on different jurisdictions with varying attitudes to security and RoT transactions.[19]

The lack of the international uniform substantive rules governing creditors' rights in such types of equipment as aircraft, railway and space objects has in the past generated uncertainty and affected the availability of financing, which is particularly significant given the high cost of these objects.[20] The main purpose of the Convention, which is supported by three equipment-specific Protocols, is to provide the much needed uniform legal regime for the creation, registration and protection of the interests of a secured creditor, conditional seller and lessor held in these types of objects.[21] One of the Convention's unique features is that it provides for the creation of an autonomous international interest in these types of equipment, which does not depend on any domestic law.[22] Another important creation of the Convention is an electronic asset-based International Registry (IR), where creditors can register their interests held in aircraft objects.[23] The international registries for the registration of interests in railway objects and space assets are expected to follow in due course. The creditor's international interest is supported by an elaborate system of remedies exercisable in the case of the debtor's default or insolvency.[24] These features of the Convention and the Protocols are aimed at promoting predictability and transparency in the financing of mobile equipment, which should reduce the risks and costs of borrowing to the benefit of all stakeholders.

The Convention and Aircraft Protocol were concluded at the Diplomatic Conference held in Cape Town in October–November 2001 under the auspices of the International Institute for the Unification of Private Law (UNIDROIT)[25] and the International Civil Aviation Organization (ICAO).[26] The Cape Town Convention (CTC or 'the Convention') and Aircraft Protocol came into force on 1 March 2006, when the number of ratifications

[19] R Goode, *Official Commentary to the Convention on International Interests in Mobile Equipment and Protocol Thereto on Matters Specific to Aircraft Equipment*, 3rd edn (Rome, UNIDROIT 2013) 14–15; G Mauri and B Itterbeek, 'The Cape Town Convention on International Interests in Mobile Equipment and its Protocol on Matters Specific To Aircraft Equipment: A Belgian Perspective' (2004) 9 *Unif L Rev* 547, 550.

[20] R Goode, 'International Interests in Mobile Equipment: A Transnational Juridical Concept' (2003) 15 *Bond L Rev* 9, 10.

[21] See the Convention's Preamble.

[22] Art 2 CTC. See L Weber and S Espinola, 'The Development of a New Convention Relating to International Interests in Mobile Equipment, in Particular Aircraft Equipment: a Joint ICAO-UNIDROIT Project' (1999) 4 *Unif L Rev* 463, 463–65.

[23] Art 16 CTC. R Cuming, 'Considerations in the Design of an International Registry for Interests in Mobile Equipment' (1999) 4 *Unif L Rev* 275, 276–79.

[24] See chapter three.

[25] For the history and purposes of the UNIDROIT, see http://www.unidroit.org/about-unidroit/overview.

[26] See generally www.icao.int/about-icao/Pages/default.aspx.

reached eight as required by the Protocol.[27] The Rail Protocol was concluded in Luxembourg on 23 February 2007[28] and the Space Protocol was adopted at a Diplomatic Conference in Berlin in March 2012.[29] The Luxembourg and the Space Protocols are not yet in force.[30] The Convention establishes a set of rules to be utilised if it is considered useful and feasible to extend its application to the objects not currently covered by it, provided that such objects are uniquely identifiable.[31] Presently, extensive work is being undertaken by UNIDROIT on the development of a fourth Protocol, relating to agricultural, construction and mining equipment ('the MAC Protocol').[32]

The idea that a uniform legal regime for the creation and protection of security interests in mobile equipment should be established was first advocated by Mr TB Smith QC, a Canadian member of the Governing Council of UNIDROIT presiding over the Diplomatic Conference in Ottawa in 1988.[33] The desirability and feasibility of the project was further confirmed by the positive responses to a questionnaire prepared by Professor Ronald Cuming. Great care was taken not only in the drafting of the substantive provisions of the Convention and the Protocols, but also in ensuring that all interest groups were involved in their development. The exploratory working groups and several specialist groups set up to examine specific issues (such as the Aircraft Working Group (AWG), the Registration Working Group, the Insolvency Working Group and the Public International Working Group) consisted of a mixture of academic and practising lawyers from different legal systems, representatives of the relevant business organisations and, in the case of the Aircraft Protocol, participants from organisations such as ICAO and the International Air Transport Association (IATA).[34] The consistent and close cooperation of various interest groups in preparing the Convention and the Protocols was vital in ensuring that the resulting documents reflected the needs and gained support of the industries concerned.

[27] Art XXVIII of the Aircraft Protocol.

[28] See generally R Goode, *Official Commentary to the Convention on International Interests in Mobile Equipment and Luxembourg Protocol Thereto on Matters Specific to Railway Rolling Stock*, (Rome, UNIDROIT 2008).

[29] See generally R Goode, *Official Commentary to the Convention on International Interests in Mobile Equipment and Protocol Thereto on Matters Specific to Space Assets* (Rome, UNIDROIT 2013).

[30] Art XXIII of the Luxembourg Protocol and Art XXXVIII of the Space Protocol, drafted in similar terms, provide that the Protocols enter into force on the first day of the month following the expiration of three months after the date of the deposit of the forth (in the case of the Luxembourg Protocol) and the tenth (in the case of the Space Protocol) instrument of ratification, acceptance, approval or accession. Both Protocols provide that they will not enter into force until the date when the IR in relation to these objects is fully operational.

[31] Art 51 CTC.

[32] See generally http://www.unidroit.org/work-in-progress/mac-protocol.

[33] R Goode, H Kronke and E McKendrick, *Transnational Commercial Law: Text, Cases and Materials*, 2nd edn (Oxford, OUP 2015) 394.

[34] See generally www.iata.org/about/pages/index.aspx.

C. Main Features of the Convention

i. Applicability

The Convention will apply if the following requirements are met. First, the parties must conclude a security agreement, a title reservation or a leasing agreement.[35] Secondly, the agreement must relate to uniquely identifiable mobile equipment, currently comprising: (a) an airframe, an aircraft engine or a helicopter; (b) railway rolling stock; and (c) space assets.[36] Once the new MAC Protocol is adopted, the types of agricultural, construction and mining equipment, covered by the Protocol will be added to this list.[37] Thirdly, the agreement must be constituted in accordance with the CTC's formal requirements. The agreement must: be in writing; relate to an object of which the chargor, conditional seller or lessor has power to dispose; enable the object to be identified in conformity with the Protocol; and, in the case of the security agreement, enable the secured obligations to be determined, but without the need to indicate the sum secured.[38]

Of these four formalities, the requirement of power to dispose may give rise to some important questions, which will be considered later in this book. The Convention does not explain the circumstances in which the power to dispose arises. It seems clear that the power to dispose includes the right to dispose, that is, where the chargor, conditional seller and lessor are the owners of the object or have the owner's authority to deal with it. But the power to dispose is wider than the right to dispose and covers other situations where a non-owner chargor, conditional seller or lessor can deal with the object in a way that will bind the true owner, even if the latter did not authorise the disposition.[39] The fact that the Convention does not explain the meaning of the requirement of power to dispose is regrettable because it brings uncertainty in relation to this significant issue. Unless this requirement is met, a valid international interest cannot be created. Another difficulty with this requirement is that it can be wrongly applied in determining priority disputes among competing interests. This book will examine the Convention's rules on priority and registration to help identify the circumstances in which the power to dispose may arise.

Finally, the Convention will only apply if its requirement relating to the connecting factor, namely the location of the debtor, is met.[40] The debtor

[35] Art 2(2) CTC.

[36] Art 2(3) CTC.

[37] Art 51 CTC. For a draft MAC Protocol, see http://www.unidroit.org/english/documents/2017/study72k/cge01/s-72k-cge01-02corr-e.pdf (last visited December 2017).

[38] Art 7 CTC.

[39] R Goode, 'The International Interest as an Autonomous Property Interest' (2004) 1 *ERPL* 18, 24.

[40] Art 3(1) CTC.

must be situated in a Contracting State at the time of the conclusion of the international interest agreement. There are several alternative ways to determine whether the debtor is located in a Contracting State.[41] If the debtor is incorporated or formed, or has a registered office or statutory seat, a centre of administration, a place of business or habitual residence in a Contracting State where it is located at the time of the conclusion of the agreement, the requirement of the connecting factor is satisfied.[42] The Aircraft Protocol provides the alternative connecting factor in relation to a helicopter or an airframe pertaining to an aircraft.[43] In the case of these objects, the Convention will also apply if the helicopter or the airframe is registered in a national aircraft register of the State of Registry. The State of Registry means the State of the national register in which the aircraft is registered and the State of location of the common mark registering authority which maintains the aircraft register in accordance with Article 77 of the Convention on International Civil Aviation 1944.[44] The alternative connecting factor cannot apply to the aircraft engines because there are, generally, no national registries in relation to these objects.

ii. The Two-Instrument Approach

In the early stages of the project, it was expected that the Convention would consist of a single document relating to all types of mobile equipment which it intended to cover. However, it soon became clear that the traditional route of international treaty making might not be the best one for the CTC.[45] The AWG was well ahead of the rail and space groups. If the Convention's drafters had been required to wait until all the equipment groups completed their work, the project's progress would have been considerably delayed. To resolve the matter, the AWG and IATA proposed a novel solution, under which the Convention would only govern the issues relating equally to all types of equipment. It would then be complemented by the Protocols, which would deal with issues specific to a particular type of equipment. The novelty of this proposal was the idea that the Protocol would prevail over the

[41] The main purpose of providing various alternative ways of establishing the connecting factor is to widen the applicability of the Convention.

[42] Art 4 CTC.

[43] Art IV(1) of the Aircraft Protocol.

[44] Art I (h), (p) of the Aircraft Protocol. The Convention on International Civil Aviation ('the Chicago Convention') is a public law treaty designed to promote safe and secure flights, whereas the CTC is a private law treaty and its main objective is to facilitate financing and leasing of aircraft, railway and space objects. The CTC should not be, generally, interpreted by reference to the Chicago Convention.

[45] R Goode, 'The Preliminary Draft UNIDROIT Convention on International Interests in Mobile Equipment' (1999) 4 *Unif L Rev* 265, 269–71.

Convention in the case of an inconsistency between the two instruments.[46] Another alternative was to have a set of stand-alone Conventions relating to each type of equipment. It was soon realised that this would multiply the work, as each time the drafters would have to reconsider and evaluate the provisions of the original Convention. More importantly, this approach could undermine the CTC's integrity and uniform application.

In contrast, the novel solution of the base Convention, supplemented by the equipment-specific Protocols, had several advantages and was ultimately adopted at the Diplomatic Conference. It allowed each equipment-specific working group to proceed at its own speed.[47] Leaving the issues relating to various types of equipment to the Protocols also meant that the CTC's text could be kept as simple as possible. At the same time, the Protocols could be drafted in a way which would better reflect the nature of the equipment and the needs of the industry concerned.[48] Finally, the separation of the base Convention and the Protocols allowed Contracting States to choose which Protocol to ratify and that, in turn, helped secure a greater number of ratifications.

iii. The International Interest

The Convention is mostly concerned with three types of financing of mobile equipment, namely a secured loan, a conditional sale and a lease.[49] Some jurisdictions, such as the United States, Canada and New Zealand, characterise conditional sale and some leases as security interests. Other jurisdictions distinguish between the 'true' security interests on the one hand, and conditional sale and leases on the other hand, and subject them to different legal regimes. Reaching an agreement on the uniform approach to the characterisation of the CTC's interests was impracticable and it was decided that this issue should be left to the applicable domestic law. But a solution that would reflect the differences between a security interest, conditional sale and a lease and still treat them in a similar manner was needed under

[46] C Chinkin and C Kessedjian, 'The Legal Relationship between the Proposed UNIDROIT Convention and its Equipment Specific Protocols' (1999) 4 *Unif L Rev* 323, 323–25.

[47] Goode, Kronke and McKendrick (n 33) 402–06.

[48] *Ibid* 402–06.

[49] The Convention does not govern outright sale of objects. However, the Aircraft Protocol makes an exception for an outright sale and a prospective sale (which do not constitute international interests) of the aircraft objects, which can be registered in the IR. See Arts III, V of the Aircraft Protocol. Similarly, Art IV of the Space Protocol extends the application of this Protocol to an outright sale and a prospective sale. The Luxembourg Protocol takes a different approach and only permits registration of a notice of sale (but not the prospective sale) for information purposes, so that the holder of such an interest cannot benefit from the CTC's priority rules. See Art XVII of the Luxembourg Protocol.

the Convention. This gave rise to the creation of the truly unique concept of the 'international interest'.[50]

An international interest can take the form of a security interest, title reservation or lease.[51] All three types of international interests are subjected to the same rules regarding creation, registration and priority. The distinction between them becomes important when the creditor needs to exercise its remedies, because this is the moment when the nature of its title in the object becomes relevant. This is why the CTC provides for separate remedial rules for the secured creditor and the conditional seller and lessor.[52]

The Convention delegates the issue of the interest's characterisation to the applicable law.[53] At the same time, it provides definitions of security agreement, title reservation agreement and leasing agreement.[54] The meaning of these terms under the Convention and the applicable law may not always coincide, which raises an important issue of the relationship between the two routes of defining these interests and the types of transactions that fall into the Convention's scope. The Official Commentary (OC) advances the view that the Convention's definitions should be used for the 'initial' characterisation of an interest to decide whether the transaction falls into its scope. Provided that this issue is resolved positively, the applicable domestic law should then be used to characterise the transaction again.[55] However, it is suggested that this two-stage exercise can create dissonance between the characterisations under two different legal regimes. Under the OC's approach, it is not clear whether the transaction would fall within the Convention's scope and, if so, how broad or specific should the characterisation be under the applicable law.

This book examines these issues and suggests a different explanation of the relationship between the Convention and the applicable domestic law in relation to the characterisation of interests.[56] It will be argued that to determine whether the transaction falls within the Convention's scope, the agreement should be characterised by the applicable domestic law.[57] Once this issue is established, the interest arising out of this agreement is subjected to the CTC's legal regime and its definitions. Under this approach, the transaction is only characterised once, so there is no danger of it being re-characterised later. It can also bring predictability to the creditor in relation to its remedies. The role of the applicable law should cease after the

[50] Art 2 CTC. Goode (n 19) 266–68.
[51] Art 2(2) CTC.
[52] Arts 8, 9, 10 CTC.
[53] Art 2(4) CTC.
[54] Art 1(q), (ii), (ll) CTC.
[55] Goode (n 19) 267.
[56] See chapter one.
[57] As prescribed by Art 2(4) CTC.

creditor's interest is characterised. For example, an interest characterised by the applicable law as that of the conditional seller cannot avoid the requirement of the registration in the IR to attain the CTC's priority even if the registration would not be required under the domestic law.

iv. The International Registry

Another unique feature of the Convention is that it establishes an electronic asset-based notice-filing International Registry (IR) for the registration of registrable interests in mobile equipment.[58] At present, only the aircraft IR, which is situated in Dublin, is in operation. Registration allows a registrant to give notice of the international interest's existence to third parties, secure its priority among competing interest holders and ensure that the registered interest is effective in the case of the debtor's insolvency. The registrations and searches must be made against the object and not the name of the debtor. For this reason, the objects should be uniquely identifiable. Consequently, international interests in future or after acquired property cannot be registered in the IR. This raises an interesting question whether it is possible to create and register a floating security interest in the aircraft and other objects under the Convention, an issue considered in this book.[59]

The IR is extensively used by aircraft manufacturers, financiers and other stakeholders, with the number of registrations exceeding 100,000 in 2014.[60] The fact that it is electronic and operational 24 hours 7 days a week means that it can be accessed globally, a factor of great significance in cross-border transactions. The IR is regulated by the Convention, the Aircraft Protocol and the Regulations and Procedures. The latter two documents lay down the rules for the IR's practical operation and can be revised when the need arises. This innovative approach enables constant development and further improvement of the IR to reflect the needs of its user community. For instance, when the IR was first established, the interests held in several aircraft objects, such an airframe and the engines pertaining to it, had to be registered in separate registration sessions. This practice was repetitive and wasteful of time and resources. As soon as it became technologically possible, the IR developed a new facility, 'multiple object registration', allowing a registering party to group several objects and register interests held in them in a single registration session. Similarly, the Regulations have recently been revised to implement a new facility, the 'closing room', enabling several financiers to assemble the information required for multiple registrations relating to one or several aircraft objects, collect consents and negotiate the

[58] Art 16 CTC.

[59] See chapter two.

[60] See the IR's Annual Statistical Report at www.internationalregistry.aero/ir-web/annualStatisticalReport/findAll (last visited July 2016).

chronological order of the registrations before this information is released into the IR so as to become searchable.[61] The main features and the process of the registration in the IR as well as some challenges presented by its electronic nature and the first cases emerging from its operation are examined in this book.

v. Remedies

A registered international interest which cannot be enforced will not be of great value to its holder. To ensure that the international interest can be protected, the Convention establishes remedial rules exercisable in the case of the debtor's default or insolvency.[62] Since the conditional seller and lessor are often considered as owners of the object, the Convention distinguishes between the remedies available to them and those exercisable by the secured creditor.[63] On the debtor's default, the secured creditor can enforce its international interest by taking possession or control, selling, or leasing the object.[64] The secured creditor can also collect or receive any income or profits arising from the management or use of the object to obtain repayment of the debt.[65] In addition, if at any time after default, the debtor and other interested persons agree, the ownership (or any other interest held by the debtor) of the object covered by the security agreement can be vested in the secured creditor in or towards the satisfaction of the debt.[66] In contrast, the remedies of the conditional seller and lessor are confined to the power to terminate the agreement and repossess or take control of the object.[67]

The Convention also provides for the remedy of 'speedy relief' pending final determination of the claim, inspired by the remedy of interim relief known to many domestic legal systems.[68] The Convention's speedy relief is viewed by some commentators as the form of an advance enforcement of default remedies.[69] This book explores the nature of the remedy of speedy relief and argues that it cannot be equated with the advance enforcement of default remedies. Although speedy relief is akin to the remedy of interim relief, it has its own unique features and, being the CTC's creature, must be interpreted according to its principles and policies.[70]

[61] See chapters three and four.
[62] Chapter III CTC.
[63] Arts 8, 9, 10 CTC.
[64] Art 8(1) CTC.
[65] Art 8(1)(c) CTC.
[66] Art 9(1) CTC.
[67] Art 10 CTC.
[68] Art 13 CTC.
[69] G Cuniberti, 'Advance Relief under the Cape Town Convention' (2012) *Cape Town Convention Journal* 79.
[70] See further chapter six.

In addition to the CTC's remedies, the Protocols also provide for equipment-specific remedies. For instance, the Aircraft Protocol provides for the remedies of de-registration and export and physical transfer of the object to another jurisdiction. These remedies should enable the creditor to cancel the aircraft's current registration in a national registry and re-register the aircraft in a different jurisdiction which may be more favourable to the protection of its interests. The remedy of de-registration has been recently enforced in a decision of the High Court of New Delhi.[71] The Luxembourg Protocol also provides that in the case of the debtor's default, the creditor may physically transfer a railway object from the territory in which it is situated, to another country.[72] However, the Convention recognises that the repossession of railway rolling stock may cause disruption to the carriage of passengers and freight. For this reason, the exercise of this remedy is subject to the public service exemption.[73] If the railway object is habitually used to provide a service of public importance, it cannot be repossessed by the creditor. One issue considered in this book in the light of this exception is whether the creditor's interest is adequately protected and whether it can still obtain repayment of the debt. Similar issues arose in the drafting of the Space Protocol, as space assets often play a central role in delivering services of public importance.[74] This resulted in the imposition of the limitations on the creditor's exercise of the remedies in respect of the space assets providing public service.[75]

The Convention offers an elaborate remedial scheme exercisable in and out of the debtor's insolvency and this book assesses its effectiveness. It examines the concept of a default, amounting under the Convention to such 'a default which substantially deprives the creditor of what it is entitled to expect under the agreement'.[76] The Convention does not explain what amounts to the creditor's expectation under the agreement and its substantial deprivation. This book explores what factors are relevant when considering these issues. Further, the remedies must be exercised in a commercially reasonable manner, but the meaning of this requirement and the consequences of a failure to comply with it are not specified in the Convention. The scope of application, the meaning and general considerations relating to the requirement of commercial reasonableness in the context of specific remedies are extensively examined in chapter six.

[71] *Awas 39423 Ireland Ltd & Ors v Directorate General of Civil Aviation & Anr* (WP(C) 871/2015) and *Wilmington Trust SP Services Ltd v Directorate General of Civil Aviation & Anr* (WP(C) 747/2015). For the discussion of this case, see chapter six.

[72] Art VII(1) of the Luxembourg Protocol.

[73] Art XXV of the Luxembourg Protocol.

[74] See J Atwood, 'A New International Regime for Railway Rolling Stock Asset-Based Financing' (2008) 40 *UCC LJ* 3, Art 2.

[75] Article XXVII of the Space Protocol.

[76] Art 11 CTC.

vi. System of Declarations

Another important feature of the Convention and its Protocols is their elaborate system of declarations.[77] There are opt-in declarations which must be made if a particular provision is to have effect in a Contracting State. For example, the Convention does not normally apply to pre-existing rights or interests (PERI), which remain subject to the priority rules under the applicable law. However, a Contracting State can make a declaration under Article 60, indicating that the priority rules of the Convention will apply to PERI if certain conditions are met.

If a Contracting State wishes to exclude the application of certain provisions of the Convention, it can make an opt-out declaration. For instance, some jurisdictions do not allow an extra-judicial exercise of remedies. An opt-out declaration under Article 54(2) could preclude the creditor from exercising remedies under the Convention without resorting to a court. One of the remedies exercisable by a chargee on the debtor's default is the right to grant a lease of the object. This remedy is available subject to a declaration of a Contracting State, precluding the grant of a lease of the object while it is located on or controlled from its territory.[78] A Contracting State may also make a declaration, excluding the Convention's provisions dealing with relief pending final determination and issues of jurisdiction.[79]

Some declarations are mandatory and must be made by a Contracting State to enable it become a party to the Convention. Examples of these types of declarations can be found in Article 48(2), regarding matters within the exclusive competence of the regional economic integration organisation and Article 54(2), on whether the remedies which, under the Convention do not require application to a court, may be exercised only with the leave of court. There are also declarations which can be made by a Contracting State in relation to matters of its own law. A declaration relating to non-registrable non-consensual rights or interests (NCRIs) under Article 39 falls into this category. A Contracting State depositing such a declaration may indicate that certain NCRI which, under that State's law, do not require registration and prevail over an interest which is equivalent to the international interest, should be treated in priority to registered international interests under the Convention.

Finally, there are declarations which may be made under the Protocols. The Aircraft Protocol provides for two alternative sets of rules (Alternative A and Alternative B) in relation to the creditor's right of repossession exercisable

[77] The list presented here is not exhaustive. Declarations can also be made under Arts 40, 50, 52, 53 CTC.

[78] Art 54(1) CTC.

[79] Arts 13, 43, 55 CTC.

in the case of the debtor's insolvency.[80] The Luxembourg Protocol adds a third alternative, Alternative C, to these options.[81] The Contracting State can declare which of the alternatives it chooses to apply on the occurrence of an insolvency related event or in the case of the debtor's insolvency. If none of the options is chosen, the domestic insolvency rules will continue to apply. The complex system of declarations under the Convention and the Protocols may be criticised as undermining their uniform application. At the same time, the strength of this regime is that it allows Contracting States to retain their positions on important policy issues, which may help secure a greater number of ratifications.[82]

D. Interpretation of the Convention

A common feature of many international private law conventions is the requirement for uniform application and respect for their international character.[83] Similar to other conventions, the CTC must be interpreted *autonomously*, that is in accordance with its own concepts and definitions. The provisions of the Convention should not be interpreted with reference to any domestic law.[84] This is clear from Article 5(1), which provides that:

> In the interpretation of this Convention, regard is to be had to its purposes as set forth in the preamble, to its international character and to the need to promote uniformity and predictability in its application.

Article 5(2) provides guidance on how to proceed if a particular matter is not expressly settled in the Convention:

> Questions concerning matters governed by this Convention which are not expressly settled in it are to be settled in conformity with the general principles on which it is based or, in the absence of such principles, in conformity with the applicable law.

If the Convention does not expressly deal with a particular matter, it must, first, be ascertained whether this issue is *governed* by the Convention at all. As stated above, the Convention applies to asset-based financing and

[80] Art XI of the Aircraft Protocol.

[81] Art IX of the Luxembourg Protocol.

[82] See J Wool, 'Rethinking the Notion of Uniformity in the Drafting of International Commercial Law: A Preliminary Proposal for the Development of Policy-Based Unification Model' (1997) 2 *Unif L Rev* 46, 46–53.

[83] See Art 31(1) of the Vienna Convention on the Law of Treaties 1969; Art 7(1) of the Vienna Convention on International Sale of Goods 1980; Art 6 of the Convention on International Financial Leasing 1988; Art 4 of the Convention on International Factoring 1988.

[84] M Gebauer, 'Uniform Law, General Principles and Autonomous Interpretation' (2000) 5 *Unif L Rev* 683, 686–87.

leasing of uniquely identifiable mobile equipment and there is a plethora of issues which may arise in this regard. These issues will be addressed in this book. Once it is established that the matter is governed by the Convention, it should be resolved in accordance with the general principles underlying the Convention. These principles include: party autonomy, reflecting the fact that the parties engaged in the kind of transactions covered by the Convention will be knowledgeable and experienced and, for this reason, their agreements should, generally, be enforced; predictability in the application of the Convention, which is reflected in clear rules on priority; transparency, which can be found in the rules on registration, making the interests of senior and junior creditors visible to other parties; and the protection and ready enforceability of remedies in the case of the debtor's default or insolvency.[85] If the matter is found not to be governed by the Convention, it should be settled in accordance with the applicable law.[86]

E. Aims of this Book

The area of cross-border security interests is fraught with numerous complex issues, which stem from the multiplicity of jurisdictions with varying attitudes to security interests. Another reason for the complexity in this area of the law stems from the variety of legal issues which have to be considered before a comprehensive security agreement can be put together. For instance, before a security agreement is entered into, a prospective secured creditor needs to ascertain whether the aircraft object is already encumbered and evaluate its potential priority standing among other creditors. This task may be difficult to accomplish because some interests, such as non-registrable NCRI, may be binding even though they are not visible in the IR and other interests, such as prospective international interests, which are visible, may no longer be in existence.

The CTC aims to provide a uniform set of substantive rules for the creation, perfection, priority and enforcement of security interests and interests of conditional sellers and lessors in mobile equipment, which, given the complexity of this area of the law, is an ambitious task. One aim of this book is to examine the provisions of the Convention and the Protocols and to test whether the legal regime created by it can operate successfully and help facilitate financing and leasing of aircraft, railway and space objects. To test the effectiveness of the Convention, its provisions will be evaluated in the context of various factual scenarios, which, considering the limited number of cases which have been brought under the Convention,

[85] Goode (n 19) 22–25.
[86] Art 5(2) CTC.

were largely inspired by the experience of some major domestic jurisdictions, such as the UK and the US.[87] This exercise may shed some light on the strengths and weaknesses of the Convention and the Protocols in comparison with these systems.

The evaluation of the Convention will also involve the identification of questions the answers to which are not entirely clear. For instance, the concept of 'deficiency' is not expressly mentioned in the Convention, which gives rise to the question whether the secured creditor may claim the remainder of the debt if the sale of the repossessed object did not generate enough proceeds to extinguish the debt. This book identifies such issues and proposes solutions and/or possible interpretations of the relevant provisions of the Convention.

This book primarily deals with the issues of the definition, creation, registration, priority and enforcement of security interests under the Convention. Security interests in aircraft, railway and space objects are one of the most frequently used mechanisms, employed to ensure the repayment of the debt and to support the financing of these types of equipment. It is their significance, effectiveness and frequency of use that explains this book's focus and scope. But the category of international interest is not confined to security interests and includes the interests of a conditional seller and lessor. For this reason, these international interests will be examined to the extent that they help illuminate the concept of security interests. The Convention also deals with the effect, formal requirements and priority of assignment of associated rights and international interests. Since the main focus of this book is on security interests, the issues relating to the assignment of associated rights and international interests are only briefly touched upon in the part that deals with the registrable interests under the Convention.

The present chapter addresses the following issues. Part II examines the concept of a security interest and the definition of a security agreement under the Convention. It also explores the essence of the *formal v functional* divide, relating to the understanding of what amounts to a true and *quasi* security interest. Part III examines the concept of an international interest and the two routes of characterising a transaction. It also suggests an explanation of the relationship between the two routes of defining eligible interests under the Convention. Finally, Part IV considers the legal nature of international interests. The Convention does not expressly specify whether international interests are personal or proprietary. It will be argued that its provisions, in particular those relating to the priority of registered interests,

[87] There have been a few cases decided under the Convention concerning the operation of Art 44 and the issue of jurisdiction to make orders against the Registrar to discharge bogus registrations. However, the substantive provisions of the Convention have not yet been tested in court. The cases concerning the discharge of registrations are examined in chapter four.

ability to be traced into the proceeds, and effectiveness in the debtor's insolvency, confirm their proprietary nature.

II. THE CONCEPT OF A SECURITY INTEREST

A. What is a Security Interest?

The definition of a security interest is approached differently by various legal systems. Rather than starting with a definition of security, some legal systems tend to examine a transaction by looking at the balance of rights and obligations of the parties to decide whether it falls into one of the forms of recognised security interests.[88] Other legal systems look at the function of the transaction. If it performs the functions of a security, that is, if it secures the performance of the main obligation, ensures that the creditor enjoys priority among other creditors and is able to survive the debtor's insolvency, it is recognised as the transaction giving rise to a true security interest even if labelled differently by the contracting parties.[89] As a result, a transaction can be considered as a security interest by some legal systems and not seen as such by others.[90]

In spite of diverse approaches to the question of what amounts to a security interest, it seems that the general understanding of the concept of a security is shared by most legal systems. Generally speaking, a security interest involves a grant of a right in a property by an obligor (the debtor) to an obligee (the creditor) to secure or ensure that the obligor performs its obligation.[91] For instance, a debtor manufacturing an aircraft will need finance to cover its expenses. A financier which may be willing to provide the loan will need some assurance that the debt will be repaid to it. To this end, the financier can take a security interest in the financed aircraft. By granting a security interest, the debtor recognises that, in the case of its

[88] Jurisdictions such as those of England and Wales, Hong Kong, Malaysia and Singapore follow this approach. See P Ali, *The Law of Secured Finance: An International Survey of Security Interests Over Personal Property* (Oxford, OUP 2002) 15. For the position under English law, see *Agnew v Commissioner of Inland Revenue* [2001] UKPC 28, [2001] AC 710 at [32]; *Re George Inglefield* [1933] Ch 1; *Helby v Matthews* [1895] AC 471; *Welsh Development Agency v Export Finance Co Ltd* [1992] BCLC 148; *Smith v Bridgent CBC* [2001] UKHL 58, [2002] 1 AC 336. See also Beale, Bridge, Gullifer and Lomnicka (n 8) 75–97.

[89] For instance, §1-201(b)(35) of the United States Uniform Commercial Code (UCC) defines a security interest as 'an interest in personal property ... which secures payment or performance of an obligation'. As long as the transaction performs this function, it is considered as a security. See J White and R Summers, *Uniform Commercial Code*, 6th edn (St Paul, Minn, West Group 2010) 1153–55.

[90] S Worthington, *Proprietary Interests in Commercial Transactions* (Oxford, Clarendon Press 1996) 11.

[91] Gullifer (n 9) 3.

default, the financier will be able to exercise its remedies, including repossession and sale of the object to discharge the debt. The threat of enforcement of the security interest can serve as a strong incentive for the repayment of the debt. The grant of a security in the object also means that even in the case of the debtor's insolvency, the financier will, generally, be able to obtain the discharge of the debt before the other creditors of the debtor.

B. The Definition of a Security Agreement under the Convention

The Convention defines a security interest as 'an interest created by a security agreement'.[92] Article 1(ii), in turn, provides that a security agreement as 'an agreement by which a chargor grants or agrees to grant to a chargee an interest (including an ownership interest) in or over an object to secure the performance of any existing or future obligation of the chargor or a third person'.[93] Several points flow from this definition. First, because Article 1(ii) refers to an 'agreement', only consensual forms of security interests are included in this definition.[94] This does not mean that non-consensual security interests are excluded from the Convention's scope altogether. For instance, Article 40 allows a Contracting State to make a declaration that NCRI can be registered in the IR and then be treated as registered international interests. Thus, provided that a Contracting State made the appropriate declaration, a right of a creditor arising out of a legal right of detention where an aircraft engine has been taken for repair and the work has not been paid for by the debtor, can be registered. A registered NCRI will be considered as an international interest and take priority over a subsequently registered and unregistered interest.[95]

Secondly, a security interest can ensure the performance of the existing and future obligations of the chargor or a third person. This means that a security agreement can be used as a continuing facility, which may be particularly convenient in long-term projects. When the value of the collateral is greater than the loan, the parties can use the same collateral for further advances. This will allow the parties to cut unnecessary transaction costs associated with legal fees and the negotiation of the terms of the agreement. Crucially, the Convention distinguishes between security over a future obligation and security in future property. The registration in the asset-based IR is effected against a uniquely identified object and, for this reason, it is

[92] Art 1(jj) CTC.
[93] Art 1(ii) CTC.
[94] B.P Honnebier, 'The New International Regimen Proposed by UNIDROIT as a Means of Safeguarding Rights *in Rem* of the Holder of an Aircraft under Netherlands Law' (2001) 6 *Unif L Rev* 5.
[95] See chapter three for the discussion of registrable NCRI.

not possible to use as collateral an object which does not yet exist, such as an aircraft which does not have the manufacturer's serial number because it has not yet been constructed. At the same time, provided that the collateral is sufficiently identifiable, it is possible to use it as a security for all obligations owed by the debtor to the secured creditor now or in the future.[96] The definition of the security agreement also indicates that a chargor can use the collateral to secure performance of an obligation owed to the chargee by a third person. This position of the Convention reflects a common feature of modern financing where companies forming part of a corporate group provide the lender with cross-guarantees securing performance of obligations of its member companies.[97]

Thirdly, a security interest can arise by a grant of an interest (including an ownership interest) in or over an object. The following points emerge from this part of the definition.

i. An Interest in a Uniquely Identifiable Object

The Convention's security interest must be created in or over an 'object', which is defined as 'an object of a category to which Article 2 applies'.[98] These categories currently comprise: (a) airframes, aircraft engines and helicopters; (b) railway rolling stock; and (c) space assets.[99] These objects must be uniquely identifiable in accordance with the Protocols' requirements.[100] For instance, the Aircraft Protocol provides an exhaustive description of the types of airframes, aircraft engines and helicopters by reference to their jet propulsion, shaft horsepower and other technical particulars.[101] It further provides that the requirement of the unique identification is satisfied if the description of an aircraft object contains its manufacturer's serial number, the name of the manufacturer and its model designation.[102] Similarly, the Luxembourg and Space Protocols provide definitions of the railway rolling stock[103] and the space assets falling into their scope.[104] However, these Protocols override the Convention's requirement of the unique identification of objects for the constitution of international interests. This is because

[96] Goode (n 19) 54.

[97] See *Re Conley* [1938] 2 All ER 127; *Saltri Iii Ltd v MD Mezzanine Sa Sicar* [2012] EWHC 3025 (Comm). See also Gullifer (n 9) 10.

[98] Art 1(u) CTC.

[99] Art 2(3) CTC.

[100] Art 2(2) CTC.

[101] Art I of the Aircraft Protocol.

[102] Art VII of the Aircraft Protocol.

[103] Art I(e) of the Luxembourg Protocol.

[104] Art I(k) of the Space Protocol.

the unique identification is only required when the interest in the object needs to be registered in the asset-based IR.[105] Both Protocols delegate the issue of the unique identification of objects to the Regulations.[106] With the addition of the new MAC Protocol, the current categories will be extended to agriculture, construction and mining equipment. The draft MAC Protocol replicates the bifurcated approach to object identification adopted by the Luxembourg and Space Protocols. While the MAC equipment can be described in general terms in the agreement constituting an international interest, it will have to be uniquely identified for the registration of interests in the IR, which is envisaged to be asset based.[107]

ii. The Debtor Need Not be the Owner of the Charged Object

A security interest can arise by a grant by a chargor to a chargee of 'an interest (including an ownership interest)' in or over the object. Thus, the CTC recognises a security by way of ownership transfer, pledge, or charge, or any other form of consensual security in personal property.[108] At the same time, the size, and ability to speedily cross national borders, of aircraft, railway and space objects can dictate the way in which financial transactions involving them are structured, rendering some forms of security interest more advantageous than others. For instance, a pledge involving the delivery of possession of the object as a security of the performance of an obligation is unlikely to be frequently used in cross-border transactions involving objects governed by the CTC.[109] This is because a debtor, situated in jurisdiction A and intending to acquire a railway rolling stock in jurisdiction B to operate it in jurisdiction C, may find it commercially impractical if, in order to obtain finance for its acquisition, it needs to deliver possession of the object to the financier, situated in jurisdiction D. Likewise, the financier, such as a bank, may find it inconvenient if, in order to secure the repayment of the debt, it has to take possession of the object, thereby not only depriving the debtor from the opportunity to generate profit from its use, but also incurring expenses relating to its maintenance.

[105] See Art V of the Luxembourg Protocol and Art VII of the Space Protocol indicating that the railway rolling stock and the space assets can be broadly defined in the agreement. Art XXX of the Space Protocol delegates the issue of unique identifications of space assets to the Regulations.

[106] Art XXX of the Space Protocol and Art XIV of the Luxembourg Protocol delegate the issue of unique identifications to the Regulations.

[107] See Art V and Art XVI of the draft MAC Protocol.

[108] Goode (n 19) 263.

[109] M Bridge and R Stevens (eds), *Cross-Border Security and Insolvency* (Oxford, OUP 2001) 18–19.

In contrast, a transfer of ownership by way of security, such as a mortgage, represents a better practical solution.[110] This way, the debtor can transfer ownership of the object as a security for the performance of an obligation to the financier and retain its possession. It will then be able to use the object and repay the debt out of proceeds received from its operation. Once the debt is repaid, the ownership will revert back to the debtor. Not all jurisdictions recognise the transfer of ownership in movable objects as a valid security interest and the Convention's express permission for the constitution of such a security may create an incentive for reform in such jurisdictions.[111]

The CTC does not insist that the debtor must be the owner of the object in order to grant a security interest in it. Article 1(ii) specifically provides that a chargor can grant to a chargee '*an interest* (including an ownership interest)'.[112] The debtor can transfer any interest it holds in the object even if it is less than ownership. For instance, an airline-lessee can grant a security interest to the secured creditor in an aircraft object held by it even though its interest in that object is merely possessory and does not amount to ownership.

Moreover, the 'grant of an interest' does not seem to exclude the creation of a new interest not amounting to ownership or possession. Thus, the debtor can grant an interest to the secured creditor in the form of an encumbrance on the object by way of a charge or hypothecation. This means that both ownership and possession remain with the debtor, but the object is appropriated to the satisfaction of the secured obligation, entitling the secured creditor to enforce its security in it to discharge the debt in priority to the debtor's unsecured and junior creditors.[113] Security by way of a charge may be potentially beneficial both to the debtor and the secured creditor in cross-border transactions because it allows the debtor to retain possession and use the object and at the same time keep it encumbered by the debt.[114]

An English floating charge is unlikely to arise under the Convention. English law distinguishes between a fixed and a floating charge, both of

[110] Under English law, ownership may be transferred by way of security by a mortgagor to a mortgagee. Once the secured obligation is performed, the ownership reverts back to the mortgagor. See *Keith v Burrows* (1876) 1 CPD 722; *Santley v Wilde* [1899] 2 Ch 474; *Maugham v Sharpe* (1864) 17 CB NS 443, 141 ER 179; *Kreglinger v New Patagonia Meat and Cold Storage Company Ltd* [1914] AC 25; *Ulfraframe (UK) v Fielding* [2005] EWHC 1638. Transfer of ownership by way of security is used in some other countries too. See Drobnig (n 1) 58.

[111] Mauri and Itterbeek (n 19) 549.

[112] emphasis added.

[113] *Carreras Rothmans Ltd v Freeman Mathews Treasure* [1985] Ch 207 at 227; *National Provincial and Union Bank of England v Charnley* [1924] 1 KB 431. See also Gullifer (n 9) 36.

[114] Bridge and Stevens (n 109) 23.

which may be taken against the present and future property.[115] While the parties can in principle create a charge in respect of the present property, they cannot do so in relation to future aircraft objects, since the Convention does not permit the use of a future property as collateral.[116] The fixed charge allows a secured creditor to take a security in the debtor's specific asset(s) and can, for this reason, be created and registered under the Convention.[117] In contrast, the floating charge does not attach to a particular asset until some specified crystallising event occurs (eg the debtor's default or insolvency).[118] Instead, the floating charge hovers over a specified fund of assets, comprising constantly changing objects, which allows the debtor to dispose of any of them without obtaining the creditor's consent.[119] Until such crystallisation occurs, the secured creditor does not have an interest in any specific property of the debtor.[120] Because Article 2(2) prescribes that the interest of the creditor should relate to a uniquely identified object, it seems unlikely that the constitution of a floating charge is possible under the Convention in relation to aircraft objects.

iii. The Interest is Granted for the Purpose of Securing the Obligation

A security agreement is concluded only for the purpose of securing performance of an obligation. Once the obligation is performed, the secured creditor's interest ceases to exist and the debtor's interest in the object reverts back to it or resumes its unencumbered state. The transfer of an interest to the secured creditor cannot be absolute even if it is by way of the transfer of

[115] *Holroyd v Marshall* (1862) 10 HL Cas 191. See, generally, S Atheton, 'Charges over Chattels: Issues in the Fixed/Floating Jurisprudence' (2005) *Comp Law* 10; R Goode, 'Charges over Book Debts: A Missed Opportunity' (1994) *LQR* 592; R Goode, 'Charge-Backs and Legal Fictions' (1998) 114 LQR 178; M Bridge, 'Fixed Charges and Freedom of Contract' (1994) *LQR* 340.

[116] The position is different in relation to the railway objects, space assets and the MAC equipment because all three Protocols permit description of existing and future objects in broad terms in the international interest agreement. However, even if a floating security interest is created in these types of equipment, its registration in the IR will require unique identification of each object which means that floating security in future unidentified property cannot be registered. Lack of registration will not invalidate the international interest, but will preclude its holder from securing its priority position among others interest holders. This will severely limit the effect of the international interest.

[117] *Agnew v Commissioner for the Inland Revenue* [2001] AC 710.

[118] *Re Florence Land and Public Works Company* (1871) 10 Ch D 530 CA; R Pennington, 'The Genesis of the Floating Charge' (1960) 23 *MLR* 630; R Gregory and P Walton, 'Fixed and Floating Charges—A Revelation' [2000] *LMCLQ* 123.

[119] *Evans v Rival Granite Quarries Ltd* [1910] 2 KB 979; *Re Panama, New Zealand and Australian Royal Mail Company* (1870) 5 Ch App 318; *Hodson v Tea Company* (1880) 14 Ch D 459.

[120] *Re Cosslett (Contractors) Ltd* [1998] Ch 495.

ownership. In contrast, an agreement stating that the debtor agrees to transfer the property absolutely without the opportunity of redemption cannot amount to a security interest.

iv. Security is by Grant and Not RoT

Finally, security interest arises by a 'grant' of an interest. Consequently, a security interest cannot be created by the RoT by the creditor. Thus, a conditional sale agreement, involving a RoT by the seller, cannot amount to a security interest. This way, the Convention preserves the distinction between the traditional forms of security interests and other financial arrangements, such as conditional sale or lease, which perform a similar function to security interests but are not considered as such by some legal systems. The distinction between true and *quasi* security interests lies at the heart of the so-called *formal v functional* divide.

C. The Essence of the Formal v Functional Divide

i. The Formal Approach: True Security Interests and Quasi Security Interests

Under the *formal* approach, followed by most civil law jurisdictions, the United Kingdom and other legal systems belonging to the common law family outside North America and New Zealand, the law broadly distinguishes between *the grant* by the debtor of an interest by way of security and *the reservation of title* by the creditor under the RoT agreements such as conditional sale, hire purchase and leasing.[121] According to this approach, true security interests generally arise when the debtor transfers or grants an interest in the collateral to the creditor as security for the performance of an obligation.[122] For instance, under German law, the debtor can transfer its title in the property to the secured creditor, or it can deposit the goods with the creditor and confer on it a right of sale, or it can unconditionally assign receivables due to it to the creditor as a security.[123]

English law traditionally recognises only four forms of consensual security, namely the pledge, the contractual lien, the mortgage and the charge.[124] The debtor may grant by way of security its ownership (mortgage)[125]

[121] R Goode, *The Hamlyn Lectures: Commercial Law in the Next Millennium* (London, Sweet & Maxwell 1998) 63.
[122] Gullifer (n 9) 3–5.
[123] See B Jakel in Bridge and Stevens (n 109) 99–101.
[124] Gullifer (n 9) 5.
[125] *Santley v Wilde* [1899] 2 Ch 474; *Re Sir Thomas Spencer Wells* [1933] Ch 29.

or deliver actual or constructive possession of the collateral (pledge),[126] or encumber the property as a security for the performance of the obligation (charge).[127] A contractual lien, arising out of the express terms of the contract or, if not explicitly provided for in the contract, by operation of law, can arise when the goods are initially delivered for the purpose other than security.[128] For instance, the goods delivered for repair may be used as a security for the payment due to the creditor from the debtor. Other financial and business arrangements, performing the function of a security, are not viewed as such by English law.

Another example can be provided by the Polish Civil Code, stating that for the creation of a valid mortgage over real property, the contract should, among other things, unequivocally declare that the owner of the property agrees to *grant* its interest by way of mortgage as a security for the performance of the secured obligation.[129] A Polish possessory pledge is created when the debtor, who must be the owner of the pledged property, delivers it to the creditor or another agreed third party.[130] The Civil Code of the Russian Federation[131] and the Federal Law on the Hypothec (the Pledge of Immovable Property) of the Russian Federation[132] indicate that both possessory and non-possessory pledges of property presuppose that the pledgor grants to the pledgee its interest (which can be less than ownership) in the property as security for the performance of the obligation.[133] Finally, French law on security interests prescribes that, as a general rule, security over tangible movable property is created and perfected by physical delivery of the collateral to the pledgee or other agreed third party.[134] In each of these examples, it is the debtor—clothed in such terms as the pledgor, the mortgagor or the chargor—which must grant the interest held by it to the secured creditor for a true security to arise.

[126] *Coggs v Bernard* (1703) 2 Ld Raym 909; *Donald v Suckling* (1866) LR 1 (QB) 585; *Halliday v Holgate* (1868) LR 3 (Exch) 299; *Singer Manufacturing Company v Clark* (1879) 5 Ex D 37; *Mathew v Sutton* [1994] 1 WLR 1455.

[127] On the difference between a charge and a mortgage, see *Swiss Bank Corporation v Lloyds Bank Ltd* [1982] AC 584, 595.

[128] *George Barker (Transport) Ltd v Eynon* [1974] 1 WLR 462.

[129] L Choroszucha, 'Secured Transactions in Poland: Practicable Rules, Unworkable Monstrosities and Pending Reforms' (1994) 17 *Hastings Int'l Comp L Rev* 389, 400.

[130] Polish law recognises non-possessory pledges, but these are only available to banks. See Choroszucha (n 128) 404–06.

[131] '*Гражданский Кодекс Российской Федерации, Части Первой*', The Civil Code of the Russian Federation, Part One, 30 November 1994, N 51-ФЗ.

[132] '*Федеральный Закон об Ипотеке (Залоге Недвижимости)*', The Federal Law on the Hypothec (the Pledge of Immovable Property), 16 July 1998, N 102-ФЗ, approved by the Council of the Federation on 9 July 1998, adopted by the Parliament ('*Gosudarstvennaya Duma*') on 10 July 1998. This federal law was first officially published in *Финансовая Россия* (Financial Russia), 1998, N 27 and *Российская Газета* (Russian Gazette), 1998, N137.

[133] B Bennett, 'Secured Financing in Russia: Risks, Legal Incentives, and Policy Concerns' (1999) 77 *Tex L Rev* 1443, 1447.

[134] M Gdanski in Bridge and Stevens (n 109) 59.

Security interests recognised by domestic laws are not the only means which a financier can employ to provide its customer with the required finance while, at the same time, ensuring that it will be repaid. Various business arrangements, broadly defined as RoT transactions, can perform a function similar to that of a security and at the same time possess other features which parties to a transaction may find more advantageous. Because of their chameleon-like nature, allowing them to serve as a security, RoT agreements are often described as *quasi* security interests. These financial arrangements include RoT clauses in conditional sale agreements, sales and lease-backs, hire purchase and leasing agreements.

a. Retention of Title

The term 'retention of title' can be used to describe various financial devices where the ownership of an object remains with the creditor as a security for the performance of an obligation (usually payment of money) and the possession is transferred to the debtor. For example, hire purchase and lease can be described as RoT agreements.[135] In addition, the term 'retention of title' is also used to refer to the RoT clauses, frequently found in conditional sale agreements.[136] While there exist many varieties of RoT clauses, their general purpose seems to be universal. By means of such a clause, the seller intends to reserve the ownership of the goods delivered to the buyer until the latter performs certain conditions, often amounting to the payment of the purchase price.[137]

A valid RoT clause can be used by the conditional seller as a security designed to ensure that the buyer pays the purchase price.[138] Similar to security interests, the RoT clause protects the conditional seller in the case of the buyer's insolvency.[139] Since the conditional seller retains ownership of the goods, they do not become part of the buyer's estate on insolvency and the unpaid seller is generally entitled to repossess the goods. In contrast with the traditional security interests, RoT clauses, generally, do not require registration.[140] This circumstance is particularly advantageous to the parties

[135] Beale, Bridge, Gullifer and Lomnicka (n 8) 235.

[136] The legal basis of RoT clauses under English law is to be found in Sale of Goods Act 1979, s 2(3) and s 19(1). See also *Clough Mill Ltd v Martin* [1985] 1 WLR 111; *Armour v Thyssen Edelstahlwerke AG* [1991] 2 AC 339 and *Hendy Lennox (Industrial Engines) Ltd v Graham Puttick Ltd* [1984] 1 WLR 485.

[137] G McCormack, 'Personal Property Security Law Reform in England and Canada' (2002) *JBL* 113, 133.

[138] Worthington (n 90) 41.

[139] *Clough Mill Ltd v Martin* [1985] 1 WLR 111, 122.

[140] The position is different under the US UCC, adhering to the functional approach, which states that the interest of unpaid seller under the RoT clause amounts to a registrable security interest. See §1-201(35) UCC.

intending to enter several sales agreements, as registering each clause every time a new agreement is concluded is burdensome.[141]

In spite of the fact that RoT clauses perform the function of a security, English law, in line with the formal approach, does not consider them as true security interests. The main reason for this is that, in contrast with true security interests, the conditional seller (the creditor) does not rely on the debtor's grant of an interest, but retains its ownership until the obligation is performed.[142] Curiously, while English courts have accepted the validity of 'simple' clauses, under which ownership to the goods is not to pass to the buyer until the purchase price under the contract is paid, as well as the 'current account' or 'all monies' clauses, allowing the seller to retain ownership until *all* debts and not just the purchase price due from the buyer are paid, they have refused to treat more extended forms of RoT clauses as such.[143] When the conditional seller attempts to retain its ownership in the original goods used by the buyer in the process of mixture or manufacture of new products, or in the proceeds received by the buyer as a result of the sale of original goods, English courts usually treat these clauses as charges and not RoT clauses.[144] This generally seems to happen because title to the goods is deemed to have passed to the buyer at the moment of the irreversible mixture of the original goods with the other goods of the buyer, or the sale of the original goods to a third party.[145] On this view, the interest held by the conditional seller is considered to have been obtained by the grant by the buyer and not RoT by the seller.[146]

The difference between the true security interests by the grant and *quasi* security interests by the RoT is followed with varied rigidity by various jurisdictions. While English law maintains strongly that the true security interests arise by the grant of an interest by the debtor to the creditor and not the RoT by the creditor, other legal systems adopt a slightly different approach. Thus, German law, similar to English law, does not consider such RoT agreements as leasing as a true security interest: the lessor is deemed to retain the unconditional title to the leased goods and is entitled to terminate

[141] McCormack (n 136) 124.

[142] The position is different in the jurisdictions adhering to the functional approach, where the conditional seller is considered as a secured creditor and both ownership and possession are transferred to the conditional buyer. See J Sampson and B Brown, 'Retention of Title under New Zealand's Personal Property Securities Act 1999' (2002) 17 *JIBL* 102; M Bridge, R Macdonald, R Simmonds and C Walsh, 'Formalism, Functionalism, and Understanding the Law of Secured Transactions' (1999) 44 *McGill LJ* 567, 587–98.

[143] *Borden (UK) Ltd v Scottish Timber Products Ltd* [1981] Ch 25; *Armour v Thyssen Edelstahlwereke AG* [1991] 2 AC 339.

[144] *Re Peachdart* Ltd [1984] Ch 131.

[145] See *Borden (UK) Ltd v Scottish Timber Products Ltd* [1981] Ch 25, where it was held that the supplier's title in the resin disappeared once it was used in the process of chipboard manufacture.

[146] *Ian Chisholm Textiles Ltd v Griffiths* [1994] BCC 96.

the lease and repossess the goods in case of the lessee's default.[147] At the same time, RoT clauses, allowing the unpaid seller to retain ownership until the buyer performs conditions precedent to the transfer of the title, are seen as true security interests.[148]

b. Hire Purchase[149]

Hire purchase can be considered as a form of a RoT agreement aimed at providing the creditor with security against the debtor's default.[150] Hire purchase is essentially a contract, whereby the owner (the creditor) lets the goods on hire to the hirer (the debtor) in return for the payment of rentals.[151] It is similar to conditional sale in that the hirer, like the conditional buyer, obtains possession of the goods and can use them in its business in return for periodic payments. The two arrangements are also similar as they both perform a security function. In both cases, the owner/conditional seller retains ownership of the goods to ensure that the hirer/conditional buyer makes timely payments.[152] Some legal systems, however, distinguish between a hire purchase and a conditional sale on the basis that unlike the conditional buyer, who is obliged to purchase the goods, the hirer has merely an option to do so, but may choose not to exercise that option.[153] Another difference between the two under English law is that because hire purchase is not considered to be a sale, the hirer cannot transfer good title to a bona fide third party, should it decide to sell the hired goods.[154] Since hire purchase does not involve a grant of an interest by the hirer and is accomplished by the retention of title by the owner, English law, for instance, does not consider it as a true security interest.[155] As a consequence, hire purchase does not, generally, require registration as many security interests do.

[147] Jakel in Bridge and Stevens (n 109) 104.

[148] I Fletcher and O Swarting, *Remedies Under Security Interests* (London, Kluwer Law International 2002) 135.

[149] See, generally, R Goode, *Hire Purchase Law and Practice*, 2nd edn (Butterworth & Co Publishers 1970); AG Guest, *The Law of Hire Purchase* (Sweet & Maxwell 1966).

[150] A Diamond, 'A Review of Security Interest in Personal Property', HMSO, DTI, 1989.

[151] Beale, Bridge, Gullifer and Lomnicka (n 8) 255.

[152] *Ibid* 256; H Johnson, 'Problems with Hire Purchase' (1993) 12 *IBFL* 39.

[153] *Jobson v Johnson* [1989] 1 WLR 1026.

[154] M Bridge, 'Form, Substance and Innovation in Personal Property Security Law' (1992) *JBL* 1, 6. But see s 27 of the Hire Purchase Act 1964 indicating that, under English law, a trade or finance purchaser of a motor vehicle from the hirer takes subject to the interest of the owner. At the same time, an innocent private purchaser takes free from such interest. See further Beale, Bridge, Gullifer and Lomnicka (n 8) 486.

[155] *McEntire v Crossley Bros Ltd* [1895] AC 457.

c. Leasing

Leasing involves the transfer of possession of the goods by the lessor to the lessee for a certain period of time in return for the rentals.[156] There are different ways of structuring the transaction, but in a basic form it usually starts with a lessee, who, having found the equipment it needs, approaches the lessor so that the latter can buy this equipment and lease it to the lessee.[157] In some cases, when the lessor does not wish to purchase the equipment itself, the lessee, who has better knowledge of the particulars of the equipment it needs, may buy such equipment, sell it to the lessor and lease it back. This is often referred to as sale and lease-back, whereby 'the buyer' (lessor) agrees to allow 'the seller' (lessee) to retain possession of the equipment in return for the payment of a rent. Alternatively, instead of leasing the equipment back, the seller may agree to re-purchase it at a later stage.[158]

English law distinguishes between conditional sale, hire purchase and lease on the basis that unlike conditional sale or hire purchase, leasing does not impose on the lessee an obligation or option to purchase the goods.[159] In fact, the title is never intended to be transferred to the lessee and is retained as security for the rentals by the lessor. There are different forms of leases reflecting the needs of particular industries and lessees, but the most commonly accepted classification is that between operational and finance leases. The operational lease usually denotes a short-term hire contract, whereby goods having a reasonably long economic life are let on hire for short periods of time to different lessees.[160] In contrast, a finance lease is a true financial tool involving a lessor who hires the goods out for the duration of their useful economic life to a lessee in return for rental payments.[161] Such rental payments amount to the return of sums which the lessor spends on the acquisition of the goods and its profit. Like RoT clauses under conditional sale, finance lease operates 'in the nature of security'. Thus, the lessee has the possession of the goods, while the lessor secures periodic payments through the retention of title in them as the true owner.[162]

[156] See, generally, *Tolley's Leasing in the UK*, 4th edn (Butterworths Tolley Ltd 2002).

[157] Beale, Bridge, Gullifer and Lomnicka (n 8) 260–65.

[158] *Ibid* 266.

[159] The distinction between these transactions may become less clear if, as is often the case, the lessee under a finance lease is given the right to receive the proceeds of sale of the equipment. See *On Demand Information plc v Michael Gerson (Finance) Ltd plc* [2004] 4 All ER 734.

[160] The operational leases do not perform the function of security. See Law Commission Consultation Paper No 164, *Registration of Security Interests: Company Charges and Property other than Land*, para 7.30 (hereafter '*Consultation Paper*').

[161] *Ibid* 7.30–7.34.

[162] *On Demand Information plc v Michael Gerson (Finance) Ltd plc* [2004] 4 All ER 734, 743.

ii. The Choice between a True Security and a Quasi Security Interest and Aspects of Characterisation

The types of transactions discussed above illustrate that, apart from recognised security interests, there also exist other ways of meeting the debtor's needs by providing it with finance or possession of the required goods and at the same time securing the creditor's position.[163] The parties to a transaction can opt for either a true security or a *quasi* security interest because they are treated differently by law which, in turn, has important practical implications. First, while security interests often require registration,[164] *quasi* security interests generally do not, which helps cut costs associated with the registration and ensure that the transaction's particulars remain confidential.[165] Secondly, if, following the debtor's default, the creditor repossesses and sells the collateral at the price exceeding the amount of debt, it will be entitled to keep the surplus in the case of a *quasi* security, but will have to hand it over to the debtor in the case of a true security. Thirdly, the retained ownership of the object as a *quasi* security will also provide the creditor with a super-priority badge on the debtor's insolvency. Since the object belongs to the creditor, it will not constitute part of the insolvent debtor's estate and will have to be handed back to the owner before the distribution among other secured and unsecured creditors begins.[166]

The main reason why *quasi* security creditors enjoy super-priority stems from the nature of their interest in the object. As true owners, they simply claim something that belongs to them and do not assert their rights in the debtor's property, as secured creditors do. There may be other reasons for opting for either a true or a *quasi* security. For instance, the financier can be precluded from lending a loan to the borrower, but allowed to provide the same finance by other means, such as by buying and re-selling the equipment to the borrower. The taxation implications may differ depending on the choice of the parties and the accounting considerations may also play a role when the choice is made by the parties.[167]

In some cases, the *quasi* security interests mimic the functions of the true security interests to such an extent that it is difficult to distinguish one

[163] For a detailed examination of these and other functionally similar devices, see Beale, Bridge, Gullifer and Lomnicka (n 8) Chapter 7.

[164] Thus, under English law, many charges created by companies are registrable under s 859A of the Companies Act 2006. But possessory security interests, such as pledge, usually do not require registration on the basis that possession in itself signals the existence of the interest. See Gullifer (n 9) 82. For a similar position in French law see Gdanski in Bridge and Stevens (n 109) 65.

[165] *Consultation Paper* (n 159) 6.3.

[166] *Re George Inglefield Ltd* [1933] Ch 1, 26–27, per Romer LJ.

[167] Beale, Bridge, Gullifer and Lomnicka (n 8) 81.

from the other. For instance, a railway operator wishing to raise finance to acquire a new rolling stock may sell some of its existing equipment to a finance house and agree to buy it back later. Such an arrangement can be considered as a true sale and buy-back transaction, whereby ownership passes to the creditor and the debtor agrees to retain possession and buy the property back by making instalment payments. This way, the debtor can receive the required funds and continue to use the property. The creditor, in contrast, can be considered as providing a loan to the debtor on the security of equipment, which is being repaid by periodic payments with interest. In this case, the court will have to decide whether the transaction amounts to a security or a genuine sale and buy-back agreement. If it is found to be a genuine sale/buy-back, all is well. If, as the case may be, the court decides that the transaction is in fact a disguised loan on security, it may be found void for a lack of registration or some other formality with which a true security must comply. The problems of characterisation and the necessity to subject true and *quasi* security interests to different legal regimes raises a question whether *quasi* security should be treated as a true security interest. Some commentators in the common law jurisdictions consider the *formal* approach, which divides economically similar devices into different categories, as artificial and unnecessarily complicating the law.[168] This issue has been considered by many legal commentators and was most clearly emphasised in the Diamond Report on security interests.[169] Professor Diamond suggested, among other things, that security interests and the functionally equivalent *quasi* securities, such as RoT agreements, should be equated and subjected to the same requirements of notice-filing or registration. His proposals were based on the United States Article 9 UCC, which essentially treats all devices intended to provide a security as true security interests. The proposals in the Diamond Report have not been adopted in the UK so far. Some legal scholars suggest that it is merely a question of time and eventually the courts will accept the *quasi* security interests into the category of true security interests.[170] Other jurisdictions, notably, Canada and New Zealand have shown more flexibility and, following legal reforms, adopted the functional approach.[171]

[168] Goode (n 120) 62–63.

[169] A Diamond, 'A Review of Security Interest in Personal Property', HMSO, DTI, 1989. For the discussion of the Diamond Report and other reports on the subject, see Consultation Paper (n 159) paras 1.27–1.31.

[170] Bridge (n 153).

[171] See, generally, I Davies, 'Floating Charges and Reform of Personal Property Legislation' (1988) *Comp Law* 47; N Howcroft, 'Canada: Security for Lending—Personal Property Security Act' (1988) *JIBL* 157.

iii. The Functional Approach: The Unitary Concept of Security Interest

The distinction between a true and *quasi* security interest is largely extinguished by the *functional* approach, treating all security devices as security interests. The *functional* approach originated in the US law under Article 9 UCC.[172] The pre-Code US law on secured transactions, somewhat similar to the formal approach, recognised distinctions between various security devices and governed them by different laws.[173] This was changed by the 1962 Article 9, which introduced a new *unitary* concept of a security interest, taking under its umbrella all old forms of security devices in personal property without regard to their form or location of the title.[174]

The key provisions of Article 9 for understanding whether a transaction is governed by it are mainly §1-201(35) on 'security interests', §9-109 on the 'scope' and §9-102 on the 'definitions'. §1-201(35) defines a security interest as 'an interest in personal property or fixtures which secures payment for performance of an obligation'. Accordingly, a transaction which confers only personal rights on the creditor will not be sufficient to create a valid security interest. In contrast, so long as the security device denotes some interest in the personal property it may amount to a security interest 'regardless of its form'.[175] This means that in addition to the traditional security interests, such as pledges, mortgages and charges, Article 9 regards many others, including some leases, consignments, RoT clauses under conditional sales, account receivables financing, factoring, deposit accounts and other security devices, as security interests.[176] At the same time, as broad as Article 9 appears to be, some devices will be out of its reach. For instance, the subordination agreements, allowing one creditor of the debtor to agree to subordinate its claim to that of another creditor, and negative pledges, prohibiting the debtor from creating a new security interest in its property until the debt to the present secured creditor is paid, are not considered as security interests.[177]

[172] The UCC, the drafting of which was initiated by Mr William A Schnader in 1940, was first published as the '1952 Official Text' under the auspices of the National Conference of Commissioners on Uniform State Laws (NCCUSL) and the American Law Institute (ALI). The UCC is a comprehensive code dedicated to commercial issues comprised of 11 Articles, Article 9 being titled as Secured Transactions. The UCC has been revised on many occasions and the last revision was conducted in 2009–2010. See W Schnader, 'A Short History of the Preparation and Enactment of the Uniform Commercial Code' (1967) 22 *U Miami L Rev* 1.

[173] See, generally, D Baird and T Jackson, *Security Interests in Personal Property: Cases, Problems, and Materials*, 2nd edn (New York, The Foundation Press, Inc 1987); G Gilmore, *Security Interests in Personal Property* (Boston & Toronto, Little, Brown and Company 1965).

[174] Broude in Bridge and Stevens (n 109) 50.

[175] §9-109(a)(1) UCC.

[176] D Garland, 'Revised Art 9: Understanding the Changes to Secured Transactions' (2001) 64 *Tex Bar J* 974.

[177] White and Summers (n 89) 1154.

Article 9 provides a comprehensive set of legal rules guiding a security interest through its major development stages: attachment, perfection, priority and enforcement. Attachment refers to all necessary steps to be taken for the creation of a security interest which will be valid between the creditor and the debtor. Perfection of security generally denotes the steps to be taken by the parties to secure the position of the secured creditor against third parties. One usually 'perfects' by filing the financing statement or taking control or possession of the collateral in order to publicise its position as a secured creditor to the world at large. At the stages of priority and enforcement, the secured creditor's position in the line of other secured creditors is determined and it is then able to exercise the remedies under Article 9.[178]

Article 9 has been characterised as 'fundamentally sound',[179] 'rational and modern',[180] 'awe inspiring, scary and spectacular'[181] and simply 'genius'.[182] Such countries as New Zealand,[183] Canada (with the exception of the civil law province of Quebec),[184] Gaza and the West Bank drafted their Personal Property Security Acts on the model of Article 9.[185] It has inspired several international initiatives in the field of security interests in personal property.[186] It is generally thought to eliminate problems associated with the formal approach such as compartmentalisation, complexity and difficulty in determining priorities. Instead of grouping different security devices into various compartments and subjecting them to different laws, Article 9 provides a single uniform legal regime for all of them, ridding the system of unnecessary complexity.

[178] For detailed examination of these stages, see White and Summers (n 89) Chapters 23–26.

[179] H Ruda, 'Art 9 Works—How Come?' (1994) 28 *Loy L A L Rev* 309, 309.

[180] J Ziegel, 'The New Personal Property Security Regimes—Have We Gone too Far?' (1989–90) 28 *Alta L Rev* 739, 741.

[181] H Hughes, 'Aesthetics of Commercial Law—Domestic and International Implications' (2007) 67 *Louisiana L Rev* 689, 730–32.

[182] R Cuming, 'Article 9 North of 49: The Canadian PPS Acts and the Quebec Civil Code' (1996) 29 *Loy L A L Rev* 971, 989.

[183] On the discussion of the New Zealand Personal Property Security Act, see H Gabriel, 'The New Zealand Personal Property Securities Act: A Comparison on the North American Model for Personal Property Security' (2000) 34 *Int'l L* 1123; R Carnachan and M King, 'New Zealand: Personal Property Securities Act 1999' (2001) 3 *J Int'l Fin Markets* 80; C Taylor and M King, 'New Zealand: Personal Property Securities Act' (1999) 1 *J Int'l Fin Markets* 75.

[184] See, generally, Howcroft (n 170); R Cuming and C Walsh, 'Revised Art 9 of the Uniform Commercial Code: Implications for the Canadian Personal Property Security Acts' (2000–2001) 16 *Bank Fin L Rev* 339; M Sheppard and L Champion, 'The Personal Property Security Act of Alberta—Implications for Oil and Gas Lenders' (1991) 29 *Alta L Rev* 33.

[185] Bridge, Macdonald, Simmonds and Walsh (n 141) 569.

[186] J Spanogle, 'A Functional Analysis of the EBRD Model Law on Secured Transactions' (1997) *NAFTA: L Bus Rev Americas* 82; F Dahan and G McCormack, 'International Influences and the Polish Law on Secured Transactions: Harmonisation, Unification or What?' (2002–3) 7 *Unif L Rev* 713; I Davies, 'The New *Lex Mercatoria:* International Interests in Mobile Equipment' (2003) 52 *ICLQ* 151, 154.

The unitary concept of Article 9 and the functional approach in general is not, however, welcomed by all. Some have commented that the unitary concept of security interests brought more confusion than clarity as regards the very essence of a security interest and that this concept should not be taken at face value.[187] For instance, RoT clauses, under which ownership is reserved by the conditional seller, are treated as a security interest under Article 9. The traditional English law distinction between 'simple' and 'all debts' RoT clauses and more advanced 'proceeds' and 'products' RoT clauses, construed as charges, is irrelevant under Article 9.[188] The conditional seller is considered as a secured creditor.[189] Once the debtor (conditional buyer who becomes the owner of the goods) obtains possession of the goods, the creditor's (conditional seller's) claim is equated with that of the claim of a secured creditor. It follows that to compete with other secured creditors of the buyer, the conditional seller must file the financing statement or, in other words, perfect its security, to avoid being treated as an unsecured creditor. The 'super-priority' enjoyed by the conditional seller as a true owner, which was previously taken for granted, is denied to it under the functional approach and must be clawed back by filing the financing statement or complying with the Article 9 requirements for the perfection of the purchase money security interest.[190] Another consequence of the functional approach applied to the RoT is that on repossession, the conditional seller is no longer entitled to deal with the goods as the owner. As a secured creditor, it has to sell them and account for any surplus to the buyer. Viewed from this perspective, the functional approach may seem to disrupt the general perception shared by business persons of what conditional sale and RoT clauses are.[191]

Furthermore, a substantial body of US case law on the distinction between true leases and security interests demonstrates that the problem of the characterisation persists under the functional approach.[192] True leases are governed by Article 2A UCC and need not be perfected or filed under Article 9 as a security interest.[193] If the lessor is in reality a secured

[187] Bridge, Macdonald, Simmonds and Walsh (n 141) 574.

[188] McCormack (n 5) 39–99.

[189] §9-110 UCC provides in part that a security interest arising under §2-401 (seller who retains title as security interest), §2-505 (seller who ships under RoT), §2-711(3) (buyer in possession of rejected goods) is subject to Article 9.

[190] Purchase money security interest (PMSI) is generally said to arise when the creditor provides the debtor with funds to enable it to purchase specific goods. PMSI is granted super-priority status which upsets the general rule of priority according to which priority is granted on the basis of the first-to-file criterion. See White and Summers (n 89) 1196–99.

[191] McCormack (n 136) 113.

[192] See, for example, *Leasing Services Corp v American Nat Bank & Trust Co*, 1976 WL 23674, 19 UCC (DNJ 1976); *In re Lerch*, 147 BR 455, 20 UCC Rep Serv 2nd 260 (Bankr C D Ill 1992).

[193] M Livingston, 'Certainty, Efficiency and Realism: Rights in Collateral under Art 9 of the Uniform Commercial Code' (1994) 73 *North Carolina L Rev* 115, 125–26.

creditor retaining a security to ensure performance of the debtor's obligation, Article 9 applies and the secured creditor loses its privileged position unless it complies with its requirements, such as the filing of the financing statement.[194] The issue is rather complex and some have even suggested that both true leases and those leases amounting to security interests should be subjected to the requirements of filing to eliminate the need for the characterisation.[195] To summarise, Article 9 is sometimes described as the 'most modernised, rational and comprehensive system of security interests in the present world'.[196] While this may be the case, many legal systems have chosen to retain the formal approach to the definition of security interests.

III. THE CONCEPT OF THE INTERNATIONAL INTEREST

A. What is an International Interest?

One of the main objectives of the Convention is to establish an effective international legal framework for the creation, perfection, priority and enforcement of international interests held in the uniquely identifiable high value mobile equipment. The international interest is the key category of the interests governed by the Convention.[197] Provided that the interest is created in accordance with Articles 2 and 7 CTC, it will constitute a valid international interest even if it would not have had such an effect under the national law.[198] Likewise, an interest validly created under the domestic law will not constitute an international interest unless it complies with the Convention's requirements.[199] If the formal requirements for the constitution of the international and national interests coincide, they will come into existence simultaneously. In this case, the creditor can exercise the rights given to it by domestic law as long as they do not conflict with the Convention's provisions. At the same time, a registered international interest can give the secured creditor stronger protection since it will enjoy priority over a domestic interest, as well as subsequently registered and unregistered Convention interests, and will survive the debtor's insolvency.[200]

Although the international interest is the key category of registrable interests, the CTC does not provide a comprehensive definition of this concept.

[194] White and Summers (n 89) 1155–63.

[195] D Baird and T Jackson, 'Possession and Ownership: An Examination of the Scope of Art 9' (1983) 35 *Stan L Rev* 175, 189–94. For the opposite view, see C Mooney, 'The Mystery and Myth of 'Ostensible Ownership' and Art 9 Filing: A Critique of Proposals to Extend Filing Requirements to Leases' (1988) 39 *Alabama L Rev* 683.

[196] McCormack (n 136) 141.

[197] For an overview of other interests governed by the Convention, see chapter three.

[198] Goode (n 19) 266–68.

[199] Goode (n 20) 12.

[200] Goode (n 19) 56.

Instead, its meaning has to be ascertained from Articles 2 and 7. First, the international interest must be either: (a) granted by the chargor under a security agreement; (b) vested in a person who is the conditional seller under a title reservation agreement; or (c) vested in a person who is the lessor under a leasing agreement.[201] Secondly, the international interest must relate to one of the objects of mobile equipment listed in Article 2(3), namely aircraft and railway objects or space assets.[202] Thirdly, an international interest agreement must be: (a) in writing; (b) relate to the object of which the chargor, conditional seller or lessor has power to dispose; (c) enable the object to be identified in conformity with the Protocol; and (d) in the case of security agreement, enable the secured obligation to be determined, but without the need to state the maximum sum secured.[203]

To establish an international interest one should, among other things, determine whether a transaction can be characterised as a security, title reservation or a leasing agreement. It is not clear whether the issue of characterisation should be dealt with under the applicable law or under the Convention. First, Article 2(4) provides that it is the applicable law that should deal with this issue. The applicable law is said to refer to the 'domestic law of the State whose law is applicable by the rules of private international law of the forum'.[204] Secondly, the meaning of these terms can be ascertained from the definitions provided by Article 1 CTC. The section below considers both routes of characterising a transaction and explains the relationship between them.

B. Defining the International Interest: Applicable Law or the Convention?

i. Article 2(4) Route: Applicable Law

Article 2(4) provides that it is the applicable law and not the Convention that determines whether an interest is a security agreement, title reservation or a leasing agreement. The reason why this characterisation was left to the applicable domestic law was that finding a uniform approach on this issue was thought to be impracticable.[205] This is due to the sharp divide between the formal and functional approaches adopted by various legal systems in defining security interests and other functionally similar devices.[206] Initially, the sub-committee of the Study Group responsible for the preparation of

[201] Art 2(2) CTC.
[202] Art 2(2), (3) CTC.
[203] Art 2(2) CTC and Art 7 CTC.
[204] Art 5(3) CTC.
[205] Goode (n 19) 267.
[206] *Ibid* 267.

the uniform rules on security interests concluded that the draft Convention should adopt the functional approach to the definition of security interests, embracing the notions of the RoT and lease.[207] This was in line with the proposals of Professor Cuming expressed in his Report[208] and was confirmed by the positive response to the Questionnaire on the issues of security interests distributed among banks, financial institutions, buyers and sellers.[209] However, some delegates from the legal systems adhering to the formal approach and the representatives of the European Leasing Industry, insisted on preserving the distinction between the traditional security interests and the RoT and lease.[210] This is why the uniform characterisation of interests seemed impracticable and it was decided to leave this issue to the applicable law.

Since the transaction can be viewed differently by various legal systems, its characterisation by the applicable law may result in it being considered either as a security, RoT or a lease. The difference between these categories under the CTC is primarily relevant to the creditor's remedies.[211] If the agreement is characterised as a title reservation agreement, the creditor can exercise the remedies available to it under Article 10 CTC and can terminate the agreement and take possession or control of the object. Since the creditor is the owner of the object, the debtor cannot claim an interest in the surplus which can be generated by the object's subsequent sale. In contrast, if the agreement is defined as a security agreement, the creditor will have to proceed under Articles 8 and 9 CTC as a secured creditor. Provided that the debtor agrees, the creditor can take possession or control of the object, sell or grant a lease, or collect or receive any income or profits arising from the object's management or use.[212] These remedies must be exercised in a commercially reasonable manner[213] and in the case of the proposed sale or lease the creditor must give prior written notice to all interested persons.[214] Sums collected by the creditor must be applied towards discharge of the secured obligation and any surplus must be distributed among the holders of the subsequently ranking interests and the debtor.[215]

The delegation of the issue of characterisation to the applicable domestic law allows the Convention to stay outside the long-standing debate between

[207] Davies (n 185) 161.

[208] R Cuming, 'International Regulation of Aspects of Security Interests in Mobile Equipment' UNIDROIT 1989, Study LXXII Doc 2.

[209] Davies (n 185) 158–59.

[210] *Ibid* 161.

[211] Goode (n 19) 267.

[212] Art 8(1) CTC.

[213] Art 8(3) CTC. For the examination of the requirement of commercial reasonableness, see chapter six.

[214] Art 8(4) CTC.

[215] Art 8(6) CTC.

the formal and functional approaches. It is a compromise solution allowing Contracting States to adhere to the approach they adopted.[216] The fact that Article 2(2) expressly distinguishes between the security agreement, title reservation and leasing agreements indicates that the legal systems adopting the formal approach can utilise these categories to introduce the transaction into the bigger category of the international interest.[217] From the functional approach perspective, the true security and *quasi* security interests can be subsumed under the Article 2(2)'s category of a 'security agreement'.

This mechanism allows both formal and functional approaches to co-exist at the stage of the constitution of the international interest. United as 'international interests', all three types of interests are then subjected to the Convention's uniform legal regime governing creation, registration and priority.[218] The distinctions between the three categories do not, however, become wholly irrelevant and when the issue of the remedies arises, the transaction's characterisation once again becomes important. The remedies of the secured creditor are more detailed than those of other holders of international interests because a secured creditor, unlike a conditional seller and lessor, is not considered to be the owner of the object.[219] In countries following the functional approach, the RoT and some leases are treated as security interests. When the transaction is characterised as such, the creditor will only be able to exercise the remedies available to it as a secured creditor, and not as the conditional seller or lessor.[220] This is the effect of Article 2(2) providing that the categories enumerated therein are mutually exclusive. Once a transaction has been characterised as, for instance, a title reservation agreement it cannot be later re-characterised as a security interest.

ii. Article 1(q), (ii), (ll) Route: The Convention

Although Article 2(4) prescribes that it is the applicable law that determines whether a transaction amounts to a security, RoT or a lease agreement, Article 1 also provides for the definitions of these types of interests and agreements. It appears that the Convention provides for two different routes of determining whether a transaction falls into one of the categories of Article 2(2) and does not explain the relationship between these routes. This issue is important because the characterisation under the applicable law and the Convention may not always coincide.

216 See R Goode, 'Rule, Practice, and Pragmatism in International Commercial Law' (2005) *ICLQ* 539, 560.

217 Honnebier (n 94) 17–22.

218 For instance, Art 16(1)(a), enumerating the registrable interests does not distinguish between security, title reservation and lease and defines them as 'international interests'.

219 Goode (n 19) 280–81.

220 *Ibid* 280.

Consider an agreement whereby an owner is letting an aircraft object on hire to the hirer, the latter having an option to purchase the object. Such an agreement will have to be characterised to establish whether it can qualify as the Convention's international interest. If Article 2(4) is relied upon and, say, English law applies, the agreement may be characterised as a hire purchase and will not fall into either of the categories of Article 2(2).[221] In contrast, if the agreement is defined under the Convention, it may be considered as a lease and amount to an international interest. English law distinguishes a lease and hire purchase on the basis that while a lease does not entail an option to purchase and the object must be returned to the lessor at the end of the agreement, hire purchase provides the hirer with this option.[222] In contrast, the broad definition of the leasing agreement under Article 1(q) includes any agreement by which 'one person (the lessor) grants a right to possession or control of an object (with or without option to purchase) to another person (the lessee) in return for a rental ...'. This definition would allow characterising this agreement as a lease and the lessor's interest could qualify as an international interest.

The uncertainty relating to the characterisation of interests may be seen as being clarified by the OC's comment relating to the definition of a lease under Article 1(q): 'leasing agreement ... covers leases and sub-leases ... with or without an option to purchase ... *whether or not* the transaction would be characterised by national law as a leasing agreement, *though under Article 2(4) it is left to the applicable law to determine whether the agreement is to be characterised as a security agreement or a title reservation agreement*'.[223] This comment confirms that the characterisation of the transaction can differ under the Convention and the national law. It also seems to suggest that the characterisation under the Convention is a two-stage exercise. First, the CTC's definitions must be used for the 'initial characterisation' to determine whether a transaction gives rise to an interest which, in principle, can be governed by the Convention.[224] If, applying Article 1, a creditor's interest can be defined as that of a secured creditor, conditional seller or the lessor, this interest will be governed by the Convention. Secondly, once this is established, then the transaction should be characterised by the applicable domestic law for the purpose of other provisions of the Convention and, in particular, those, relating to the creditor's remedies.[225]

221 See Beale, Bridge, Gullifer and Lomnicka (n 8) 255.

222 This distinction between hire purchase and lease may become less clear if, as is often the case, the lessee is given the right to receive any proceeds of sale of the goods at the end of the lease. See Beale, Bridge, Gullifer and Lomnicka (n 8) 261.

223 Goode (n 19) 257 (emphasis added).

224 *Ibid* 267.

225 *Ibid* 267.

In line with this view, the agreement of hire of the aircraft object with the option to purchase should be initially characterised as a lease under Article 1 CTC. This will bring the agreement within the Convention's scope. Once the international interest of the lessor is constituted, the interest must, once again, be characterised under the applicable law pursuant to Article 2(4). The subsequent characterisation is needed to determine which interest-sensitive provisions of the Convention should apply to it. Thus, if the interest of the owner/lessor is later re-characterised by the applicable law as a security interest, it will exercise the remedies of a secured creditor and not those of a lessor.

The OC's explanation of the relationship between the two routes of defining various interests is not entirely satisfactory. For instance, a transaction initially characterised by the Convention as a lease with an option to purchase may later be re-characterised as a hire-purchase agreement by the applicable domestic law. In this case, it is not clear whether such an interest would fall within the Convention's scope. It would be an undesirable outcome breeding uncertainty if a transaction characterised as falling within the Convention's scope at the first stage could later be excluded from its legal regime due to its subsequent re-characterisation by the applicable domestic law at the second stage of this exercise.

In support of the view expressed in the Commentary, it is potentially arguable that characterisation under the applicable law should have the effect of simply distinguishing between security interests and RoT agreements in the broad sense. If this is correct, then a hire purchase agreement with an option to purchase could be re-characterised under the applicable law as the title reservation agreement in the sense that the owner retains its title until the hirer pays the rentals and decides to exercise the option to purchase. This argument can probably be supported by the OC's remark relating to the definition of the lease that 'under Article 2(4) it is left to the applicable law to determine whether the agreement is to be characterised *as a security agreement or a title reservation agreement*'.[226] This view would correspond to the Convention's general distinction between the interests of a secured creditor and the conditional buyer and lessor as far as the remedies are concerned. Indeed, the Convention does not distinguish between the remedies of the conditional seller and lessor. Accordingly, it is irrelevant whether the applicable law views the transaction as a hire purchase, lease or conditional sale. Provided that it is a transaction involving the retention of title by the owner/lessor or the conditional seller, the holder of such an interest can exercise the Convention's remedies designed to suit the needs of the conditional seller and lessor.

[226] Goode (n 19) 257 (emphasis added).

The approach adopted in the Commentary is difficult to justify because it is not supported by the text of the Convention. Article 2(4) expressly provides that it is the applicable law that should determine whether an interest is a security interest, a title reservation or a lease. In addition, the fact that its drafters did not intend the Convention to be used for this purpose flows from Article 2(4) of the Draft Convention, which reads as follows: '[t]he Convention does not determine whether an interest to which paragraph 2 applies falls within sub-paragraph (a), (b) or (c)'.[227] This wording confirms that the definitions of the security, title retention and lease contained in Article 1 should not be used to decide whether a transaction falls into one of the categories of Article 2(2).

The intention of the CTC's drafters is also evident from the comments to the Draft Convention presented by the delegation from Japan:

> since the characterisation is always the first step to determine the applicability of relevant provisions, i.e. the remedies under the Convention, and thus, this paragraph seems to be so important to be argued and interpreted repeatedly by the relevant parties in future, the explicit provision [that it should be governed by the applicable law and not the Convention] is preferable to avoid future confusions and misunderstandings.[228]

Further, Article 1, defining the CTC's terms, provides that these definitions should only be used as long as the context of the Convention does not require otherwise. Therefore, it is clear that Article 2(4) should be given priority over the definitions of a security, title retention and lease provided in Article 1 for the characterisation of a transaction.

It is suggested that the transaction must be characterised by the applicable domestic law to ascertain whether it falls into one of the categories of Article 2(2). Once characterised by the applicable law, the meaning of the terms 'security interest', 'retention of title' and 'lease', whenever they appear in other provisions of the Convention, should be read in accordance with Article 1. This approach is different to the one adopted in the Commentary in that the Convention's definitions are not used for the initial characterisation of the creditor's interest. Instead, the interest is characterised by the applicable domestic law, as required by Article 2(4), to establish whether it is governed by the Convention. The proposed approach can also eliminate the possibility of the re-characterisation of the creditor's interest at a later stage and bring predictability to the creditor in relation to its remedies. Once the interest is characterised by the applicable domestic law, it is

[227] Convention on International Interests in Mobile Equipment and Protocol Thereto on Matters Specific to Aircraft Equipment: Diplomatic Conference to Adopt a Mobile Equipment Convention and an Aircraft Protocol—Acts and Proceedings. Draft [UNIDROIT] Convention on International Interests in Mobile Equipment, DCME Doc No 3, 6 April 2001.

[228] *Ibid* 186. DCME Doc No 32, 31 October 2001.

subjected to the legal regime of the Convention, including its defined terms. Consequently, in relation to other provisions of the Convention, such as the rules on priority and registration, the creditor's interest should be defined in accordance with Article 1.

For example, if the creditor's interest is characterised by the applicable domestic law as that of the conditional seller, it does not mean that such an interest need not be registered and should be granted super-priority simply because the creditor is considered as the owner of the object, even if this would be the consequence of its characterisation under the applicable law. The role of the applicable law ceases once the creditor's interest is characterised as that of the conditional seller. After that, it should be considered in accordance with the definitions in Article 1. Thus, the conditional seller will not be granted super-priority and will have to register its interest in the IR to secure its priority against subsequently registered and unregistered interests.

IV. THE LEGAL NATURE OF INTERNATIONAL INTERESTS: PROPRIETARY OR CONTRACTUAL?

Consider the following situation. A creditor is willing to make a loan to the debtor to manufacture a new satellite. To assure the creditor that the loan and the interest will be repaid, the debtor transfers the ownership in the satellite to the creditor by way of a security. The parties agree that once the debt is discharged, the ownership in the satellite will revert back to the debtor. The satellite will be operated at low Earth orbit and thus out of reach of any jurisdiction known to the creditor. Concerned about possible practical complications relating to taking possession or selling the satellite in the case of the debtor's default, the creditor wishes to support its security by some other means.[229]

To achieve this end, the directors of the debtor company provide the creditor with the personal guarantees whereby they undertake to repay the borrowed sums together with the interest, should the debtor default. Both arrangements are entered into to assure the creditor that the borrowed sums will be repaid. For this reason, some jurisdictions treat such arrangements as different types of security interests. For instance, the Russian Civil Code considers a personal guarantee as one of the means of securing performance of an obligation and treats it alongside other forms of security, such as a hypothec over movable and immovable property, a pledge, a right

[229] Unlike other Protocols, The Space Protocol covers not only interests in tangible space assets, but also rights assignments and rights reassignments which must be linked to the physical space assets. See D Panahy and R Mittal, 'The Prospective UNIDROIT Convention on International Interests in Mobile Equipment as Applied to Space Property' (1999) 4 *Unif L Rev* 303, 306. See also Goode (n 29) 164, 421–22.

of retention and others.[230] Other legal systems take the view that the legal nature of these two arrangements is so different that it is necessary to treat them almost as different institutions of the law.[231]

The arrangement between the creditor and the debtor provides the former with a *proprietary* interest in the property of the latter and is often referred to as a *real* security. By obtaining ownership in the satellite as a means of securing repayment of the debt, the creditor obtains an interest in the property itself. Because it is an interest in the object and not simply a right against a particular contracting party with respect to the object, the creditor will, in theory, be able to pursue the satellite into the hands of a third party, should the debtor sell it and dissipate the proceeds of sale.[232] By earmarking this particular satellite to the discharge of the debt, the creditor can also ensure that, in the case of the debtor's insolvency, it will be able to obtain repayment by means of realising its security in priority to the other creditors. The property encumbered by the creditor's real security will no longer be available for distribution among the insolvent debtor's unsecured creditors. Generally speaking, the creditor holding a real security in the debtor's object will be able to take this object out of the insolvent debtor's estate, sell it and use the proceeds towards the discharge of the unpaid debt.

In contrast, the arrangement between the creditor and the directors with respect to the personal guarantee confers no such powers on the creditor. Similar to the real security, a personal guarantee affords the creditor additional security in that it may rely on the directors for the repayment of the debt should the debtor default. However, a personal guarantee, whereby the guarantor undertakes to honour the obligation owed to the creditor by the debtor, is a mere contractual obligation and confers no proprietary interest in the property of the directors on the creditor. For this reason, such a security is often called a *personal* security as opposed to the *real* one.[233]

Assuming that the Convention applies and that the domestic law characterises both arrangements as security interests, can both of them amount to international interests? On the one hand, Article 2(4) provides that it is the applicable domestic law that should characterise agreements as a security, title retention or lease, which necessarily implies that the Convention has no role to play in this exercise. On this view, both agreements can be considered as international interests. On the other hand, the Convention's provisions demonstrate that it governs the international interests of a proprietary

[230] The Civil Code of the Russian Federation, Part One, 30 November 1994, N 51-ФЗ. See Chapter 23, in particular Art 329, Arts 361–367 of the Civil Code.

[231] Gullifer (n 9) 5.

[232] See R Goode, 'Ownership and Obligation in Commercial Transactions' (1987) *LQR* 433, 433–34.

[233] Ali (n 88) 176.

rather than personal nature.[234] It follows that although the Convention does not state so expressly, the proprietary nature of an interest is a necessary criterion to be met for it to fall within the Convention's scope.

Since the contractual and proprietary interests attract different legal consequences, the distinction between them is of considerable practical significance. Many legal systems recognise that a property interest implies exclusive dominion over the object which can be asserted against the whole world.[235] In contrast, a contractual obligation, or a personal right, merely reflects the rights and obligations of the contracting parties.[236] The universality of property interests can explain their major feature: in principle, property interests remain valid in the case of the debtor's insolvency.[237] This consequence flows from a widely recognised principle of insolvency law, according to which only those assets which belong to the insolvent company are available for the distribution among its creditors. If the creditor demonstrates that it has a property and not simply a personal right in an identifiable asset of the insolvent debtor, such property will no longer be considered as available for distribution among its other creditors. For this reason, the unpaid seller who has validly retained ownership of the goods can, in principle, take them back if the buyer is struck by insolvency. Since the unpaid seller has a property interest in the goods until it is paid the purchase price, such goods cannot be treated as the property of the insolvent debtor. Similarly, if the secured creditor holds a proprietary interest by way of a security in the insolvent debtor's object, it can, in principle, segregate this object from other assets of the debtor and obtain the repayment of the loan from the proceeds of sale. The liquidator or trustee in bankruptcy of the insolvent debtor will not be able to keep the holder of the property interest on the sidelines while it pays the debts owed by the insolvent debtor to its general creditors. This does not mean that the personal right is completely destroyed by the insolvency of the debtor. Rather, it is transformed into a right to prove for its monetary value along with other creditors of the insolvent debtor.[238] Since the value of the assets of the insolvent debtor is often considerably smaller than its liabilities, the holder of a personal right usually has only minuscule chances of obtaining the discharge. This feature of property interests on its own makes it clear why a creditor may be eager to establish that it has a property rather than a personal right over some identifiable assets of the insolvent debtor.

[234] Goode (n 19) 38.

[235] U Mattei, *Basic Principles of Property Law: A Comparative Legal and Economic Introduction* (Contributions in Legal Studies, N 93, Greenwood Press 2000) 78–79; M Bridge, *Personal Property Law*, 4th edn (Oxford, OUP: Clarendon Law Series 2015) 1–3.

[236] S Panesar, *General Principles of Property Law* (Pearson Education 2001) 219.

[237] Calnan (n 4) Chapter 2.

[238] McKendrick (n 2) 29.

The Convention does not explicitly define international interests as either personal or property interests. The representatives of the aviation industry, taking part in the drafting of the Convention and the Aircraft Protocol, insisted that its final text should reflect the vital principles of asset-based finance and leasing and ensure that the interest acquired by the holder of the international interest is of a proprietary nature.[239] Likewise, the Restricted Working Group (RWG), which consisted of representatives of financial institutions, industries and practicing lawyers, concluded that the international interest should denote a proprietary interest in the asset of the debtor. The RWG stated that as a proprietary interest, the international interest should afford its holder an opportunity to *follow* the asset into the hands of third parties and to obtain the discharge of the debt *prior* to other creditors of the debtor.[240]

Although the Convention does not explicitly refer to international interests as proprietary interests, its provisions allow one to conclude that the holder of the international interest acquires a property rather than simply a personal right in the object.[241] For example, Article 30 provides that in the insolvency proceedings against the debtor an international interest remains 'effective' if registered in the IR prior to the commencement of such proceedings. 'Effective' is said to reflect the proprietary nature of the international interest,[242] which means that, as a general rule, registered international interests will rank ahead of the claims of the junior secured and unsecured creditors of the insolvent debtor.[243]

A proprietary international interest will not only be effective during the insolvency proceedings, but is also likely to survive the debtor's insolvency. Although no cases decided under the Convention have yet been reported to support this point, one English case may prove to be useful in this regard.[244] In this case, Hugh Lind, in return for a loan, mortgaged the possibility of becoming possessed in the future of a share of his mother's personal estate first to the Norwich Union Life Insurance Society and three years later to another lender—HL Arnold. In the same year he was adjudicated bankrupt and obtained his discharge. Neither Norwich Union nor Arnold tried to enforce their security at that time. Six years later, Mr Lind's mother died and he became entitled to a share in her estate. He assigned this share to the plaintiffs.

[239] J Wool, 'The Case for a Commercial Orientation to the Proposed UNIDROIT Convention as Applied to Aircraft Equipment' (1999) 4 *Unif L Rev* 289, 291.

[240] Davies (n 185) 159–60.

[241] See Goode (n 19) 38, stating that proprietary nature of international interests is reinforced by the Convention's choice of words that the security interest is 'granted' by the chargor to the chargee and that the interest of a conditional seller and lessor is 'vested' in it.

[242] Goode (n 19) 343.

[243] Panahy and Mittal (n 228) 311.

[244] *In Re Lind, Industrial Finance Syndicate, Limited v Lind* [1915] 2 Ch 345.

The plaintiffs argued that the security interests of the first two lenders were of no value. This was based on the bankruptcy and the discharge of the debtor and that after the discharge the debtor was entitled to a 'fresh start' free from the old contractual obligations.[245] The court's reasoning turned on the question whether assurances of Mr Lind to the prior creditors rested in the contract, or whether they amounted to a real security in the potential share of Mr Lind and became enforceable once such property came into existence. It was held that because the assurances given to Norwich Union and Arnold were security interests and conferred on the secured creditors a proprietary and not merely a personal right in the share of Mr Lind, these security interests survived his bankruptcy and had to be ranked ahead of the plaintiff's interest. By analogy with this case, if the holder of a registered international interest fails to enforce its security at the start of the debtor's insolvency proceedings, its security should not simply disappear. Since the security interest is of proprietary nature and 'effective' in insolvency, it is likely to survive the debtor's insolvency and rank ahead of the junior secured and unsecured creditors of the debtor.

Article 29 CTC serves as another indicator of the proprietary nature of the international interests. Article 29(1) provides that 'a registered interest has priority over any other interest subsequently registered and over an unregistered interest'.[246] The privileged treatment of the prior registered international interest can be explained by its proprietary nature. Once the debtor transfers its proprietary interest in the object to the secured creditor, who registers its interest, it becomes the holder of such a proprietary interest.[247] As the holder of the registered property interest in the object, the secured creditor is entitled to take this object in priority to the holders of the subsequently registered and unregistered interests.[248]

The priority enjoyed by the secured creditor over the unsecured creditors or the liquidator of the insolvent debtor is evident from many cases decided under English law.[249] In one case, a company obtained a loan from

[245] *Ibid* 357.

[246] Priority, along with effects in insolvency and ability to pursue the asset into the hands of a third party are often said to be common incidents of property rights. These incidents are frequently considered to be integral to security interests *because* of its proprietary nature. Presumably, if one can find all three incidents in an interest (such as international interest under the Convention), its legal nature must necessarily be proprietary.

[247] L Ponoroff and F Knippenberg, 'Having One's Property and Eating it Too: When the Article 9 Security Interest Becomes a Nuisance' (2006) 82 *Notre Dame L Rev* 373, 393–95.

[248] *Ibid* 393–95.

[249] Priority enjoyed by the secured creditor is often subjected to the restrictions imposed by the law in various jurisdictions for policy reasons (eg to protect vulnerable unsecured creditors). For instance, under English law, failure to register a registrable charge within 21 days of its creation will invalidate it in the case of the debtor's liquidation which may have effect on the order of priority among the debtor's other creditors. See Companies Act 2006, s 861(3); Gullifer (n 9) 108, 191–92.

the plaintiffs in exchange for a security in 'all the stock, plant, chattels, and effects which may from time to time be held by the company'.[250] Before the principal money became due or the interest had fallen into arrears, the debtor went into liquidation. The liquidators of the insolvent company took possession of all its property and were about to apply it for the benefit of its ordinary creditors. In the dispute between the secured creditors (the plaintiffs) and the liquidators of the insolvent company, the court gave priority to the secured creditors even though the time for the repayment of the debt had not yet arrived. It was held that once the company had become insolvent, security had become immediately enforceable and the secured creditor should not be kept on the sidelines while unsecured creditors obtained their discharge out of the property encumbered by security.

The priority flowing from the proprietary nature of the interest held by the secured creditor was also evident in another case, where the insolvent company owed money both to unsecured and secured creditors.[251] One of the unsecured creditors obtained judgment against the insolvent company. Instead of approaching the insolvent company for the repayment of the debt, the unsecured creditor served a garnishee order nisi on the debtor of the insolvent company. In accordance with the garnishee order nisi, the debtor was required to pay its debt to the unsecured creditor instead of its original creditor. The secured creditor argued that the debt belonged to the insolvent company and was for this reason encumbered by security. It was held that the garnishee order nisi did not transfer the ownership in the debt from the insolvent company to the unsecured creditor. The debt remained encumbered by the security and the secured creditor was able to obtain the discharge out of this money prior to the unsecured creditor. The proprietary nature of the security and the privileged treatment which it affords to a secured creditor allowed it to extend its hands to such property of the insolvent debtor which had not yet even reached its intended recipient!

Finally, another case demonstrates just how strong a privileged position of the secured creditor can be.[252] In this case, a company obtained a secured loan and duly paid all interest to the secured creditor. The principal sum had not yet become payable and the debtor was not in breach of contract between itself and the secured creditor. At this stage, another creditor of the debtor obtained a judgment against it, ordering the debtor to repay sums due to this creditor. The secured creditor appointed a receiver, with the result that the debtor was unable to deal with its property and pay to the judgment creditor. The court held that since the secured creditor was the

[250] *Hodson v Tea Company* (1880) 14 Ch D 859. See also *Wallace v Universal Automatic Machines Company* [1894] 2 Ch 547; *In Re Crompton & Co Ltd* [1914] 1 Ch 954 for similar results.

[251] *Norton v Yates* [1906] 1 KB 112.

[252] *Campbell v London Pressed Hinge Company, Limited* [1905] 1 Ch D 576.

holder of a proprietary interest in the property of the debtor, it could enforce the security on the ground that such security was in jeopardy. Although Buckley J felt that the outcome of the case was possibly unjust with respect to the judgment creditor, he stated that 'the creditor never had any right as between himself and the debenture-holder [secured creditor] to enforce payment in priority to the debenture-holder'.[253]

Finally, Article 29(6) CTC is also indicative of the proprietary nature of the international interests. According to this provision, 'any priority given by this Article to an interest in an object extends to proceeds'. The ability to follow the object or trace its proceeds in the case of an unauthorised disposition is often considered as another incident of a property interest held in such an object. As a general rule, the owner (or the holder of a lesser proprietary right) is entitled to take its property back from a third party.[254] Article 1(w), however, defines 'proceeds' restrictively, limiting them to monetary or non-monetary proceeds resulting from total or partial loss of the object (such as insurance payments) or total or partial confiscation, condemnation or requisition. For instance, if a debtor sells a train wagon, encumbered by a security, to a third party and retains the proceeds of sale in its bank account, a secured creditor who has a registered international interest in the wagon will not be able to pursue the collateral into the proceeds of sale. If the secured creditor were able to do so, it would broaden the Convention's scope beyond the categories of objects listed in Article 2(3).[255] In contrast, if the charged object is insured against a loss and is later destroyed by collision with another object, the secured creditor's interest in the collateral will extend to the insurance proceeds.[256]

[253] *Ibid* 582, *per* Buckley J.

[254] This general rule may be subjected to exceptions allowing a third party to override the title of the initial owner. See Ali (n 88) 30; A Oakley, 'Proprietary Claims and Their Priority in Insolvency' [1995] *CLJ* 377, 378–81; J Beatson and N Andrews, 'Common Law Tracing: Springboard or Swan Song?' (1997) 113 *LQR* 21.

[255] Another reason why 'proceeds' are narrowly defined by the Convention is to avoid it from covering issues which are already governed by the UN Convention on the Assignment of Receivables in International Trade 2001. See Goode (n 19) 100–01.

[256] *Ibid* 100–01.

2

The Constitution of Security and other International Interests under the Convention and the Protocols

I. INTRODUCTION

TO PROTECT ITS interest in the debtor's equipment, the creditor[1] must ensure that a valid international interest is created in it. To achieve this end, transacting parties must follow the formal requirements in Article 7. An interest is constituted as an international interest where the agreement creating a security interest or providing for an interest[2] of a conditional seller or lessor: (a) is in writing; (b) relates to an object of which the chargor, conditional seller or lessor has power to dispose; (c) enables the object to be identified in conformity with the Protocol; and (d) in the case of a security agreement, enables the secured obligations to be determined, but without the need to state a sum or maximum sum secured.[3] The identification requirements for the purposes of Article 7(c) are provided for by the Protocols.

The constitution of an international interest raises a number of questions. First, although the agreement for the international interest must be in writing, it is not clear whether it must be contained in a single document or whether a multiplicity of documents demonstrating the presence of an agreement is acceptable. Secondly, the chargor, conditional seller or lessor

[1] Art 1(i) CTC defines 'creditor' as a chargee under a security agreement, a conditional seller under a title reservation agreement or a lessor under a leasing agreement.

[2] The agreement between the parties is said to '*create*' the interest in the case of a security agreement and '*provide for the interest*' in the cases of RoT and lease agreements. Such wording reflects the way in which the interests of the creditors are obtained. While a secured creditor's interest is usually *created* by its agreement with a debtor, the conditional seller's and lessor's interests precede their agreements with the buyer and lessee. Consequently, the international interest will arise not at the moment when the interests of the conditional seller and lessor in the object are acquired, but when they enter into the agreements with the conditional buyer and lessee. See R Goode, 'The International Interest as an Autonomous Property Interest' (2004) 1 *ERPL* 18, 22.

[3] Art 7 CTC.

must have the power to dispose of the object, but this term is not defined by the Convention and it is not clear when the power to dispose arises. Thirdly, what degree of precision is required to identify the object in the international interest agreement? Finally, is it possible to create a floating security under the Convention? These questions are considered in turn.

II. THE EFFECT OF THE CONSTITUTION OF THE INTERNATIONAL INTEREST

The Convention is silent as to the effect of the creation of the international interest in that it does not state whether, once constituted, it becomes valid only between the parties to the agreement or whether it also becomes effective against third parties. It can be argued that, once the international interest is constituted it becomes effective only as between the parties to the agreement.[4] Indeed, to make its interest enforceable against third parties, the creditor is required to take a further step and register its interest in the International Registry (IR). However, this position is difficult to justify because the Convention's international interests are of a proprietary rather than personal nature. It follows that, once constituted, such interests should be effective both against the debtor and against third parties.[5] The only moment when the proprietary interest in the object can be granted to the secured creditor is the moment of the constitution of the international interest. By registering its international interest, the creditor cannot convert an interest previously effective only between itself and the debtor into an interest enforceable against third parties.

Since the international interest is effective against the debtor and third parties from the moment of its creation, the creditor is entitled to privileged treatment and can, in principle, take the asset to the exclusion of third parties to discharge the liability of the defaulting debtor.[6] If the secured creditor, intending to take possession of the collateral, learns that its only competitors are the debtor's unsecured creditors, the secured creditor will be, generally, entitled to take the collateral in priority to these creditors as the holder

[4] For the position under English law, see L Gullifer (ed), *Goode on Legal Problems of Credit and Security*, 5th edn (London, Sweet & Maxwell 2013) 63.

[5] See, generally, P Ali, *The Law of Secured Finance: An International Survey of Security Interests Over Personal Property* (Oxford, OUP 2002) 52.

[6] The position appears to be similar under the US Article 9 UCC referring to the process of creation of a security interest as *attachment*. §9-203(b) provides that once the formal requirements are met, the security interest becomes 'enforceable against *the debtor and third parties* with respect to the collateral' (emphasis added). However, an attached but unperfected security interest can be defeated by a perfected security interest of a third party. To protect the security interest from the attacks of third parties, its holder should 'perfect' it by filing or other means. See *Uniform Commercial Code: Official Text and Comments*, 2009–2010 edn (Thomson West 2009) 882–83.

of the proprietary international interest in the debtor's object. In practice, the secured creditor will often have to compete with holders of other international interests in the same object. As holders of proprietary interests, the secured creditor and holders of other international interests will, generally, be entitled to cut off the claims of the debtor's unsecured creditors, but will have to find a way of ordering their own claims. This may result in the interest of the secured creditor being postponed to the holders of competing interests. However, this does not mean that the interest, created in accordance with Article 7, is only effective between the secured creditor and the debtor and not enforceable against third parties. It only means that as between two or more holders of proprietary international interests, one of such holders will have to give way to the others.

To allow the secured creditor to determine its priority position among other interest holders, the Convention provides for an additional mechanism, namely registration in the IR, enabling creditors to learn about other interests in the object, give notice of the existence of their own interest and establish their priority.[7] One of the effects of registration is the ability of the secured creditor to defeat the claims of some other interest holders. But this does not mean that it is only on registration, or 'perfection' as it is often referred to in some legal systems, that the security interest will become effective against third parties.[8] By registering its interest, the creditor can perfect the existing proprietary international interest in the asset, not create one.

III. THE AUTONOMOUS NATURE OF THE INTERNATIONAL INTEREST

The Convention's formal requirements are essential for the constitution of an international interest.[9] Once these requirements are met, a valid autonomous international interest comes into existence even if such requirements would not be sufficient to create a similar interest under the applicable domestic law.[10] Conversely, non-compliance with these formalities means

[7] The registration is not a formal requirement under the Convention. For a different position under some other legal systems, see J Wilson, 'Movable Equipment Financing in Latin America: Application of the OAS Model Law, the Cape Town Convention and the Luxembourg Rail Protocol' (2007) *Unif L Rev* 473, 483.

[8] 'Perfection' is a process of giving third parties notice of the security interest's existence that can be accomplished by various means, such as registration, possession or control. See Gullifer (n 4) 77–80.

[9] R Goode, 'International Interests in Mobile Equipment: A Transnational Juridical Concept' (2003) 15 *Bond L Rev* 9, 12; B Honnebier and J Milo, 'The Convention of Cape Town: The Creation of International Interests in Mobile Equipment' (2004) 1 *ERPL* 3, 7; M Stanford, 'The New Regimen: Its History and Future after South Africa' (2004) 1 *ERPL* 9.

[10] C Mooney, 'The Cape Town Convention: A New Era for Aircraft Financing' (2003) 18 *Air Space Law* 4.

that no international interest is created and its purported registration is ineffective.[11] Another consequence of the international interest's autonomous nature is that compliance with Article 7 may result in the creation of an interest that has no equivalent in the domestic law of some jurisdictions.[12] For example, under Belgian law, aircraft can only be pledged and not mortgaged.[13] One of the requirements of a validly created pledge is the delivery of possession of the collateral to the creditor. Since dispossession of the debtor would make it impossible for it to operate the aircraft and generate income to repay the loan, the pledge is not normally used as it was intended by the legislator.[14] Instead, the industry has developed a different financial arrangement, whereby the parties create a third company, acting as the aircraft's purchaser or a lessor. Once the company obtains ownership of the aircraft, it pledges the object to the creditor. The creditor, in turn, delivers the aircraft to the debtor, which holds the object on behalf of the creditor.[15] The effect of this cumbersome structure is that, on the one hand, the pledgor delivers the possession of the collateral to the pledgee as required by the legislator, while, on the other hand, the debtor is able to operate the aircraft. Since the Convention does not require delivery of the object, creation of a non-possessory international interest would remove the necessity to construct this tri-partite structure.

Some legal systems restrict the range of parties who can act as a creditor or a debtor under a security agreement. For instance, the law of secured transactions of Venezuela confines the definition of debtors to the owners of the object.[16] In contrast, the CTC's chargor does not have to be the owner of the collateral. Mere power to dispose of the object will suffice for the creation of a valid international interest.[17] Another example can be found in Polish law on security interests. Recognising the limitations of the

[11] J Wool, 'The Next Generation of International Aviation Finance Law: An Overview of the Proposed UNIDROIT Convention on International Interests in Mobile Equipment as Applied to Aircraft Equipment' (1999) 20 *U Pa J Int'l Econ L* 499, 517.

[12] R Goode, *Official Commentary to the Convention on International Interests in Mobile Equipment and Protocol Thereto on Matters Specific to Aircraft Equipment*, 3rd edn (Rome, UNIROIT 2013) 275.

[13] G Mauri and B Itterbeek, 'The Cape Town Convention on International Interests in Mobile Equipment and its Protocol on Matters Specific to Aircraft Equipment: A Belgian Perspective' (2004) 9 *Unif L Rev* 547, 549.

[14] V Sagaert, 'The UNIDROIT Convention on International Interests in Mobile Equipment: A Belgian Perspective' (2004) 1 *ERPL* 75, 77.

[15] *Ibid* 77.

[16] H Gutierrez-Machado, 'The Personal Property Secured Financing System of Venezuela: A Comparative Study and the Case for Harmonisation' (1998) 30 *U Miami Inter-American L Rev* 343, 352. See also B Kozolchyk, 'What to do About Mexico's Antiquated Secured Financing Law?' (1995) 12 *Ariz J Int'l Comp L* 523.

[17] R Cuming, '"Hot Issues" in the Development of the (Draft) Convention on International Interests in Mobile Equipment and the (Draft) Aircraft Equipment Protocol' (2000) *34 Int'l L* 1093, 1097.

possessory pledge over movables, Polish law has introduced the concept of a non-possessory pledge. However, the class of creditors who can take the non-possessory pledge is limited to state-owned and other Polish banks.[18] The Convention does not have such restrictions, enabling a much broader category of businesses to act as creditors and debtors.

Further, since the Convention's formal requirements are for the most part simple,[19] the interest created under national law may at the same time constitute the CTC's international interest.[20] The holder of such interests will be entitled to the protection available under the applicable domestic law with respect to the national interest.[21] To obtain priority under the CTC, the holder of the international interest will still have to register it in the IR.[22] Finally, although the international interest is autonomous from the national law, some issues in relation to its constitution, such as the parties' capacity to contract and the effect of the vitiating factors on the contract's validity, are outside of the Convention's scope and must be governed by the applicable domestic law.[23]

IV. THE FORMAL REQUIREMENTS

A. 'Writing'

i. The Definition of 'Writing' and the Requirement of Approval of the Record

An agreement for the international interest must be put into writing. The advantage of the written form is that it provides the parties with clear evidence of the existence of the agreement and the terms to which they agreed.[24]

[18] L Choroszucha, 'Secured Transactions in Poland: Practicable Rules, Unworkable Solutions and Pending Reforms' (1994) 17 *Hastings Int'l Comp L Rev* 389, 406–08.

[19] Some legal systems prescribe a more extensive list of formal requirements. See P Honnebier, 'The Dutch Real Rights of Airlines Can be the Basis of International Interests Under the Convention of Cape Town, Just Like Their Equivalent American Security Interests' (2004) 1 *ERPL* 46, 49; P Erbacher and K Gunther, 'Aspects of Aircraft Leasing in Germany' (1992) *Int'l Comp Com L Rev* 52, 54; G Monti, 'The Future of Reservation of Title Clauses in the European Community' (1997) *ICLQ* 866.

[20] Goode (n 12) 275.

[21] *Ibid* 56.

[22] *Ibid* 56.

[23] *Ibid* 51.

[24] See, generally, P Birks, 'Before We Begin: Five Keys to Land Law' in S Bright and J Dewar (eds), *Land Law: Themes and Perspectives* (Oxford, OUP 1998) 457, 482–83; A Clarke and P Kohler, *Property Law: Commentary and Materials* (Cambridge, Cambridge University Press 2005) 461; C di Luigi, 'Divergences of Security and Property Law in the European Union: The Need for Action' (2008) *JBL* 526; L Fuller, 'Consideration and Form' (1941) 41 *Columbia L Rev* 799, 800; J Perillo, 'The Statute of Frauds in the Light of the Functions and Disfunctions of Form' (1974–75) 43 *Fordham L Rev* 39, 53.

'Writing' is defined as 'a record of information (including information communicated by teletransmission) which is in tangible or other form and is capable of being reproduced in tangible form on a subsequent occasion and which indicates by reasonable means a person's approval of the record'.[25] This definition covers traditional paper documents and electronic forms of communication. Thus, a paper document is a 'record of information … in tangible form' and an electronic document is a 'record of information … communicated by teletransmission' which can be 'reproduced in tangible form on a subsequent occasion'.[26] Since both paper and electronic forms of communication are simply called a 'record' and are not subjected to different treatment under the Convention, they have equal legal force. It follows that an agreement for an otherwise valid international interest cannot be invalidated for the simple reason that it is not put into a paper form. Provided that it can be 'reproduced in tangible form', such an agreement is valid.

The Convention's explicit permission to use electronically created and stored documents reflects commercial reality. Some banks are already exploring and using the possibility of granting loans online to the debtors. Similarly, in some cases, equipment can be leased to the lessees using online electronic lease forms.[27] Taking into account the international nature of the transactions covered by the Convention, the possibility of conducting business electronically is more efficient than creating an agreement by means of paper documents, since electronic documents can usually reach the recipient faster than their paper versions. The CTC does not clarify what can be considered as 'electronic and other forms of teletransmission'. Presumably, a copy of an agreement contained on a floppy disc, a USB memory stick, a compact disc or on a hard drive which can be printed out when required should fall within the definition. This is probably also true in relation to the agreements concluded by email, which can be stored in the electronic form and do not have to be transferred into a tangible form to become valid.

Although Article 7 does not require the agreement to be signed, the CTC makes it clear that regardless of whether the agreement is in a paper or an electronic form it will have to indicate 'by reasonable means a person's approval of the record'.[28] One way of demonstrating such an approval is by signing the document. A signature placed at the foot of the document conveys a certain degree of completeness and finality to the document. Transacting parties usually sign the agreement after its terms have been discussed and agreed upon. A signature at the end of the agreement also signifies

[25] Art 1(nn) CTC.
[26] Goode (n 12) 52.
[27] W Agin, 'Electronic Signatures and Instruments' (2005) 1 *J Bankr L Practice* 2.
[28] Art 1(nn) CTC.

the parties' intention to be committed to its performance. Since 'writing' encompasses paper and electronic documents, the person's approval of the record can be indicated by means of a manual and/or electronic signature. An 'electronic signature' is a generic term used to describe signatures incorporated into documents by electronic means. Examples of electronic signatures include the type-written name of the signing person at the foot of the email;[29] and where the name of the person sending the email does not appear at the end of the document, the requirement of a signature is satisfied by the header of the email bearing the sender's name.[30] Other examples of an electronic signature include a scanned version of a manual signature incorporated into a document, and the clicking of an 'I Accept' button which is found at the end of some web pages.[31]

An electronic signature can also take the form of a digital signature that is unique to its user and capable of protecting the data from non-authorised use by third parties.[32] Digital signatures usually involve the use of complementing asymmetric keys: one private key, unique to the sender, and one public key, given to the recipient, enabling it to open and read the electronic document and to determine whether it was interfered with in the process of transmission. Digital signatures are not yet widely used worldwide and, because they are not expressly required by the CTC, it seems that a simple electronic rather than a digital signature should suffice to approve the record.

ii. A Single Document and a Multiplicity of Documents

The Convention does not indicate whether the international interest agreement must be contained in a single document or whether the requirement of writing can be satisfied by a multiplicity of documents cumulatively giving rise to the international interest. This may give rise to the issue of what documents can be used to establish that the international interest agreement was validly created. For example, in the absence of a written agreement, can a certificate of registration amount to such an agreement? The answer must be 'no'. The registration of the interest has limited informative value to a searcher. For instance, the searcher will not be able to determine whether the registered interest is a prospective or current interest because the search

[29] For the position under the US law, see *Faulks v Cameron* (2004) 32 Fam LR 417; *Wilkens v Iowa Insurance Commissioner*, 457 NW 2d 1 (1990).

[30] See *International Casings Group Inc v Premium Standard Farms Inc*, 358 F Supp 2d 863 (2005).

[31] S Christensen, S Mason and K O'Shea, 'The International Judicial Recognition of electronic Signatures—Has Your Agreement Been Signed?' (2006) *Communications Law* 150, 151.

[32] P Cerina, 'The New Italian Law on Digital Signatures' (1998) *Computer and Telecommunications L Rev* 193, 194.

certificate will simply state that the person named in it either has or intends to acquire an interest in the object.[33] Indeed, the registration of the international interest does not amount to proof of its creation, validity or even its existence. Rather, the purpose of the registration is to give public notice of the possible existence of the interest and secure its holder's priority.[34] Consequently, the registration certificate alone cannot amount to or substitute an international interest agreement.

What if the registration certificate is supported by other documents? It is conceivable that the secured creditor may present such documents as a list itemising the same assets of the debtor as indicated in the registration certificate, documents showing that the loan has been advanced to the debtor and correspondence between the parties negotiating the terms of the security agreement. Could such documents, taken together and supported by the registration certificate, amount to a written agreement for the international interest? This issue has not yet been tested in courts, but it may be helpful to examine cases in domestic legal systems revealing the relevant factual settings and considerations. For example, §9-203 UCC provides that to create a valid security interest the following formal requirements must be met: (1) a secured party must give value; (2) the debtor must have rights in the collateral; (3) there must be a security agreement describing the collateral; and (4) either the security agreement must be in writing and signed by the debtor or there must be some other authenticating event. In relation to the requirement of writing, §9-203 does not state whether the security agreement must be contained in a single document or whether a multiplicity of documents is sufficient to create a valid security interest.

Under the US law, a financing statement, which is the CTC's counterpart of the registration certificate, cannot be equated with a valid security agreement.[35] Similar to the Convention's registration certificate, the main function of the financing statement is to provide third parties with a notice that a person who has filed its interest *may* have a perfected security interest in the collateral.[36] A financing statement alone cannot establish that a security agreement was in fact entered into by the parties. Furthermore, a financing statement, even if signed by both parties, does not, generally, express the debtor's intention to grant a security interest to the creditor.[37]

[33] Art 22(3) CTC.

[34] Goode (n 12) 76.

[35] *American Card Co v HMH Co*, 97 R I 59, 196 A 2d 150 (1963); *Shelton v Erwin*, 472 F 2d 1118, 1120 (8th Cir 1973); *Mitchell v Shepherd Mall State Bank*, 458 F 2d 700 (10th Cir 1972); *In re Mancini Meat & Provision Co*, 23 UCC Rep 1037, 1977 WL 25609 (D Conn 1977); *Flores De New Mexico v Banda Negra International*, 155 B R 571, 20 UCC 2d 1353.

[36] *In the Matter of Numeric Corp*, 485 F 2d 1328, 12 UCC 416 (1973), at 1331.

[37] *In Re John Oliver Co*, 129 BR 1, 15 UCC 2d 1031.

The importance of such granting words was highlighted in *In re Arctic Air*,[38] where a secured creditor claimed almost half of the proceeds of sale of its insolvent debtor's assets generated as a result of a public auction. In the absence of a written security agreement, the secured creditor presented a financing statement together with the copies of invoices showing that the goods were sold and delivered to the debtor. It was held that these documents could not amount to a valid security agreement as neither of them contained any language evidencing the intention of the debtor to grant a security interest to the creditor.[39]

A different conclusion was reached in *In the Matter of Numeric Corp*,[40] where the parties intended to enter into a security agreement covering the debtor's machinery, but it could not be established whether such an agreement came into existence and whether it was signed. The creditor presented a financing statement covering the machinery coupled with the resolution of the directors of the bankrupt debtor itemising the same machinery and stating that a security agreement in favour of the creditor did in fact exist. It was held that these documents taken together were sufficient to create a valid security interest, allowing the creditor to claim the machinery in the bankruptcy proceedings.[41] The court stated that a separate formal document titled a 'security agreement' was not always necessary under §9-203. If the presented documents, even though not labelled as a security agreement, adequately describe the object and provide evidence of the parties' agreement to create a security interest, these documents satisfy the §9-203 writing requirement and amount to a valid security agreement.[42]

Since the purposes of the writing requirement of §9-203 and the functions of a financing statement appear to be similar to the purposes and functions of their counterparts under the Convention, it can be argued that the writing requirement in Article 7 should, in principle, be interpreted in a similar way. In the absence of a single written agreement, the multiplicity of documents, identifying the object in conformity with the Protocols and expressing the intention of the parties to create an international interest, taken together with the registration certificate, can constitute a valid international interest agreement.[43] This solution gives sufficient weight to the explicit writing

[38] *In re Arctic Air*, 202 BR 533, 31 UCC 2d 233 (1996).

[39] See *Gibbs v King*, 263 Ark 338, 564 SW 2d 515 (1978); *In re Cambridge*, 37 UCC Rep 618, 34 BR 88 (1983); *In re Wolsky*, 68 BR 526 (1986); *In re Shinville Assoc, Inc*, 46 BR 352 (1985).

[40] 485 F 2d 1328, 13 UCC 416 (1973).

[41] See *Casco Bank & Trust Company v Cloutier*, 398 A 2d 1224 (Supr Jud Ct Maine 1979); *In re Rite-Cap*, 7 BR 113 (Bankr RI 1980); *In re Frace*, 17 BR 198 (Bankr D Maine 1982).

[42] 485 F 2d 1328, 13 UCC 416 (1973), at 1331. See also *In re Carmichael Enterprises, Inc*, 334 F Supp 94, 105 (ND Ga 1971); *Nunnemaker Transp Co v United Cal Bank*, 456 F 2d 28 (9th Cir 1972).

[43] Art 20(1) CTC indicates that the registration may only be effected by either party with written consent of the other party, which can prevent improper registrations.

requirement and, at the same time, it takes account of the possibility that even though there is no single written contract between the parties, there may be sufficient documentary evidence showing the parties' intentions to create the international interest. This approach takes account of the concerns for certainty and predictability which underlie the writing requirement, but at the same time avoids rigidity, by introducing a mechanism for reaching a fair result in the circumstances.

B. 'Power to Dispose'

In the case of the debtor's default, the secured creditor may attempt to enforce its security interest by taking possession and selling the collateral. At this point, the secured creditor may learn that the object was only delivered to the debtor for repairs or that the debtor merely had a right to possession of the object as a lessee or conditional buyer. The secured creditor may be confronted by the true owner of the object, arguing that as the debtor did not have the power to dispose, the creditor's security interest did not attach to the object.

To prevent such an outcome, the Convention provides that the international interest agreement must relate to the object of which the chargor, conditional seller or lessor has power to dispose.[44] The meaning of this requirement is not clear, which is regrettable because this is a lack of clarity in relation to a point of significance. The requirement is important because unless it is satisfied, an international interest agreement will not be validly created and even its registration in the IR will be ineffective. Another difficulty is that, due to its uncertainty, it may wrongly be used to deal with priority disputes between competing interests for which it was not designed.

For instance, consider an object which belongs to the debtor but which is in the possession of a repairer while undergoing maintenance. The debtor grants a security interest in its object to secured creditor 1 (SC1) and the repairer, holding the same object, grants a security interest in it to secured creditor 2 (SC2), which registers its interest before the registration of SC1's interest occurs. In this situation the Convention's rules of priority will grant priority to the first registered interest holder, that is SC2.[45] However, SC1 may attempt to reverse the order of priority by claiming that the repairer, which only held the object to perform maintenance work, did not have the power to dispose and that SC2's international interest was not validly created. If SC1's claim is successful, SC2 will lose its priority.

[44] Art 7(b) CTC.
[45] Art 29(1) CTC.

Furthermore, uncertainty as to the meaning and the circumstances when power to dispose arises may lead to a situation where the Convention's requirement is supplanted by similar concepts in national law. This can lead to non-uniform interpretation of the notion of power to dispose under the Convention and undermine the principle of predictability on which it is based. Indeed, the Commentary indicates that if the issue whether the relevant party has the power to dispose cannot be determined under the Convention, it should be resolved by the applicable domestic law.[46] It is suggested that whether the issue of power to dispose is to be delegated to the national law must be determined in accordance with the rules in Article 5 CTC. First, Article 5(1) prescribes that in interpreting the Convention, regard is to be had to its international character and the need to promote uniformity and predictability in its application. To achieve these objectives, national courts must avoid interpreting the Convention in accordance with their own domestic law and instead have regard to the Convention's purposes set out in the preamble.[47]

Secondly, if the issue is governed by the Convention but is not expressly settled in it, it needs to be settled in conformity with the general principles on which it is based. Power to dispose is one of the key elements of the constitution of the international interest, a unique creature of the Convention that has its own autonomous status and does not have an analogue in national laws. The formal requirements for the constitution of the international interest are expressly provided for in the Convention. They are intended to be as simple as possible to ensure that the process of the international interest's constitution is speedy and not burdened by unnecessary complexity. This aim will be difficult to achieve if one of the formative elements of the international interest is to be ascertained under the applicable national law. Since power to dispose is expressly stipulated in the Convention as an element necessary for the formation of the international interest, it is undoubtedly a matter governed by it. Although the meaning of this concept is not expressly settled in it, it needs to be ascertained in conformity with the general principles, such as party autonomy and predictability, on which the Convention is based. Thirdly, it is only when such principles cannot be found, that the interpretation of the requirement of power to dispose should be delegated to the applicable law.[48] For these reasons, it is important to ascertain what the power to dispose amounts to under the Convention.

The power to dispose includes the right to dispose, that is, where the chargor, conditional seller or lessor are owners of the object or have the

[46] Goode (n 12) 275.
[47] Art 5(1) CTC.
[48] Art 5(2) CTC.

owner's authority to deal with it.[49] For instance, an owner of the object has the right to dispose of it by granting senior and junior security interests in it to its creditors. Similarly, if a head lease allows the lessee to create a sub-lease in the object, the lessee acting as the sub-lessor, has the authority and, consequently, the right to dispose of its interest in the object. However, the power to dispose is wider than the right to dispose and covers other situations whereby a non-owner chargor, conditional seller or lessor deals with the object in a way that binds the true owner.[50] Thus, a non-owner lessee, lacking actual authority to grant a security interest in an object, can be held out by the true owner as having apparent authority to dispose of its interest and, consequently, the power to dispose to grant a security interest.

According to the Commentary, 'the word "dispose" covers every form of disposition encompassed within the power ... whether taking the form of a grant of a security interest, a sale under a reservation of title or a lease'.[51] This explanation does not indicate the circumstances in which the power to dispose arises. For instance, it is not clear whether a bailee, entrusted with the object's safekeeping, a repairer, holding the object until payment is made to it, or a manufacturer's dealer without possession have sufficient power to dispose.

The Commentary suggests that the Convention's priority and registration rules can help identify the circumstances in which the power to dispose arises.[52] The Convention provides that a registered interest has priority over the subsequently registered and unregistered interest.[53] If the debtor grants a security interest to secured creditor 1 (SC1), which does not register its interest, and to secured creditor 2 (SC2), which immediately registers its interest, SC2's interest will take priority over the unregistered interest of SC1. This rule demonstrates that the debtor has the power to dispose of the interest greater than the one it holds. The result would be different if the creditors registered their interests in the order of creation. SC1's previously registered interest would gain priority over the subsequently registered interest of SC2. In other words, the debtor would only be able to transfer to SC2 the interest which it holds, namely, the interest subject to SC1's security. In both situations, the debtor has sufficient power to dispose of its interest in the object and the issue becomes one of priority between competing interest holders.

The Commentary suggests that the rule that the registered interest prevails over subsequently registered and unregistered interest means that not only the debtor-chargor, but also the lessee or the conditional buyer have

[49] Goode (n 12) 276.
[50] *Ibid* 276.
[51] *Ibid* 276.
[52] *Ibid* 276.
[53] Art 29(1) CTC.

power to dispose of the object.[54] If a lessor grants a security interest to SC1, which does not register its interest, and the lessee wrongly grants a security in the object to SC2, which registers its interest, the unregistered interest of SC1 will be postponed to SC2's registered interest. Since SC2 has priority over SC1, it must follow that the lessee had sufficient power to dispose of its interest in that object. Similarly, a conditional seller's SC1, which fails to register its interest in the object before the buyer improperly grants a security interest in the object to SC2, which immediately registers its interest, will be subordinated to that registered interest. It follows that although the Convention does not expressly state that the conditional buyer has the power to dispose, the fact that the registered interest of SC2 is preferred to the unregistered or subsequently registered interest of SC1, means that the conditional buyer has sufficient power to dispose of its interest in the object.

Although this argument is attractive, it fails to explain whether the lessee and the conditional buyer had the power to dispose in the first place. It is true that the registered interest prevails over the unregistered or subsequently registered interest and for this reason the earlier registered interest of SC2, taking the security interest from the lessee or the conditional buyer, will enjoy priority. But this outcome must be based on the premise that the party acting as the conditional buyer or lessee had the power to dispose in the first place. To make a valid registration, it is not sufficient to register whatever interest the lessee or the conditional buyer purports to transfer to the secured creditor. Unless the lessee or the conditional buyer had the power to dispose, the registration by the secured creditor will simply be ineffective. If this is the case, SC2's earlier registered security interest will not take priority over the subsequently registered interest of the lessor's or the conditional seller's SC1. The mere fact of registration cannot prove that the lessee or the conditional buyer had sufficient power to dispose of its interest in the object. It is only if the international interest is validly created, meaning, among other things, that the party making the disposition has the power to dispose, that the registration will be effective and confer priority on its holder. The rule that a registered interest prevails over a subsequently registered or unregistered interest is not able to show whether the party making the disposition had the power to dispose. It is a priority rule that becomes operative provided that the conditional buyer and lessee have the power to dispose. At best, it demonstrates that it is possible that the conditional buyer and lessee *may* have the power to dispose and caters for such a possibility, but it does not explain in what circumstances the power to dispose arises.[55]

[54] Goode (n 12) 276.

[55] See S Saidova, 'The Cape Town Convention: The Constitution of the International Interest' [2012] *LMCLQ* 285, 291–92.

This position can be further supported by the way the Convention treats the priority of a prospective international interest, which can be registered first and created later. Once the formal requirements are met, the prospective interest turns into the actual one and its priority dates back to the original registration.[56] However, a failure to comply with these requirements, including power to dispose, will result in the registration being ineffective and in the loss of the priority. Therefore, although the Convention provides for the priority and registration rules relating to the prospective international interest, this does not mean that the person granting such an interest, or selling or leasing it has the power to dispose.

It has also been argued that the lessee should be treated as having the power to dispose because the Convention requires the lessor to register its interest. On this view, the registration is essential to protect the lessor from the adverse disposition by the lessee. Since such adverse disposition is possible, it must mean that the lessee has sufficient power to dispose.[57] However, the possibility of non-authorised disposition by the lessee is not the only reason why the lessor may decide to register its interest. For instance, if the lessor grants a security interest over the object to a secured creditor, the outcome of the priority dispute between the secured creditor and the lessee will depend on whether and when the lessor has registered its interest.[58] If the lessor has registered its interest before the secured creditor, the lessee's interest will be protected.[59] Conversely, if the lessor did not register or registered after the secured creditor, the latter will be able to take possession of the object.[60] Since the protection against possible non-authorised disposition by the lessee is not the only reason why the lessor can choose to register its interest, the requirement of registration alone cannot prove that the lessee has the power to dispose.

This discussion does not mean that the lessee or the conditional buyer do not have the power to dispose under the Convention. Another way of demonstrating that the party making the disposition has the power to dispose is to consider whether it holds possession of the object. Possession should not be required if the party making the disposition is the owner or has the right to dispose. However, in the absence of the right to dispose, the power to dispose can be found where the transferor holds the possession of the object because possession can create an impression of ownership.[61] In addition, the person in possession can dispose of the object with relative ease.[62]

[56] Art 18(3).
[57] Goode (n 2) 24.
[58] Art 29(4) CTC.
[59] Art 29(4)(b) CTC.
[60] Art 29(4)(a) CTC.
[61] M Bridge, L Gullifer, G McMeel and S Worthington, *The Law of Personal Property* (London, Sweet & Maxwell 2013) 48.
[62] Goode (n 12) 54.

Consequently, the disposition by the lessee or the conditional buyer, which holds possession, should bind the true owner. At the same time, possession in itself does not invariably signal the presence of the power to dispose. Possessory interests in goods vary from transient interests, such as an interest of a repairer, to a more extensive interest of a lessee under a long term lease of the object.[63] One way of determining whether possession confers the power to dispose could be through analysing the terms of the agreement to establish the capacity in which the person in possession holds it. It is suggested that if the transferor holds possession in a capacity that demonstrates the owner's agreement that the transferor can deal with the object in the course of its business, then the transferor should have the power to dispose of its interest in the object.

For instance, a lessee, holding possession of the aircraft object, can grant a security interest in it to SC1 and transfer the object to the repairer. The repairer, in turn, can grant a security interest in the object to SC2. Before considering the issue of priority and registration, the interest holders may raise the question whether the lessee and the repairer had the power to dispose. This is when the capacity in which the object is held by the parties may become relevant. Under the lease, used to finance the acquisition of the object, ownership remains with the lessor but its economic benefits, such as an ability to use the object and the hardship of ownership, such as responsibility to repair it, belong to the lessee.[64] The purpose of the lease is to enable the lessee to have possession and deal with the object as if it belongs to it by using the aircraft in its business, and at the same time to repay the lessor the sum spent on the acquisition together with the profit.[65] Since the benefit of ownership under the lease belongs to the lessee and it can use the object in its business, the lessee should have the power to dispose by granting security interest, sub-leasing or even selling the aircraft to the transferor. For this reason, the lessee should be able to grant a security interest to SC1 and provided that SC1 registers it in time, it can benefit from the Convention's priority rules. In this regard, the position of the lessee is similar to the position of the conditional buyer. The sale on retention of title (RoT) terms often envisages that the buyer will deal with the goods in the course of its business, which may even lead to considerable changes to the nature of the original goods, but strives to preserve the ownership with the conditional seller until the relevant conditions, such as payment of the purchase price, are met. Consequently, the conditional buyer, which is able to exercise control over the object, should also have the power to dispose.

[63] Bridge, Gullifer, McMeel and Worthington (n 61) 66.
[64] *Ibid* 116.
[65] *Ibid* 116.

In contrast, the purpose for which the object is transferred to the repairer is limited to the performance of the required works. The transferor does not intend to confer on the repairer any benefits of ownership or to allow the repairer to deal with the object as if it were its own. Thus, even though, generally, the repairer can hold on to the possession until it receives payment for its service, it cannot dispose of the object by granting security interest, leasing or selling the object. The limited purpose for which the possession is transferred to the repairer cannot confer on it the power to dispose.

C. 'Object Identified in Conformity with the Protocol'

i. General

The international interest agreement must enable the object to be identified in conformity with the Protocols.[66] The Convention does not establish any criteria for the identification of mobile equipment. It merely states that an international interest is an interest in mobile equipment in a uniquely identifiable object of one of the categories listed in it.[67] These categories are presently comprised of: (a) airframes, aircraft engines and helicopters; (b) railway rolling stock; and (c) space assets,[68] but may be added to by future Protocols.[69] Indeed, in 2005, the UNIDROIT Governing Council recommended to the UNIDROIT General Assembly to start work on the preparation of the fourth Protocol on matters relating to mining, agricultural and construction equipment, all three industries being of commercial significance worldwide and in particular in developing countries.

The aims of the MAC Protocol are twofold: first, to facilitate the financing and leasing of these types of equipment by reducing risks for the creditors; secondly, to allow manufacturers of such equipment to access markets previously closed to them.[70] In 2006, the UNIDROIT Governing Council presented a list of the types of equipment, which can be governed by the MAC Protocol. Extensive work, involving questionnaires to assess the need and feasibility of the project, consultation with the industry and economic analysis of the proposed Protocol, was undertaken and in 2016 the preliminary draft Protocol was ready for submission to the Governing Council with a recommendation that the Committee of Governmental Experts be convened to further examine the Protocol. The current draft MAC Protocol

[66] Art 7(c) CTC.
[67] Art 2(2) CTC.
[68] Art 2(3) CTC.
[69] Art 51(1) CTC.
[70] For information relating to the preparation of the MAC Protocol, see http://www.unidroit.org/work-in-progress/mac-protocol (last visited 28 December 2017).

contains three annexes providing the harmonised system codes for the types of the MAC equipment governed by it.

ii. Aircraft Objects

The Protocols' provisions relating to the definition of objects not only describe their nature, but also help determine which objects are covered by the Convention and which objects are likely to be excluded.[71] The term 'aircraft object' is a generic term used to describe all types of objects listed in Article 2(3)(a) CTC, namely, airframes, aircraft engines and helicopters. Aircraft objects used in military, custom or police services are excluded from the scope of the Convention. 'Airframe' means an aircraft frame certified by the competent aviation authority to transport: (i) at least eight persons including crew or (ii) goods in excess of 2,750 kilograms together with all installed, incorporated or attached accessories, parts and equipment and all data, manuals and records relating to the aircraft.[72] The Protocol uses the test of minimum carrying capacity of the aircraft (persons or weight of cargo) to exclude smaller airframes from the scope of the Convention and to confine its application to high value objects.

The term 'airframe' includes all attached parts and accessories, excluding the aircraft engine. Thus, a fuselage, the central body of the aircraft, the wings, empennage (tail assembly) and the landing gear are included. The smaller parts of these and other structures of the airframe should also be included as 'accessories and parts.' For instance, the landing gear may include wheels with shock absorbers, or skis for snow or floats for water. An aircraft's wings have a complex structure and include ailerons (movable flaps of the wings controlling the aircraft's rolling and banking movements) and other parts. So too, the data, manuals and records relating to the aircraft are treated as part of the airframe. Since these parts are constituent parts of the airframe, it is not possible to create and register a separate interest in them and the creditor's interest must relate to the airframe as a whole.

The Protocol defines 'aircraft engines' as engines powered by jet propulsion or turbine or pistol technology and sets a minimum engine capacity to cut off lower value units from its scope.[73] Since the Protocol considers an aircraft engine as an independent aircraft object it is possible to create and register a separate international interest in it even if the creditor does not hold an interest in the airframe on which the engine is installed.[74]

[71] Arts I(2) and VII of the Aircraft Protocol.

[72] Art I(2)(e) of the Aircraft Protocol.

[73] Art I(2)(b) of the Aircraft Protocol.

[74] Article XIV(3) of the Aircraft Protocol. See also L Clark, 'The 2001 Cape Town Convention on International Interests in Mobile Equipment and Aircraft Equipment Protocol: Internationalising Asset-Based Financing Principles for the Acquisition of Aircraft and Engines' (2004) 69 *J Air L Com* 3, 10.

This approach reflects the industry's perception that aircraft engines are high value and easily detachable items frequently leased or exchanged between various aircraft users.[75]

In contrast, *installed* helicopter engines are not considered as separate objects or as aircraft objects at all and no international interest can be created or registered in relation to such engines. This is regrettable, because similar to aircraft engines, helicopter engines can be exchanged and separately financed. It is, however, possible to establish an international interest in a helicopter engine *before* it is installed on the helicopter or *after* it has been removed from it.[76] The rights created in the helicopter engine *before* its installation will be preserved during the period when it is installed on the helicopter.[77]

Finally, helicopters are defined as heavier-than-air machines certified to transport: (i) at least five persons or (ii) goods in access of 450 kilograms.[78] As with the other aircraft objects, the Protocol uses the carrying capacity to emphasise that only high value helicopters are covered by it. Once it is established that an aircraft object falls within the CTC's scope, the parties will have to describe this object for the purpose of Article 7. The description of the aircraft object must contain three elements, namely, manufacturer's name, serial number and model designation.[79] Only when all three elements are indicated in the international interest agreement will it be possible to create a valid interest in this object.

iii. Railway Objects

Railway rolling stock is defined as 'vehicles movable on a fixed railway track or directly on, above or below a guideway, together with traction systems, engines, brakes, axles, bogies, pantographs, accessories and other components, equipment and parts, in each case installed on or incorporated in the vehicles, and together with all data manuals and records relating thereto'.[80] The broad definition of the railway rolling stock includes conventional trains, such as locomotives, with no payload capacity of their own, and multiple unit trains used for passenger and freight transportation. But trams, mountain trains, maglev, metro trains and monorail trains are also included in the definition because they either hover above, or move

[75] P Honnebier, 'New Protocols and the Financing of Aircraft Engines' (2006) 21 *Air Space Law* 15, 16.

[76] Goode (n 12) 171–72.

[77] Art XIV(3) of the Aircraft Protocol. See Goode (n 12) 171.

[78] Art I(2)(l) of the Aircraft Protocol.

[79] Art VII of the Aircraft Protocol.

[80] Art I(e) of the Luxembourg Protocol.

below or beside guideways.[81] At the same time, trolley buses and road trains (such as the ones used in Argentina, Australia and Mexico to move several trailers connected with one tractor unit) are not covered by the Protocol because they do not move on a fixed track.[82] Since it is not always possible to differentiate between train systems which cross borders and those which can potentially cross borders, the Protocol's drafters decided that both types of railway rolling stock should be included in the definition.[83]

In contrast with the Aircraft Protocol, the Luxembourg Protocol does not consider engines as separate objects.[84] Locomotives, which can be seen as engines because they provide motive power to the train, are not considered as such under the Protocol. Consequently, it is possible to create and register an international interest in a locomotive separately from the train which it pulls. But other types of engines, such as the ones installed in a multiple unit train, are treated as integral parts of the train carriage.[85]

To identify a railway rolling stock object for the constitution of an international interest, the agreement must describe it either by: (a) item; (b) type or (c) in a statement that the agreement covers all present and future railway rolling stock; or (d) in a statement that the agreement covers all present and future rolling stock except for specified items or types.[86] An interest in the future railway rolling stock, identified in conformity with these requirements, can be created as a valid international interest as soon as the chargor, conditional seller or lessor acquires the power to dispose of such an object without the need for any new act of transfer.[87]

The Luxembourg Protocol's identification requirements differ from those of the Aircraft Protocol, in that no unique identification of railway objects is required to constitute an international interest. The reason why these two Protocols approach this issue differently is because there are only a few big commercial aircraft manufacturers of global significance, and the limited number of such manufacturers has enabled them to develop a permanent

[81] R Castillo-Triana, 'The Relevance of the Luxembourg Protocol for Central and South America' (2007) *Unif L Rev* 46, 468.

[82] See, generally, R Goode, *Official Commentary to the Convention on International Interests in Mobile Equipment and Luxembourg Protocol Thereto on Matters Specific to Railway Rolling Stock* (Rome, UNIROIT 2008) 288; H Kronke, 'The Luxembourg Protocol to the Cape Town Convention: A Pillar for the Bridge to the Future of Rail Transportation' (2007) *Unif L Rev* 420.

[83] However, Art 50(2) CTC allows a Contracting State to exclude its application to the type of railway rolling stock equipment used exclusively in internal transactions. See H Rosen, 'The Luxembourg Rail Protocol: A Major Advance in the Railway Industry' (2007) *Unif L Rev* 427, 431.

[84] Consequently, there is no separate definition of a train engine in the Protocol. See Art I(e) of the Luxembourg Protocol.

[85] Goode (n 82) 288.

[86] Art V(1) of the Luxembourg Protocol.

[87] Art V(2) of the Luxembourg Protocol.

identification system for aircraft objects.[88] In contrast, there are many railway rolling stock manufacturing companies worldwide. These companies use different identification criteria making it impractical to search for a unique identifier of railway objects.[89] The identification numbers given to individual train wagons by various manufacturers are not permanent and can be painted on or wiped out from the wagon. Consequently, while the requirement of the unique identification was not difficult to comply with under the Aircraft Protocol, a new approach to identifying the railway objects was required under the Luxembourg Protocol.

An object needs to be uniquely identified so that an interest held in it can be registered in the asset-based IR. Since registration is not necessary for the creation of an international interest, there is no need to provide the unique identification of a railway object at the stage of the constitution of the international interest. For this reason, the Luxembourg Protocol has introduced two identification points: one at the stage of the constitution of the international interest, and the other at the stage of its registration in the IR.[90] While at the stage of the constitution, it is possible to identify the railway object in general terms, such as a long distance passenger train or a high speed train crossing the English Channel, this will not be sufficient for registration, when the object's unique identifier will have to be provided. To ensure the uniqueness of the railway object's identification, the CTC's Registrar is required to provide such an object with a unique identifier, which is either: (a) affixed to the object; (b) associated in the IR with the manufacturer's name and its identification number which is affixed to the object; or (c) associated in the IR with a national or regional identification number affixed to the object.[91]

iv. Space Assets

Similar to the Luxembourg Protocol, the Space Protocol distinguishes between the broad identification requirements for the constitution of the international interest and the strict identification requirements for its registration, which must ensure that the space assets can be uniquely identified.[92]

[88] H Rosen, 'Creating an International Security Structure for Railway Rolling Stock: an Idea Ahead of its Time?' (1999) 2 *Unif L Rev* 313, 318.

[89] H Rosen, 'The Regimen of the Railway Rolling Stock Protocol' (2004) 1 *ERPL* 26, 33.

[90] Art V and Art XIV of the Luxembourg Protocol.

[91] Art XIV(1) of the Luxembourg Protocol.

[92] Art VII and Art XXX of the Space Protocol. The issue of the space assets' definition was much debated because of its connection to the issues of public interest and national security of the Contracting States. For the general information on the (Draft) Space Protocol, see O Ribbenik, 'The Protocol on Matters Specific to Space Assets' (2004) 1 *Unif L Rev* 37; D Panahy and R Mittal, 'The Prospective UNIDRIT Convention on International Interests in Mobile Equipment as Applied to Space Property' (1999) 2 *Unif L Rev* 303; P Larsen, 'Future Protocol on Security Interests in Space Property' (2002) 67 *J Air L Com* 1071; P Larsen and

The definition and identification of space assets have been challenging issues because space assets includes a much broader range of objects than aircraft or rail objects. The Protocol provides that a space asset means any man-made uniquely identifiable asset in space or designed to be launched in space.[93] The space assets must fall into one of the three following categories, namely: (i) a spacecraft; (ii) a payload, in respect of which a separate registration can be made in accordance with the Regulations; (iii) a part of a spacecraft or a payload, in respect of which a separate registration can be made in accordance with the Regulations.[94]

The Protocol provides a non-exhaustive list of examples for each category. A satellite, space station, space module, space capsule, space vehicle or reusable launch vehicle are all examples of a spacecraft.[95] A payload, the second category, denotes whatever is carried on the platform to perform the set task, such as telecommunication, navigation, observation or a scientific mission. Only the payload in relation to which a separate registration can be made in accordance with the Regulations (yet to be developed) will be considered to be a space object.[96] The third category comprises a part of a spacecraft or payload, such as a transponder, which must be uniquely identifiable to be capable of separate registration.[97] Although the list of the categories of the space assets is closed, each category is broad enough to accommodate any newly invented space assets.

Once it is established that the space asset falls into one of the prescribed categories, it is important to ascertain how it should be identified for the constitution and registration of the international interest held in it. To comply with the object identification requirement, it is sufficient for the identification of the space asset in the international interest agreement to contain: (a) a description of the space asset by item; (b) a description of the space asset by type; (c) a statement that the agreement covers all present and future space assets; or (d) a statement that the agreement covers all present and future assets except for specified items or types.[98] Thus, the identification for the constitution of the international interest need not be specific and it is possible to create an interest in a future space asset. In this case,

J Heilbock, 'UNIDROIT Project on Security Interests: How the Project Affects Space Objects' (1998–99) 64 *J Air L Com* 703; S Davies, 'Unifying the Final Frontier: Space Industry Financing Reform' (2001) 106 *Comm LJ* 455.

[93] Art I(k) of the Space Protocol. See, generally, R Goode, *Official Commentary to the Convention on International Interests in Mobile Equipment and Protocol Thereto on Matters Specific to Space Assets* (Rome, UNIROIT 2013) 422–23.

[94] Art I(k) of the Space Protocol.

[95] Art I(k) of the Space Protocol.

[96] Art I(k) of the Space Protocol.

[97] Art I(k) of the Space Protocol.

[98] Art VII of the Space Protocol.

an international interest will be constituted as soon as the chargor, conditional seller or lessor acquires the power to dispose of the asset without the need for any new act of transfer.[99]

In contrast, the space asset's identification for the registration of an international interest held in it will require a unique identifier, an issue delegated by the Protocol to the Regulations.[100] The process of the development of the unique identifier is complex and lengthy for several reasons. First, the range of space assets is broad and, in contrast with the aircraft objects, not all of them can be identified by a standard set of criteria. The Regulations must develop unique identifiers for different types of space assets. Secondly, some space assets are already in space and fixing the identifying marks on them is difficult or impossible. Finally, there is always a possibility that new types of space asset will be invented in the future. The unique identification criteria must be flexible enough to ensure that they can be used on these new assets.

v. Mining, Agriculture and Construction (MAC) Objects

The MAC Protocol is still under development and its final text is not yet available. It will govern three types of equipment used in very different industries. To ensure a sufficient number of ratifications and realising that some Contracting States may wish to limit the Protocol's application to some, and not all, types of equipment, the UNIDROIT Secretariat suggested that the lists of the mining, agricultural and construction equipment should be severable to allow Contracting State to opt in or out of each of the three areas governed by the MAC Protocol.[101] Exactly what kind of MAC equipment falls within the Protocol's scope is decided in accordance with the global Harmonised System (HS), established by the World Customs Organization, to achieve the uniform classification of goods in international trade.[102] This system uses a six-digit code to identify the equipment and provides states with an opportunity to increase this code to a ten-digit number.

The draft Protocol includes three separate annexes, listing the types of the MAC equipment together with the HS code. For instance, types of agricultural equipment such as self-propelled bulldozers, angledozers, graders, levelers, scrapers, mechanical shovels, excavators, shovel loaders, tamping machines and road rollers are included. Examples of mining equipment

[99] Art VII(2) of the Space Protocol.

[100] Art XXX of the Space Protocol.

[101] See, generally, http://www.unidroit.org/work-in-progress/mac-protocol (last visited December 2017).

[102] Art I of the draft MAC Protocol defines 'Harmonised System' as the 'Harmonised Commodity Description and Coding System governed by The International Convention on the Harmonised Commodity Description and Coding System'.

include interchangeable tools for hand tools, whether or not power-operated, or for machine tools (for example, for pressing, stamping, punching, tapping, threading, drilling, boring, broaching, milling, turning or screw driving), including dies for drawing or extruding metal and rock drilling tools or earth boring tools. Finally, construction equipment such as ships' derricks, cranes, including cable cranes, mobile lifting frames, straddle carriers and works trucks fitted with a crane are included.[103] All these objects are supplied with a six-digit HS code.

It is envisaged that the MAC Protocol, similar to the Luxembourg and Space Protocols will adopt a dual identification approach to the constitution and registration of the international interest. To constitute an international interest in MAC equipment, its identification should contain: (a) a description of the equipment by item; b) a description of the equipment by type; (c) a statement that the agreement covers all present and future equipment; or (d) a statement that the agreement covers all present and future equipment except for specified items or types.[104] No unique identification is required at this stage and it is possible to create an international interest in future objects.[105] In relation to the identification requirements for the registration of the international interest, the draft Protocol adopts a slightly different approach to other Protocols. It provides that the MAC equipment must be identified by a combination of the manufacturer's name and serial number and that these identifiers can be added to by the Regulations. Together, these criteria will amount to the 'necessary and sufficient' identification requirements.[106]

vi. The Possibility of a Floating Charge

A floating charge can be described as a security in a fund or a class of assets rather than in the specific objects of which the fund is comprised.[107] A floating security allows the debtor to acquire new objects which are automatically covered by the existing security and dispose of such assets free from the charge. The main advantage of the floating security is that the debtor is left free to conduct business as it thinks fit and the secured creditor can be certain that it has a present security interest in the assets included in the fund. When the debtor defaults or some other crystallising event occurs, the floating security crystallises into a fixed security and captures all the assets found

[103] See Annexes to the draft MAC Protocol and the Legal Analysis of the UNIDROIT Secretariat, available at http://www.unidroit.org/work-in-progress/mac-protocol#a2 (last visited December 2017).

[104] Art V of the draft MAC Protocol.

[105] Art V(2) of the draft MAC Protocol.

[106] Art XVI of the draft MAC Protocol.

[107] *Re Yorkshire Woolcombers Association Ltd* [1903] 2 Ch 284, 295.

in the fund at this moment. Only then will the issue of the identification of assets arise as the secured creditor will need to know the objects against which the security can be enforced. For this reason, unique identification of an object is not required at the stage of the creation of the floating security and it can be granted in the debtor's present and future property.

Since the Aircraft Protocol requires the aircraft objects to be uniquely identified by manufacturer's name, serial number and model designation at the stage of the constitution of the international interest, it is not possible to create a floating security interest in the debtor's future, unidentified aircraft objects. In contrast, in relation to railway objects, space assets and MAC equipment, the Protocols' flexible identification requirements mean that the collateral can be broadly described in the international interest agreement by type or item, or may relate to present and future objects. Accordingly, a floating security over present and future railway, space or MAC objects can be created under the Protocols. However, the strict identification requirements for registering the interests in these objects will prevent the registration of a floating security in them. The effect of an unregistered floating security will be limited as it will be postponed to the interests registered in the IR.

D. 'Identification of Secured Obligations'

If the international interest is based on a security agreement, it must enable the secured obligations to be determined, but without the need to state a sum or a maximum sum secured.[108] The security agreement can secure performance of the existing and future obligations and describe the nature of the secured obligations in general terms. For instance, an agreement securing the repayment of 'all sums due from the debtor to the secured creditor now or in the future' will be sufficient under the Convention. To require the parties to indicate the exact or maximum amount of the secured obligation would be impractical for two reasons. First, if the amount of the future indebtedness is not certain at the time of the creation of the security agreement, the creditor may simply state a sum in excess of what is required

[108] Art 7(d). The CTC's approach is different to the position of some other legal systems. See B Bennet, 'Secured Financing in Russia: Risks, Legal Incentives, and Policy Concerns' (1999) 77 *Tex L Rev* 1443, 1450; T Rodrigues, 'International Regulation of Interests in Aircraft: the Brazilian Reality and the UNIDROIT Proposal' (2000) 65 *J Air L Com* 279, 291; F Dahan and G McCormack, 'International Influences and the Polish Law on Secured Transactions: Harmonisation, Unification or What?' (2002) 7 *Unif L Rev* 713, 723; T Josipovic, 'The Rail Protocol and Croatian Secured Transactions Law' (2007) 12 *Unif L Rev* 489, 496–97; Gutierrez-Machado (n 16) 354–55.

by the debtor.[109] Secondly, even if the exact amount of the secured debt is indicated in the security agreement, it cannot reveal how much of this debt has already been repaid.[110] A potential secured creditor willing to take a security interest in the debtor's object will not be able to determine exactly how much is still owed to the previous secured creditor. To obtain this information, the potential creditor will need to ask the parties to the security agreement for further details. Consequently, an indication of the exact or maximum amount of the secured obligation would be of limited value to a third party.

[109] Goode (n 12) 277.
[110] *Ibid* 277.

3

Registering an Interest in the International Registry

I. INTRODUCTION

BEFORE EXTENDING A loan to a debtor, a creditor will need to know whether the object offered to it as collateral is already subjected to a *prior* security or other international interest. This information will help the creditor assess the risks associated with the repayment of the debt. If the object is encumbered by another security interest, the creditor may realise that, in the case of the debtor's insolvency, it will not have immediate access to the object and will have to wait for the prior secured creditor to satisfy its claim first. By the time the creditor gains access to whatever is left of the collateral, there may not be enough to cover the repayment of the debt. Once the creditor obtains the information about the prior interests, it may decide not to lend at all, to include the risks in the cost of the credit, or to enter into an agreement with the prior creditor in order to change its priority position.[1] If the creditor is the first to be granted a security in the debtor's object, it can be more certain that in the case of the debtor's default or insolvency it will be able to sell the collateral and apply the proceeds for the repayment of the debt.

Once the loan is provided, the secured creditor will need to ensure that any *subsequent* creditors of the debtor will be aware of the existence of its security interest. This will be particularly important if the debtor retains the possession of the object and uses it in the course of its business, which may create the appearance of 'false wealth'.[2] Since the existence of a security will not be apparent from the object's visual examination, the subsequent secured and unsecured creditors may be induced to believe that it is not subjected to any prior interest. As a result, the creditors may act on the understanding that they will be the first ones to be granted security interests in the collateral. Similarly, the unsecured creditors may be confused by the

[1] S Harris, 'The International Rail Registry' (2007) *Unif L Rev* 531, 536.

[2] See P Wood, *Comparative Law of Security Interests and Title Finance*, 2nd edn (London, Sweet & Maxwell 2007) 141–42.

debtor's appearance of wealth and assume that the pool of assets available for the distribution to them is larger than it actually is.

One way to learn whether the collateral is subject to any prior claims and to notify the subsequent creditors about the existence of the security is to ask the debtor to provide information regarding the former and to let the prospective creditors know about the security interest of the creditor. In this case, the creditor will have to rely on the debtor to reveal any previous claims to the collateral and monitor whether the debtor has obtained any subsequent loans and has given notice to its other creditors about the existence of its security interest.[3] While some jurisdictions find this approach acceptable, it may be both naïve to expect the debtor to fully disclose information regarding its prior creditors (as it may prejudice the credit's cost and availability) and inefficient for the secured creditor to constantly monitor the debtor.[4]

Another way to achieve these objectives is to take possession of the collateral.[5] This will put the subsequent creditors on notice that since the debtor cannot use the object as its own, it may be subjected to some prior security interest.[6] However, this approach can be commercially impractical as the secured creditor may find it prohibitively expensive to store the collateral and the debtor will usually need the object to generate funds for the repayment of the debt. Furthermore, giving possession merely shifts the problem from the debtor to the creditor. Once the latter obtains possession, it may appear to its own creditors as being the owner of the object.

[3] This is the position under the Civil Code of the Russian Federation, Part I, Chapter 23, Art 342(3), (4) applicable to charges (zalog) in general. It seems that it continues to apply to the aircraft charges despite the recently introduced requirement that charges and other proprietary interests in the aircraft should be registered in the Common State Registry of Interests in Aircraft in accordance with the Federal Law of 14 March 2009 N31-ФЗ 'On State Registration of Interests and Contacts relating to Aircraft', Chapter 2, Art 9. Given that the aircraft registry is a public registry and can be checked by prospective creditors, it is unclear why the creditor should continue to rely on the debtor's cooperation.

[4] See B Bennett, 'Secured Financing in Russia: Risks, Legal Incentives, and Policy Concerns' (1999) 77 *Tex L Rev* 1443, 1455–56.

[5] A possessory pledge is not usually registrable because the owner's dispossession of the object is considered to be sufficient for the purposes of publicity. See A Greco, 'National Report on the Transfer of Movables in Italy' in W Faber and B Lurger (eds), *National Reports on the Transfer of Movables in Europe, Volume I: Austria, Estonia, Italy, Slovenia* (Sellier, European Law Publishers 2008) 364. On the nature of the pledge in English law which is also non-registrable, see *Donald v Suckling* (1866) LR 1 QB 585. For an argument that a pledge created by a written attornment by the debtor should be registrable, see L Gullifer (ed), *Goode on Legal Problems of Credit and Security*, 5th edn (London, Sweet & Maxwell 2013) 82.

[6] E Adams, S Nickles, S Sande and W Shiefelbein, 'A Revised Filing System: Recommendations and Innovations' (1995) *Minn L Rev* 877, 883. The position is similar under French law where no public register to record pledges over tangible personal property exists and physical delivery of the object is both necessary and sufficient to perfect the pledge. See M Gdanski, 'Taking Security in France' in M Bridge and R Stevens (eds), *Cross-Border Security and Insolvency* (Oxford, OUP 2001) 65.

In contrast, the registration of interests in a public registry offers a more effective solution. By searching the register, the creditor can ascertain whether the object is already encumbered by a *prior* interest. Similarly, by registering an interest, the creditor can ensure that the *subsequent* creditors discover its existence if they search the registry before granting a loan to the debtor. This is precisely what the International Registry (IR) established under the Convention aims to achieve.[7] The main objective of the IR is to make asset-based financing and leasing of mobile equipment transparent, in line with one of the main principles on which the Convention is based, in order to help reduce the risks and cost of the credit.[8] This can be achieved by making the IR a reliable source of information about various interests held in the objects. The IR is the central point of reference enabling a creditor to learn about the possible existence of the prior interests in the collateral and give notice about its own interest in it to other interest holders.

However, in the case of the debtor's default, the mere knowledge of the possible existence of competing interests is not sufficient. The secured creditor will need to know whether its security can be immediately enforced or is likely to be postponed to a prior interest. For this reason, the Convention puts the registration of interests in the IR at the centre of its priority rules.[9] By providing that a registered interest has priority over the subsequently registered and unregistered interests,[10] the Convention allows the creditor to ascertain its priority status among other interest holders. Finally, the registration of an interest in the IR allows its holder to preserve its effectiveness during the debtor's insolvency, provided that such registration was effected prior to the commencement of the insolvency proceedings.[11]

The Convention envisages that different registries will be established to register and search for the interests held in various categories of the objects governed by it.[12] At present, only the IR for aircraft objects is in operation.[13] It was established in 2006 and is operated by Aviareto Ltd,

[7] For a general overview of the reports of the International Registry Task Force, see J Standell, 'The Role of the International Registry Task Force (I.R.T.F.) in the Development of the International Registry for Interests in Aircraft' (2006) *Unif L Rev* 8.

[8] R Goode, *Official Commentary to the Convention on International Interests in Mobile Equipment and Protocol Thereto on Matters Specific to Aircraft Equipment*, 3rd edn (Rome, UNIDROIT 2013) 23.

[9] Goode (n 8) 298.

[10] Art 29 CTC. See chapter five for detailed treatment of the Convention's priority rules.

[11] Art 30(1) CTC. For a historical overview of the insolvency provisions of the Convention, see K Zwieten, 'The Insolvency Provisions of the Cape Town Convention and Protocols: Historical and Economic Perspectives' (2012) *Cape Town Convention Journal* 53.

[12] Art 16(2) CTC. See B Honnebier, 'The Fully-Computerised International Registry for Security Interests in Aircraft and Aircraft Protocol that will Become Effective Toward the Beginning of 2006' (2005) *J Air L Comm* 63, 71.

[13] The IR for the aircraft objects is accessible at www.internationalregistry.aero/ir-web.

based in Dublin, Ireland.[14] The IR has proved to be successful and is actively used by aircraft manufacturers, financiers and lessors globally.[15] The registries for railway objects and space assets are still in the process of development, but it is expected that they will follow the approach taken by the IR for aircraft objects as far as possible. At the same time, such registries will have to reflect features specific to rail and space equipment. The purpose of this chapter is to examine the defining features of the IR for aircraft objects, the role of the Supervisory Authority, the main objectives of effecting a registration and the interests which can be registered in the IR. Chapter four, in turn, focuses on the process of registering an interest in the IR.

II. DEFINING FEATURES OF THE INTERNATIONAL REGISTRY

A. Electronic International Registry

The IR is a global fully electronic Internet-based system accessible for effecting and searching registrations 24 hours a day, 7 days a week.[16] The advantage of there being only *one* IR is that the location of the collateral, the debtor or the creditor is irrelevant when effecting a registration or making a search.[17] The registry is public and can be accessed by any searcher. However, for the purposes of security, the data available in the IR free of charge is limited.

Another advantage of the IR's electronic nature is the speed with which all operations in it can be performed. For instance, applications for effecting, amending and discharging registrations can be considered speedily and usually dealt with within one or two working days.[18] Further, the IR's electronic format dictates the manner in which communications with it are conducted. Accordingly, registration data can only be transmitted to the IR in an electronic format and a hard copy of the documents must not be

[14] Aviareto is a joint venture company of SITA (an air transport telecommunications and IT solutions company, created and owned by air transport community) and the Irish Government. For more information on Aviareto, see www.aviareto.aero.

[15] R Cowan and D Gallagher, 'The International Registry for Aircraft Equipment—The First Seven Years, What We Have Learnt' (2014) 45 *UCC LJ* 225, 227.

[16] This is subject to maintenance works which should be performed outside peak periods. See sec 3.4 of the Regulations and Procedures for the International Registry (International Civil Aviation Organisation, Doc 9864, 6th edn 2014) (hereafter 'the Regulations').

[17] Although the IR is accessible worldwide, the Convention will apply if the debtor is situated in a Contracting State at the time of the conclusion of the agreement creating or providing for the international interest. See Art 3, 4 CTC.

[18] The Legal Advisory Panel of the Aviation Working Group, 'Practitioners' Guide to the Cape Town Convention and the Aircraft Protocol' (Aviation Working Group 2015) 96–97 available at http://awg.aero/assets/docs/VED%20Practitioner's%20Guide%209.9.15.pdf (last accessed July 2016).

sent to the Registrar.[19] This approach can be contrasted with some other domestic registration systems, whereby the registering data is submitted in a hard copy and either stored as such or entered manually or electronically to an electronic database by the registry staff.[20] This process is time consuming and costly. It also creates the possibility of errors both by the registrant (when submitting the data) and the registry staff (when entering it in the registry).[21]

In contrast, the electronic IR is efficient and secure because avoiding human intervention reduces the risk of errors in the registration data, which may help preserve the priority status of the registrant and ensure that a searcher can obtain reliable information relating to the object.[22] In addition, there is no need to keep the paper documents at a certain physical location, which reduces the risk of these documents being lost and cuts the cost of storage. To minimise the possibility of errors, the registrant is required to use the IR's drop-down menus.[23] For example, information relating to the manufacturer's name, generic model designation and the serial number of the aircraft object must be transmitted to the Registrar by selecting the relevant data from the IR's drop-down menu. Exceptionally, when the aircraft object cannot be found on the IR's list, the registering party can make a 'free text' entry of the identification information relating to the aircraft object.[24]

Despite these advantages, the IR's electronic nature presents certain challenges. First, it is clearly more difficult to detect any interference with an electronic document in comparison with a paper-based document, where alterations will usually be visible to the eye.[25] This is why utmost care must be taken to preserve the integrity of the electronically stored data held in the IR.[26] To alleviate this risk, the IR requires all parties to formally confirm the registration by sending a digitally signed consent to the IR. In addition, the IR uses a Tamper Check alarm, which is software, specifically designed for the registry, alerting it to any unauthorised changes to the stored data.[27]

[19] Sec 5.1 of the Regulations. SV Erp, 'The Cape Town Convention: A Model for a European System of Security Interests Registration?' (2004) *ERPL* 91, 98.

[20] R Cuming, 'Considerations in the Design of an International Registry for Interests in Mobile Equipment' (1999) *Unif L Rev* 275, 281.

[21] *Ibid* 281.

[22] However, it has been suggested that a purely electronic system may be too rigid and if it is not flexible enough to accommodate possible errors in the data submitted by the registrant, it may be commercially impractical. R Cuming, 'Article 9 North of #49: The Canadian PPS Acts and the Quebec Civil Code' (1996) 29 *Loyola of Los Angeles L Rev* 971, 983–84.

[23] Sec 5.1 of the Regulations. See also J Atwood, 'The Status of the Mobile Equipment (Cape Town) Convention—Arrival of an International Registration System' (2006) 39 *UCC LJ* 1 Art 3.

[24] Sec 5.1 of the Regulations.

[25] Cowan and Gallagher (n 15) 231.

[26] *Ibid* 231.

[27] *Ibid* 231.

Another challenge, associated with the electronic nature of the IR, relates to the storage of data and the technological advances. In particular, it is important to ensure that even when new technology becomes available and the registration system is aligned with such technological developments, old records can still be stored and accessed when required.[28] Finally, the electronic nature and the possibility of conducting an anonymous search can present a security risk. The registration information relates to high value objects and has substantial commercial value in itself. To protect the integrity of the data, the IR limits the kind of information that can be accessed by a searcher free of charge. It also uses a sophisticated 'public key infrastructure' (PKI) technology, employed to digitally sign and encrypt data to protect the integrity of the system and ensure privacy.[29]

B. Notice Filing v Transaction Filing

Another key feature of the IR is that it is based on *notice filing* rather than a *contractual document* or *transaction filing*.[30] The latter usually involves the filing of a copy of the contract creating a security interest.[31] The main advantage of the transaction filing system is that it allows a prospective creditor to examine the documents without the need to contact the previous creditor. By checking the documents at the public registry, the creditor may also ascertain how much was borrowed by the debtor and what interest must be paid to the creditor.

However, the documents creating the charge will not reveal how much of the debt has currently been repaid to the creditor. Consequently, the searcher may still have to contact the prior creditor to obtain this information before providing the debtor with the loan.[32] Another unsatisfactory feature of the transaction filing system is that the registration does not, generally, determine the order of priority between competing interests and serves only as a perfection requirement.[33] Finally, since the transaction filing system involves

[28] *Ibid* 228.

[29] *Ibid* 233.

[30] Art 17(2)(i) CTC.

[31] G McCormack, *Secured Credit under English and American Law* (Cambridge, CUP 2004) 133. This is the position under English law. Companies Act 2006 (Amendment of Part 25) Regulations 2013, reg 859A requires the registrar to register a charge when the company or any person interested in the charge (usually a creditor) delivers to it a statement of particulars and a certified copy of the instrument creating or evidencing the charge within 21 days of its creation.

[32] Law Commission Consultation Paper N164, *Registration of Security Interests: Company Charges and Property other than Land* (London, TSO 2002) 50.

[33] In the context of English law, adhering to a transaction filing registration system, the Law Commission has recently proposed to make the registration a priority point. The proposal was not implemented and under the current system, the registering party, generally, has 21 days

the registration of a copy of the charge document, this means that each transaction creating a charge must be separately registered and the whole credit relationship between the debtor and the creditor cannot be registered in a single registration session.[34]

In contrast, the notice filing system, which has its origins in the US Article 9 of the Uniform Commercial Code (UCC), does not involve the registration of the transaction documents. Instead, what is registered or *filed* under the UCC system, is a simple financing statement, providing some basic information regarding, among other things, the names of the debtor and the creditor and identification of the collateral, covered by the financing statement.[35] Similar to the UCC, the Convention adopts a notice filing registration system. The Convention's registration system requires the registrant to provide basic information, allowing a searcher to discover that a certain transaction may have given rise to an interest in an aircraft object and the names of the parties involved. The searcher can then approach the creditors named in the certificate to obtain more detailed information in relation to such a transaction.

The Convention's registration system has several advantages. First, since the registration data is only basic, confidential details of the business arrangements between the debtor and its previous creditors remain undisclosed.[36] The searcher can obtain the relevant information by making further enquiries from the creditors, which are named in the search certificate.[37] Secondly, the minimalistic content of the registration information, required under the

from the creation of the charge to effect the registration. As long as the interest is registered within this time, the charge is effective against third parties. This may create an invisibility problem, whereby a prospective creditor, searching the register within the 21-day period of the creation of the previous charge that is not yet registered, may be misled by a clear search. Such a prospective creditor can extend the credit on the understanding that it will be the first secured creditor. Even if the prospective creditor registers its interest first, and the previously created charge is registered after it, but within the 21-day period, this will not necessarily mean that the first registered interest will have priority over the subsequently registered one. See Gullifer (n 5) 92.

[34] See G McCormack, 'Rewriting the English Law of Personal Property Securities and Article 9 of the US Uniform Commercial Code' (2003) *Comp Law* 69, 71. In English law, these unsatisfactory features of the transaction registration system prompted calls for reforms along the lines of the notice filing systems under the United States Article 9 UCC as well as Canadian, New Zealand and Australian Personal Property Security Acts. See Gullifer (n 5) 92.

[35] See, generally, J White and R Summers, *Uniform Commercial Code*, 6th edn (West Group 2010) Ch 23. See also D Beran, 'Financing Statements, Descriptions, Collateral and Confusion: Arkansas Courts Tackle the New Article 9' (2005) 57 *Arkansas L Rev* 951.

[36] R Cuming, 'The International Registry for Interests in Aircraft: An Overview of its Structure' (2006) *Unif L Rev* 18, 26.

[37] *Ibid* 28. However, previous creditors are not under an obligation to respond to the inquiry of the searcher. For a different position under the Canadian law, see I Davies, 'The Reform of Personal Property Security Law: Can Article 9 of the US Uniform Commercial Code be a Precedent' (1988) *ICLQ* 465, 489.

notice filing system, reduces the possibility of entering erroneous data.[38] Thirdly, the need to provide only basic information, coupled with the electronic nature of the IR, creates a more cost efficient mechanism than the transaction documents system, which requires digitalisation and registration of the entire documents creating an international interest.[39] Fourthly, the minimalistic approach of notice filing means that the registration data may not reveal whether the interest was *actually* created or only *intended* to be created. This approach allows for the registration of a prospective international interest, which can be accomplished before the agreement constituting the actual international interest is entered into. Thus, the searcher is only able to ascertain that a prior creditor *may* have an international interest in the object held by the debtor. The parties may agree for the prospective interest relating to a uniquely identifiable object to be registered while they negotiate the terms of the agreement which will create the actual international interest. Once the international interest is created, there will be no need to re-register it and the priority of the creditor will date back to the moment when the prospective interest was registered.[40] Further, because the registration in the notice filing system is not linked to a particular transaction or a document creating the international interest, it is possible to cover subsequent loans by the initial registration.[41] Finally, under the Convention's notice filing system, the time of registration determines the order of priority between competing interests. The direct link between the registration and the priority status of the registrant creates a strong commercial incentive to register the interest as quickly as possible. This is because a failure to, or delay in, registering an interest may result in a loss of the priority position. This feature of the Convention's registration system helps to obviate the need to impose a time period, within which the interest holders must register their interests to ensure validity. It also helps to ensure that the IR is a transparent and reliable system in that the registrant can be certain that only those interests that are registered in it at the time of the registration of its own interest will bind it.[42]

C. Asset-based International Registry

The IR is an asset-based system, which means that all registrations and searches in it are conducted against a uniquely identifiable aircraft object.[43]

[38] Cuming (n 20) 279.
[39] *Ibid* 278.
[40] Art 19(4) CTC.
[41] Harris (n 1) 537. See chapter five for a more detailed discussion of this issue.
[42] This is subject to the exceptions to the general rule discussed later in the chapter.
[43] Goode (n 8) 77.

This approach can be contrasted with a debtor-based system, where the registrations are effected and searched against the debtor's name. The advantage of a debtor-based system is that it is not tied to a specific object, which enables the registrant to register an interest in the debtor's future or after-acquired property. In contrast, in an asset-based system, the registrant can only register an interest in the existing object, which is uniquely identifiable at the time of the registration. It is for this reason that the Convention and the Protocols require the object to be uniquely identified at the stage of the registration.[44]

The debtor-based system is well suited for the registration of the interests in such collateral as inventory or accounts because it obviates the need to make a new registration each time the collateral is changed.[45] However, this system offers the secured creditor 1 (SC1) little certainty where debtor A changes its name to B and grants a new security interest in the same collateral to the secured creditor 2 (SC2). Before granting a loan, SC2 will search the registry against the name of the debtor known to it (ie B) and will not be able to discover SC1's interest. Even if the debtor does not change its name or sell the collateral to another party, a single mistake in the debtor's name, such as a misspelling by one letter or the use of a nickname instead of a legal name, may preclude a proper search revealing any registered interests in the debtor's property.[46] These problems can be avoided in an asset-based system, showing all potentially existing interests in the object, irrespective of any changes in the debtor's name or identity. The objects governed by the Convention are of exceptionally high value and are less likely to be used as inventory. Moreover, these objects can, generally, be uniquely identified. For these reasons, the Convention's asset-based system is better suited for the registration of the interests in these types of objects than the debtor-based system.

[44] Art 18(1) CTC; Art XX(1) of the Aircraft Protocol and sec 5.3(c) of the Regulations; Art XXX of the Space Protocol; Art IX of the Luxembourg Protocol.

[45] Cuming (n 22) 981.

[46] Misspellings of the debtor's name or use of the incorrect names in financing statements are a major problem under Art 9 UCC filings. If the mistake is such that the correct filing cannot be located, it invalidates the financing statement of the secured creditor and results in a loss of priority. This problem has generated some considerable case law. See, for example, *Clark v Deere and Co (In re Kinderknecht)* 308 BR 71 (10th Cir BAP 2004), where the use of a debtor's nickname, Terry, instead of his legal name, Terrance, by the secured creditor, had an invalidating effect on the financing statement. See, also, *In re FV Steel and Wire Co*, 310 BR 390; *In re Nittolo Land Dev. Ass'n*, 333 BR 237 (Bankr SDNY 2005), where a financing statement reciting the debtor's name as 'Nittolo Land Development Associates, Inc' instead of the correct name of 'Nittolo Land Development Association, Inc' was held to be invalid. Similarly, the decision in *Pankratz Implement Co v Citizens Nat'l Bank*, 281 Kan 209, 130 P 3d 57 (Kan Sup Ct, 2006) leaves a secured creditor no room for an error in the debtor's name. In this case, only one letter was omitted and instead of Rodger House, the debtor's first name was misspelled as Roger, invalidating the financing statement.

An essential feature of an asset-based system is that the objects in which the interests are registered should be capable of unique identification. The Protocols adopt different approaches in the search for the objects' unique identifier. The aircraft industry benefits from a longtime global tradition of aircraft objects' unique identification by serial number, manufacturer's name and model designation. The Aircraft Protocol uses these criteria to identify the aircraft objects at the stages of the constitution and registration of the international interests held in them. These criteria are used to identify both the airframes and the aircraft engines, which are considered by the Protocol as distinct aircraft objects even if they form part of the same aircraft.[47] This approach reflects existing commercial practice because, similar to the airframes, aircraft engines are high value, mobile and frequently interchangeable objects, which are often separately financed.[48]

In contrast, a helicopter is considered as an aircraft object as a whole, including any *installed* engines.[49] This means that, as a general rule, while it is installed on the helicopter, the engine cannot constitute a distinct aircraft object and no interest can be registered in it. However, in certain circumstances, a helicopter engine can be considered as a separate aircraft object. In particular, a helicopter engine will constitute an aircraft object *before* it is installed on a helicopter and *after* it is removed from it.[50] Accordingly, as long as the engine is physically separated from the helicopter, it should be possible to register a separate interest in it and this interest will continue to exist even after the engine is installed in and subsequently removed from the helicopter.[51] The Protocol's treatment of helicopter engines in this manner is unfortunate and difficult to justify. Helicopter engines, similar to aircraft engines, are often interchanged between different helicopters and financed separately from the frame. To solve this problem, the Commentary offers a practical solution of registering a prospective international interest in the engine installed on the helicopter.[52] Once the engine is removed, the prospective interest in it will turn into the actual international interest with priority dating back to its registration. While registration of the prospective interest may offer protection to the holder of the international interest, it seems that the denial of a separate object status to an installed helicopter engine is confusing and unnecessary.

In contrast to the aircraft industry, the railway industry was not able to draw on a widely accepted tradition of rail equipment registries in which security interests were recorded, because not many countries maintained

[47] Art I(2)(c) of the Aircraft Protocol.
[48] Goode (n 8) 29, 429.
[49] Art I(2)(l) of the Aircraft Protocol.
[50] Goode (n 8) 29.
[51] Goode (n 8) 171–72. Art XIV(3) of the Aircraft Protocol.
[52] Goode (n 8) 172.

such registries.[53] There are no uniform unique identification criteria applicable to railway objects worldwide. While it is customary to use the manufacturer's and the operator's serial numbers in many countries, there is no guarantee that these numbers can uniquely identify the railway object or that they will not change if the object undergoes a major rebuild or if it is transferred to a different operator.[54] The absence of a universal system providing unique identification of railway objects meant that the simple approach taken by the Aircraft Protocol could not be adopted under the Luxembourg Protocol. To tackle the issue of unique identification of railway objects, a special Unique Rail Vehicle Identification System (URVIS) was developed.[55] The URVIS is a 20-digit number allocated to the railway object on its first registration in the IR, intended to be kept permanently.[56] This identification number is either: (a) affixed to the object; (b) associated in the IR with the manufacturer's name and identification number; or (c) associated in the IR with a national or regional identification number.[57] Unlike the Aircraft Protocol, the Luxembourg Protocol does not consider railway engines as separate railway objects. Instead, the railway engines are regarded as parts of the railway rolling stock and interests in them are not separately registrable.[58]

It is envisaged that the registrations under the Space Protocol will also be made against a uniquely identifiable space assets and not against the debtor's name. However, the identification of the space assets for the registration has proved to be a difficult matter. First, in contrast to the aircraft objects, which are confined to airframes, aircraft engines and helicopters, the space assets comprise a much broader range of assets. That is why the definition of the space assets is complex, having been debated for several years.[59] Space assets comprise three groups, namely: (i) a spacecraft, such as a satellite, space station, space module, space capsule, space vehicle or reusable launch vehicle; (ii) a payload in respect of which a separate registration may be effected in accordance with the regulations which will be developed in the future under the Space Protocol. The payload includes transponders, filtering systems, cameras and other equipment needed to enable the satellite to perform its aim (telecommunication, navigation, observation, scientific or other); (iii) a part of the spacecraft or a payload such as transponder,

[53] M Fleetwood and P Bloch, 'The Cape Town International Rail Registry and the Development of State Registries' (2014) *Cape Town Convention Journal* 95.

[54] *Ibid* 106.

[55] *Ibid* 106.

[56] *Ibid* 106.

[57] Art XIV(1) of the Luxembourg Protocol.

[58] Art 1(2)(e) of the Luxembourg Protocol.

[59] R Goode, *Official Commentary to the Convention on International Interests in Mobile Equipment and Protocol Thereto on Matters Specific to Space Assets* (Rome, UNIDROIT 2013) 166.

in respect of which a separate registration may be effected.[60] Space assets are often complex in their composition, and while a spacecraft and a payload can amount to the distinct space assets, some of their parts can also qualify as separate space assets.[61]

Not all space assets can be uniquely identified by a consistent set of identifiers such as serial numbers, manufacturers' names and model designations. This means that the unique identification criteria may vary, depending on the type of the space asset. Furthermore, the formulation of the identification requirements will have to take into account space assets that are already in space. In relation to these assets, it may be difficult or impossible to view or place any identification marks on them. The identification of space assets already launched into space must also be consistent with their identification prior to the launch to avoid confusion and uncertainty affecting priority of competing creditors.[62] Due to the complexity of this issue, the Space Protocol leaves the identification requirements for the registration to the Regulations and Procedures which are expected to be issued by the Supervisory Authority.[63]

III. THE SUPERVISORY AUTHORITY AND THE REGISTRAR

It is envisaged that there will be different registries where interests held in various categories of objects governed by the Convention can be registered.[64] Each IR will be operated by the Registrar, who will be appointed and dismissed by the Supervisory Authority.[65] In the case of aircraft objects, the Supervisory Authority is the Council of the International Civil Aviation Organization (ICAO) and the Registrar, appointed for the period of five years, is Aviareto. The Supervisory Authority is responsible for the establishment of the IR and ensuring the continuity of its effective operation in the case of a change of the Registrar.[66] It is for this reason that the Supervisory Authority is given the ownership of all proprietary rights in the database and archives of the IR.[67] The ownership of proprietary rights vested in the Supervisory Authority is essential for ensuring that the new Registrar is assigned all necessary rights for the effective operation of the IR. Other functions of the Supervisory Authority include the publication

[60] Art 1(k) of the Space Protocol.

[61] M Sundahl, *The Cape Town Convention: Its Application to Space Assets and Relation to the Law of Outer Space* (Lieden/Boston, Martinus Nijhoff Publishers 2013) 52.

[62] *Ibid* 53.

[63] Art XXX of the Space Protocol.

[64] Art 16(2) CTC.

[65] Art 17(2)(b) CTC.

[66] Art 17(2)(a), (c) CTC.

[67] Art 17(4) CTC.

of the Regulations, establishment of administrative procedures for making complaints concerning the operation of the Registry, providing guidance to the Registrar at its request and the review of the fees associated with the services of the IR.

In the case of the railway objects, in relation to which the registry is not yet in operation, a slightly different structure was adopted. The Supervisory Authority will consist of the representatives of at least 10 Contracting States to the Luxembourg Protocol and will be assisted in the performance of its functions by the Secretariat.[68] The Intergovernmental Organisation for International Carriage by Rail (OTIF) will act as the Secretariat and its headquarters in Berne (Switzerland) will be used by the Supervisory Authority during the discharge of its functions.[69] The Supervisory Authority will have international legal personality and its employees will enjoy immunity from legal or administrative processes.[70] This means that the Supervisory Authority will have a legal personality distinct from its members and can enter into agreements with other parties for the performance of its functions under the Convention and the Protocols. The Supervisory Authority is exempt from taxes and may enjoy other privileges provided by the host State in which it is located. The IR's assets, documents, databases and archives will be inviolable and immune from seizure, but such immunity can be waived by the Supervisory Authority when, for example, a person making a claim against the Registrar needs to access this information to support its claim.[71]

Unlike the Supervisory Authority, the Registrar is not immune from legal and administrative processes and is liable for the loss suffered by a person directly resulting from the Registrar's error or the IR's malfunction.[72] But the liability of the Registrar is not absolute and damage caused by the malfunction of the system, which occurred as a result of an event of inevitable and irresistible nature that could not have been prevented, will not be within its liability.[73] Similarly, the Registrar is not liable for any factual inaccuracy it receives or transmits in the form in which such information was originally received.[74] Since the IR is an electronically operated system, it is difficult for the Registrar to check the external information transmitted to it by the registrant. For this reason, the Registrar is entitled to assume the correctness of the information and should not be liable if, for example, the information

[68] Art XII of the Luxembourg Protocol.

[69] G Kafka, 'The Supervisory Authority and its Secretariat According to the Luxembourg Protocol' (2007) *Unif L Rev* 554–55.

[70] Art 27(1) CTC.

[71] Art 27(4), (5), (6) CTC.

[72] Art 28(1) CTC.

[73] Art 28(1) CTC. See, generally, H Bollweg and K Schnell, 'Liability of the Registrar for the Registration of International Interests Pursuant to the Luxembourg Protocol' (2007) *Unif L Rev* 559.

[74] Art 28(2) CTC.

submitted by the registrant contains errors in relation to the identification of the object.[75] Finally, the Registrar is required to cover its liability by insurance or a financing guarantee to the extent determined by the Supervisory Authority.[76]

IV. OBJECTIVES OF THE REGISTRATION AND REGISTRABLE INTERESTS

A. Objectives of the Registration

The IR is unique in that for the first time it is possible to register the international interests in aircraft objects in a global registry, not tied to any specific national legal system. The fact that such a registry was established and operates successfully can serve as a powerful impetus to those jurisdictions where a registry, recording security interests in the aircraft objects, does not yet exist. An effective registration system was once called 'the centre pole that holds up the entire personal property security tent' and it has been suggested that 'without such a system, lenders would go wary, commerce would be hobbled, and the manifold commercial ends that are met by commercial lenders would be stunted, rendered more costly, or stymied together'.[77] At the same time, the registration of security interests in personal property and in aircraft objects in particular is not a universally accepted phenomenon. Indeed, some jurisdictions do not have registries to record security interests at all.[78] The fact that secured financing can still flourish in such jurisdictions may suggest that there is really no need for the IR's existence, since the information available there can perhaps be obtained from the debtor or the examination of the financial accounts of the company. The examination of the main objectives of the IR will help ascertain whether its establishment was warranted and why a registrant would wish to record its interest in an aircraft object in it.

i. Notice of Possible Existence of the Registered Interest

One of the main purposes of effecting a registration in the IR is to provide notice of the possible existence of a registered interest to third parties.[79]

[75] Goode (n 8) 330.

[76] Art 28(4) CTC. See H Rosen, 'The Luxembourg Rail Protocol: A Major Advance for the Railway Industry' (2007) *Unif L Rev* 427, 435–38.

[77] J White, 'Reforming Article 9 Priorities in Light of Old Ignorance and New Filing Rules' (1995) 79 *Minn L Rev* 529, 530.

[78] For example, there is no central registry for security interests in tangible and intangible movables in such countries as Germany, the Netherlands or Austria. See Wood (n 2) 155.

[79] R Castillo-Triana, 'The Relevance of the Luxembourg Protocol for Central and South America' (2007) *Unif L Rev* 461, 467.

As noted, before extending a loan, the creditor will need to know whether the aircraft object offered to it as a security is already encumbered by a prior interest.[80] After the loan is granted, the creditor will wish to ensure that any subsequent creditors can discover its interest in the object before providing the debtor with funds.[81] The creditor can obtain information regarding any previous claims in the object and give notice to subsequent creditors by searching the IR and registering its own interest in the object in it. Similarly, a trustee in bankruptcy, a liquidator or a creditor which has obtained a court order for the satisfaction of the debt owed to it by the company, will wish to search the IR to establish which of the creditor claims must be honoured first or how heavily the asset is encumbered.

What can the notice of the registered interest tell the searcher? First, a registration in the IR does not guarantee that the international interest exists.[82] A search certificate will only indicate that the creditor named in the registration *has acquired or intends to acquire* an international interest in the object.[83] It will not reveal whether what is registered is an actual international interest or a prospective international interest, even if this can be ascertained from other registered information.[84] The certificate's neutral language allows the parties to register a prospective interest while the terms of the security agreement are being negotiated. Once the agreement has been concluded, and provided that the registered data is sufficient to support the registration of the international interest, there will be no need to register a new international interest.[85] Although this means that the searcher will not be able to ascertain from the certificate alone whether the registration refers to the prospective or actual international interest, such registration may allow the registrant to secure its priority at the stage of the negotiations with the debtor. This is because the Convention treats the interest which is first registered as a prospective interest and this later becomes an international interest as registered from the time of the prospective interest's registration rather than from the time of its creation as an actual international interest.[86] Since priority of competing interests is, generally, determined by the order of registration,[87] the registration of a prospective interest may

[80] Similarly, under English law, Buckley J noted in *Re Jackson and Bassford Ltd* [1906] 2 Ch 467, at 476, that the object of the registration is that 'those who are minded to deal with the limited company shall be able, by searching a certain register, to find whether the company has encumbered its property or not'.

[81] For a similar view, see *Re Cardiff Workmen's Cottage Co Ltd* [1906] 2 Ch 627, at 629, where it was noted that the purpose of registration is 'to ensure the means of notice to those who contemplate giving credit to the company'.

[82] Goode (n 8) 84.

[83] Art 22(3) CTC.

[84] Art 22(3) CTC.

[85] Art 18(3) CTC.

[86] Art 19(4) CTC.

[87] Art 29(1) CTC.

allow the creditor to secure its claim at an earlier stage. At the same time, the certificate will provide the searcher with the names and addresses of any creditors. The searcher should then be able to contact them to obtain more information about the nature of the registered interest.

Secondly, the registration is not proof that the international interest was validly created.[88] Registration is not necessary for the *creation* of the international interest and, for this reason, cannot be used as proof of its existence.[89] If the formal requirements for the creation of the international interest are not met,[90] its registration will simply be ineffective. It is, of course, possible to register an interest (as a prospective interest) before the agreement creating it is entered into. But should it later transpire that, for example, the negotiations between the parties did not result in the creation of the actual international interest, that the secured obligations cannot be determined from the security agreement, or that the chargor did not obtain the power to dispose of the object, the security agreement will not be considered as validly created. Consequently, the registration of the interest arising from such an agreement will also be invalid.

Thirdly, to effect a registration, the registrant must obtain consent of the other party.[91] However, the existence of the registration cannot be used as proof that such consent was validly obtained. This consequence flows from the IR's electronic nature. Since the process of the registration and search involves no human intervention, the Registrar cannot evaluate and assess the facts external to the transmitted data.[92] For this reason, the Registrar is not under a duty to enquire whether consent to the registration has in fact been given or is valid. Once consent to make a registration is electronically transmitted and provided that all other necessary requirements are met, the Registrar will have to effect the registration. If consent was not in fact validly obtained, the registration will be invalid, even if this cannot be ascertained from the IR.[93]

Finally, the registration is not a guarantee that the registered interest was not discharged. Once the obligations secured by the security agreement have been performed, the security interest ceases to exist and the debtor's interest in the object becomes unencumbered. In this case, the holder of the

[88] Goode (n 8) 84. This position is not universal. For example, under the Croatian law, both the creation and priority depend on and are determined at the moment of the registration of a security interest. See T Jocipovic, 'The Rail Protocol and Croatian Secured Transactions Law' (2007) *Unif L Rev* 489, 503.

[89] In contrast, Art 6.2 of the EBRD Model Law on Secured Transactions states that a registered charge is created by entering into a 'charge instrument' and by registering the charge.

[90] Art 7 CTC. See further chapter two.

[91] Art 20(1) CTC.

[92] Goode (n 8) 311.

[93] Art 19(1) CTC. Goode (n 8) 311.

registered interest, for example, the secured creditor, the conditional seller or lessor, has to arrange for the interest to be discharged from the IR.[94] The discharge must be procured after a written demand by the debtor is delivered to or received at the address of the registrant.[95] In the case of the aircraft objects, the discharge should occur no later than five working days after receipt of the demand.[96] Since there is a five-day period during which the discharge can be reflected in the IR, some registered interests appearing as current may have in fact already ceased to exist.

To reiterate, the registration in the IR cannot amount to a notice of existence of the registered interest or to proof that the registration was validly effected. Nor can it guarantee that the registered interest was validly created and was not discharged. The purpose of such a notice is to draw to the searcher's attention that a registered interest *may* have been created. It is then for the searcher to enquire from the creditors, named in the registration information, about the status of their registered interest.

One possible criticism of this system is that the information given in the IR is too vague to be of any value. Effectively, it is merely a list of *possible* creditors who *may* have an interest in the object. Searching the IR may not be sufficient to make a decision in relation to the loan for the debtor. The searcher will still have to approach the creditors named in the search certificate. Since the Convention does not impose a duty on the registrants to disclose the information to the searchers, the latter may also need to run an independent credit check on the debtor to clarify its financial position and assess its ability to repay the debt.

Another possible criticism is that not only may the list of the registrations provided by the IR be inconclusive, but it may also not be comprehensive. Some of the registered interests may appear as current, but in fact may never have come into existence or have already been discharged at the time of the search. Other interests may not appear on the register because they cannot be registered and yet be binding on the searcher. Although the general rule is that a registered interest has priority over an unregistered interest even if the holder of the former knows of the existence of the latter,[97] this rule is subject to a number of exceptions.[98]

The first exception concerns the non-registrable non-consensual right or interest (NCRI) in relation to which a Contracting State has made a declaration under Article 39 CTC. Examples include liens on an aircraft for unpaid navigation charges, taxes or repairs.[99] Although the searcher will not be able

[94] Art 25(1) CTC.
[95] Art 25(1) CTC.
[96] Art XX(2) of the Aircraft Protocol.
[97] Art 29(1) CTC.
[98] See further chapter five.
[99] Goode (n 8) 375.

to find these interests in the IR, they will take priority over the registered international interests.[100] But the Convention does not leave the searcher with no means of discovering the existence of a NCRI. The searcher may be able to find out about their possible existence by making a separate search in the IR, revealing the relevant declarations.[101] Therefore, there is no need to investigate whether a Contracting State's national law provides that certain non-registrable NCRIs are treated in priority to the registered interests. The IR serves as a central point of inquiry for this purpose. If the search does not reveal a declaration, the searcher is entitled to assume that such a NCRI will not be able to trump its priority in the debtor's insolvency. Finally, the scope of the Article 39 exception is limited to those rights and interests, which under the law of the Contracting State, have priority over an interest equivalent to the international interest, namely, to the interests of a chargee, conditional seller and lessor.

In contrast, some other domestic registration systems have much longer lists of interests, not requiring registration and still binding a searcher. For example, §9-309 of Article 9 UCC contains a list of various transactions, such as purchase money security interests in consumer goods, a sale of payment intangibles and a sale of promissory notes, which do not have to be filed or registered to obtain priority and are, generally, automatically perfected once attachment is complete.[102] Similarly, English law does not require registration of pledges, liens, hire purchase, RoT agreements and leases. The holders of such interests enjoy priority because they are either in possession or are the owners of the object and can, in principle, claim it back in the case of the debtor's insolvency.[103] Despite the fact that domestic registration systems recognise that there may be various non-registrable rights and interests, which can still bind the registered interest of a secured creditor, the advantages of a central public registry seem to outweigh this inconvenience.[104]

The second exception to the general rule that a registered interest takes priority over an unregistered or subsequently registered interest, relates to the position of a conditional buyer and lessee, which do not have registrable interests and, for this reason, cannot protect themselves against the creditor of the conditional seller or lessor.[105] To shield the conditional buyer or lessee

[100] Art 39 CTC.

[101] Sec 7.5 of the Regulations.

[102] On the meaning of the automatic perfection under the US law, see White and Summers (n 35) 1195–1202.

[103] JD Lacy, 'Constructive Notice and Company Charge Registration' (2001) *Conveyancer and Property Lawyer* 122, 124; I Davies, 'Reservation of Title Clauses in France' (1991) *Int'l Banking Law* 417.

[104] White (n 77) 530.

[105] R Goode, 'International Interests in Mobile Equipment: A Transnational Juridical Concept' (2003) *Bond L Rev* 9, 15.

from the possible claims to the object, which may come from a secured creditor of a defaulting conditional seller or lessor, the Convention provides the following. If the conditional seller or lessor registers its interest before its creditor registers its own interest in the IR, the creditor's registered interest will be postponed to the unregistered interest of the conditional buyer or lessee.[106] The Convention's protection of the interests of the conditional buyer and lessee can be justified by the fact that the creditor will have an opportunity to search the IR before granting a loan to the conditional seller or lessor and find out about the existence of the conditional sale and leasing agreements.[107]

The third exception relates to the treatment of an outright buyer of an object, which is not registrable under the Convention. Article 29 provides that such a buyer acquires its interest in the object free from the unregistered interest even if it has actual knowledge of it.[108] Conversely, the buyer's interest in the object will be subjected to the interest registered at the time of the acquisition of that interest.[109] The effect of this provision is that the buyer is given priority over an existing interest which is not registered until after the buyer's acquisition of the object. For example, if the seller grants a security interest to a secured creditor and sells the object to the buyer before the interest of the secured creditor is registered, the buyer will take it free from the security interest even if it is registered later.[110] However, this exception implies that the seller has the power to dispose of the object. If the seller sells the object to the buyer first, the seller's power to dispose of it will be extinguished. Consequently, any grant of a security and its registration by the seller's secured creditor *after* the sale to the buyer will not have any effect on it. This will not be the result of the exception, but will flow from the lack of validity of the security interest. Finally, this exception does not apply to aircraft objects because the interest of an aircraft buyer is made registrable by the Aircraft Protocol.[111] Consequently, the priority status of the buyer will be determined by the order of registration.

These exceptions are widely adopted in many domestic registration systems and may not be a novelty to the users of the IR.[112] In addition, the information provided by a notice filing registry need not be perfect or detailed in order to be valuable.[113] Since it provides preliminary information

[106] Art 29(4) CTC.

[107] R Goode, 'The Cape Town Convention on International Interests in Mobile Equipment: A Driving Force for International Asset-Based Financing' (2003) 36 *UCC LJ* 2 Art 1.

[108] Art 29(3)(b) CTC.

[109] Art 29(3)(a) CTC.

[110] Goode (n 8) 336.

[111] Art III of the Aircraft Protocol.

[112] Goode (n 107) 15.

[113] P Alces, 'Abolish the Article 9 Filing System' (1995) 79 *Minn L Rev* 679, 695.

and enables the searcher to ask the relevant questions, such as who the creditors of the debtor are and what the nature and extent of their registered interests are, the system is commercially valuable.[114] Additional credit and other financial checks will still be required, but the high value of aircraft objects and the amount of financing involved justify creditors' inquiries.

ii. Registration and Priorities

The CTC's registration system plays vital role in determining priorities between competing interests.[115] Generally, a valid registration ensures the priority of the registrable interest over any subsequently registered and unregistered interest.[116] This remains the case even if the holder of the first registered interest had actual knowledge of other interests.[117] For example, if SC2 knows that the debtor granted SC1 a security interest in an airframe and registers its international interest in the IR before SC1 registers its interest, SC2 will enjoy priority over the subsequently registered interest of SC1. By searching the IR before extending the loan, the creditor may assess how its priority status would relate to other registered interests and this may help deciding whether to grant a loan to the debtor and on what terms. If the creditor discovers that its security interest will be the first to be registered, it may assume that in the case of the debtor's insolvency, it will, generally, be able to enforce its security in priority to the subsequently registered or unregistered interests in the same object. Consequently, the creditor may be relatively certain that its interest will not be postponed to other interests and that the debt will be repaid. If the search of the registry reveals that the object is already encumbered by previously registered interests, the creditor's place in the queue of holders of such interests may be shifted. This may increase the risk of non-repayment and result in an increased cost of credit but it will still help the creditor to clarify its priority status.

Since the first creditor to register is generally superior to the subsequently registered and unregistered interests, the registration not only allows the creditor to determine its priority position, but also to validate its claim against other creditors.[118] Once the registration is effected and becomes searchable, the subsequent creditors will consider it as an effective registration and accept its superiority. This explains the importance of the existence

[114] *Ibid* 695.

[115] This is not the case under the English registration system where the main purpose of the registration of charges is to provide information about their existence to third parties. For a view that this should be changed and priorities between competing creditors should be determined by the order of the registration, see Lacy (n 103).

[116] Art 29(1) CTC.

[117] Art 29(2)(a) CTC.

[118] See, generally, J Ayer, 'Some Comments on Bowers' (1995) 79 *Minn L Rev* 745, 747.

of the IR. The information contained in the IR is not there simply to provide a notice to third parties; it is valuable in itself because it allows the creditor to publicly mark its claim in the object and to ensure that it will be recognised by the subsequent creditors of the debtor.

Finally, the registration of the international interest in the IR prior to the commencement of the insolvency proceedings against the debtor ensures the effectiveness of that interest in insolvency.[119] This protection shields not only international interests, but also other registrable interests, such as notices of national interests[120] and registrable NCRIs[121] which, once they are registered, are treated as international interests.

B. Interests Which Can be Registered in the International Registry

The CTC provides for the list of registrable interests comprising: (a) international interests, prospective international interests and registrable non-consensual rights and interests; (b) assignments and prospective assignments of international interests; (c) acquisitions of international interests by legal or contractual subrogations under the applicable law; (d) notices of national interests; and (e) subordinations of any of the mentioned interests.[122] This list is not conclusive and some other interests specified in the Convention and the Protocols can also be registered in the IR. For example, the CTC does not, generally, apply to a right or interest created in a Contracting State prior to the 'effective date' of the Convention.[123] However, a Contracting State can make a declaration relating to pre-existing rights or interests (PERIs), so that the Convention's regime applies to them to determine priority.[124] In this case, PERIs become a distinct registrable category in the IR, although they are not mentioned in the Convention's list of registrable interests.[125]

Another example of interests which are not indicated in the list of registrable interests, but can be registered in the IR relates to the interests of a conditional buyer and lessee. These interests cannot be registered by themselves, but can attain protection if the conditional seller and lessor register their international interests prior to the registration of the interests of their

[119] Art 30(1) CTC.

[120] Art 50(2) CTC.

[121] Art 40 CTC.

[122] Art 16(1) CTC.

[123] Art 60(1) CTC. According to Art 60(2) CTC, the 'effective date' means either the time when the Convention enters into force or the date when the State where the debtor is situated becomes a Contracting State.

[124] Art 60(3) CTC.

[125] Art 60(3) CTC does not apply to the space assets as it is disapplied by Art XL(1) of the Space Protocol. See also Goode (n 59) 76.

own creditors.[126] Thus, if a lessor grants a security interest to a secured creditor, the lessee's non-registrable interest will only be protected if the lessor registers its international interest in the object prior to the secured creditor's registration. To pierce this protection, the secured creditor can enter into a subordination agreement with the lessee. The subordination of the lessee's interest can be registered in the IR even though it is not mentioned in the CTC's list of registrable interests.[127]

The CTC's list of registrable interests is further expanded by the Protocols. For instance, the interests of an outright buyer and a prospective buyer are not registrable under the Convention. However, the Aircraft Protocol[128] and the Space Protocol[129] render an outright sale and a prospective sale of the aircraft objects and space assets registrable in the IR. Once registered, these interests are viewed as the international and prospective international interests for the purposes of priority. In contrast, the Luxembourg Protocol[130] and the draft MAC Protocol[131] do not allow for the outright sale to be registered, but allow for a notice of sale to be registered. The notice of sale is registrable merely to provide information and has no other consequences under the Convention.

The Space Protocol further adds several new registrable interests to the Convention's list.[132] For instance, if a debtor and a public service provider enter into a contract, relating to a space asset providing a public service in a Contracting State, the parties and the Contracting State may agree to register a public service notice in the IR.[133] Further, subject to the Contracting State making the required declaration, the creditor can also register a notice in the IR, informing searching parties that it may exercise its remedies if the debtor fails to cure its default within the specified period.[134] The Space Protocol also adds such new registrable interests as rights assignments, rights reassignments and acquisitions of debtor's rights by subrogation, which can be recorded against a registered international or registered prospective international interest.[135] The following section examines the interests registrable in the IR for aircraft objects.

[126] Art 29(4) CTC.

[127] The same applies to the subordination of a conditional buyer's non-registrable interest, Sec 5.8 of the Regulations. Art 16(1)(e) CTC refers to the subordinations of interests 'referred to in any of the preceding sub-paragraphs', which does not include the non-registrable interest of a lessee.

[128] Art III; Art V(3) of the Aircraft Protocol.

[129] Art IV(1); Art V(3) of the Space Protocol.

[130] Art XVII of the Luxembourg Protocol.

[131] Art XVIII of the draft MAC Protocol.

[132] Art XXXII(1) of the Space Protocol.

[133] Art XXVII(1) of the Space Protocol.

[134] Art XXVII(4) of the Space Protocol.

[135] Goode (n 59) 297.

i. International Interests, Prospective International Interests and Registrable Non-Consensual Rights and Interests

a. International Interests[136] and Prospective International Interests

The international interest, the main category of registrable interests, comprises interests that are granted by a chargor under a security agreement, vested in a conditional seller under a title reservation agreement or a lessor under a leasing agreement.[137] Since the IR is not a title registry, the registration of the interests based on the title reservation and lease does not guarantee the creditor's ownership. Instead, such registration signals to potential searchers that the creditor holds its interest in the object as a conditional seller or lessor.[138] Consequently, the interests of a conditional seller and lessor do not become registrable as international interests until a conditional sale or a leasing agreement have been concluded.

The international interest can be actual or prospective. An actual international interest is created once all the formal requirements are satisfied.[139] It is also possible to register a *prospective* international interest, which is an international interest, intended to be taken in the identifiable object in the future.[140] A prospective international interest can be registered in the IR *before* it takes the form of an actual international interest. The registration of a prospective interest may help the parties preserve the creditor's priority while the terms of the agreement creating the international interest are being negotiated. Once the requirements for the creation of the international interest are met, and provided that the registered information is sufficient to support this interest, there will be no need to procure a new registration and the prospective international interest will automatically turn into an actual international interest.[141]

b. Registrable Non-Consensual Rights and Interests

Another category of a registrable interest is that of a non-consensual right or interest (NCRI). As its name suggests, the NCRI does not arise as a result of an agreement between the parties. Instead, it is conferred by the law of a Contracting State and can take the form of a registrable or non-registrable NCRI. The Contracting State can make a declaration either

136 See further chapters one and two.
137 Art 2(2) CTC.
138 Goode (n 8) 299–300.
139 Art 2, 7 CTC.
140 Goode (n 8) 31.
141 R Goode, 'The International Interest as an Autonomous property Interest' (2004) *ERPL* 18, 24–25.

under Articles 39 or 40 CTC in relation to NCRIs.[142] Under Article 40, the Contracting State can declare which categories of NCRI can be registered in the IR. If registered, these are viewed by the CTC as if they are international interests.[143] Consequently, a registered NCRI will enjoy priority over any other subsequently registered and unregistered interest.

The Article 40 declaration must provide a list of specific NCRIs registrable in the IR.[144] Some examples include liens in favour of an airline's employees for unpaid wages, arising prior to the time of a default declared by the airline,[145] rights of a person obtaining a court order permitting attachment of an aircraft object in partial or full satisfaction of a legal judgment[146] and liens or other rights of a State entity, relating to taxes or other unpaid charges.[147] One advantage of making the Article 40 declaration is that once registered, the NCRI can be easily discovered by a searcher which may help it ascertain its priority position. Another advantage is that the registration of the NCRI can help the IR to provide potential searchers with a more complete picture of the interests burdening the object.

A Contracting State can also make a declaration under Article 39 in relation to the NCRIs not covered by the Article 40 declaration. These NCRIs cannot be registered in the IR, but can still gain priority over the registered interests. Article 39 allows for two types of the declarations to be made by a Contracting State. First, it is possible to declare under Article 39(1)(a), either generally or specifically, the categories of NCRI which under the law of the Contracting State are treated in priority to an interest equivalent to that of a holder of the registered international interest, that is, the interest of a secured creditor, a conditional seller or lessor.[148] A failure to make a declaration or to list all non-registrable NCRIs in the declaration will result in the loss of priority of the NCRI to the registered international interests, reflecting the general rule that first to register gets priority.

Some examples of non-registrable NCRIs which may arise under the Article 39 declaration can be provided by the English case law. For instance, in *Channel Airways Ltd v The Lord Mayor*,[149] a company (an air transport

[142] Art 1(s), (dd) CTC.

[143] Art 40 CTC.

[144] As of December 2015, 32 Contracting States have made declarations under Art 40.

[145] See the Declaration by Malaysia, available at http://www.unidroit.org/depositary-2001capetown?id=440.

[146] See the Declaration by Oman at http://www.unidroit.org/depositary-2001capetown?id=440.

[147] See the Declaration by the Republic of South Africa at http://www.unidroit.org/depositary-2001capetown?id=440.

[148] As of December 2015, 50 Contracting States have made the Art 39(1) declaration. See J Pritchard and D Lloyd, 'Analysis of Non-Consensual Rights and Interests under Article 39 of the Cape Town Convention' (2013) *Cape Town Convention Journal* 3, 18.

[149] *Channel Airways Ltd v The Lord Mayor, Aldermen and Citizens of the City of Manchester* [1974] 1 *Lloyd's Rep* 456.

operator) granted a registered charge over its property to a bank. The company also owed a debt to Manchester Corporation for the airport charges, relating to an aircraft's landings and departures. When the aircraft landed, it was detained by the corporation in accordance with the Manchester Corporation Act 1965. In a priority dispute between the registered charge and a non-registrable statutory right of detention, the court held that the corporation's right of detention prevailed.[150]

Another case, *Bristol Airport plc v Powdrill*,[151] concerned the interaction between the powers of an administrator of a failing business and the statutory right of detention under the Civil Aviation Act 1982. Paramount Ltd, an insolvent charter airline, was in administration, the main purpose of which was either to restore it to financial health or to sell it as a going concern. The administrators were negotiating a sale of the airline's business, which could not be concluded unless all aircraft were transferred to a prospective purchaser. Prior to the administration, Paramount incurred debts to two airport operators in respect of landing, fuel and other airport charges. The airport operators detained the airline's aircraft in exercise of their statutory right of detention.

The conflict between the airport operators' right of detention and the administrators' aim to sell the business as a going concern was obvious. On the one hand, high mobility of the aircraft meant that if the operators allowed them to leave the airport, it was likely that they would not return. The inability to have access to the aircraft would diminish the operators' prospects of receiving repayment of the debt. On the other hand, the administrators needed the company's assets, including the aircraft, to be unencumbered in order to sell the business for the benefit of the failing company's creditors. To enable an administrator to perform its functions, the Insolvency Act 1986[152] prohibits the enforcement of 'security' over a company's property without the court's leave or the administrator's consent. It was important to ascertain whether the statutory right of detention amounted to 'a lien or other security' and it was held that it did.[153] The operator enforced its security by serving a notice of lien on the aircraft captain and placing a lorry in front of the aircraft to prevent it from leaving the airport. In the absence of the administrator's consent, such enforcement required the court's leave. The court refused to grant the leave to exercise the right of detention and the administrators were allowed to proceed with the sale.

150 *Ibid* 461. On the facts, it was held that the corporation agreed not to exercise its right and for this reason detention could not be justified.

151 *Bristol Airport plc v Powdrill, Re Paramount Airways Ltd* [1990] BCC 130.

152 S 11(3)(c) of the Insolvency Act 1986.

153 *Ibid* 760.

In November 2015, the United Kingdom ratified the Convention, giving it effect by the International Interests in Aircraft Equipment (Cape Town Convention) Regulations 2015. One question which may arise post-ratification is whether the statutory rights of detention arising under such instruments as the Manchester Corporation Act and the Civil Aviation Act can now be considered as examples of NCRIs having priority without registration under the Regulations.[154] This question requires examination of several issues. First, the United Kingdom made a general declaration under Article 39(1)(a) CTC, providing that 'all categories of non-consensual rights or interests ... which at the date of this declaration or created after that date have priority over an interest in an object equivalent to that of the holder of a registered international interest ... shall to that extent have priority over a registered international interest'.[155]

The Regulations[156] giving effect to this declaration, list two categories of NCRI, namely: (a) a possessory lien in respect of work done on the aircraft object on the express or implied authority of any persons lawfully entitled to possession of the aircraft object;[157] and (b) any right to detain the aircraft object under an enactment (including an Act of the Scottish Parliament, of the Northern Ireland Assembly or of the National Assembly for Wales). The statutory rights of detention both in the *Channel Airways* and in the *Bristol Airport plc v Powdrill* case arose under such 'enactments'. Therefore, it seems likely that these rights could amount to NCRIs for the purposes of the Regulations.[158] Furthermore, being an interest at least akin to a possessory lien,[159] the right of detention does not require registration[160] and is clearly non-consensual.

[154] The International Interests in Aircraft Equipment (Cape Town Convention) Regulations 2015 (SI 2015/912) give effect in UK law to the Cape Town Convention and the Aircraft Protocol.

[155] For the full text of the declaration, see http://www.unidroit.org/depositary-2001 capetown?id=438.

[156] Reg 17(2) of the International Interests in Aircraft Equipment (Cape Town Convention) Regulations 2015 (n 154).

[157] For an example of what would probably be covered by this declaration post-ratification, see *Wilmington Trust Company, Orix Aviation Sytems Limited v Rolls-Royce plc, IAE Aero Engines AG* [2011] CSOH Number 151.

[158] Statutory rights of detention may arise under other enactments too. See *Global Knafaim Leasing Ltd and another v Civil Aviation Authority & Anor, Eurocontrol & Ors* [2010] EWHC 1348 (Admin), where statutory right of detention and fleet lien arose under s 88(1)(ii) of the Civil Aviation Act 1982, reg 83 of the Transport Act 2000 and the Civil Aviation (Chargeable Air Services) (Detention and Sale of Aircraft for Eurocontrol) Regulations 2001 (SI 2001/494).

[159] *The Sierra Nevada* (1932) 42 LILR 309 Ct of Session.

[160] Since possession serves as notice of the security interest to other creditors, there is, generally no requirement to register such an interest. See *Seka Pty Ltd (In provisional liquidation) v Fabric Dyeworks (Aust) Pty Ltd* (1991) 4 ACSR 455. See also H Beale, M Bridge, L Gullifer and E Lomnicka, *The Law of Security and Title-Based Financing*, 2nd edn (Oxford University Press 2012) 135.

The second issue is whether a statutory right of detention has priority over an interest which is 'equivalent' to that of the holder of a registered international interest. In other words, the question is whether it has priority over the interests of a secured creditor, conditional seller or lessor under English law. It seems that to satisfy this requirement,[161] the NCRI does not have to enjoy priority over *all* equivalents of the international interests under the national law. It may well be that while the national law treats the NCRI in priority to security interests, this priority does not extend to the interests of a conditional seller or lessor.[162] The Convention cannot be used as a means of expanding priority enjoyed by the NCRI under the national law.[163] Likewise, since Article 39 is concerned with priority under the national law, the CTC cannot be used to deny priority on the basis that the national law elevates the NCRI over some, but not all, equivalents of international interests. For example, if a national law grans priority to the NCRI over a security interest, but not over the interest of a conditional seller, the same result should be achieved under the CTC. In *Channel Airways*, the corporation's statutory right of detention prevailed over the secured creditor's interest. Accordingly, if the case were considered post-ratification, the statutory right of detention would amount to a non-registrable NCRI under the Convention and granted priority over a registered international interest based on a security interest.

Some support for the view that the statutory right of detention will not be defeated by the interest of an owner (such as a conditional seller or lessor) can be found in *Bristol Airport plc v Powdrill* considered above.[164] In this case, the aircraft, detained by the airport operators, were leased by Paramount from a third party (lessor). Still, the statutory right of detention was not defeated by the interest of the true owner-lessor.[165] This outcome confirms that post-ratification, the statutory right of detention can amount to a non-registrable NCRI, prevailing over the registered international interests, based on the title reservation and lease.

This position can further be strengthened if the analogy with the repairer's lien is drawn.[166] For instance, in *Wilmington Trust Company v Rolls-Royce plc*,[167] the owners of two aircraft and engines leased them to a lessee, which was unable to make payments, leading to the termination of the lease. The lessee was contractually required to arrange for maintenance of the aircraft

[161] Art 39(1) CTC.

[162] Pritchard and Lloyd (n 148) 18.

[163] Goode (n 8) 375.

[164] *Bristol Airport plc v Powdrill, Re Paramount Airways Ltd* [1990] BCC 130.

[165] For the discussion of this case, see Beale, Bridge, Gullifer and Lomnicka (n 160) 540.

[166] *Ibid* 540.

[167] *Wilmington Trust Company, Orix Aviation Sytems Limited v Rolls-Royce plc, IAE Aero Engines AG* [2011] CSOH Number 151.

objects and to pay the lessor the 'maintenance reserves' to ensure that the work could be paid for. The lease also prohibited the lessee from subjecting the aircraft objects to any encumbrances, including lien unless it was a 'permitted lien'.[168] The lessee sent the engines for maintenance to IAE, which placed the work with Rolls-Royce. The latter conducted the necessary works and was paid by IAE. The repairer agreed to keep the engines until the lessee paid IAE for the work. Thus, the engines were delivered to the lienholder (IAE) not by the owners, but by the lessee, which merely had the possession of the aircraft objects.

Despite the contractual prohibition, it was held that the lessee had the authority to have the work done by the repairer. This remained true even though the repairer did not conduct the work itself, but sub-contracted it to Rolls-Royce. It was held that IAE had possession of the engines and that its lien could not be defeated by the interests of the owners. These cases illustrate that the statutory right of detention (by analogy with the repairer's lien) can bind not only a secured creditor, but also a true owner, such as a conditional seller and lessor. Consequently, it is likely that, post-ratification, the statutory right of detention is likely to amount to a NCRI enjoying priority over the registered international interests as a result of the Article 39(1) declaration made by the United Kingdom.

Since the NCRI cannot be registered, the holder of a registered international interest may only learn about the existence of a NCRI if it is either revealed by the debtor or asserted by the holder. The option of making a general rather than a specific declaration relating to non-registrable NCRIs adds to the uncertainty which the creditor may experience when attempting to establish what interests encumber the object. However, the fact that a Contracting State is given an opportunity to make such a declaration has its benefits. By searching the IR and finding that a declaration (even a general one) exists, the creditor is put on notice that certain NCRIs may take priority over its own registered interest.[169] It is then up to the creditor to clarify who the holders of these NCRIs may be and, possibly, even extinguish the debtor's debt, in an attempt to preserve the priority of its registered interest. If nothing is done, the holder of the NCRI may be able not only to detain, but also to sell the aircraft.[170] Once the aircraft is sold and the NCRI (and other senior interests) are satisfied, little may be left for the creditor.

Another advantage of the Article 39 declaration is that it can reassure the creditor that only those NCRIs that are listed in it may present a threat

[168] *Ibid* para 14.

[169] G Mauri, 'The Cape Town Convention on Interests in Mobile Equipment as Applied to Aircraft: Are Lenders Better Off Under the Geneva Convention?' (2005) *ERPL* 641, 646.

[170] *International Nederlanden Aviation Lease BV & Ors v The Civil Aviation Authority & Anor* [1997] CLC 43.

to the priority of its registered interest.[171] From the perspective of the Contracting State, a general, rather than specific, declaration enables it to ensure that any newly created types of NCRI in its national law can be covered by the original declaration, obviating the need to change it in the future.

The second type of a declaration that can be made by a Contracting State under Article 39(1)(b) aims to protect the rights of arrest or detention of an object, which do not directly arise under its national law, but flow from a contract.[172] For instance, the Article 39(1)(b) declaration can cover charges collected by organisations such as EUROCONTROL, an international organisation providing air navigation facilities and coordinating the provision of such services by national providers.[173] EUROCONTROL can collect these charges in its own name, but the declaration itself must be made by a Contracting State and not by a private organisation.[174]

Finally, a NCRI covered by an Article 39 declaration will, generally, have priority over a registered international interest if the declaration was deposited *prior* to its registration.[175] This rule allows a potential creditor searching the IR to identify any NCRI which can affect its priority before deciding to extend the credit. However, a Contracting State can also declare that a NCRI will have priority over the international interests registered *before* the declaration was made.[176] In this case, the creditor's priority may still be postponed to the NCRI if the declaration is submitted after the creditor's interest is registered.

ii. Assignments and Prospective Assignments of International Interests[177]

Article 16(1)(b) renders assignments[178] and prospective assignments of international interests registrable in the IR. The CTC only governs contractual assignments conferring on the assignee the associated rights with or without the related international interest.[179] A prospective assignment relates to an assignment intended to be made in the future on the occurrence

[171] Mauri (n 169) 646.

[172] Art 39(1)(b) CTC.

[173] For example, the Civil Aviation Authority, established under the Civil Navigation Act 1971, for regulating civil air transport in the UK. Charges relating to air navigation services can be paid to the CAA or EUROCONTROL and these organisations can, in some cases, have rights of detention and sale of an aircraft. See, for example, *Irish Aerospace (Belgium) NV v European Organisation for the Safety of Air Navigation and Civil Aviation Authority* [1992] 1 Lloyd's Rep 383.

[174] Goode (n 8) 377.

[175] Art 39(3) CTC.

[176] Art 39(4) CTC.

[177] See, generally, Goode (n 8) 346–70.

[178] See, generally, R Goode, 'Contractual Prohibitions against Assignments' [2009] *LMCLQ* 300.

[179] Art 1(b) CTC.

of a stated event irrespective of whether the occurrence of this event is certain.[180] Assignment can only be made by a creditor, namely by a chargee, conditional seller or a lessor.[181] The creditor may decide to assign its interest in the object held by the debtor if, for example, it needs funding and approaches its own creditor to obtain a loan. Once the creditor's debt to the assignee is discharged, its interest in the object will be returned to it.

Assignment can be made outright or by way of a security.[182] In an outright assignment, the lessor of the aircraft object can register its international interest and later assign its rights under the leasing agreement to the assignee. As a result, the assignee will receive not only the associated rights (for example, rights to the rentals under the lease), but also the lessor's international interest. Once the assignee is registered as the holder of the assigned international interest, it will be able to assert the same priority status as the original lessor and to obtain the rentals from the debtor (lessee). In contrast, if the assignment is by way of a security and the lessor discharges its debt to the assignee, the interest of the latter will be extinguished and the right to the remaining rentals under the lease will revert to the lessor. Associated rights denote all rights to payment or other performance by the debtor under the agreement. For example, rights to repayment under a secured loan, payment of the price under a conditional sale agreement as well as other forms of performance, such as insurance and maintenance[183] of the object are considered as associated rights. Associated rights are said to be *secured by* the security agreement and *associated with* the retention of title or a lease agreement.[184]

Since Article 16(1)(b) renders assignment and a prospective assignment separate categories of registrable interests, they can be registered even if the international interest to which these interests relate is not itself registered. But the priority of a registered assignee is of limited effect under the Convention. The registration of an assignment of the unregistered international interest will help the assignee defeat the interests of the subsequently registered and unregistered assignees of the same assignor.[185] However, such an assignment will be subordinated to the holder of a subsequent international interest, and its assignees, which registers its interest ahead of the prior unregistered international interest.[186] Finally and unless the parties

[180] Art 1(x) CTC.
[181] Goode (n 8) 347.
[182] Art 1(b) CTC.
[183] See *Sunrock Aircraft Corporation Limited v Scandinavian Airlines System Denmark-Norway-Sweden* [2007] EWCA Civ 882, exemplifying lessee's maintenance obligations regarding an engine's Limited Life Parts (LLP) and 'scab patches' on the aircraft fuselage.
[184] Art 1(c) CTC.
[185] Goode (n 8) 350.
[186] *Ibid* 350.

agree otherwise, the assignment of associate rights transfers to the assignee the assignor's international interest and the priority status. But if the international interest itself is not valid, its assignment will also be ineffective.

iii. Acquisitions of International Interests by Legal or Contractual Subrogation under the Applicable Law

Article 16(c) makes acquisitions of international interests by legal or contractual subrogation arising under the applicable law a registrable interest. The applicable law is generally viewed by the CTC as a law different from the Convention itself. However, in this particular instance, the Official Commentary provides that the right of subrogation under Article 9(4) should be considered as the right given by the applicable law of the Contracting State.[187] Article 9(4) provides that where after the debtor's default and before the charged object is sold, the full payment of the amount secured is made by an interested person other than the debtor, that person is subrogated to the rights of the chargee.[188]

iv. Notices of National Interests

The CTC does not define the mobility of objects or the international character of the transactions governed by it, these features being considered as inherent in the nature and intended use of the equipment. This omission may lead to situations where a purely internal transaction, in that the parties and the equipment are located in the same Contracting State, may be covered by the Convention. While this situation is unlikely to occur with respect to aircraft and space assets, the position may be different in relation to railway objects. To this end, the Luxembourg Protocol provides that if a security agreement, title reservation or a leasing agreement relates to the railway rolling stock that is only capable, in its normal use, of being operated on a single railway system within one Contracting State, such a transaction shall be considered as an internal transaction.[189]

The CTC allows Contracting States to make a declaration under Article 50(1) excluding internal transactions from its ambit. To be considered as an internal transaction, a security agreement, title reservation or a leasing agreement must be structured in a way that: (a) the centre of all main interests of all parties to it and the object itself must be located in the same

[187] Goode (n 8) 371–372.

[188] For an example of the right of subrogation arising under English law see, for example, *Banque Financier de la Cite v Parc (Battersea) Ltd* [1998] 1 All ER 373; *Boscawen v Bajwa* [1995] 4 All ER 769.

[189] Art XXIX(2) of the Luxembourg Protocol.

Contracting State at the time of the conclusion of the contract; (b) the interest created by the transaction is registered in a national registry of that Contracting State; and (c) the Contracting State has made the declaration under Article 50(1). An interest created by the internal transaction and held by the creditor in the object covered by the declaration, is defined as a national interest by the Convention. While the national interest itself cannot be registered in the IR, it is possible to register *a notice,* stating that the national interest was created. The Article 50(1) declaration has a limited effect in that the CTC's provisions on registration and priority will still apply to such notices. Once the notice of a national interest is registered in the IR, it is protected against subsequently registered and unregistered interests. In contrast, a failure to register a notice of the national interest will result in the loss of the priority to a registered interest. The Convention's remedial rules do not apply to notices of national interests.

v. Subordinations of Interests Referred to in Any of the Preceding Sub-Paragraphs

When a debtor needs a new loan in addition to the one that it has already taken, the creditor may be willing to provide it with the funds. The new loan can stimulate further investment by the debtor and help it repay the debt. But if the debtor's financial position is not strong, the creditor may decide that additional lending can increase the risk of non-repayment and decline to extend the funds. Instead, the creditor may be prepared to yield its priority to a subsequently registered or a new creditor willing to provide the debtor with a fresh advance.[190] By subordinating its priority to a subsequent creditor, the yielding creditor may actually increase the prospect of being repaid by the debtor. The subordination agreement changing the priority positions of the creditors is registrable in the IR.

The subordination agreement can relate to any of the CTC's registrable interests. For example, a registered notice of a national interest can be subordinated to a subsequently registered international interest and the subordination agreement to that effect can itself be registered in the IR. Article 29(5) further reinforces the importance of the need to register the subordination agreement. This provision does not create a new registrable interest but rather, first, stipulates that the parties may vary the priority of their competing interests and, secondly, provides that an assignee of a subordinated interest will not be bound to yield that interest unless the subordination agreement is registered at the time of the assignment. Consider secured creditor 1 (SC1) and secured creditor 2 (SC2) registering their interests in an object in turn. Later, SC1 agrees to yield its security interest

[190] See, generally, Beale, Bridge, Gullifer and Lomnicka (n 160) 356.

to SC2 which fails to register the subordination agreement. Should SC1 decide to assign its interest to A1, the latter will not be bound by the unregistered subordination agreement and will enjoy priority over SC2 even if it had actual knowledge of the agreement. Otherwise, the assignee could wrongly assume that a senior priority position was transferred to it without the means to discover the subordination agreement between its assignor and the other party.

4

The Process of Registration

I. INTRODUCTION

THE INTERNATIONAL REGISTRY (IR) established under the Convention is the first online global facility for registering and searching international interests in aircraft objects. It is actively used by the aircraft manufacturers, financiers and other stakeholders worldwide. When the IR first became operational in 2001, over 32,000 registrations against aircraft objects were made. In 2014, this number increased to over 100,000 registrations.[1]

The IR's electronic nature and the fact that it is an asset-based and a notice filing system were important factors contributing to its success. Another key element boosting the IR's success is the way in which it uses the technology to achieve its aims. The IR is closely attuned to the commercial needs of its user community and continues to develop new features to ensure the promotion of asset-based financing. For example, when the IR was established, interests held in several aircraft objects had to be registered separately. Thus, the registration of international interests in an airframe and two engines, pertaining to it, required three registration sessions. This practice was repetitive, wasteful of time and resources and increased the possibility of errors in the registration data. In response, the IR developed a new feature, 'multiple object registration', allowing a registrant to group several objects and register interests held in them in a single registration session.[2]

To allow the IR to take advantage of technological developments, the CTC's drafters adopted an innovative technique in the way it is regulated. All general issues, such as the establishment and the general framework of the IR's operation, its structure, the list of registrable interests and the rules on effecting, searching and discharging a registration are governed by the CTC.[3] The Aircraft Protocol deals with more detailed issues specific to

[1] See the Annual Statistical Report of the IR at https://www.internationalregistry.aero/ir-web/annualStatisticalReport/findAll (last visited July 2016).

[2] See W Piels and TS Huay, 'Generation II of the International Registry Website. The Closing Room: A Transactional Approach to Registrations' (2013) *CTCJ* 165, 168–69 for more detail.

[3] Art 16 CTC.

aircraft equipment. For instance, the Convention indicates that there should be some criteria for the unique identification of objects to effect and search the registrations, but states that these criteria should be specified by the relevant Protocols.[4]

The Convention and the Aircraft Protocol are the foundation blocks on which the IR stands, but they are not the only instruments governing its operation. The practical issues, such as who can effect a registration, an amendment or a discharge and what information is required to effect and search a registration, are covered by the Regulations issued by the Supervisory Authority.[5] The Regulations also provide a sophisticated security system to safeguard the IR's integrity. This is achieved through the rules regulating access to the IR and the system of authorisations and consents for effecting, amending and discharging the registrations. The Regulations are further supported by the Procedures issued by the Supervisory Authority, relating to the IR's administrative processes.[6] The Procedures cover issues such as the functions of the administrator and registry users and the way in which the help desk can be accessed should technical support in relation to the IR be required. In contrast to the Protocols which may prevail over the Convention,[7] the Regulations and Procedures must fully comply with it.

The fact that the IR is governed by four different instruments, that is, the Convention, the Aircraft Protocol, the Regulations and the Procedures, may seem unnecessarily complex. Indeed, even the question whether there should be a distinct Convention and several equipment-based Protocols was debated at the Diplomatic Conference.[8] The question is whether the additional layer of the Regulations and Procedures was necessary and why the issues governed by these documents could not be incorporated into the Aircraft Protocol. One answer lies in the extremely technical nature of the issues covered by the Regulations and Procedures. These documents are essential to the IR's operation and use. They provide how the registrations can be effected, amended, extended, discharged and searched for and who may be eligible to do so. The Protocols would be too technical and cumbersome if these issues were incorporated in their texts.

Another advantage of separate Regulations and Procedures is that they can be revised when the need arises. In contrast, modifying the provisions

[4] Art 18(1) CTC.

[5] Art 17(2)(d) CTC; Art XVIII of the Aircraft Protocol.

[6] Sec 15 of the Regulations and Procedures for the International Registry (International Civil Aviation Organisation, Doc 9864, 6th edn 2014) (hereafter 'the Regulations').

[7] Art 6 CTC.

[8] R Goode, 'The Preliminary Draft UNIDROIT Convention on International Interests in Mobile Equipment' (1999) 4 *Unif L Rev* 265, 269–71; C Chinkin and C Kessedjian, 'The Legal Relationship between the Proposed UNIDROIT Convention and its Equipment-Specific Protocols' UNIDROIT Document Study LXXII-Doc 47 and ICAO Ref LSC/MEE-WP/12, reproduced (1999) 4 *Unif L Rev* 323, 323–25.

of the Convention can only be triggered by a request of not less than 25 per cent of the States Parties to the Depository. Once the request is received, the Depository is expected to consult the Supervisory Authority to consider whether a Review Conference should be convened.[9] The separately issued Regulations and Procedures allow the Supervisory Authority not only to constantly test and improve the IR's practical operation, but also to keep it in touch with the commercial needs of its users.

The Regulations have been recently revised to implement the rules relating to the new facility called the 'closing room', developed by the IR. The closing room can be used in complex transactions involving several financiers of aircraft objects.[10] It can be created and managed by a coordinator responsible for assembling the information required for the multiple registrations of several aircraft objects, collecting consents and negotiating the chronological order of the registrations. The coordinator can electronically invite other participants to review the information in the closing room. Once satisfied that the registration information is assembled and accurately reflects the participants' intentions, the coordinator can 'lock' the closing room. When the closing room is locked, the information in it will still be available for review and for providing consents to the registrations, but it can no longer be edited. When all consents are assembled, the registrations contained in the closing room can be released into the IR so as to become searchable and this is when they become effective. The closing room is a complex facility, but it can bring flexibility and assist in coordinating multiple registrations before they go live in the IR.[11]

This chapter focuses on the process of registering an interest in the IR. Part II explains who can effect registrations. Part III examines how to establish an account with the IR. Part IV analyses the formal requirements for effecting a registration and some problems relating to errors in the identification of aircraft objects. Part V focuses on the validity of registrations. Part VI deals with searches and search certificates that can be issued by the IR. Finally, Part VII analyses the issues relating to the discharge of registrations from the IR and examines some of the first cases decided under the Convention.

[9] Art 61(2)(d) CTC.

[10] See Sec 5.18 and Appendix to the Regulations. See further Piels and Huay (n 2).

[11] The Legal Advisory Panel of the Aviation Working Group, Practitioners' Guide to the Cape Town Convention and the Aircraft Protocol (Aviation Working Group, Chicago, 2015) 102 (hereafter the *Practitioners' Guide*). For the discussion of other innovations introduced by the IR, such as 'transferrable right to discharge' and registration of fractional interests in aircraft objects, see R Cowan and D Gallagher, 'The International Registry for Aircraft Equipment—The First Seven Years, What We Have Learnt' (2014) 45 *UCC LJ* 225.

II. WHO CAN EFFECT REGISTRATIONS IN THE INTERNATIONAL REGISTRY?

The Regulations introduce a number of terms, defining the parties who can access the IR. A legal entity or a natural person intending to be a named party in a registration can establish an account and access the IR as a transacting user entity (TUE).[12] A law firm or an internal legal department of TUE, providing professional services in connection with the transmission of information to the IR is referred to as a professional user entity (PUE).[13] Alternatively, the registration information can be transmitted through an entity, established by a Contracting State as an entry point.[14] The Regulations define an entry point, through which the registration information shall or may be directly transmitted to the IR as a direct entry point (DEP).[15] Together, the TUE, PUE and DEP are called a registry user entity (RUE).[16] The Regulations refer to the employees of a TUE, PUE, DEP or RUE as a transacting user (TU), professional user (PU), direct point entity user (DPEU) or registry user (RU) respectively.[17]

An RUE cannot directly effect registrations unless it appoints an administrator, who has the authority to act on behalf of RUE on administrative matters in dealing with the IR. The RUE can only have one administrator at a time.[18] Apart from the administrator, registrations can also be effected, amended or discharged by its employee, that is, an RU. But the RU will not be able to access the IR unless the RU obtains the administrator's electronic approval and authorisation.[19] After such approval and authorisation, the Registrar will send an email to the RU, containing a link to a digital certificate, which should be used when effecting the registrations in the IR.[20]

In addition to these two approaches, the TUE can also instruct a PUE to effect the registrations in relation to the specific types of aircraft objects in the IR. But the PUE will have to appoint an administrator too, and ultimately registrations will be made by the PUE's administrator or by the PUE's professional user, approved and authorised by the administrator of the TUE.[21] Many large aircraft operators choose this approach to registrations because a single PUE can effect registrations for several TUEs and coordinate complex set of transactions before registrations are entered on the IR.[22]

12 Sec 2.1.17 of the Regulations.
13 Sec 2.1.12 of the Regulations.
14 Art 18(5) CTC; Art XIX of the Aircraft Protocol.
15 Sec 12.1(b) of the Regulations.
16 Sec 2.1.15 of the Regulations.
17 Sec 2.1.17; 2.1.12; 2.1.8; 2.1.15 of the Regulations.
18 Sec 5.3 of the Procedures.
19 Sec 4.2 of the Regulations; Sec 6.1; 6.2; 12.5 of the Procedures.
20 Sec 5.7 of the Procedures.
21 Sec 6.2(b) of the Procedures.
22 *Practitioners' Guide* (n 11) 99.

Clearly, the Regulations confer extensive powers on the administrator and RUE should exercise care when selecting and appointing its administrator to prevent abuse of power.[23] For example, once the TUE's administrator is approved by the Registrar, it is automatically authorised to effect, amend, discharge, consent to registrations or communicate on other matters with the IR on behalf of the TUE.[24] The administrator is entitled to delegate its powers to an acting administrator for a period not extending three months and the RUE will be bound by the acts of the acting administrator.[25] One way to minimise the potential for abuse is to appoint one of the RUE's current employees as an administrator. The Procedures provide that the administrator may, but need not be, an employee of RUE. An internal appointment can give the RUE a degree of control over the administrator's actions.[26] Another benefit of the internal appointment is that the RUE will be able to effect the registrations directly via internal administrator at a reduced cost and increased speed. This is why this method of effecting the registrations is often used in simpler transactions. It is expected that with the introduction of the closing room facility this method will be more commonly used.[27]

Alternatively, it is possible to appoint an external administrator effecting the registrations on behalf of the RUE.[28] In this case, the relationship between the RUE and the administrator is regulated contractually and the RUE must exercise diligence in securing contractual protection to prevent potential for abuse of power by the administrator.[29] The Regulations also require the RUE to designate a back-up contact. Should the account of the administrator be subject to a security breach that could reasonably be expected to result in unauthorised access to and use of the IR, the Registrar and the RUE can take corrective actions, including blocking or disabling the inappropriately used account.[30]

The IR's sophisticated security system provided by the Regulations and Procedures means that the creditor will have to make some prior arrangements by finding and appointing a suitable administrator to make registrations. But once these arrangements are put in place, the same administrator can be used to effect future registrations which may be a relatively small price to pay to ensure the overall security of the IR.

The need to obtain approvals and authorisations are not the only preconditions, which must be satisfied by a registrant, before its interest can be

[23] Sec 4(a) of the Procedures.
[24] Sec 5(4) of the Procedures.
[25] Sec 4(1) of the Regulations; Sec 4(b) of the Procedures.
[26] Sec 5.1 of the Procedures.
[27] *Practitioners' Guide* (n 11) 99.
[28] *Practitioners' Guide* (n 11) 100.
[29] *Practitioners' Guide* (n 11) 100.
[30] Sec 5.12; 5.13 of the Procedures.

registered. The CTC empowers the Contracting States to designate an entity or entities in its territory to serve as entry points.[31] The purpose of the entry points is either to authorise transmission of the registration information or to directly transfer submitted data to the Registrar.[32] Where a Contracting State has designated an entry point, the registrant will not be able to register its interest directly in the IR and will have to submit the registration information to the entry point first. The registration information will then be either directly sent to the IR or authorised to be sent there by the registrant.

It is also open to the Contracting State to set additional requirements, which must be satisfied by the registrant, before the registration information can be transmitted to the IR. These requirements may differ from the CTC's requirements and may, for instance, include an additional fee, the signature of both the creditor and the debtor, a copy of the security agreement giving rise to the international interest, or proof of title of the conditional seller or lessor.[33] In relation to the aircraft objects, the Regulations preclude the use of entry points with respect to the registration of interests in aircraft engines.[34] In addition, the entry points cannot be used for the registration of notices of national interests and registrable non-consensual rights or interests (NCRIs) arising under the law of another State.[35]

The use of entry points can further support the IR's security system by ensuring that mistaken registrations are not made in it. The entry points can be used as the additional filter, checking that submitted information is correct and reflects the agreement between the parties. The Contracting States may also wish to use the entry points to collect a stamp duty or tax or to gather statistical data. Since the CTC's drafters envisaged that the Contracting States would use the existing agencies of civil aviation authorities as the entry points, the expense of their establishment is unlikely to be significant. Furthermore, the designation of entry points is not mandatory and it is for the Contracting States to decide whether such entities are needed at all.[36]

At the same time, because the Regulations already provide for robust control mechanisms, the additional check at the entry point adds little to

[31] Art 18(5) CTC.

[32] Sec 12 of the Regulations.

[33] R Cuming, 'The International Registry: An Overview of Its Structure' (2006) *Unif L Rev* 18, 34–36.

[34] The reason for this is mainly historic. While almost all States now have recording offices where aircrafts and helicopters can be registered as to nationality, such offices do not usually distinguish between airframes and engines. It was envisaged that Contracting States would use existing offices as entry points. Since these offices do not usually distinguish between airframes and engines, there was no need to require that interests in engines should be approved by entry points. See Cuming (n 33) 34–36.

[35] Art XIX(1) of the Aircraft Protocol.

[36] As of January 2016, Albania, Brazil, China, Mexico, Spain, Ukraine, United Arab Emirates, the United States of America and Vietnam had declared that entry points should be established on their territories.

the IR's security. Moreover, the authorisation to transfer the data to the IR may be turned down at the entry point even if all the formalities prescribed by the Regulations have been met. This can happen if one of the additional requirements of the entry point was not complied with and, for example, an incorrect application form was used by the registrant. Furthermore, the creditor may be required to physically deliver the necessary documents, and since entry points need not be operational 24 hours a day 7 days a week, this requirement may delay the authorisation process.[37] Finally, there may be a gap between the time when the information is submitted to the entry point and the time when the necessary authorisation from it is received by the registrant. Since the Convention does not prescribe that entry points should act within a specified period, the process of checking the information and issuing the authorisation can take some time. During this time, the registrant may be ready to effect a registration in the IR, but unable to do so because of the delay at the entry point. Even in the case of a DEP, the registrant will have to wait until the information is actually transferred to the IR and becomes searchable in it. Until this moment, the registration will not be effective and the registrant will not be able to secure its priority among other creditors.

III. ESTABLISHING AN ACCOUNT WITH THE INTERNATIONAL REGISTRY

Once the administrator is appointed, RUE or its administrator has to submit an electronic application form to the Registrar to obtain the latter's approval and to establish an account.[38] The applicant must provide information such as the legal name, entity type, email address and phone number of the RUE as well as the administrator's own legal name, email address and phone number.[39] During the application process, the IR will generate a pair of public and private keys. The public key infrastructure (PKI) is a password protected digital signature technology, tied to a specific computer used by the administrator when dealing with the registrations. The aim of this technology is to bolster the IR's security. If the password is lost, it cannot be recovered and the account application process will have to be started afresh.[40]

[37] Entry points have to be operational during working hours in their respective territories. Art XX(4) of the Aircraft Protocol.

[38] Sec 4.1 of the Regulations; Sec 2(1)(a) of the Procedures.

[39] Sec 10 of the Procedures; *Practitioners' Guide* (n 11) 96.

[40] J Winn, 'The Cape Town Convention's International Registry: Decoding the Secrets of Success in Global Electronic Commerce' (2012) *CTCJ* 25, 41.

The Registrar may approve the application when it can reasonably conclude that: (a) the RUE and the administrator are who they claim to be and (b) on the basis of the information submitted, that the administrator is entitled to act on the RUE's behalf.[41] The Regulations do not clarify what steps must be taken by the Registrar to arrive at such a 'reasonable conclusion' before granting the approval. For example, the Registrar could be required to make external inquiries to verify the accuracy of the submitted information. This could include contacting a state authority in the country of the RUE's incorporation to confirm its existence. The Registrar may also seek to verify that the administrator's mandate to act on the RUE's behalf is valid and was not revoked due to some changed circumstances, such as the latter's bankruptcy.

However, requiring the Registrar to make external enquiries could undermine the IR's aim of providing a speedy and low cost service of registering interests in the aircraft objects. Furthermore, the role of the Registrar in operating the IR is purely administrative and it is, generally, not expected to verify external facts. For example, once the registration information and the necessary consents are submitted to the Registrar, the Registrar is required to release the registration information into the IR to make it searchable. The Registrar is not expected to verify the accuracy of the submitted information and cannot be held liable should it later transpire that the registered interest was not validly created.[42] Consequently, it is unlikely that the Registrar is required to conduct external verifications before it can reasonably conclude that the applicant can be granted access to the IR.

The Regulations provide some guidance on compliance with the standard of reasonable conclusion by stating that when deciding whether to approve an application, the Registrar is not expected to undertake a 'specific legal analysis'.[43] But this guidance does little to clarify the meaning of the requirement of reasonable conclusion as it could mean that while a *specific* legal analysis should not be conducted, some *general* legal analysis is still necessary. For instance, can the Registrar peruse submitted documents and, provided that they appear to be in order on their face, approve the application? If this is the case, the standard of reasonable conclusion can be diluted to an extent where it becomes meaningless as the Registrar will be expected to accept all the documents appearing to be in order. While making external enquiries may be excessive in the light of the resources available to the Registrar and the underlying aims of speed and low cost underpinning the IR's operation, blanket acceptance of the documents appearing to be in order

[41] Sec 4.1(a), (b) of the Regulations.
[42] Cowan and Gallagher (n 11) 236.
[43] Sec 4.1 of the Regulations.

may also fail to meet the requirement of reasonable consideration of the application.

Instead, it is suggested that the Registrar has to take a balanced approach to ensure that the decision to approve is reasonable. The Procedures entitle the Registrar to run 'reasonable identity checks' of the administrator and the registry user and the same principle should apply to the RUE.[44] For example, when the application form, containing email addresses and phone numbers along with the legal names of the parties is submitted, the Registrar can send a confirmation notice indicating that the application form was received to the email address indicated in the form. It should be equally possible to check whether the phone number provided by the applicant is accurate. These checks can be performed quickly and at low cost. They should enable the Registrar to arrive at a reasonable conclusion in relation to the accuracy of the submitted information. At the same time, if the documents verifying the existence of the entity or the authority to act, such as a certificate of good standing or a certificate to act are submitted on the letterhead and are signed by the applicant, the Registrar should be entitled to consider these documents as valid and should not be expected to check their accuracy by making enquiries from third parties.[45]

Another point of uncertainty relates to the duration of the approval process. The Registrar's approval must be issued 'as soon as is *reasonably practicable* and [the Registrar] will endeavor to complete the approval process *within forty eight hours of receipt* of the application'.[46] The relationship between a reasonably practicable period and the 48-hour period is unclear. Can the applicant argue that, on the basis of the information provided in the application form, it would be reasonably practicable for the Registrar to issue the approval, say, within 24 rather than 48 hours? The delay in processing the application could result in the delayed registration leading to the loss of priority.

Alternatively, can the Registrar take longer than 48 hours to issue the approval if it considers it reasonably practicable to do so? Since the Registrar is required only to 'endeavor' to complete the process within 48 hours, it seems that this period does not constitute a cutting-off point on the expiration of which the Registrar is expected to make the decision. If the examination of the application invites further inquiries, the Registrar should be able to take longer than 48 hours and issue the approval as soon as is reasonably practicable. At the same time, the 48-hour period can certainly be viewed as an indication that the approval process is expected to take one to two days rather than weeks.

[44] Sec 5.14 of the Procedures.
[45] *Practitioners' Guide* (11) 96.
[46] Sec 10.6 of the Procedures (emphasis added).

IV. FORMAL REQUIREMENTS FOR REGISTRATION

A. General

The formal requirements for effecting a registration and for making searches are for the most part simple. The CTC itself does not stipulate what information should be transmitted to the Registrar to effect a registration and delegates this issue to the Regulations and Procedures.[47] The Regulations provide a list of detailed formal requirements, tailored to a particular type of a registrable interest.[48] The information required to effect registrations can be divided into two broad categories.

First, some formal requirements can be defined as general requirements because the information relating to them must be submitted to the Registrar in the cases of most registrable interests. These formal requirements include the information as to the identification of the aircraft objects, the names of TUEs, the electronic signature of the registrants, the electronic addresses of the persons to which the IR is required to send information notices, the information relating to the name of the creditor, holding a sole right to consent to the discharge of a registration and the information, relating to the registration's lapse date. Secondly, the Regulations provide for specific requirements which are tailored to a particular type of a registrable interest and must be submitted to the Registrar in addition to the general requirements. For example, if the interest being assigned is a registered interest, the file number of the registration of that interest must be indicated by the registrant.[49] If the interest being assigned is not a registered interest, the registering party must still describe the assigned interest and the debtor under that interest.[50] This allows for the link between the original (registered and unregistered) interest and the assignment of that interest to be visible to other parties.

Consider secured creditor 1 (SC1) which, after registering its interest, assigns it to A1. A1 also registers its interest and indicates the file number of SC1's interest. If the debtor grants another security interest in the same aircraft object to secured creditor 2 (SC2), which registers and assigns its interest to A2, both SC2 and A2 will be able to discover the interest of A1 and assess their priority before registering their interests in the object. The Convention does not provide how accurate the transmitted information must be, but it seems that while the accuracy of some of these requirements is vitally important for the effectiveness of the registration, the inaccuracy

[47] Art 18 CTC.
[48] Sec 5 of the Regulations.
[49] Sec 5.5(c) of the Regulations.
[50] Sec 5.5(d) of the Regulations.

or absence of some other requirements is less likely to make the registration defective. This issue is considered in more detail below.

B. Identification of the Object and Errors in the Registration Data

Since the registrations and searches in the IR must be effected against a uniquely identifiable object, the transmission of correct information identifying the aircraft object in the process of effecting a registration is critically important because it enables a searcher to locate such registration. A mistake as to a serial number of the aircraft object or the model designation when effecting a registration may mean that the searcher will not be able to locate the registration and may be misled by a clear search and assume that its interest will be the first to be registered.[51] To reduce the possibility of mistakes, the IR limits transmission of free text to identify the aircraft object. The registrant is required to select the object identification information from the IR's drop-down menu provided and updated by the aircraft manufacturers.[52] The registrant should use the free-text facility to type the information in the prescribed form only when a manufacturer does not provide the aircraft object identification information.[53]

To register an international interest in the aircraft object, the registrant must indicate: (i) the manufacturer's name; (ii) the manufacturer's generic model designation; and (iii) the serial number assigned to the aircraft object by the manufacturer.[54] The same information should be sufficient to search registered interests in the aircraft object.[55] The manufacturer's serial number (MSN) can be entered as free text into the search application form. Once the serial number is entered, the searcher is invited to select the name of the manufacturer from the list provided in the form. If, for example, MSN 3000 and Airbus as the name of the manufacturer are selected, the system will then list the types of model designations used by this manufacturer. The model designations relate to the different aircraft families produced by the manufacturer and the searcher may select, for example, an A320 model from the menu, rather than type it in as free text. Although the possibility

[51] The result would be different in debtor-based registration systems, not requiring unique identification of the object. See, for example, *Cunard Steamship Company, Limited v Hopwood* [1908] 2 Ch 564, where one ship was substituted for another, but new registration of a security was not required because prescribed particulars only asked for the object's general description.

[52] Sec 5.1 of the Regulations.

[53] R Goode, *Official Commentary to the Convention on International Interests in Mobile Equipment and Protocol Thereto on Matters Specific to Space Assets*, 3rd edn (Rome, UNIDROIT 2013) 202.

[54] Sec 5.3(c) of the Regulations.

[55] Art 19(6) CTC; Art XX(1) of the Aircraft Protocol; Sec 7.1 of the Regulations.

of mistakes in transmitting the information identifying the aircraft object is reduced by making the use of the drop-down menu mandatory,[56] errors may still occur where an incorrect element of the aircraft object description is chosen or where the registrant enters the object identification information as free text.

The CTC does not explain the legal consequences flowing from such mistakes, namely whether the registration remains effective despite the mistake. It is submitted that although the Convention does not expressly deal with this issue, the effect of mistakes in the objects' identification on the validity of the registration should still be governed by the Convention.[57] This should be the case because this issue relates directly to the registration process in the IR, the creature of the CTC. Since the Convention does not expressly deal with the consequences of mistakes in the registration data, this matter should be settled in conformity with the general principles on which it is based.[58] On the one hand, it can be argued that such principles as predictability and transparency, which underpin the Convention and its registration system, suggest that any error in the registration data, however slight, should invalidate the registration. If the searcher knows that any mistake in the transmitted information will render the registration invalid, it can safely rely on the search result even if it is clear and no registration can be found against the aircraft object. Should it later transpire that a previous registration relating to the same aircraft object, in fact did exist, but that this registration could not have been located because of a mistake relating to the object identification, the principle of predictability would seem to dictate that the mistaken registration should not bind the searcher.

The application of the principle of transparency would seem to lead to the same result. This principle operates through the rules of registration by rendering the international interest visible to potential searchers. Consequently, if the interest cannot be seen in the IR as a result of the mistake in the object identification, the registration should not bind the searcher. While a validly created international interest may still be effective, the registration, containing mistakes in the object identification will be ineffective.

On the other hand, it can be argued that the invalidation of a registration due to any mistake, however insignificant, may be too harsh on the registrant. Since human intervention cannot be avoided when the registration information is entered for transmission to the Registrar, the possibility of mistakes will always exist. Holding that mistakes in the data will necessarily invalidate the registration may be commercially impracticable. If the effect of any mistake leads to the loss of priority, the price of effecting a

[56] Sec 5.1 of the Regulations.
[57] Art 5 CTC.
[58] Art 5(2) CTC.

registration may be too high. As a result, the creditor may decline to provide a loan or increase the cost of credit to such an extent that it may no longer be affordable to the debtor. This approach may lead to a decrease in the use of the IR and hinder the promotion of the Convention's objective to facilitate asset-based financing and leasing of mobile equipment. For this reason, it is submitted that mistakes in the information transmitted to the Registrar should not necessarily invalidate the registration, and a more flexible solution should and can be found within the Convention.

First, the Convention provides that the registration information may be amended if required.[59] Consequently, following the submission of the registration information to the Registrar, the registrant, noticing a mistake in the data, still has an opportunity to amend the initial registration to correct this mistake. The fact that the Regulations expressly allow amendments of the registration information means that mistakes in the data should not lead to automatic invalidation of the registered interest and that the amended registration can remain effective. Secondly, whether erroneous data will render the registration ineffective should arguably depend on the gravity of the mistake.[60] For instance, if the mistake relates to the duration of the registration, stating that it will last for five instead of seven years, this information can be easily amended. This mistake should not prevent the searcher from discovering that the registered interest exists in the aircraft object and will allow it to approach the named registrant for further information.

The suggestion that this type of a mistake should not invalidate the registration seems to be supported by the approach taken by the Regulations to the priority of amended registrations. The Regulations draw a distinction between amendments not affecting the registrant's priority and amendments shifting its priority status. If the amendment relates to the duration of the registration, the registrant will retain the same priority position as it had at the time of the original registration.[61] This must mean that the amended registration remains effective and binding on the searcher. This result accords with one of the main objectives of the registration system, namely to provide a notice of *possible* existence of the registered interests in the object. If the information, albeit erroneous, allows the searcher to discover the registered interest and approach the registrant for more details, mistakes in the data should not invalidate the registration.

The situation is radically different when the erroneous data relates to the identification of the aircraft object. This information is of vital importance to the searcher because it allows it to determine whether the aircraft object

[59] Art 16(3) CTC states that the term 'registration' includes, where appropriate, an amendment, extension or discharge of registration.

[60] Goode (n 53) 85.

[61] Sec 5(11)(c) of the Regulations.

is encumbered by prior registered interests. Consequently, if the registrant mistakenly enters an incorrect manufacturer's serial number or a model designation, the searcher will not be able to find the correct registration. The information identifying the aircraft object is the only criterion allowing the searcher to locate the prior registrations. In addition, a mistake as to a serial number or the name of the manufacturer will probably mean that the registrant will appear to have an interest in another aircraft object. It is submitted therefore that a mistaken registration relating to a wrong aircraft object must be ineffective. Until amended, a mistaken registration will mean that the searcher will not be able to locate the correct registration. Such erroneous registration should be ineffective and should not bind the searcher. It is, of course, possible to register an amendment, rectifying the object's identification mistake. But the original priority of the registrant will be lost. The amended registration will be considered as a new registration and its priority will rank from the time when the amendment is complete.[62]

To summarise, the Regulation's approach seems to support the view that if the mistake relates to the information helping the searcher to locate the registration relating to the aircraft object, it has the effect of invalidating the registration. In this case, the registrant can either discharge the initial registration and make a new registration or amend the existing registration. Its priority position will shift to the moment of effecting the new registration or amending the existing one. In contrast, if the mistake relates to the information which does not prevent the searcher from discovering the registered interest, such a mistake should not invalidate the registration or affect its priority.

V. VALIDITY AND TIME OF REGISTRATION

A. Time of Registration

Since priorities among competing creditors are determined by the order of registration, the time of registration is of paramount importance to them. The registrant will want to know precisely at what moment its registration becomes effective so as to be binding on the subsequent creditors. There are different moments in time when the registration could be deemed to be effective. The registration could be effective once the registration information is transferred to the Registrar, when the Registrar confirms its receipt or when the data is entered in the IR.

[62] Sec 5(11)(c) of the Regulations.

For example, under English law, a registrable charge has to be registered within 21 days from the time of its creation.[63] Once the registrant delivers a statement of particulars and a certified copy of the instrument creating the charge to the Registrar, and provided that this is done within the prescribed period, the charge is considered as validly registered even if the information is not yet entered in the register. Since the registrant has 21 days to deliver the documents and because the registration does not, generally, determine the order of priorities,[64] subsequent creditors searching the registry may be misled by a clear search. This may happen if the subsequent creditor searches the registry within the 21-day period, but before the registrant delivers the documents to the Registrar, and assumes that no charge exists in relation to the debtor's object. If the registrant registers its charge within the prescribed period, the registration may still affect the subsequent creditor.

This result would not be satisfactory under the Convention, since the time of registration is essential for determining the order of priorities. If the subsequent creditor cannot rely on the search, it will not be able to clearly assess its priority position before deciding whether to provide a loan to the debtor. To ensure that the registration becomes effective as quickly as possible and to enable the searcher to make an informed decision based on its priority perspectives, the Convention provides that the registration shall be effective or *complete* upon entry of the required information into the IR so as to be searchable.[65] The registration becomes searchable once: (a) the IR has assigned to it a sequentially ordered file number and (b) the registration

[63] See reg 859A(4) of the Companies Act 2006 (Amendment of Part 25) Regulations 2013 (SI 2013/600). The time of registration can be extended pursuant to a court order. The late registration is usually allowed subject to a proviso that the order is issued without prejudice to the rights of parties acquired prior to the time of actual registration. See *In re Spiral Globe, Limited* [1902] 1 Ch 396; *In re Joplin Brewery Company Limited* [1902] 1 Ch 79; *Re Chantry House Developments plc* [1902] BCC 646. *In re Ehrmann Brothers, Limited* [1906] 2 Ch 697. At the same time, if the winding up of the company commenced or if the liquidation is imminent, the order extending the time of registration is likely to be refused. See *In re Abrahams & Sons* [1902] 1 Ch 695; *Re Barrow Borough Transport Ltd* (1989) 5 BCC 646; *In re Ashpurton Estates Ltd* [1983] Ch 110. It has been argued that the 21-day period, which can be extended to allow for a late registration, accentuates the ostensible ownership of the chargor and highlights the necessity of reform in this area of the law. See I Davies, 'Floating Charges and Reform of Personal Property Legislation' (1988) *Comp Law* 47.

[64] Since registration does not, generally, determine the priority status, the registrant has no incentive to effect registration quickly. As long as this is done within 21 days of the creation of the charge, the registration should be valid. The position is different in relation to the registration of the aircraft mortgages, whereby the priority status depends on the time of registration. In addition, Mortgaging of Aircraft Order 1972 allows for the registration of a priority notice, stating that a mortgage or a charge is to be granted over the aircraft. If mortgage or charge is in fact registered in UK Mortgage Register within 14 days of the notice, the priority of security interest will date back to the time of registration of the notice of priority. See P Thorne, 'Aircraft Mortgages' in N Palmer and E McKendrick (eds), *Interests in Goods*, 2nd edn (LLP, London 1998) 712.

[65] Art 19(2) CTC.

information, including the file number, is stored in a durable form and may be accessed at the IR.[66] The IR's electronic nature helps ensure that the entry of the registration information in a searchable form can be accomplished in a speedy manner.[67]

B. Valid Registrations and Grounds for Invalidity

The interest registered in the IR will only survive the debtor's insolvency and provide its holder with priority if the registration of that interest is valid. To effect a valid registration or to amend, extend or discharge the existing one, the registrant must comply with the formal requirements set by the Convention, Regulations and Procedures. In addition, the registrant must obtain an electronically transmitted consent from the other party.[68] The requirement of prior consent provides an important safeguard against improper or incorrect registrations. If the registration is made without the consent of the relevant party, it will be ineffective.[69]

While the Convention stipulates which parties' consents must be secured by the registrant,[70] the Procedures prescribe the steps that must be followed to obtain consents.[71] First, the registrant enters the registration information on the IR website. Once this is completed, each named party will be sent a request to submit its consent to the proposed registration through the IR.[72] The electronic consent should be transmitted to the Registrar prior to the registration becoming searchable and within 36 hours from the time of the request.[73] A failure to send the consent within the prescribed period will result in the registration being automatically aborted.[74] It may well be that to effect a registration, the registrant will need to obtain consent of several named parties. If this is the case, the Registrar will wait until the final consent of the last of the named parties[75] is received[76] before automatically issuing a confirmation of the registration to all parties entitled to receive it.[77]

Since the registration only becomes effective and searchable after the consent of the other party is obtained, it is difficult to see how it can be

[66] Art 19(3) CTC.
[67] Goode (n 53) 311.
[68] Art 20 CTC; Sec 12.3–12.4 of the Procedures.
[69] Art 19(1) CTC. See Goode (n 53) 310–21.
[70] Art 20 CTC.
[71] Secs 12.3–4 of the Procedures.
[72] Sec 12.3 of the Procedures.
[73] Sec 12.3(b) of the Procedures.
[74] Sec 12.3 of the Procedures.
[75] See Sec 2(e) of the Procedures providing the definition of the final consent.
[76] But no longer than 36 hours from the moment the request for consent is sent to all relevant parties.
[77] Sec 12.4 of the Procedures.

effected without the prior consent. But the consent may have been transmitted by a person who was not entitled to do so and the Registrar, not having the means to verify the facts external to the registration process, may have proceeded with the registration.[78] In this case, the registration will not be valid even if it appears to be.[79] The Convention does not expressly list other grounds invalidating the registration, but if, for example, some formal requirements necessary for the creation of the international interest are not complied with, the purported registration of that interest will not be effective. So, too, the registration of a registrable NCRI and the registration of a notice of a national interest in the IR would only be effective if these rights and interests were validly created under the applicable national law. Similarly, if the agreement creating or providing for the international interest was concluded at the time when the debtor was not situated in a Contracting State, the interest would not be valid and its registration would have no effect.[80]

VI. SEARCHES AND SEARCH CERTIFICATES

To effect a registration, the registrant must comply with the Regulations and Procedures of the IR. This is likely to involve making prior arrangements with the Registry, employing an administrator, complying with the formal requirements and obtaining the consent of the other party. In addition, if a Contracting State has designated an entry point, the registration information must be submitted to the entry point before it can be transmitted to the IR to become searchable. The main purpose of these measures is to ensure that the IR is reliable and that it is not burdened by improper or incorrect registrations.

In contrast, the searches in the IR can be electronically conducted by any person whether or not the searcher has a specific interest in the aircraft object.[81] The registration of interests in the IR is made against a uniquely identifiable aircraft object. For this reason, a search criterion, which consists of several elements, is also made up of the information identifying the object. The search can be carried out using information regarding: (i) manufacturer's name; (ii) manufacturer's general model designation; and (iii) manufacturer's serial number for the aircraft object.[82] Once the search is ordered and the prescribed fee is paid, the Registrar is required to issue the searcher with an electronic search certificate digitally signed by it.[83]

[78] Goode (n 53) 310.
[79] This is the effect of Art 19(1) CTC.
[80] Goode (n 53) 311.
[81] Sec 7.1 of the Regulations.
[82] Sec 7.1 of the Regulations.
[83] Sec 13.5 of the Procedures.

It is possible to order three types of searches, two of which, namely a priority search and a Contracting State search, are official, while the third, the information search, does not have any significance for the purpose of priority. The aim of the information search is to provide the searcher with sufficient information to enable it to conduct a priority search.[84] The information search can be conducted when the searcher does not have sufficient information to identify the object. In this case, the IR can still provide the searcher with a list of possible matches and registered data in relation to such objects.[85]

The priority search is essentially a search for any registered interests which may exist in the aircraft object. Once the Registrar receives a request for the priority search, it must issue an electronic priority search certificate indicating all those interests which are registered in the IR in relation to the aircraft object together with the names of the interest holders.[86] The searcher should then be able to contact the holders of prior registered interests and obtain more detailed information in relation to the status and extent of their interests in the debtor's object. The certificate should also provide the searcher with a transactional history of each registered interest.[87] For example, if the duration of the registered international interest was extended for five years, or if the registered interest was subordinated to another creditor, or if it was assigned to another party, these changes should be reflected in the certificate. The certificate must also state the date and time of the registration of the information and all registrations should be listed in the chronological order.[88] This information can help the searcher to assess what its position would be in the queue of other creditors should the debtor be struck by insolvency. The priority search certificate should be issued even if no interests were registered in relation to the object.[89] In this case, the certificate will simply state that no information was recorded in respect of the object.

Some interests, such as a non-registrable NCRI, may be binding on the searcher even if they cannot be registered in the IR. This may be the case if a Contracting State makes a declaration under Article 39 CTC. Although the searcher cannot establish whether these NCRIs exist from the IR, it can order a Contracting State search certificate revealing all declarations made by the Contracting State.[90] There is, therefore, no need to seek this information elsewhere and the IR can be used as a central point for ascertaining the existence of these declarations. The list of declarations and their

[84] Sec 13.2 of the Procedures.
[85] Sec 7.3 of the Regulations.
[86] Art 22(2) CTC.
[87] Sec 7.4(b)(ii) of the Regulations.
[88] Art 22(2) CTC; Sec 7.4(b)(i) of the Regulations.
[89] Art 22(2)(b) CTC.
[90] Sec 7.5 of the Regulations.

withdrawals is searchable in the IR against the name of the declaring State.[91] The Contracting State certificate may help the searcher establish whether certain unregistered interests can be binding on it and the dates when the declarations in relation to such interests came into effect.[92]

Finally, the certificate issued by the IR is *prima facie* proof that it was in fact so issued and no additional evidence needs to be presented unless the authenticity of the document is challenged.[93] The certificate is proof of the facts recited in it, including the date and time of the registration and, as such, can be used to assert the priority status of its holder.[94]

VII. DISCHARGE OF REGISTRATION

A. General

Once the debtor performs the obligations secured by the registered international interest or when the obligations giving rise to a registered NCRI have been fulfilled, the debtor is entitled to obtain a discharge from the IR.[95] Whether it is possible to obtain a discharge of a prospective international interest or prospective assignment of an international interest depends on the intending creditor's or assignee's commitment to give value. If the intending creditor or assignee has not yet provided any funds to the debtor and negotiations between the parties cannot be continued, the debtor is entitled to have the prospective interests discharged. In contrast, if the intending creditor or assignee has made at least partial payment to the debtor, the registered interest cannot be discharged until the debt is fully repaid.[96] The Convention also provides that where the obligations secured by a national interest specified in a registered notice of a national interest have been performed, the registration relating to the interest will be discharged.[97] Finally, where the registration has been made improperly or incorrectly, the debtor is entitled to the discharge or amendment which should be procured by the holder of such an interest.[98] The discharge of the registration from the IR does not mean that the registered information will be removed from the register. Instead, a new record, stating that the interest has been discharged,

[91] Art 23 CTC.
[92] Art 23 CTC.
[93] Art 24 CTC. See Goode (n 53) 320.
[94] Art 24(b) CTC.
[95] Art 25(1) CTC. In contrast, registration of a contract of sale (but not of a prospective sale) of aircraft object cannot be discharged as it continues indefinitely. Art V(3) of the Aircraft Protocol.
[96] Art 25(2) CTC.
[97] Art 25(3) CTC.
[98] Art 25(4) CTC.

will appear on the system, to preserve registration history affecting the relevant aircraft object.[99]

The Convention and the Protocols prescribe a procedure to be followed to discharge a registered interest. First, the registration may only be discharged by or with the consent in writing of the party in whose favour it was made.[100] Secondly, to obtain a discharge, the debtor should deliver to the holder of the registered interest a written demand, requesting the discharge. The demand should be 'delivered to or received at its address' indicated in the registration.

This wording may create some uncertainly as it may not be clear whether the moment of delivery of the demand will necessarily coincide with its receipt. For example, the demand may be delivered on Wednesday 11 November, but the post may be opened or 'received' on Friday 13 November. In this case, it may not be clear when the demand will be considered as properly communicated to the holder of the registered interest. Alternatively, the two temporal points of the communication of the written demand may coincide, with the effect that once the demand is delivered to the address it is deemed to have been received at that address. This issue is important because the obligation of the holder of the registered interest to procure the discharge of the registration arises upon the delivery or receipt of the demand.

There is no indication as to whether the demand can only be sent to the holder of the registered interest or whether it can also be sent to its agent or its legal team. It seems that, provided that the demand is delivered to the address indicated in the registration information, it can be delivered either to the holder of the registered interest, its agent or the legal team. This issue arose in *Belair Holdings Ltd v Etole Holdings Ltd*,[101] a case decided under the Convention. In this case, the written demand to discharge a registration of a NCRI was sent by Belair, the debtor, to Etole's agent instead of Etole's lawyers but this was held effective because the agent's address was indicated in the registration information.

The Convention does not provide what should be indicated in the written demand sent by the debtor. Presumably the demand should, at least, specify the object or the file number of the registration that is to be discharged and the reason for the requested discharge. In most cases, once the obligations are performed, it is likely that the parties will mutually agree that the registration should be discharged. In this case, it is unlikely that the creditor will insist on the indication of the reasons for the requested discharge in the demand. However, it is still advisable to include this information in the demand because the creditor may later dispute the basis or validity of the

[99] Goode (n 53) 86.
[100] Art 20(3) CTC.
[101] *Belair Holdings Ltd v Etole Holdings Ltd* [2015] IEHC 596.

demand. In addition, a clear statement of the reasons for the discharge, the file number of the registration, or the aircraft object in relation to which the registration should be discharged can assist the creditor in effecting the discharge if it holds several registered interests in various aircraft objects of the debtor and only some of them need to be discharged. At the same time, it seems that, provided that it is clear which particular registration is required to be discharged, the demand will be deemed effective even if it contains superfluous information. For example, in *Belair* the demand contained a request to 'discharge and remove' the registration. Clearly, the registrations are never removed from the IR. Instead, a separate record is made to signify the discharge of the registration, enabling other parties to view the registration history affecting the aircraft object. This led Etole to argue that the request to 'remove' the registration could not be honoured as it was 'beyond its powers' and that the demand was invalid. The court rejected this argument and held that Belair's demand was effective as it was clear what registered interest had to be discharged.

Thirdly, upon receipt of the complying demand, the creditor should procure the discharge without undue delay. In the *Belair* case, the applicant required Etole to discharge the registration within 24 hours of the demand's receipt and Etole argued that this requirement imposed a legally ineffective time limit on it. It was held that provided that Etole responded in a 'substantive manner' the fact that the discharge could not have been effected in such a short period could not have given rise to a complaint by the applicant. In other words, it seems that the obligation to procure the discharge without undue delay does not translate into the obligation to comply with a timeframe set by the debtor. While, the discharge can, in principle, be effected within 24 hours of the demand's receipt, a longer period can be taken to discharge a registration and still comply with the requirement to do this without undue delay.

Moreover, the Aircraft Protocol provides that the holder of a registered prospective international interest or a registered prospective assignment of the international interest, or a person in whose favour a prospective sale has been registered, shall take such steps as are within its power to procure the discharge of the registration not later than five working days following the receipt of the demand.[102] Similarly, the Luxembourg[103] and Space Protocols[104] provide that the creditor should take the necessary steps to discharge the registration not later than 10 calendar days after the demand's receipt. These timeframes clearly indicate that there is no expectation that the discharge should occur within 24 hours of the demand's receipt and that

[102] Art XX(2) the Aircraft Protocol.
[103] Art XV(2) of the Luxembourg Protocol.
[104] Art XXXII(3) of the Space Protocol.

provided that the creditor takes such steps that are within its power and responds to the demand in any 'substantive manner' (eg by communicating to the debtor its intention to procure the discharge), the discharge, which happens within the timeframe stipulated in the Protocols, should be deemed as complying with the Convention's requirement. Finally, even though the Protocols provide some indication as to the timeframe for the discharge of registration, the obligation to procure the discharge within the specified period imposed by the Protocols is not a strict one, because the holder of the registered right is only required to take such steps as are 'within its power' to effect the discharge.[105]

B. Failure or Refusal to Discharge a Registration

In most cases, the debtor will send the demand requesting the discharge to its creditor when both parties agree that the debtor's obligations are performed. So too, if the parties agree that the registration should not have been made or that it is erroneous, the person in whose favour the registration was made can procure the discharge or amendment of the offending registration. But how can the debtor ensure that the registration is discharged where the holder of the registered right fails or refuses to procure the discharge? This is exactly what happened in one of the first decisions under the Convention, involving a bogus registration.

In *PNC Equipment Finance LLC v Aviareto Limited and Link Aviation LLC*,[106] the debtor became the registered owner of the United States registered aircraft, financed by the secured creditor. The secured creditor duly registered the international interests in the airframe and aircraft engines in the IR. The debtor leased the aircraft to the lessee and also registered its international interests in the aircraft objects in the IR. Both the lessor and the lessee were founded in the United States. A year later, the lease was terminated and the lessee purported to register a NCRI relating to the aircraft in the IR. The registration of a registrable NCRI does not require the consent of the other party, enabling its holder to effect the registration without cooperation of the party affected by it. Further, PNC Equipment acquired the debtor's indebtedness relating to the financed aircraft from the secured creditor in order to take possession and sell it. To conclude the sale, PNC Equipment had to demonstrate to the prospective purchaser that title to

[105] Goode (n 53) 477.

[106] *PNC Equipment Finance LLC v Aviareto Limited and Link Aviation LLC*, case 2012 397 MCA, 19 December 2012 (not reported). See D Gallagher, 'The Unique Jurisdiction of the Irish High Court under the Cape Town Convention' (2014) 1 *Irish Business Law Review* 47, 52–53 for a detailed analysis of the case.

the aircraft was not encumbered. It is for this reason that PNC Equipment needed the bogus registration discharged from the IR.

The US court ordered the lessee to procure the discharge, but the registration remained undischarged. Since the role of the Registrar under the Convention is purely administrative, it could not be involved in adjudicating the factual dispute between the parties relating to the effectiveness of the registration.[107] For this reason, the Registrar could not discharge the registration at PNC Equipment's request without a court order. This meant that PNC Equipment had to obtain a court order, directing the Registrar to discharge the offending registration. The Convention confers exclusive jurisdiction on the courts of the place where the Registrar has its centre of administration to award damages or make orders against the Registrar.[108] In the case of the IR for aircraft objects, the Registrar, Aviareto Ltd, is based in Dublin and orders against the Registrar can only be made by Irish courts.[109] The CTC and Aircraft Protocol were given effect in Irish law by the International Interests in Mobile Equipment (Cape Town Convention) 2005 Act.[110] Section 7 of the 2005 Act indicates that proceedings against the Registrar should be brought in the High Court of Ireland. The Convention provides that where a person fails to comply with an order of a court having jurisdiction under it, or in the case of national interest, with an order of a court of competent jurisdiction requiring it to amend or discharge the registration, the courts of the Registrar's jurisdiction may give effect to the order of the national court by directing the Registrar to amend or discharge the registration.[111]

In *PNC Equipment*, Irish High Court accepted the correctness of the order of the US court and held that the registration of the NCRI effected by the lessee in the IR should not have been made. The Convention enables a Contracting State to make a declaration under Article 40 and list the categories of NCRI which can be registered in the IR. Once registered, such NCRIs are treated as international interests. The United States did not make the Article 40 declaration and, for this reason, the lessee's purported registration of a NCRI was invalid. The High Court applied Article 44(3) CTC and directed the Registrar to discharge the registration of the NCRI if the lessee did not procure the discharge within 21 days of the order. The registration was duly discharged by the Registrar.

[107] Goode (n 53) 90.

[108] Art 44(1) CTC.

[109] See SI No 31/2008, Rules of the Superior Courts (Cape Town Convention) 2008 available at www.irishstatutebook.ie/eli/2008/si/31/made/en/print amending the rules of the Superior Courts in Ireland to facilitate bringing of the proceedings against the Registrar.

[110] Sec 2 of the 2005 Act.

[111] Art 44(3). See Goode (n 53) 387.

Several points emerge from the *PNC Equipment* case. It illuminates how Article 44 CTC, dealing with the issue of jurisdiction to make orders against the Registrar, operates. Although the Registrar is based in Dublin, the registrations in the IR can be made from anywhere in the world by parties based in different countries with no connection to Ireland. The international nature of the parties, the transactions in relation to which registrations are made, and the functions performed by the Registrar could expose it to multiple proceedings in different countries and potentially conflicting orders should a dispute between the parties relating to the validity currency or accuracy of registrations arise. It is for this reason that the Convention confers exclusive jurisdiction on the courts of the place of the Registrar's centre of administration to award damages or make orders against it and no other court can make such orders against the Registrar.[112]

At the same time, the courts of the Registrar's jurisdiction are not likely to be suitable for resolving the disputes relating to the registrations arising between the parties based in different countries.[113] Accordingly, Article 44(3) provides for a two-stage procedure to be followed in the case where the beneficiary of the registration refuses or fails to discharge it after a written demand was served on it. In the first place, it is important to obtain an order, directing the discharge or amendment of the registration from the court, having jurisdiction under the Convention. This is a court of a Contracting State chosen by the parties to the transaction as having jurisdiction in respect of the claims under the Convention.[114] Secondly, once the order of a national court chosen by the parties is received, a claim against the Registrar can be brought in the courts having exclusive jurisdiction over it. This court, currently the High Court of Ireland, may issue an order directing the Registrar to amend or discharge the registration in accordance with the order obtained from the national court. This procedure was followed in the *PNC Equipment* case and the order requiring the Registrar to discharge the offending registration was expeditiously issued by the High Court.

A question arising in this regard is whether it is possible to bring a claim against the Registrar in the court of its jurisdiction directly, ie without obtaining an order from the national court. The Convention expressly states that direct proceedings against the Registrar can be initiated where a person required to procure the discharge fails to respond to a written demand made to it and where that person has ceased to exist or cannot be found.[115] In this case it may be difficult to initiate proceedings against that person and Article 44(2) enables the debtor or the intending debtor to proceed against the Registrar to obtain an order requiring it to discharge the registration.

[112] Goode (n 53) 387.
[113] *Ibid* 90.
[114] Art 44(3) CTC, Art 42(1) CTC.
[115] Art 44(2) CTC.

The obvious limitation of this provision is that it is only possible to invoke it in the case where the party benefiting from the registration ceases to exist or cannot be found. However, in *Transfin-M Ltd v Stream Aero Investments SA and Aviareto Limited*,[116] another case decided under the Convention involving the discharge of a registration, the High Court held that its jurisdiction was not so limited. This case involved a proposed sale of an aircraft registered in the UK from Transfin-M Ltd, a Russian based entity, to Stream Aero, a Panamanian-based entity. Both Russia and Panama are Contracting States of the Convention, but they have not made the Article 40 declarations. Transfin and Stream Aero signed a letter of intent, but the negotiations were not successful and the sale was not concluded. Unknown to Transfin, Stream Aero acted as a broker and intended to resell the aircraft to Star Jet (Hong Kong) Limited. After the negotiations between Transfin and Stream Aero had broken down, Transfin sold the aircraft to Star Jet directly. Stream Aero sought payment of a percentage of the total selling price as a commission allegedly owed to it. Stream Aero also registered a NCRI against the aircraft in the IR and failed to procure its discharge following a written demand made by Transfin.

In contrast to the *PNC Equipment* case, Transfin did not have a court order directing Stream Aero to discharge the offending registration enabling the High Court to exercise its jurisdiction under Article 44(3). Article 44(2) could not be employed because Stream Aero clearly did not cease to exist and could be found. In these circumstances, Trasfin sought the order to discharge the registration directly from the High Court in Ireland. Although the Convention's provisions expressly granting the jurisdiction did not apply, the High Court held that its own rules provided it with jurisdiction and that the proceedings were covered by Order 11, Rule 1(f) and/or Rule 1(g) of the Rules of Superior Courts. These provisions state that the High Court has jurisdiction whenever:

> '(f) the action is founded on a tort committed within a jurisdiction; or
>
> (g) any injunction is sought as to anything to be done within the jurisdiction, or any nuisance within the jurisdiction is sought to be prevented or removed, whether damages are or are not also sought in respect thereof'

Since neither of the Contracting States made the Article 40 declarations, the registration by Stream Aero of the NCRI was not only baseless, but also ineffective. The court determined that the registration amounted to a tort and/or nuisance existing in Ireland, because this was the place where the Registrar was based. The Court determined that it had jurisdiction and

[116] *Transfin-M Ltd v Stream Aero Investments SA and Aviareto Limited*, 2013 No 112 MCA (not reported). See Gallagher (n 106) 53–54 for a detailed discussion of this case.

ordered Stream Aero and, concurrently, the Registrar to procure the discharge of the registration. Stream Aero did not comply with the order and the registration was discharged by the Registrar.

The decision of the court to accept jurisdiction to make direct order against the registering party in the case of an invalid or improper registration clearly benefits the party affected by the offensive registration. The possibility of bringing direct proceedings in Ireland obviates the need to initiate proceedings and wait for a court order in another jurisdiction.[117] After the court order in the alternative jurisdiction is issued, the registering party may refuse or fail to comply with it, necessitating the application to the High Court in Ireland. The applications for orders to courts in different jurisdictions coupled with the 21-day period during which the registrant may appeal the decision of the High Court may mean that the party adversely affected by the offending registration will have to wait a considerable time before the registration can be discharged. Time and financial costs can be reduced if the applicant can bring simultaneous proceedings against the Registrar and the registering party ordering them to discharge the registration directly in Ireland.[118]

Another case, confirming that Irish High Court can accept jurisdiction even if the Convention's procedural rules do not apply, is *Belair Holdings Ltd v Etole Holdings Ltd* considered above.[119] This case also concerned an improperly registered NCRI in the IR. Etole, a prospective purchaser based in British Virgin Islands and Belair, the aircraft owner based in Cayman Islands, signed a letter of intent for the purchase of the aircraft stipulating that Belair should not offer or sell the aircraft to a third party, and this is exactly what Belair purported to do. Faced with the possibility of losing its deposit and the aircraft, Etole sought injunctive relief in a New York court in an attempt to prevent the sale. Etole also registered a NCRI against the aircraft in the IR. Belair did not have a court order from a national court directing Etole to discharge the registration from the IR and applied directly to the High Court both against Etole and, concurrently, the Registrar. The issue of jurisdiction did not arise, because Etole submitted to it. The debtor, Belair, whose interest in the aircraft was burdened by the registered NCRI, was based in a non-Contracting State at the time of the conclusion of the agreement. This meant that the Convention did not apply. However, the court stated that even if the Convention did apply, none of the relevant Contracting States made the Article 40 declaration and the registration should not have been made by Etole. As in the previously considered cases, the registrant was able to effect a registration because the registration of a NCRI

[117] Gallagher (n 106) 54–55.
[118] *Ibid* 54–56.
[119] *Belair Holdings Ltd v Etole Holdings Ltd* [2015] IEHC 596.

did not require the consent of the other party. The purely administrative role of the Registrar also meant that it could not verify the details of the registration before it was entered on the IR. In these circumstances, the High Court held that the court should not 'condone a misleading registration' and made the order directing the discharge.

The *PNC Equipment*, *Transfin* and *Belair* cases demonstrate how Article 44 operates and show that Irish courts are willing to assume jurisdiction even where the Convention's jurisdictional provisions do not apply, in circumstances where the court's own jurisdiction rules can provide it with jurisdiction and where the respondent submits to the jurisdiction. At the same time, all three cases concerned improperly made registrations of NCRIs, which were undeniably invalid due to the lack of the Article 40 declarations by the Contracting States. The question remains as to whether Irish High Court will accept jurisdiction to determine a dispute on a substantive matter relating to the validity of the registration where, for example, the validity of a registered interest is challenged.[120] Another limitation of Article 44(2) is that the application to the court having exclusive jurisdiction over the Registrar must be made by the debtor or intending debtor. This means that if a party, whose interest in the aircraft object is affected by the registration, but who cannot be considered as the debtor or the intending debtor, obtains an *in personam* order from a court, having a jurisdiction under the Convention or under the *lex fori*, then unless the exclusive jurisdiction under Article 44(1) is interpreted broadly, these parties will not be able to ensure the discharge of the registration in the event such order is not complied with.[121] So far, the cases involved parties seeking the discharge who acted as 'debtors' under the Convention. It remains to be seen whether the High Court will be prepared to accept a broader jurisdiction where the party cannot be considered as such.

[120] Gallagher (n 106) 55–56.
[121] Goode (n 53) 388–89.

5

Priority of Competing Security and other International Interests

I. INTRODUCTION

THE SECURED CREDITOR providing a loan to the debtor is unlikely to be the only creditor claiming an interest in the equipment held by it. The debtor may have already granted a security interest to a previous creditor, leased the asset to a lessee, or negotiated its sale with an outright buyer. In addition, a holder of a non-consensual right or interest (NCRI), such as a repairer who did not receive payment for its services, or a holder of a national interest,[1] which has registered its notice in the International Registry (IR), may also attempt to establish its claim in the debtor's asset. If the debtor remains solvent and capable of meeting its obligations, the secured creditor may rest assured that the loan will be repaid. However, should the debtor become insolvent, it may not have enough assets to meet the obligations it owes to various creditors. In this case, creditors will need to know whether the debts will be repaid on a 'first-come-first-served' basis or whether the repayment will depend on the size of the debt, the time when the obligation was incurred, or some other criteria.

The main function of the priority rules is to establish the order in which competing creditors can satisfy their claims from the object held by their common debtor.[2] In addition, a clear set of priority rules can help the creditor ascertain its position in the queue of creditors in advance, which can influence its decision to extend the loan. By assessing its position among other creditors, the potential secured creditor can estimate whether the debtor will have enough funds to repay the loan after all previous claims have been met. If the object is already heavily encumbered and the secured creditor is unlikely to receive full repayment, it can decide to enter into a subordination agreement with one of the senior creditors in order to change its priority position. Alternatively, the secured creditor may decide

[1] For the discussion of NCRIs and national interests, see chapter three.

[2] T Jackson and A Kronman, 'Secured Financing and Priorities Among Creditors' (1978–79) 88 *Yale LJ* 1143, 1144.

to increase the cost of the credit or not to lend at all.[3] Finally, the priority rules accepted by all creditors can help the creditor to validate its claim, because once the priority position of the secured creditor is established it will be recognised by other interest holders. In other words, the creditor's priority can help protect its stake in the object from the competing claims, which may be one of the reasons for taking a security interest rather than extending an unsecured loan.[4]

The CTC's priority rules are tied to the time of registration in the IR.[5] The general rule is that a registered interest has priority over a subsequently registered and unregistered interest irrespective of whether the unregistered interest is registrable in the IR.[6] An important advantage of the Convention's priority scheme is that it renders registration the only mode of perfection and the only requirement for obtaining a priority. Indeed, some international instruments recognise that the priority system, based on the use of the public registry, is 'the most effective way to provide creditors with the means to determine their priority with a high degree of certainty at the time they extend credit'.[7] All that the holder of a registrable interest has to do to determine its priority is to search the IR, which should reveal its potential position among the holders of competing interests. By registering its interest, the secured creditor can crystallise its priority among other interests and ensure that it is visible to searchers.

The position is more complicated in some national legal systems which, for instance, recognise that to perfect a security interest in certain types of

[3] See further P Coogan, 'Article 9 of the Uniform Commercial Code: Priorities among Secured Creditors and the "Floating Lien"' (1959) 72 *Harv L Rev* 838, 859–60.

[4] V Finch, 'Security, Insolvency and Risk: Who Pays the Price?' (1999) 62 *MLR* 633, 634. See also R Mann, 'Strategy and Force in the Liquidation of Secured Debt' (1997–98) 96 *Mich L Rev* 159.

[5] Art 29(1) CTC. See R Goode, *Official Commentary to the Convention on International Interests in Mobile Equipment and Protocol Thereto on Matters Specific to Aircraft Equipment*, 3rd edn (Rome, UNIDROIT 2013) 332–42.

[6] Art 29(1) CTC. Priority extends to proceeds, defined narrowly by Art 1(w) and confined to 'money or non-money proceeds of an object arising from the total or partial loss or physical destruction of the object or total or partial confiscation, condemnation or requisition'. The Convention's general priority rule is similar to the rule under the US UCC. §9-322(a)(1) provides that as between two security interests, first to file gets priority. In contrast, English law gives priority to the first-in-time of creation, but this rule is subject to exceptions. See R Calnan, 'Taking Security in England' in M Bridge and R Stevens (eds), *Cross-Border Security and Insolvency* (Oxford, OUP 2001) 26.

[7] See the UNCITRAL Legislative Guide on Secured Transactions (2007) para 33, p 193. The position is different under the Model Law on Secured Transactions, developed by the European Bank for Reconstruction and Development (EBRD). Art 17.2 of the Model Law provides that, subject to exceptions, priority between competing charges is determined in accordance with the time of their creation or deemed time of creation. Generally, the unpaid vendor's charge (Art 17.3), the possessory charge over negotiable instruments or negotiable documents (Art 17.4) and a security right arising by operation of law for money due for services in relation to a thing or right held (Art 17.6) are given super-priority over previous charges.

objects, the secured creditor may either register or file a financing statement at a filing office or take possession or control over the collateral.[8] Such systems may have several hierarchies of priority rules.[9] If competing interests are perfected by the same mode of perfection, such as filing, then as between two filed security interests, first to file will take priority.[10] If competing security interests are perfected by different modes, such as control and filing, the resolution of the conflict between them will depend on which type of perfection is given priority by the legislator. Should perfection by control be granted priority, then a security interest perfected in this way will take priority over the filed competing interest, even if the latter was perfected earlier than the former.[11]

The Convention's priority rules, rendering the time of registration the only focal point for determining priority, are much simpler, which is particularly valuable in international transactions involving high value mobile equipment. In these types of transactions, the debtor, its creditors and the financed objects are often located in different jurisdictions, which may complicate the process of determining and validating the priority status of various stakeholders. The Convention's approach, providing a single and easily accessible reference point, namely the IR, for ascertaining one's priority and cementing this priority position among other interest holders, offers a simple, clear and transparent solution.[12] Furthermore, since registration is the only way of perfecting and obtaining the priority, the only relevant distinction between competing interests is that of registered and unregistered interests.[13] Other considerations, that may be important in some legal systems, such as location of the title to the object, are irrelevant. For example, some legal systems provide that interests of a conditional seller and lessor do not require registration to gain priority over a registered security interest.[14]

[8] See §9-313(a) (perfection by possession or delivery) and §9-314(a) (perfection by control) UCC, exemplifying this position. See P Coogan, 'A Suggested Analytical Approach to Article 9 of the Uniform Commercial Code' (1963) *Colum L Rev* 1, 28–29.

[9] R Picker, 'Perfection Hierarchies and Nontemporal Priority Rules' (1999) 74 *Chi-Kent L Rev* 1157.

[10] §9-322(a)(1) UCC. See J White and R Summers, *Uniform Commercial Code*, 6th edn (West Group, 2010) Chapters 23 and 25.

[11] Picker (n 9) 1164–65.

[12] The position is different under English law, where registration is irrelevant for determining priorities. However, if a registrable interest is not registered within 21 days of creation, it becomes void against the liquidator and creditors of the company, promoting other security interests into the place of the avoided security. See H Beale, M Bridge, L Gullifer and E Lomnicka, *The Law of Security and Title-Based Financing*, 2nd edn (Oxford University Press 2012) 451.

[13] Art 1(cc) CTC defines 'registered interest' as an international interest, a registrable NCRI or a national interest registered in the IR. According to Art 1(mm), 'unregistered interest' means a consensual interest or NCRI (but not the interest covered by Art 39), which has not been registered, irrespective of whether or not it is registrable in the IR.

[14] This is the position under English law. See Beale, Bridge, Gullifer and Lomnicka (n 12) 473.

Since they retain title in the object, this exempts them from the necessity to register and justifies their priority over registered security interests. In contrast, the Convention does not grant super-priority to selected types of interests and a conditional seller or lessor will have to register their interests to protect their priority. This rule injects the Convention's priority scheme with a high degree of predictability and clarity in that an unregistered or subsequently registered interest of a conditional seller or lessor will not be given priority over an earlier registered interest.

This chapter examines the following issues in the following five parts. Part II considers the two limbs of the general priority rule and examines its consequences. It also analyses the difficult issue of whether the debtor, registering its interest in the IR ahead of its own creditor, can assert priority over it. According to the Official Commentary (OC), the debtor's interest should be subordinated to the interest of its creditor because the former should not act inconsistently with the rights it has granted to the latter. After putting this position to the test, Part III proposes a different position, namely that the debtor, acting in a different capacity, should be able to overtake its creditor if it registers its interest in the IR first. Part IV considers the need for and possibility of creating and registering a purchase money security interest (PMSI) under the Convention. Further, similar to other legal systems, the Convention's general priority rule is subject to a number of exceptions. These exceptions can affect the position of an outright buyer, conditional buyer and lessee, the holder of a non-registrable NCRI, the holder of a pre-existing right or interest (PERI) as well as the position of the parties entering a variation agreement. Part V tests the effectiveness of these exceptions. It also examines the issue of whether it is possible for a holder of two separately registrable interests to achieve a 'cross over' protection if it registers only one, but not the other of such interests. Taking a position different to that in the OC, this work argues that it is possible to achieve 'cross over' protection. Part VI considers the international interest's effectiveness in insolvency. Finally, one of the effects of granting a security interest is that the secured creditor can satisfy its claim in priority to a claim of an unsecured creditor.[15] On the one hand, it may seem unfair that by concluding a private security agreement, the debtor and the secured creditor may alter the position of an unsecured creditor and reduce its chance of obtaining the repayment in the case of the debtor's insolvency.[16] On the other hand, it can be argued

[15] For a view that priority of secured creditors should not be disturbed because unsecured creditors are unlikely to benefit from that, see D Baird, 'The Importance of Priority' (1997) 82 *Cornell L Rev* 1420.

[16] For a discussion reflecting similar concerns in the context of Canadian Personal Property Security Acts, see J Ziegel, 'The New Personal Property Security Regimes—Have We Gone too Far?' (1989–90) 28 *Alta L Rev* 739. See also R Mokal, 'Priority as Pathology: The Pari Passu Myth' [2001] *CLJ* 581. For a debate on the position of unsecured creditors and propositions to cut full priority of secured creditors, see L Bebchuk and J Fried, 'The Uneasy Case for the

that voluntary unsecured creditors can reduce their risks by charging higher interest rates[17] and that the debtor should be able to alienate its property rights in the objects by way of security as freely as possible.[18] The Convention does not deal with the issues of priority between secured and unsecured creditors and is only concerned with priority conflicts between registered and unregistered interests. For this reason the issues of justification of the privileged position enjoyed by secured creditors in relation to unsecured creditors are not addressed in this chapter.

II. THE GENERAL RULE: FIRST-IN-TIME, FIRST-IN-RIGHT

A. Rule 1: The First Registered Interest Gets Priority

The general priority rule consists of two parts. First, as between two registered interests, the first to be registered gets priority.[19] Secondly, as between a registered and an unregistered interest, the registered interest gets priority even if the unregistered interest cannot be registered in the IR.[20] This holds true even if the first registered interest was acquired with actual knowledge of the subsequently registered or unregistered interest.[21]

The Convention does not require a holder of a registrable interest to register its interest within a specified period of time once the interest is created. But the rule that the first registered interest gets priority creates a powerful

Priority of Secured Claims in Bankruptcy' (1996) 105 *Yale LJ* 857; S Schwarcz, 'The Easy Case for the Priority of Secured Claims in Bankruptcy' (1997) 47 *Duke LJ* 425; L LoPucki, 'The Unsecured Creditor's Bargain' (1994) 80 *Va L Rev* 1887; S Block-Lieb, 'The Unsecured Creditor's Bargain: A Reply' (1994) 80 *Va L Rev* 1989.

[17] Jackson and Kronman (n 2) 1148. For the discussion on the position of non-adjusting non-voluntary unsecured creditors, see S Harris and C Mooney, 'Measuring the Social Costs and Benefits and Identifying the Victims of Subordinating Security Interests in Bankruptcy' (1997) 82 *Cornell L Rev* 1348.

[18] S Harris and C Mooney, 'A Property-Based Theory of Security Interests: Taking Debtors' Choices Seriously' (1994) 80 *Va L Rev* 2021, 2022; L Ponoroff and F Knippenberg, 'Having One's Property and Eating it Too: When the Article 9 Security Interest Becomes a Nuisance' (2006) 82 *Norte Dame L Rev* 373. There were also attempts to justify the privileged treatment of secured creditors on the grounds of economic efficiency. For the detailed discussion of these issues as well as attempts to solve the so-called puzzle of the security interest, see C Hill, 'Is Secured Debt Efficient?' (2002) 80 *Tex L Rev* 1117; J Fried, 'Taking the Economic Costs of Priority Seriously' (1997) 51 *Consumer Fin LQ Rep* 328; A Schwartz, 'Security Interests and Bankruptcy Priorities: A Review of Current Theories' (1981) 10 *J Legal Stud* 1; R Mann, 'Verification Institutions in Financing Transactions' (1999) 87 *Geo LJ* 2225; R Scott, 'A Relational Theory of Secured Financing' (1986) 86 *Colum L Rev* 901; D Carlson, 'Secured Lending as a Zero-Sum Game' (1998) 19 *Cardozo L Rev* 1635; J White, 'Reforming Article 9 Priorities in Light of Old Ignorance and New Filing Rules' (1995) 79 *Minn L Rev* 529.

[19] Art 29(1) CTC.

[20] Art 29(1) CTC.

[21] Art 29(2)(a) CTC.

incentive for the holder of the registrable interest to effect registration as soon as possible. The time of registration is of cardinal importance in determining priority. All other criteria, such as the date of the interest's creation, the date when the loan was advanced or the object was delivered, are irrelevant. Thus, if the debtor grants a first security interest in an aircraft engine to the secured creditor 1 (SC1) on 1 May, which registers its interest on 10 May, and then grants a second security interest in the same engine to the secured creditor 2 (SC2) on 3 May, which registers its interest on 7 May, then SC2 will be able to obtain repayment of the loan in priority to SC1, because its interest was registered first. The result would be the same, even if SC2 had actual knowledge of the existence of the prior security interest.[22]

The rule that actual knowledge of the holder of the first registered interest about the other interest is irrelevant for the purposes of priority helps avoid factual disputes over what was known by the parties at any relevant time. The policy behind the rule is clear: making the issue of priorities turn on factual disputes based on one's state of knowledge is likely to generate uncertainty and increase litigation costs.[23] It also helps strengthen the overall aim of the priority rules, embodied in Article 29, to promote their simplicity and achieve predictability of outcomes.[24]

The link between the time of registration and priority has several consequences. One consequence, flowing from the rule that a registered interest has priority over a subsequently registered interest, is that it is possible to register the international interest first and create it later.[25] If the parties are negotiating the terms of a security agreement, providing for a secured loan for the acquisition of an airframe, the secured creditor may register its interest as a prospective international interest before the security interest is created. Once all the prerequisites for the creation of the security interest are in place, such as where the debtor obtains power to dispose of the object, the prospective interest will automatically convert into the actual international interest. In this case, priority of the security interest will date back from the time of its registration as a prospective international interest. This allows the secured creditor to prevent any intervening claims from taking priority over its security interest.

Consider the following example. The debtor/lessee (D) negotiates a lease of an airframe with a manufacturer/lessor (L) and a loan, secured by the

[22] Art 29(2)(a) CTC.

[23] The Legal Advisory Panel of the Aviation Working Group, *Practitioners' Guide to the Cape Town Convention and the Aircraft Protocol* (Aviation Working Group 2015) 28 (hereafter *Practitioners' Guide*).

[24] R Goode, 'The Priority Rules under the Cape Town Convention and the Protocols' (2012) *Cape Town Convention Journal* 95, 97.

[25] Similarly, Art 14(2)(ii) of the UK Mortgaging of Aircraft Order 1972 permits registration of a priority notice stating that a charge or a mortgage is to be granted over an aircraft. This is also the case under §9-502(d) UCC. See *Uniform Commercial Code: Official Text and Comments*, 2009–2010 edn (Thomson West 2009) 1005.

same airframe, with the secured creditor (SC). The negotiations relating to the loan start on 1 May, but SC decides not to register its security interest until after the lease is finalised and D obtains the power to dispose of the airframe. The lease is entered into on 15 August and L immediately registers its international interest. SC registers its interest on 15 September. If D defaults, L's prior registered interest will take priority over SC's subsequently registered interest. To ensure priority over L, SC should have registered its interest as a prospective international interest once negotiations with D started. The registered prospective international interest would automatically convert into the actual international interest once the requirements for its creation were met.

The registration of a prospective international interest may, in some cases, also protect the security interest from possible attacks of the insolvency administrator.[26] If the insolvency administrator has a power under the applicable domestic law to avoid a security interest, registered, say, within the 90-day period before the start of the insolvency proceedings as a preference and D became insolvent on 1 November, the insolvency administrator may be able to set aside SC's international interest if it was registered on 15 September as a security interest, but not if it was registered on 1 May as a prospective international interest.

The second consequence, flowing from the rule that a registered interest has priority over the subsequently registered interest is the following. Should SC1, which has registered its interest first, agree to advance further loans to D on the security of the same object, it may add such loans to the original loan to cover all sums by the same security interest. Provided that all loans are secured by the same collateral, there will be no need to conclude a new security agreement and register a new security interest every time the additional loan is issued. This will be the case even if in the period between when the original security interest was registered and additional loans were provided, D granted SC2 a second security interest in the same object, which was immediately registered.[27] In this case, SC1 will retain its priority over SC2 in relation to *all* loans granted to D and not only in relation to the original loan.

This arrangement can be of particular convenience to SC1 and D if the latter maintains a bank account with SC1 and is allowed to draw on this account whenever it is in need of a fresh injection of funds. All such withdrawals can be linked to the originally registered security interest and SC1 does not have to search the IR to ensure that its interest in relation to further advances is not postponed to the intervening interests of other stakeholders.

[26] Art 1(k) CTC broadly defines the insolvency administrator as a person, authorised to administer the debtor's reorganisation or liquidation. This term may cover a debtor in possession, trustee in bankruptcy, liquidator and administrator.

[27] This is the effect of Art 29(2) CTC.

This positon may, of course, disadvantage SC2, willing to provide finance to D against the security of the same collateral as the one supporting the loans advanced by SC1. However, by searching the IR before granting the loan, SC2 will notice SC1's registered interest and can contact it to clarify the details of its arrangement with D. SC2 can then consider options such as agreeing to pay SC1 to buy out its priority position in relation to its own loan, assigning its security to SC1, entering into a subordination agreement or simply asking D to provide it with different collateral.

Finally, the third consequence concerns the possibility of the registration of a floating security in the IR. If a floating security over a fund of uniquely identified objects can be registered,[28] the rule that the registered interest prevails over the subsequently registered and unregistered interests should also apply to it. It is not clear whether competing floating security interests can be taken over the same pool of objects under the Convention. English law illustrates one possible approach to this issue. For instance, in *Re Benjamin Cope & Sons, Limited,* a company created a first series of debentures charging its undertaking and all of its present and future property.[29] Ten years later, a second series of identical debentures was issued and the question arose whether the second debentures ranked *pari passu* with the first debentures or after them. It was held that the second debentures ranked after the first ones, because the fact that the second debentures covered the same assets as the first ones defeated the whole purpose of the first debentures. Conversely, had the second debenture covered only part of the same assets or different objects altogether, the result would be different. In this case, the second floating charge could take priority over the first floating charge as the creation of subsequent floating and fixed charges is considered to be within the ordinary course of the debtor's business.[30]

This reasoning is inadmissible under the Convention and the result will ultimately depend on the order of registration of competing security and other international interests. If SC2 registers its floating security before SC1, SC2 will take priority over its competitor. The time of registration will also determine the order of priority between SC1, who takes a registered floating security over objects A, B and C, and SC2, who registers a fixed security in object C. In contrast with English law, where fixed charges are accorded priority over floating charges,[31] the outcome under the Convention will depend

[28] For the possibility of creation and registration of a floating security interest over the aircraft, space and railway objects, see chapter two.

[29] *In re Benjamin Cope & Sons, Limited* [1914] 1 Ch 800.

[30] *In re Automatic Bottle Makers, Limited* [1926] Ch 412.

[31] *Re Castell & Brown Ltd* [1898] 1 Ch 315. Although the general rule is that priority between competing interests is determined by the order of creation, a fixed charge is given priority over a floating charge irrespective of the order of creation. This can be explained by the fact that a chargor under a floating charge can deal with its assets by way of granting a fixed charge as long as it is in the ordinary course of business. For a different explanation,

on which of the two secured creditors registered its interest first. This also means that, since priority under the Convention is determined by the order of registration, the floating security will not be automatically postponed to any preferential debts as is the case under English law.[32]

B. Rule 2: The Registered Interest Gets Priority over the Unregistered Interest

The second part of the general rule is that, as between registered and unregistered interests, priority goes to the registered interest irrespective of whether its holder knows of the existence of the unregistered interest.[33] This will be the case even if the unregistered interest is not registrable under the Convention.[34] For instance, if the debtor (D) delivers one of its railway objects under a pledge to the secured creditor 1 (SC1), whose interest is not registrable under the domestic law and is also not registered in the IR, and then grants a non-possessory security interest, such as an equitable charge, over the same railway object to the secured creditor 2 (SC2), which registers its interest in the IR, SC2's international interest will prevail as a registered interest. The outcome would be different under some legal systems, such as English law because, generally, a pledge, as a non-registrable interest, does not require registration to maintain priority. Moreover, as first-in-time of creation as well as being a legal interest, the pledge would usually beat SC2's equitable charge, unless the charge was authorised by the pledgee.[35]

The general rule, according to which a registered interest prevails over the subsequently registered and unregistered interests, is equally applicable to the assignment of associated rights under the Convention.[36] A holder of an

see I Chiu, 'Replacing the Default Priority Rule for Secured Creditors—Some Reservations' [2006] *JBL* 644, 646.

[32] See s 40 and s 175(2)(b) of the Insolvency Act 1986. See also *Re H&K Medway Ltd* [1997] 1 WLR 1422; *Wheatley v Silkstone and Haigh Moor Coal Company* (1884) 29 Ch D 715; *Cox Moore v Peruvian Corporation Ltd* [1908] 1 Ch 604; *Re Colonial Trusts ex p Bradshaw* (1879) 15 Ch D 465. For a discussion of the Law Commission's proposals to make the timing of registration determinative of priority, see L Gullifer (ed), *Goode on Legal Problems of Credit and Security*, 5th edn (London, Sweet & Maxwell 2013) 92.

[33] Art 29(1).

[34] Art 1(mm).

[35] *Franklin v Neate* (1844) 13 M&W 481 ER 200. See Beale, Bridge, Gullifer and Lomnicka (n 12) 461; The Convention does not distinguish between equitable and legal interests. For a discussion on the balance of interests between holders of legal mortgages and equitable interests in the context of English law, see P Omar, 'Equitable Interests and the Secured Creditor: Determining Priorities' (2006) *Conveyancer and Property Lawyer* 509.

[36] Art 35(1). Under English law, priority between competing assignments is governed by the rule in *Dearle v Hall:* the priority between assignees is governed by the order of giving notice of the assignment to the debtor. The assignee giving notice should not know of the previous assignment at the time of its assignment or when the advance is transferred. See *Dearle v Hall*

international interest can assign its interest together with associated rights (such as rights to payment under the security agreement, conditional sale or lease) to the assignee.[37] Unless otherwise agreed, the assignment transfers to the assignee all the interests and priorities of the assignor.[38] Since the assignee merely steps into the shoes of the assignor, it does not have to register its interest to retain its priority against the debtor's creditors. So if the debtor grants registered security interests in an airframe to A, B and C (registered in that order) and A assigns its registered interest to A1, A1 will have priority over B and C, even if it does not register its interest in the IR. The situation would be different if A assigned its interest in the airframe together with associated rights to A1, A2 and A3. In this case, A1 would have to register its interest to protect its priority against A2 and A3. Failing that and provided that A2 and A3 registered their interests in due course, A1's interest would be postponed to the interests of registered assignees. This is precisely where the general rule of priority becomes relevant: as between two (or more) competing assignments, the registered assignment will have priority over the one subsequently registered and over the unregistered assignment of associated rights. It should be noted that the general rule of priority applies only if at least one of the competing assignments of associated rights also transfers to the assignee the international interest and if that assignment is registered.

It is, of course, possible to transfer associated rights without the related international interest, such as where the lessor transfers its rights to rentals to the assignee, but retains its international interest.[39] But such an assignment will not be governed by the Convention because it is primarily concerned with interests in objects and not with associated rights (which, unless they are linked to the object, cannot be registered under the Convention).[40]

(1828) 3 Russell 1; *Marchant v Morton, Down & Co* [1901] 2 KB 829. Notice is relevant only to the order of priorities and not to the validity of the assignment. See *Gorringe v Irwell India Rubber and Gutta Percha Works* (1887) LR 34 Ch D 128. If the assignee does not give notice to the debtor before the debtor pays the debt to its original creditor, the assignee cannot make the debtor pay to him as well. See *Bence v Shearman* [1898] 2 Ch 582. For a suggestion that the rule should be limited to its first limb only as the second limb is not supported by a clear authority, see JD Lacy, 'The Priority Rule of *Dearle v Hall* Restated' (1999) *Conveyancer and Property Lawyer* 311. For a view that the rule in *Dearle v Hall* should be substituted to the one where priority is determined by the order of registration, see C Brown, 'Preserving Priority in Receivable Financing: Time to Revisit *Dearle v Hall*' (1995) *J Int'l Bank L* 3.

[37] Associated rights are not confined to rights to payment and may include non-monetary obligations of the debtor relating to repair, maintenance and insurance as long as they are secured by or associated with the object. See Goode (n 24) 104–06.

[38] Art 31(1)(b). The position is similar under the Canadian Personal Property Security Act 1990. See A Duggan, 'The PPSA and the Common Law' (2005) *New Zealand Bus LQ* 122, 126–28.

[39] Goode (n 5) 350.

[40] *Ibid* 350.

Thus, if two competing assignments merely transfer the associated rights and not the related international interest and if such assignments are not registered, the general priority rule and the Convention itself will not apply and the conflict should be resolved by the applicable domestic law. In contrast, if at least one of the assignments of associated rights also transfers the related international interest and if such an assignment is registered, then the CTC's priority rule will apply. In this case, the registered assignment will have priority over the unregistered assignment, even if the latter cannot be registered in the IR because it is not linked to the object.

Finally, it should be possible to assign an unregistered international interest together with the associated rights, since the Convention provides for the registration of assignments of the international interest without specifying that such an interest should itself be registered.[41] The assignee of the unregistered international interest should register the assignment or risk subordination to the holder of a subsequent international interest if the latter registers its interest before the assignee.[42]

C. The General Rule: Some Issues of Uncertainty

i. Can a Debtor Jump Ahead of Its Own Creditor by Registering First?

The general rule that a registered interest takes priority over the subsequently registered and unregistered interests aims to achieve simple and predictable outcomes. However, there are several issues of uncertainty relating to its application. First, it is not clear whether the general rule's application means that a debtor who holds a separate international interest and registers it ahead of its own creditor takes priority. Consider a scenario where a manufacturer first grants a security interest in an airframe to a secured creditor and then leases the same object to a lessee. In this case, it will act in two capacities. As opposed the secured creditor, the manufacturer will act as the debtor. As opposed the lessee, it will act as the lessor and the creditor. In this second capacity, it can register its interest arising under the lease as an international interest. The question is whether, if the manufacturer registers its international interest ahead of the secured creditor or if the secured creditor does not register its interest at all, the interest of the lessor should prevail over that of the secured creditor.

According to Article 29(1) the earlier registered interest of the lessor should prevail over the secured creditor's subsequently registered or unregistered interest. However, the OC takes a different position by stating that there exists '[a] principle that is self-evident, though not expressly stated in

[41] *Ibid* 350.
[42] *Ibid* 112–24.

Article 29 … that a debtor who itself holds an international interest cannot use its registration of that interest to assert priority over its own creditor in a manner inconsistent with the rights it has granted to the creditor. In short, it cannot deny its own creditor's title'.[43] If correct, the OC's position would amount to a powerful yet implicit exception to the general rule, granting priority to the creditor's subsequently registered or unregistered interest.[44] This exception could, potentially, cloud the transparency of the registration system, because it would mean that even if the holder of an international interest registers its interest before the subsequently registered or unregistered interest, it may not obtain priority over it if such interest is held by its own creditor. To determine whether this exception exists, it is, first, important to ascertain whether the implicit principle that the debtor cannot deny its own creditor's interest by prior registration can indeed be found in the Convention. Secondly, if this principle exists, it is important to assess whether it applies to a situation where the debtor acts in a different capacity.

If the principle that the creditor does not require registration to protect its interest from the debtor exists, it can probably be found when the relevant purposes of the registration are considered. One such purpose is to give notice to third parties about the possible existence of the creditor's interest.[45] Registration is not aimed at giving notice of the creditor's interest to the debtor simply because the debtor, being the party to the security agreement, is already aware of its existence. This is why even if the creditor does not register its interest, the debtor cannot deny its existence or act in a manner inconsistent with it.[46] Indeed, when the party acts simply as a debtor, it will usually be the creditor who will register the international interest, so the issue of priority between the creditor and the debtor will not arise.

The question which is less clear is whether this principle should apply where the debtor holds a separately registrable interest. For instance, the debtor, after granting a security interest in an object to the secured creditor, can lease the same object to a lessee. Here, in addition to being the secured creditor's debtor and quite separately from this position, it will also act as a lessor and can register its international interest. According to the view expressed in the OC, in this scenario, the lessor will not be able to obtain priority over its creditor.[47] With respect, it is not clear why this result

[43] *Ibid* 105.

[44] See M Deschamps, 'The Perfection and Priority Rules of the Cape Town Convention and the Aircraft Protocol: A Comparative Law Analysis' (2013) *Cape Town Convention Journal* 51, 61–21, considering whether a court would come to the same conclusion as the one maintained by the OC.

[45] For the analysis of the purposes of registration, see chapter three.

[46] Goode (n 5) 334.

[47] Goode (n 5) 105–06 and 334.

should follow. After all, when asserting priority against the secured creditor, the debtor will act in a different capacity, namely in the capacity of the lessor. In this new capacity, it will not be asserting priority against its own creditor. It will claim priority over a competing interest of the secured creditor, held in the same object. Indeed, the subsequently registered or unregistered interest of the secured creditor would have been postponed to an earlier registered interest of the lessor, if it did not also act as the secured creditor's debtor. Since the Convention does not distinguish between the registered interests based on their origin, it is not clear why the position should be different if the lessor also happens to be the debtor.

It is, of course, possible to argue that the purpose of the registration of the lessor's interest may be other than protection against its creditor. Thus, the lessor's prior registration will protect the non-registrable interest of the lessee against the secured creditor's subsequently registered interest.[48] In addition, by registering its interest, the lessor can protect itself against the lessee's disposition. If the lessee grants a security interest to its own creditor, the earlier registered interest of the lessor will take priority over the subsequently registered interest of the lessee's secured creditor. But this does not mean that the registration of the lessor's interest should be confined to these purposes. The Convention's registration scheme entitles the holder of the registrable interest to register its interest and encourages it to do so as soon as possible. The users of the IR, being sophisticated and experienced parties, are aware that the time of registration determines priority and they are expected to make searches and registrations to secure their positions. As the holder of the registered international interest, the lessor should be entitled to benefit from the Convention's registration and priority rules, since the secured creditor has the means of searching the IR and making its own registration.

If the principle that the creditor does not require registration to protect its interest against its own debtor is applied to the position of the debtor acting in some other capacity, this could complicate the process of determining the priority between competing interests. Consider an example where the lessor grants a lease to the lessee who immediately grants a sublease and registers its international interest as the sub-lessor. The lessor then registers its international interest and grants a security interest to a secured creditor, who also registers its interest. The interests are registered in the following order: the sub-lessor, the head lessor and the secured creditor. To a potential searcher, it will appear that the sub-lessor is the senior creditor because it registered its interest first and the secured creditor is the junior one. But if the principle that the debtor cannot deny the interest of its own creditor

[48] Art 29(4) CTC.

applies, the order of priority will be different. The sub-lessor cannot claim priority over the head-lessor and the head-lessor cannot assert priority over the secured creditor by making a prior registration. So, the correct order of priority would be as follows: the secured creditor, the head-lessor and the sub-lessor.

In addition, if the sub-lessor is considered as the lessee, whose lessor registered its interest ahead of its own secured creditor, then, according to Article 29(4), the order of priority would be as follows: the sub-lessor acting as the lessee, the secured creditor, the head lessor. This would be the case even though when the head lessor registered its interest, the secured creditor was not even on the scene. Why should the secured creditor have priority in this situation? After all, the lessor was not even its debtor when it registered the international interest. The implicit rule that the debtor, acting in a different capacity, cannot overtake its creditor by prior registration can render the registration information in the IR less reliable for the searcher. The searcher would have to make additional enquiries to ascertain whether the holders of registered interests also act as debtors in relation to holders of some other registered interests. Even if at the time of the search and enquiry the holder of a registered interest does not act as a debtor, this may change if it later grants a security interest.

It is submitted that the application of the implicit principle that the debtor cannot deny its creditor's title by making a prior registration can undermine the principles of transparency, predictability and reliability underpinning the Convention's registration system and the rules of priority. This does not mean that the principle has no place in the Convention. It clearly applies to the relationship between the creditor and the debtor. But it is argued that it has no role to play where the debtor acts in a different capacity. This may lead to harsh results because in the eyes of the creditor, the party who now acts in a different capacity remains its own debtor. But if it is accepted that the creditors are expected to search the IR before making their decision to grant a loan and that the creditors know that it is the time of registration that determines priority, then the result can be justified. After all, this is what the general priority rule is about: first-in-time of registration, first in right. Provided that the registered interest was validly created, there is no reason why its holder should not be able to benefit from its prior registration.

ii. The Double Debtor Problem

The second area of uncertainty with respect to the application of the general priority rule relates to a double debtor situation. Article 29 clearly governs the order of priorities between the creditors claiming interests in the object held by their *common* debtor. However, the Convention is silent as to whether its priority rules apply to a contest between the creditors claiming interests in the same object held by *different* debtors. Consider a scenario where the lessor of an airframe grants a security interest to the secured creditor (SC1), who immediately registers its interest. The lessee, in turn, grants a security interest in the same airframe to its own secured creditor (SC2), who also registers its interest in the IR. This means that the interests of SC1 and SC2 in the same airframe are granted to them by different debtors. If both the lessor and the lessee default, the priority contest between SC1 and SC2 will have to be resolved. The so-called 'double debtor problem' is well known to the debtor-based registration systems. If SC2 had to search the IR against the name of the debtor (lessee), it would not be able to identify SC1's interest, held in the same object, but granted by a different debtor (lessor). However, this difficulty does not arise under the Convention because the IR is asset-based and all registrations and searches in it are effected against a uniquely identified object.

Although the Convention does not expressly specify that its priority rules apply to the double debtor situation, there seems to be no reason why they should not so apply. The fact that the IR is asset-based eliminates the need to identify all potential debtors which may have granted interests in the object to their creditors. Had SC2 searched the IR before extending the loan to the debtor, it would have discovered that the airframe was already encumbered by SC1's interest. This information would have allowed SC2 to identify the holder of the previously registered interest as well as to determine its own potential priority position. On this analysis, SC2 will only be able to obtain repayment of the loan after the lessor's own creditor, that is SC1, satisfies its claim.

III. THE POSSIBILITY OF A PURCHASE MONEY SECURITY INTEREST

A. The Need for a Purchase Money Security Interest

In some legal systems, the creditor is permitted to extend a loan secured on the debtor's present and future property.[49] This can be achieved by incorporating an after-acquired property clause into the security agreement.[50] This clause allows the parties to save transaction costs in that there will be no need to conclude a fresh security agreement every time new property of the type, covered by the original security, is acquired by the debtor. This can be particularly convenient if the objects used as a security are of such nature that they are likely to be turned over frequently in the course of the

[49] See, for example, H Tjio, 'Personal Property Security Interests in Singapore and Malaysia' (1995) *Company Lawyer* 28, 30; O Pasparakis, 'Canada: Security for Lending-Purchase Money Security Interest' 2003 *J Int'l Bank L Regul* 23.

[50] Gullifer (n 32) 213–17.

debtor's business.[51] The incorporation of the after-acquired property clause also means that the secured creditor will be able to retain its original priority position in relation to the debtor's future property without the need to perfect a fresh security interest.[52] At the same time, the after-acquired property clause can create so-called 'situational monopoly', placing the debtor and its subsequent creditors into a disadvantageous position. Should the secured creditor refuse further loans to the debtor, it may be difficult for it to obtain finance from the subsequent creditors if they are to receive only a subordinate interest in the collateral.[53] Allowing the prior secured creditor to enhance its security at the expense of the subsequent secured creditor providing fresh finance to the debtor can also be inequitable.[54]

To avoid the pervasiveness of the after-acquired property clause, some legal systems allow the debtor to grant a purchase money security interest (PMSI) to its subsequent creditor.[55] The PMSI is usually linked to a specifically identified object, acquired by the debtor either on credit or with the help of the money provided by the subsequent creditor. The PMSI allows

[51] Jackson and Kronman (n 2) 1167.

[52] See R Hakes, 'According Purchase Money Status Proper Priority' (1993) 72 *Or L Rev* 323; K Meyer, 'A Primer on Purchase Money Security Interests Under Revised Article 9 of the Uniform Commercial Code' (2001) 50 *U Kan L Rev* 143; H Flechtner, 'Inflatable Liens and Like Phenomena: Converting Unsecured Debt Under UCC Article 9 and the Bankruptcy Code' (1987) 72 *Cornell L Rev* 696.

[53] N Hansford, 'The Purchase Money Security Interest in Inventory Versus the After-Acquired Property Interest—A 'No Win' Situation' (1986) 20 *U Rich L Rev* 135, 240–42.

[54] Gullifer (n 32) 213.

[55] For example, §9-324 UCC provides that a PMSI has priority over a prior conflicting security even if the PMSI is later perfected. §9-324(a) states that to assert priority over a prior security interest the PMSI holder has to perfect within 20 days after the debtor receives possession. The status of the PMSI under English law is less clear. The cases dealing with the PMSI situation are primarily concerned with prior secured creditor with a security in present and future property of the debtor and a mortgagee providing the debtor with a loan for the purchase of land. Cases decided before *Abbey National Building Society v Cann* [1991] AC 56 dealt with the priority conflict between the secured creditors by analysing whether there was a moment in time (*scintilla temporis*) when the debtor received an unencumbered title to the property during which time the first security interest could attach to it. If no such time existed, then the first secured creditor's security attached to the already encumbered title of the debtor and the second secured creditor won. *Abbey National Building Society v Cann* [1991] AC 56 rejected the *scintilla temporis* analysis and emphasised the need to look at the commercial reality of such cases: the PMSI creditor won as the acquisition of property and the mortgage money used to finance it were bound together so that the debtor never received an unencumbered title to the land. For the discussion of the PMSI problems in the context of English law, see G McCormack, 'Charges and Priorities—The Death of the Scintilla Temporis Doctrine' (1991) *Company Lawyer* 11; C Davis and H Bennett, 'Fixtures, Purchase Money Security Interests and Dispositions of Interests in Land' (1994) *LQR* 448; J Jeremie, 'Gone in an Instant—the Death of 'Scintilla Temporis' and the Growth of a Purchase-Money Security Interest in Real Property Law' (1994) *JBL* 363; JD Lacy, 'Retention of Title, Company Charges and the Scintilla Temporis Doctrine' (1994) *Conveyancer and Property Lawyer* 242. See also *Abbey National Building Society v Cann* [1991] AC 56; *Re Connolly Bros Ltd (2)* [1912] 2 Ch 25; *Wilson v Kelland* [1910] 2 Ch 25; *Church of England Building Society v Piskor* [1954] Ch 553.

the subsequent creditor to overcome the priority of the first-in-time creditor and to assert its own priority over the object, acquired by the debtor with the loan provided by it.

Since the PMSI's primary purpose is to avoid the effects of the after-acquired property clause, it will only be needed if such a clause can, in principle, be incorporated into the security agreement.[56] The creation and registration[57] of the CTC's international interests in the aircraft objects require their unique identification by manufacturer's name, serial number and model designation.[58] Consequently, it is unlikely that an after-acquired property clause, relating to future *unidentified* objects can be incorporated into the international interest agreement.[59] The position is slightly different in relation to railway objects and space assets, which need not be uniquely identified at the stage of the creation of the international interest.[60] This means that, in principle, it should be possible to include an after-acquired property clause in the international interest agreements relating to unidentified future railway objects and space assets. However, the utility of such a clause will be limited, because the registration of interests held in these objects still requires unique identification.[61]

The requirement of unique identification of the objects for the registration militates against an effective after-acquired property clause covering unidentified future objects. Consequently, there will, generally, be no need for a PMSI under the Convention and, for this reason the latter does not provide any special super-priority to such a device.[62] The prior creditor's security interest will be confined to the uniquely identified objects listed in its registration information and any new objects, acquired by the debtor will not be automatically covered by the registered interest. If the prior creditor agrees to provide finance for the acquisition of a new object, the parties will have to register a fresh international interest relating to it. If the finance is provided by a different creditor, there will be nothing to prevent the parties from registering a security interest in its favour, which will allow it to assert priority in relation to this object.

[56] D Carlson, 'Purchase Money under the Uniform Commercial Code' (1993) 29 *Idaho L Rev* 793, 795.

[57] Art 18(1) CTC provides that the Protocol and Regulations should provide the object identification requirements. Sec 5.3(c) of the Regulations and Procedures for the International Registry (International Civil Aviation Organization, Doc 9864, 6th edn 2014) provides such requirements. (Further referred to as the Regulations.)

[58] Art VII of the Aircraft Protocol.

[59] Goode (n 5) 99.

[60] Art V of the Luxembourg Protocol and Art VII of the Space Protocol.

[61] Art XIV of the Luxembourg Protocol and Art XXX of the Space Protocol provide that the Regulations will provide the necessary identification requirements.

[62] Goode (n 5) 100.

B. The Possibility of a Purchase Money Security Interest under the Convention

Although the previous section suggests that there is no possibility for the creation of a PMSI, a situation akin to it may arise under the Convention in limited circumstances. Consider the following example. A secured creditor finances the acquisition by the debtor of a uniquely identified airframe and two aircraft engines and duly registers its international interests in the IR. A year later, a computer system installed on the airframe and the engines' modules requires replacement. Assume that the computer system is easily detachable from the airframe and does not lose its identity once installed on it. The situation with the modules is less clear as, once installed, it may be difficult to distinguish which module belongs to a particular manufacturer.

Although the secured creditor refuses to provide finance to the debtor for the purchase of the necessary replacements, an aircraft manufacturer is willing to lease them to the debtor. Since computer systems and engine modules do not constitute aircraft objects under the Convention, the manufacturer/lessor is unable to register its interest in them in the IR. On the debtor's default, the secured creditor wants to take possession and sell the airframe and the engines. It considers the computer system and the modules as parts of the airframe and the engines and claims that its security automatically covers these items as they do not represent separate aircraft objects.[63] If the secured creditor is successful in its claim, it would achieve a similar result as a creditor with an after-acquired property clause in its security agreement. Admittedly, the secured creditor does not purport to cover any newly acquired aircraft *objects*, as defined by the Convention, by its existing security interest. But the effect would be similar: it would allow the secured creditor to join to its security new *items*, the acquisition of which was financed by another creditor.

The attempt of the secured creditor to extend its priority to subsequently acquired items financed by a different creditor would be in line with the doctrine of 'accession' known to many legal systems. The main idea underlying this doctrine is that if an object owned by one person is attached to the object owned by another person forming a whole product, the owner of the principal object will acquire property in the whole by way of accession.[64] The doctrine of accession can be justified by the need to preserve the integrity of the main object[65] and will, generally, apply if the removal of the

[63] See also Art I(2)(b), (e) of the Aircraft Protocol, specifying that aircraft engines and airframes include all modules and other installed, incorporated or attached accessories.

[64] A Guest, 'Accession and Confusion in the Law of Hire-Purchase' (1964) 27 *MLR* 505, 507.

[65] Goode (n 5) 339.

attached object cannot be accomplished without destruction of or serious injury to the whole product.[66]

However, these attached items often have high value and to allow the lessor the possibility of preserving its interest in them the Convention takes the following approach. While the Aircraft Protocol[67] defines an aircraft engine and an airframe as inclusive of all parts and treats them as *items* rather than *objects* so that a separate interest in them is not registrable, these definitions must be read together with Article 29(7)(a) and (b) CTC.[68] Article 29(7)(a) recognises that another party may hold an interest in an item and states that the Convention 'does not affect the rights of a person in an item, other than an object, held prior to its installation on the object if under the applicable law those rights continue to exist after the installation'. Accordingly, the Convention does not implicitly support the doctrine of accession and the lessor's ability to preserve its pre-existing rights in these items will depend on how such rights are treated under the applicable law.[69]

The computer system, which is easily detachable and does not lose its identity on installation or removal from the airframe, may be considered as a separate item, in relation to which an interest can be created under the applicable law. This means that the lessor may be able to retain its pre-existing interest in it, if the applicable law permits. In this case, the secured creditor will claim priority in the airframe and the engines and the lessor will retain its priority in relation to the computer system. This outcome will have the *effect* of the PMSI under the Convention as the second-in-time holder of a non-registrable interest in an item who financed its acquisition will gain priority over the first-in-time holder of a registered security interest. If this analysis is correct, it would mean that although it is, generally, not possible to register a PMSI under the Convention, a situation similar to the PMSI may arise under it in limited circumstances.

This is also true in relation to Article 29(7)(b), stating that the Convention 'does not prevent the creation of rights in an item other than an object, which has previously been installed on an object where under the applicable law those rights are created'. This provision envisages a situation where an item, other than an object, has been installed on an object and later removed from it and states that, if the applicable domestic law so permits, rights in such an item can be created.[70] The aim of paragraph 7(b) is not to lay down a priority rule but to ensure that if the applicable law offers protection to a right in an item when it was installed and later removed from it, the

66 See Guest (n 64) 507–10.
67 Art I(2)(b), (e).
68 Goode (n 5) 430.
69 Goode (n 24) 99.
70 Goode (n 5) 338.

Convention will indorse such protection. At the same time, if the applicable law transfers the right or interest in the smaller item to the holder of the interest in the principal object by way of accession, the pre-existing right in the item will be lost. In this way, Article 29(7) may have the effect of changing the order of priority by promoting the holder of an unregistered interest in an item ahead of the holder of the registered interest in the object.

It can be argued that the fact that the Convention delegates the issue of priorities between the interests held in an object and an item to the applicable law is regrettable. If the interests in items, and not just objects, could be registered under the Convention, it would have been possible to design a clearer rule with respect to the interests in items. However, it may well be that not all such items and spare parts are capable of unique identification and their registration in the IR would not be feasible. Since the issue is delegated to the applicable law, the results may differ in each case. For instance, the issue of modules installed on the aircraft engines may be resolved differently by various legal systems. If these items are treated as an accessory to the main object which is capable of being separately owned, then the lessor may be able to retain its rights in them. In contrast, if the modules are considered as part of the principal object by the applicable domestic law, then the lessor's interest will be transferred to the secured creditor.[71]

IV. EXCEPTIONS TO THE GENERAL RULE OF PRIORITY

A. General

Many legal systems resolve priority conflicts between competing interests based on some form of a first-in-time rule. The priorities may be determined on a first-in-time of the creation or registration basis, but the underlying idea of these rules is usually the same: once the debtor grants a security interest in its object to SC1, it cannot grant the same interest to SC2. In other words, one cannot give what one has not got.[72] All that the debtor will be able to give to SC2 is whatever is left after the disposition to SC1, namely the interest in the object encumbered by the security interest of SC1. This explains why the interest of the subsequent creditor is, generally, subjected to the interest of the previous creditor. When priorities are determined by the order of registration, the holders of competing interests may rely on the registration system. They can search the registry in order to assess their

[71] See, for example, *Hendy Lennox (Industrial Engines) Ltd v Grahame Puttick Ltd* [1984] WLR 485, where the engines, incorporated into the generators and sold subject to the retention of title (RoT) clause, could be detached from the generators, rendering the clause effective.

[72] This principle is also known as *nemo dat quod non habet*. See Beale, Bridge, Gullifer, Lomnicka (n 9) 460.

potential priority position among other creditors. Once the interest is registered, its holder may expect other searchers to recognise its priority. This is why exceptions to the general priority rule are best kept to a minimum. The CTC provides several exceptions to the first-to-register rule. These are considered below.

B. The Exception of an Outright Buyer and the Possibility of 'Cross Over' Protection

i. Outright Buyer

The first exception to the general rule relates to the position of an outright buyer. The Convention does not govern an outright sale of objects as it is primarily concerned with the interests arising out of the secured credit, conditional sale and lease. However, many legal systems recognise the importance of an outright buyer's position and this is why the Convention designed a specific rule, giving it priority in certain circumstances.[73] First, Article 29(3)(a) provides that the buyer of an object acquires its interest in it 'subject to an interest registered at the time of its acquisition of that interest'. It can be argued that this rule can hardly be considered as an exception to the general priority rule as it merely postpones the unregistered interest of the buyer to a prior registered interest. However, the buyer whose interest is not registrable in the IR and who, for this reason, may not be expected to search it, will have to do so before making the decision as to the acquisition of the object or risk subordination to a prior registered interest.[74]

Further, Article 29(3)(b) stipulates that the buyer acquires its interest in the object 'free from an unregistered interest even if it has actual knowledge of such an interest'. Although the Convention does not govern the priority between unregistered interests, in this case, as between an unregistered international interest and the unregistered interest of the buyer, the interest of the latter will have priority. This rule is a true exception to the general priority rule, but the seller must necessarily have the power to dispose of the object for it to operate.[75] For example, if a debtor grants a security interest

[73] Art 29(3). For example, the general rule that the security interest is effective against purchasers of the collateral stated in §9-201(a) UCC is subject to a number of exceptions. See *Martin Bros Implement Co v Diepholz*, 109 Ill App 3d 283, 64 Ill. Dec 768, 440 NE 2d 320 34 UCC 1749(1982); *O M Scott Credit Corp v Apex, Inc*, 97 R I 442, 198 A 2d 673, 2 UCC 92(1964); *Hempstead Bank v Andy's Car Rental System, Inc* 35 AD 2d 35, 312 NYS 2d 317, 7 UCC 932 (1972).

[74] Under English law, the buyer in the ordinary course of business is not expected to search the registry as its own interest is not registrable. See G McCormack, 'Priority of Charges and Registration' (1994) *JBL* 587, 598.

[75] Goode (n 5) 335.

in the object to a secured creditor on 1 May (who registers on 20 May) and sells the same object to the buyer on 5 May, the buyer will take free of the unregistered interest of the secured creditor even if it had actual knowledge of its interest and even if the secured creditor's interest is later registered. This way, the buyer can rely on the information found in the IR which helps maintain the system's integrity.

Although Article 29(3) introduces an exception to the general rule by granting priority to the unregistrable interest of the buyer, its effect is limited. This is because the Aircraft Protocol[76] disapplies Article 29(3) by rendering an outright sale and prospective sale of aircraft objects registrable in the IR. The order of priority between registrable interests and the interest of the buyer of an aircraft object will depend on the order of their registration. The Aircraft Protocol adopts a similar rule to the one under Article 29(1) in relation to the registrable interest of the buyer. Accordingly, a buyer of an aircraft object under a registered sale 'acquires its interest in that object free from an interest subsequently registered and from an unregistered interest'.[77] Where the debtor first grants a security interest in an aircraft engine and then sells the same engine to the buyer, the security interest will be extinguished if the secured creditor fails to register or registers its interest after the buyer registers the sale. Similar to the rule in Article 29(1), the buyer's interest in the aircraft object will be subjected to a prior registered interest.[78]

ii. The Possibility of 'Cross Over' Protection

The fact that it is possible to register a sale of an aircraft object in the IR may lead to a situation where the same party is holding two separately registrable interests: one as the buyer under the outright sale and one as the holder of some other registrable interest.[79] For example, a party who purchases the airframe from a seller can lease it to a lessee under a leasing agreement.[80] It will have two registrable interests and can register both the

[76] Art III of the Aircraft Protocol.

[77] Art XIV(1) of the Aircraft Protocol.

[78] Art IV(2) of the Aircraft Protocol. The position is similar under Art IV and Art XXIII of the Space Protocol, rendering outright sale of space assets registrable in the IR. The Luxembourg Protocol takes a different approach as it does not allow for the registration of an outright or prospective sale of the railway rolling stock. It will only be possible to register a notice of sale. See Art XVII of the Luxembourg Protocol. See R Goode, *Official Commentary to the Convention on International Interests in Mobile Equipment and Luxembourg Protocol Thereto on Matters Specific to Railway Rolling Stock* (Rome, UNIROIT 2008) 322.

[79] Goode (n 5) 218. Several registrable interests may be held by the same holder even in a situation not involving the sale. For instance, on the debtor's default, the secured creditor holding a registered international interest can repossess and lease the aircraft object. In this case, the secured creditor can register a second international interest arising under the lease.

[80] This example is provided in the Commentary, see Goode (n 5) 218.

sale (as the buyer) and the international interest (as the lessor). The issue here is whether the holder of two registrable interests can achieve overall protection against competing interests if it registers only one of such interests and not the other.

The buyer will want to protect its interest in the object against the other buyers and creditors of the seller. Similarly, when acting in the capacity of the lessor, it will want to protect its interest in the object against the buyers and the creditors of the lessee. If the buyer registers the sale, it will be protected against dispositions of its own seller. For example, the seller may first grant a security interest in an object to a secured creditor, who fails to register its interest, and then sell it to the buyer, who immediately registers the sale. In this case, the buyer's registered interest will have priority over the earlier created but unregistered interest of the secured creditor.[81] The OC states that the registration of the sale will also protect the buyer against a possible second sale of the same object by the seller to another buyer.[82] Thus, if the seller first sells the object to the buyer, who immediately registers the sale, and then sells the same airframe to the second buyer, who also registers the sale, the earlier registered buyer will gain priority. However, this situation will only rarely arise because outright sale usually involves the transfer of ownership and possession of the object. This means that when attempting to sell the same object for the second time, the seller will not have the power to dispose of it and the purported registration will be ineffective.

While the registration of the sale will undoubtedly protect the buyer from the dispositions of the seller, it is not clear whether it will also protect it from the dispositions of the lessee. The position under the OC is that the registration of only one of the registrable interests will not afford its holder protection against the consequences of a failure to register the other interest.[83] So, if the buyer registers the sale and does not register its international interest arising under the lease, this registration will protect the buyer against its own seller's creditors and buyers, but will not protect it against the buyers and the creditors of the lessee. In other words, each registrable interest requires a separate registration and registration of only one registrable interest does not provide a 'cross over' protection to its holder.[84]

What could be the rationale for the position taken by the OC? The registration of all registrable interests held by the same party has undisputable benefits. Registrable interests are different in nature and duration and, for this reason, should be registered separately. For instance, a secured creditor may register its international interest in the object and, following the

[81] Art XIV(1) of the Aircraft Protocol.
[82] Goode (n 5) 215.
[83] *Ibid* 218.
[84] *Ibid* 218.

debtor's default, take possession, lease it and register the second international interest in the same object. Once the lease expires, the international interest relating to it will be discharged. But the security interest will continue to encumber the object until the debt is repaid. In addition, the registration of all interests, held by the same party, can ensure that these interests are visible and that the registration system is transparent, which can assist the searcher in ascertaining its priority.

However, does this necessarily mean that if the holder of two separately registrable interests only registers one of them, it cannot gain 'cross over' protection against competing interests? The position, advanced in the OC, that there should be no 'cross over' protection,[85] is based on the wording of Article XIV(1) of the Aircraft Protocol, stating that 'a buyer of an aircraft object under a registered sale acquires *its interest* in that object free from an interest subsequently registered and from an unregistered interest'. The OC explains that the words 'its interest' carry the meaning that protection is only offered to the holder of the registered sale *as the buyer*. This is why the buyer cannot, by registering the sale, gain protection *as the lessor* against possible dispositions of the lessee.

It seems that the text of Article XIV(1) does not provide sufficient support for this view. The overall purpose of this provision is to extend the general priority rule, established under Article 29(1), to outright sale of aircraft objects. Article XIV(1) simply states that the buyer under the registered sale acquires its interest in the object free from the subsequently registered and unregistered interests. In contrast, if a competing interest is registered prior to the sale, this earlier registered interest will get priority over the sale.[86] Since the purpose of the provision is to extend the general priority rule to outright sale, it is natural that it refers to the buyer's interest in the object by using the words 'its interest'. These words do not necessarily carry the meaning ascribed to them by the OC. It would have been different if, for instance, the text of Article XIV(1) had stated that the buyer of an aircraft object under a registered sale acquired its interest in that object free from an interest *granted by its seller* that is subsequently registered or unregistered. This wording would clearly convey the message that the registration in the capacity of the buyer will only protect its holder against the dispositions of the seller and will not lead to cross-over protection.

More importantly, it is not clear why various registered interests should attract different types of protection as suggested by the OC. In other words, why should the scope of the protection afforded by the registration depend on the type of the registered interest, so that its holder is shielded against one line of competing interests, but not against the other line? The IR is an

[85] *Ibid* 219.

[86] Art XIV(2) of the Aircraft Protocol.

asset-based system and registrations in it are made against uniquely identifiable objects. This means that a registered interest arising under a sale or a lease will be visible to a searcher. So if the holder of two registrable interests arising under the sale and lease registers only the interest relating to the sale, this registration will be visible both to the creditors of the seller and the lessee. Since the registration of the sale will be accomplished prior to the registration of the interests held by the lessee's creditors and because this prior registration can be viewed by such creditors there seems to be no reason why the earlier registration of the buyer should not bind the subsequent registrations of the lessee's creditors. The OC indicates that in this case, the lessee's creditors may be led to believe that the buyer sold the object to the lessee and that this sale was not registered.[87] But this does not explain why the prior registered and visible interest of the buyer/lessor should not bind the subsequently registered interest of the lessee's creditor. Moreover, being a notice-based system, the IR provides only some basic information regarding the registered interests. This means that a prospective creditor will have to make enquiries once it receives the search certificate. It is not unlikely that in the course of such enquiries this uncertainty will be clarified.

To summarise, it is clearly advisable to register all interests held by the same party in the object separately. At the same time, it is submitted that there is no reason why cross-over protection cannot be achieved by the registration of one and not all of the registrable interests held by the same party. First, the text of the Aircraft Protocol does not lend clear enough support to the view that the registration of the buyer's interest under the sale will only protect it against the seller's dispositions. Secondly, since the IR is asset-based, the searcher will be able to see all registered interests encumbering the object. Consequently, the searcher, considering advancing a loan to the lessee will be able to see the registered interest of the buyer and will be bound by it, even if the buyer failed to register another registrable interest, held by it. Being the holder of the earlier registered interest, the buyer will take 'free from an interest subsequently registered' by the third party.[88] Finally, the overall purpose of Article XIV(1) of the Protocol is to extend the CTC's general rule to the outright sale of aircraft objects.[89] Apart from established exceptions, the CTC does not limit the scope of the protection available to the holder of the registered interest based on its type. So, if the creditor acts both as a secured creditor and as a lessor and registers both international interests, it is unlikely that the registered interest of the secured creditor will only protect it against the debtor's dispositions. Similarly, it is unlikely that the registered interest of the lessor will only protect it against

[87] Goode (n 5) 219.
[88] Art XIV(1) of the Aircraft Protocol.
[89] Goode (n 5) 466.

the lessee's dispositions. Article 29(1) provides that a registered interest has priority over 'any' other interest subsequently registered and over an unregistered interest. This must be correct because a third party searching the IR will find all registered interests held in the object and will be bound by them. If the purpose of Article XIV(1) of the Protocol is to extend this rule to outright sales, the same idea as the one underpinning the general rule should apply to it. For these reasons, it is submitted that the registration of sale should not confine the protection afforded to the buyer to the dispositions of the seller and can be used to shield it against other subsequently registered or unregistered interests.

C. Conditional Buyer and Lessee

The second exception to the general priority rule is designed to protect the non-registrable interests of the conditional buyer and lessee against the creditor of their seller and lessor. The Convention provides that the interest of the conditional buyer or lessee will be subjected to an interest registered *prior* to the registration of the interest held by their conditional seller or lessor.[90] For example, if a debtor first grants a security interest in an airframe to the secured creditor, who immediately registers its interest, and then leases the same airframe to the lessee and registers its interest as the lessor, the lessee will take the lease subject to the previously registered interest of the secured creditor. Consequently, if the debtor/lessor defaults, the secured creditor will be able to enforce its international interest without regard to the interest of the lessee.

In contrast, if the conditional seller or lessor registers its interest in the object *before* its own creditor, the conditional buyer or lessee will take 'free from the interest not so registered at that time'.[91] This will be the case even if the conditional buyer or lessee had actual knowledge of the creditor's unregistered interest.[92] The protection of the conditional buyer or lessee will depend on the status of the registered interest of the conditional seller or lessor. Should such interest be discharged, the protection will be lifted and the interest of the conditional buyer and lessee will be subordinated to the creditor's registered interest. The Convention's protection of the conditional buyer's and lessee's position amounts to a true exception to the general priority rule because it allows them to take their non-registrable interest free from a subsequently registered or unregistered interest of the conditional seller's and lessor's creditor.

[90] Art 29(4)(a) CTC.
[91] Art 29(4)(b) CTC.
[92] Art 29(4)(b) CTC.

However, it can be argued that the effectiveness of this protection is limited and, for this reason, not entirely satisfactory. Consider a debtor who leases an airframe to the lessee and registers its international interest as the lessor. Suppose further that the lessor grants a security interest in the same airframe to the secured creditor, who also registers its interest. In this case, the lessee's interest will be 'free' from the secured creditor's subsequently registered interest.[93] The extent of such freedom is not quite clear. If the lessor defaults both under the lease agreement (by delivering the airframe late) and the security agreement (by late payment), will 'priority' of the lessee entitle it to *enforce* its interest (for example, by claiming payment of a certain sum for late delivery) in priority to the secured creditor? Alternatively, does freedom from the subsequently registered interest of the secured creditor mean only that the lessee can *resist* enforcement of the secured creditor's interest in a manner leading to interference with lessee's possession and use of the airframe? If this is the case, then while the secured creditor may not be entitled to take possession of the airframe, it may be able to enforce its security in the manner not involving divesting the lessee of possession. In other words, can the lessor's registration of the international interest afford the lessee a fully-fledged priority as if it too were a holder of a registered interest or is the scope of priority enjoyed by the lessee limited to the protection of its possession of the object?

This issue has not yet been tested in courts and the answer to it is unclear. On the one hand, the text of Article 29(4)(b), providing that where the lessor registers its interest ahead of another holder of the international interest, the lessee takes 'free from an interest not so registered at that time', seems to suggest that the lessee should enjoy full priority. On the other hand, if the effect of the lessor's timely registration is to confer full priority on the lessee, this would mean that the lessee would have the same status as if it too were a holder of a registrable and registered interest. Had the intention of the drafters been to treat the lessee as a holder of a registrable interest, it would not have been difficult to include the interest of the lessee in the list of registrable interests. Alternatively, the Convention could have provided that where the lessor registered its interest ahead of its own creditor, the lessee should be treated as if it were the holder of a registered international interest.

Another factor indicating that it is unlikely that the lessee is entitled to enjoy full priority can be the ease with which this protection can be taken away from it. Since the protection of the lessee depends on the effectiveness of the registration of the lessor's interest, this must mean that once the interest of the lessor is discharged from the IR, the priority of the

[93] Art 29(4) CTC.

lessee's interest vanishes too.[94] Not only will the lessee's protection evaporate once the lessor's registered interest is discharged, the discharge can happen without the lessee's consent.[95] The discharge of the international interest requires consent of the 'named party' or 'parties benefiting from the registered interest' or 'the party holding the right to consent to the discharge'[96] and the debtor cannot act as any of these parties.[97] Since the lessee acts as the lessor's debtor, the lessor will not need to procure its consent to discharge its interest even though the lessee can clearly be viewed as a party benefiting from the lessor's registered interest.

Finally, it seems that the scope of protection afforded to the lessee by means of the lessor's registered interest is circumscribed by the regime of quiet possession under Article XVI(1) of the Aircraft Protocol.[98] This provision is textually linked to Article 29(4) and aims to reinforce the protection available to the conditional buyer and lessee by granting them a right of quiet possession and use of the aircraft object provided that they are not in default. It is suggested that this provision not only bolsters the protection of the lessee and conditional buyer but also outlines the limitations of this protection. The right of quiet possession can prove invaluable in practice because it can shield the interests of the lessee and the conditional buyer from third parties' claims. Although not a priority rule, the quiet possession regime can have an effect on the order of priority between competing interests. In particular, if it is successfully asserted, the right of quiet possession can afford the conditional buyer and lessee the priority over the holders of registered competing interests. The Protocol further provides that even where, as a result of Article 29(4) CTC, the interest of the conditional buyer and lessee is subjected to the earlier registered interest of the conditional seller's and lessor's creditor, the conditional buyer and lessee can still enjoy quiet possession if the holder of the earlier registered interest so agrees.[99]

The Aircraft Protocol does not provide a definition of what amounts to quiet possession and how exactly it can be breached. The OC helpfully explains that 'the concept of quiet possession denotes freedom from interference with the debtor's possession, use or enjoyment of the aircraft object'.[100] Accordingly, any such interference including 'physical seizure, disablement of the aircraft object or restriction of access to it' can amount

[94] Goode (n 5) 336.

[95] *Practitioners' Guide* (n 23) 96.

[96] Sec 5.7 of the Regulations.

[97] Sec 5.7.1 of the Regulations.

[98] Similarly, Art XXV(1) of the Space Protocol and Art XI(1) of the Luxembourg Protocol provide for the regime of quiet possession. The Aircraft Protocol extends the regime of quiet possession to an outright buyer. See Art XIV(1) and Art XVI(1) of the Aircraft Protocol.

[99] Art XVI(1)(b).

[100] Goode (n 5) 222.

to a breach of the right of quiet possession.[101] Thus, unless the lessee is in default, the lessor's repossession of the aircraft object will amount to the interference with its right to quiet possession. The cases of disablement or restriction of use can include a situation where, for instance, a lessor places a device on the computer system used in the aircraft object, enabling it to control its use. Following a dispute, the lessor can activate the device preventing the object from being used. Provided that the lessee was not in default, the lessor would be in breach of the right of quiet possession under the Protocol.[102]

The regime of quite possession poses several questions. First, the Aircraft Protocol provides that the debtor '*shall be entitled* to the quiet possession ... *in accordance with* agreement'.[103] Thus, if the agreement is silent, the Protocol cannot be utilised to invoke the quiet possession regime. It is, however, possible that even if the agreement does not expressly mention the right of quiet possession, the relevant term can still be implied in the contract under the applicable law.[104] Secondly, even if the agreement does contain a quiet possession clause, it is not clear whether it will be binding on the creditors of the conditional seller or lessor, who are not privy to that agreement. The Protocol specifies the parties against which the debtor can assert the right of quiet possession.[105] Absent default, the conditional buyer or lessor is entitled to quiet possession against its own creditor and against 'the holder of any interest from which the debtor takes free pursuant to Article 29(4) of the Convention'.[106] In other words, the Protocol protects the conditional buyer and lessee against its conditional seller and lessor and the creditors of such, provided that the conditional seller and lessor registered their interest ahead of their own creditors. This provision seems to create a direct right in the debtor, exercisable against not only the conditional seller and lessor, but also against their creditors. But even if the extended quiet possession clause,

[101] *Ibid* 222.

[102] See, for instance, *Rubicon Computer Systems Ltd v United Paints Ltd* (2002) 2 TCLR 454, where the seller supplied a computer system to the buyer. Unknown to the buyer, the seller placed a device into the computer known as the 'time lock'. Following a dispute, the seller activated the time lock, preventing the computer from being used. This case did not involve physical seizure and the object remained in the buyer's possession. Still, it was held that since the buyer could not use the computer, its quiet possession right was infringed by the seller.

[103] Art XVI(1) of the Aircraft Protocol (emphasis added).

[104] See, for instance, *Microbeads AG and Another v Vinhurst Markings Ltd* [1975] 1 WLR 218, where the seller sold to the buyer road marking machines. The sale occurred before a third party published and obtained patent in road marking machines developed by it, but the description of the machines sold to the buyer fell under the patent specification. This amounted to a breach by the seller of the implied term under s 12(2)(b) of the Sale of Goods Act 1893, stating that the buyer 'shall have and enjoy quiet possession of the goods'.

[105] Art XVI(1)(a), (b) of the Aircraft Protocol.

[106] Art XVI(1)(a) of the Aircraft Protocol.

exercisable against the debtor's own creditor and those who claim under it, is incorporated in the agreement, it is doubtful whether it will bind third parties. To give effect to Article XVI(1), it seems that the clause regarding the debtor's right of quiet possession should be included both in its agreement with its own creditor and also in the agreement between the creditor and other third parties. This may be difficult to achieve because a third party may not agree to the debtor's right of quiet possession and also because it may be difficult to identify all potential third parties that may disturb the debtor's quiet possession. If this is the case, then it seems that the Protocol's regime of quiet possession may not be as effective as the conditional buyer or lessee may have hoped. However, assuming that the right of quiet possession can be successfully asserted against the conditional seller or lessor and their creditors, the availability of this right indicates that the protection afforded to the conditional buyer and lessee under Article 29(4) CTC and Article XVI(1) of the Protocol is limited and confined to the right of quiet possession and use of the object and does not confer a fully-fledged priority to these parties.[107]

D. Non-Registrable Rights and Interests Arising as a Result of Declaration under Article 39[108]

A Contracting State can make the Article 39 declaration, which may have the effect of promoting certain non-registrable NCRIs ahead of the registered international interests. Examples of NCRIs include non-consensual liens, relating to repairs of objects in their possession, or non-consensual liens, relating to aircraft for unpaid navigation, fuel, maintenance and other charges.[109] In order to be covered by a declaration, the NCRI must have priority without registration over an interest that is considered as an equivalent of an international interest under the law of the Contracting State. For instance, the debtor may grant a security interest in an aircraft engine to the secured creditor, who registers its interest in the IR. It may later transpire that the object was delivered for repairs to A. Provided that the interest held by A in the engine is one of the NCRI in relation to which the Article 39 declaration was made, the secured creditor will be subordinated

[107] Similarly, the UNCITRAL Legislative Guide on Secured Transactions states at para 77, p 204 that, generally, 'the issue is not whether the lessee actually takes the asset free of the security right in the sense that the security right is cut off. Rather, the issue is whether the lessee's right to use the leased asset under the terms and conditions set forth in the lease agreement are unaffected by the security right. The key point is whether … the lessee can continue using the asset so long as it continues to … abide by the terms of the lease'.

[108] See further chapters two and three.

[109] See, generally, Goode (n 5) 374–78.

to the repairer's interest. In other words, A's second-in-time and unregistrable interest will take priority over the secured creditor's first-in-time registered interest.[110]

E. Pre-Existing Right or Interest

The next exception relates to the rights and interests, created before the Convention came into force or before a State became a Contracting State. There was some debate as to whether the Convention should apply to a pre-existing right or interest (PERI) and if so, whether it should require re-registration in the IR to be effective. On one view, re-registration was not necessary. On another view, it was thought that if a PERI was not required to be registered in the IR, the holders of the post-Convention interests might be subordinated to pre-Convention rights and interests, the existence of which they could not discover.[111]

Article 60 offers a compromise solution to this debate. It establishes a general rule that the Convention does not apply to a PERI and that it retains the priority it enjoyed under the applicable law before the Convention became effective.[112] The holder of such a right or interest cannot rely on the CTC's rules of priority or enforce its remedies and the matter should be resolved by the applicable law. The date when the Convention becomes effective for this purpose is either when it comes into force or when the State in which the debtor is located becomes a Contracting State.[113] The Convention becomes effective in relation to any particular category of objects when the relevant Protocol comes into force.[114]

The general rule that the Convention does not apply to a PERI may be modified by a declaration that a Contracting State can make under Article 60(3).[115] The Contracting State must indicate in its declaration a date, not earlier than three years after the declaration becomes effective, when the Convention and the Protocol will become applicable to a PERI.[116] For the Convention and the declaration to apply, the PERI must arise out of an agreement concluded when the debtor was situated in the State.[117]

[110] See, generally, A Bell, 'The Priority of General Liens' (1986) *Company Lawyer* 164.

[111] R Goode, 'The Cape Town Convention on International Interests in Mobile Equipment: A Driving Force for International Asset-Based Financing' (2003) 36 *UCC LJ* 2 Art 1.

[112] Art 60(1) CTC.

[113] Art 60(2)(a) CTC.

[114] Art 49(1) CTC.

[115] Once made, the declaration cannot be withdrawn or modified. See Arts 57(1) and 58(1) CTC.

[116] Art 60(3) CTC. Art XXVI of the Luxembourg Protocol provides that the date, indicated in the declaration, must not be earlier than three and later than 10 years. See H Rosen, 'The Luxembourg Rail Protocol: A Major Advance for the Railway Industry' (2007) *Unif L Rev* 427, 444.

[117] Art 60(3) CTC.

So, if the debtor's centre of administration, place of business or habitual residence is located in a State[118] which has not made a declaration and the debtor grants a security interest to a secured creditor in an airframe, the Convention will not apply to such a security interest. The situation may change if the State becomes a Contracting State and makes a declaration that the Convention will apply, for determining priority, to a PERI within three years after the declaration becomes effective. Re-registration in the IR will help the creditor to ensure that, once the period specified in the declaration lapses, its pre-Convention interest will continue to enjoy priority over the interest registered in the IR, and its Convention priority in relation to the subsequently registered and unregistered interests will be established.[119]

The purpose of the specified period is to provide the holders of a PERI with sufficient time to register their interests in the IR. It also helps to ensure that the holders of the post-Convention interests will not be subordinated to pre-Convention rights and interests, the existence of which they could not discover.[120] Finally, when the Convention and the Protocol become applicable under the declaration, they will only apply for determining priority, including the protection of any existing priority of a PERI.[121] It is not clear why the Convention does not allow the holders of a PERI to invoke its remedial provisions. The explanation may be found in the purpose of the declaration, namely to establish a cutting-off point, after which the PERIs would lose their priority, not to extend the Convention to them.[122]

How can a PERI constitute an exception to the CTC's general rule of priority? Consider a debtor,[123] granting security interests in an object to secured creditor 1 (SC1) and secured creditor 2 (SC2). Both SC1 and SC2 registered their interests in the national registry where priority is determined by the order of registration. A year later, the State has become a Contracting State and made the Article 60(3) declaration, specifying that the Convention would apply to a PERI on the expiration of a three-year period from the date of the declaration. A year later, the debtor grants SC3 a security interest in the same object and SC3, after searching the IR and obtaining a clear search, assumes that it will be the first holder of a registered security and immediately registers its interest. Six months later, SC2 registers its interest in the IR and, three years later, SC1 also registers its security interest there. SC2's security interest, although registered later in the IR, will have priority over SC3's interest because the declaration protects the pre-Convention priority of a PERI. Since SC1 registered outside the specified period, it lost its

118 Art 60(2)(b) CTC defines the location of the debtor for these purposes.

119 Goode (n 5) 414.

120 See, generally, Goode (n 5) 411–15.

121 Art 60(3) CTC.

122 Rosen (n 116) 445.

123 Assume that the debtor is situated in a State as required by Art 60(2)(b) CTC.

priority to other creditors. Although Article 60 may create an exception to the general rule of priority, it seems unlikely that it will become of frequent use: to date, only two Contracting States have made a declaration relating to PERIs.[124]

F. Variation Agreements

In conformity with the principle of party autonomy underlying the Convention, the general rule that a registered interest has priority over subsequently registered and unregistered interests may be varied by an agreement changing the order of priorities between competing creditors.[125] As a result of the variation or subordination agreement, a registered interest can be postponed to a subsequently registered interest and an agreement to this effect can be registered in the IR.[126] The Convention does not state whether the holders of competing interests should obtain the consent of the debtor to create a valid subordination agreement. Since the Convention is silent on this issue, obtaining consent should not be a prerequisite for a valid subordination agreement. As the debtor is obliged to satisfy the claims of all holders of international interests, the order in which this will be accomplished should be of no relevance to it.[127]

V. EFFECTS OF INSOLVENCY

A. General

It is often said that the true value of a security interest lies in its ability to retain its priority in and survive the insolvency of the debtor.[128] Although Article 30, dealing with the effects of insolvency, does not contain any rules of priority, it may have an effect on the order of priority between competing interests. When insolvency intervenes, the debtor will not usually have enough assets to satisfy all obligations it owes to its creditors. This means that in the competition between various interest holders, those who did not comply with the Convention's requirements (ie failed to register their

[124] These countries are Canada and Mexico. For the text of the declarations, see: http://www.unidroit.org/depositary-2001capetown?id=448 (last visited May 2017).

[125] Art 29(5) CTC.

[126] Art 16(1)(e) CTC. Such, generally, M Bridge, 'Failed Contracts, Subrogation and Unjust Enrichment' (1998) *JBL* 323, 324.

[127] This is the approach taken by English law. See *Cheah v Equiticorp Finance Group Ltd* [1992] 1 AC 472; R Nolan, 'Less Equal than Others' (1995) *JBL* 485.

[128] Gullifer (n 32) 175.

interests before commencement of the insolvency proceedings), will lose their priority. As a result, a subsequent secured creditor may be promoted in their place, which will change the original priority order. Even if the creditor complies with the Convention's requirements, the insolvency administrator may, in certain circumstances, avoid the security interest as a preference or a fraudulent transfer, which will cost the secured creditor the loss of its privileged position. This part of the chapter considers how the priority of international interests may be preserved in the debtor's insolvency and what techniques may be used by an insolvency administrator in an attempt to avoid such interests.

B. Effectiveness of International Interests

i. Registration as a Prerequisite of Effectiveness

An international interest registered before the commencement of the insolvency proceedings against the debtor remains effective[129] in the debtor's insolvency.[130] Consequently, the registration not only determines priority, but is also vital in ensuring that the international interest remains effective and survives the debtor's insolvency. To make the international interest effective, the registration itself must be valid.[131] Thus, if the registration relates to a prospective international interest, which never matured into an actual interest because, for example, the debtor did not obtain the power to dispose of the object, the mere fact of the registration will not render such an interest effective in the case of the debtor's insolvency.

What if the prospective international interest is registered before the commencement of the insolvency proceedings, but the debtor only obtains the power to dispose after such proceedings are started? Both priority and effectiveness of the international interest relate back to the registration date and, on this basis, it is suggested that, unless such an interest can be set aside by the domestic law as a preference or a fraudulent transfer, it should remain effective. So too, a failure to renew the existing registration will make the interest ineffective in insolvency. In contrast, if the registration is renewed before it expires, then the interest should remain effective even if the renewal was affected only hours before the commencement of the insolvency proceedings. This should be the case because renewal of the existing registration does not amount to a fresh registration: its aim is to ensure the continuance of the existing registration.

[129] See K Zwieten, 'The Insolvency Provisions of the Cape Town Convention and the Protocols: Historical and Economic Perspectives' (2012) *Cape Town Convention Journal* 53.

[130] Art 30(1) CTC.

[131] Art 30(1) CTC.

ii. Commencement of Insolvency Proceedings

The Convention provides for a cutting-off point, after which the international interest's registration will not render it effective in insolvency. The international interest will only be effective if it is registered prior to the commencement of the insolvency proceedings,[132] which means the time at which the insolvency proceedings are deemed to commence under the applicable insolvency law.[133] For example, under US bankruptcy law, a transfer of property in a bankruptcy estate can be avoided if such transfer occurs after the commencement of the bankruptcy proceedings and is not authorised by the Bankruptcy Court or under the Bankruptcy Code.[134] The bankruptcy proceedings are deemed to start at the time when the petition is filed.[135] In one case the question arose as to whether the transfer occurred before the debtor filed its petition under Chapter 11 (when the creditor received the cheque from it) or after that (when the cheque was cashed). It was held that the transfer occurred when the cheque was honoured, that is after the petition was filed and, consequently, after the bankruptcy proceedings had started. Consequently, the transfer could be avoided.[136] The cutting-off point, ie the commencement of the insolvency proceedings, which is marked by the filing of the petition, may encourage prompt registration of registrable interests and provide the creditor with certainty that it will have a date upon which the parties to the transfer can rely in their transactions.

The Convention does not expressly deal with the issue of how long before the commencement of the insolvency proceedings the registration should be made for the international interest to remain effective. For example, if the security interest in an airframe is granted and registered two days before the petition is filed, will the registration of the international interest be effective in the insolvency proceedings? The answer to this question may depend on the policies underpinning the powers of an insolvency administrator to set aside security interests and on setting a certain event as the main reference point for that. One of the objectives of stipulating a cutting-off point is the avoidance of secret security interests.[137] If security interests were allowed to be registered after the start of the insolvency proceedings, secured creditors could be persuaded to keep the transaction unpublicised until the very last moment, which would allow the debtor to continue encumbering the assets.

[132] Art 30(1) CTC.

[133] Art 1(d) CTC. For example, under French law, the 'suspect period' begins at the time when the insolvent debtor becomes unable to make payments as they become due. See M Gdanski, 'Taking Security in France' in Bridge and Stevens (n 6) 82.

[134] *In re Paxton*, 440 F 3d 233, 236 (5th Cir 2006).

[135] *In re Contractor Technology*, Ltd, not reported in F Supp 2d, 2006 WL 1118039 (SD Tex), 56 Collier Bankr Cas 2d 191, Bankruptcy case No. 05-37623-H1-7.

[136] *Ibid.*

[137] White and Summers (n 10) 1254.

This is why security interests registered after the commencement of insolvency proceedings are not effective.[138]

However, if the security interest is filed immediately before the start of such proceedings, the effectiveness of the international interest can be preserved. For example, under US law, if a trustee in bankruptcy acts as a hypothetical lien creditor it will prevail over most secured creditors if their security interests are not perfected before the commencement of the proceedings.[139] But perfection even a few minutes before the commencement of the proceedings can save the security interest.[140] The trustee in bankruptcy can still attempt to avoid the security as a preference or as a fraudulent transfer. So, if the transfer of the debtor's property was made within 90 days before the original filing of the petition, and provided that other necessary conditions were met, the trustee would be able to avoid even a perfected security interest as a preference.[141] For example, in *Barnhill v Johnson* where the question was whether the day of the transfer was when the cheque was received by the creditor or when it was cashed at the bank, it was held that the day of the transfer was when the cheque was cashed. As this day was within 90 days before the date of the filing of the petition (and the commencement of the proceedings), the trustee in bankruptcy was able to set the transaction aside.[142] Conversely, if the transfer occurred more than 90 days before the petition was filed, the security interest could not be avoided as a preference.[143]

iii. Effectiveness in Insolvency: The Rule of Validation, Not Invalidation

As noted, Article 30(1) provides that an international interest is effective if, prior to the commencement of the insolvency proceedings, that interest was registered in conformity with the Convention. Article 30(2) further stipulates that 'nothing in this Article impairs the effectiveness of an international interest in the insolvency proceedings where that interest is effective under the applicable law'. The meaning of Article 30(2) may not

[138] *Ibid* 1255.

[139] §9-317(a)(2) UCC.

[140] White and Summers (n 10) 1253.

[141] The 90 days should be counted backwards from the date of filing rather than forward from the date of alleged transfer. See *In Matter of Nelson, Co*, 959 F 2d 1269, 117 ALR Fed 751, 60 USLW 2606, 26 Collier Bankr Cas 2d 979, Bankr L Rep P 74, 518; *In re JAS Markets, Inc*, 113 BR 193, 23 Collier Bankr Cas 2d 116, 20 Bankr Ct Dec 78 United States Bankruptcy Court, WD Pennsylvania; *In re Carl Sabler Trucking, Inc*, 122 BR 318, 21 Bankr Ct Dec 273, Bankr L Rep P 73, 749.

[142] 503 US 393, 112 SCt 1386, 118 L Ed 2d 39, 60 USLW 4264, 26 Collier Bankr Cas 2d 323, 22 Bankr Ct Dec 1218, Bankr L Rep P74, 501, 17 UCC.

[143] *In re M J Sales & Distributing Company, Inc*, 25 BR 608, 7 Collier Bankr Cas 2d 884, 9 Bankr Ct Dec 1342 United States Bankruptcy Court, SD New York.

be immediately clear. On one interpretation, it can be taken as meaning that an international interest, not registered in the IR, may still be effective in insolvency proceedings. If correct, this would negate the meaning of Article 30(1)—that the international interest is effective only if so registered—and the meaning of Article 29(1)—that an unregistered interest is postponed to a registered one.

On another interpretation, it can be argued that what Article 30(2) actually refers to is not the international interest as constituted under the Convention, but its equivalent under the applicable law, ie a security interest, retention of title agreement or lease. This could be the case because Article 30(2) refers to the applicable law in relation to such an interest: the interest is first called an *international interest*, and then it is referred to as *that interest* which is effective under the *applicable law*. This could mean that Article 30(2) provides that the equivalent of the international interest, which is created under the applicable law, may still be effective in the insolvency proceedings even if not registered in the IR.[144] For example, a secured creditor may register its security interest in an airframe both in the IR (as an international interest) and in a national registry (as a charge). If, before the commencement of the insolvency proceedings, the registration in the IR expires, the international interest will lose its effectiveness.[145] But the effectiveness of the interest under the applicable law will not be impaired merely because it is not registered in the IR. In other words, the effect of Articles 30(1) and (2) is that while the international interest, not registered in the IR, will not be effective under the Convention, its equivalent may still be effective in the insolvency proceedings under the applicable law. Consequently, the loss of effectiveness under the Convention does not lead to a complete invalidation of the interest and it may retain its validity under the applicable law, provided that the validity requirements of that law are met. In this sense, it can be said that the rule in Articles 30(1) and (2) is 'the rule of validation, not invalidation' of the international interest or its equivalent.[146] If correct, this analysis may make the meaning of Article 30(2) clearer. Its effect is that the validity of interests created under the applicable law will not be disturbed if these interests are not registered in the IR. But it also makes Article 30(2) seem unnecessary. The validity of an interest under the applicable law is not within the CTC's scope. The fact that an interest which is not effective under the Convention may retain its validity under the applicable law seems self-evident, just as the fact that an interest which is not valid under the applicable law may be effective under the Convention.

[144] This view is confirmed by the Commentary's latest revision (3rd edn) 343.
[145] Art 30(1) CTC.
[146] Goode (n 5) 343.

C. Avoidance of International Interests

The Convention indorses the rules of law applicable in the insolvency proceedings, relating to the avoidance of a transaction as a preference or a transfer in fraud of creditors.[147] The insolvency administrator can only set aside or avoid the international interest on the grounds that it amounts to either a preference or a fraudulent transfer and cannot invoke any other ground which could otherwise apply under the applicable law. The two grounds selected by the Convention are commonly found in the insolvency laws of various jurisdictions.[148]

One of the main policies behind these powers of the insolvency administrator is that, in the prescribed pre-insolvency period, similarly situated creditors should be treated equally by the debtor.[149] The insolvency administrator is usually authorised to set aside transfers made within such a period so as not to allow the debtor to favour one of its creditors at the expense of the others.[150] Another policy relates to the prevention of secret security interests. But for the power to strike down a transaction as a preference, the secured creditor could take a security in the debtor's object and refrain from registering it until the very start of the insolvency proceedings. The object would appear as unencumbered to other creditors and the secured creditor's international interest would remain secret until the moment when it is most needed.

The insolvency rules relating to preferences may allow the insolvency administrator to avoid even registered international interests, provided that the necessary conditions of the applicable law are met. For example, under US law[151] if it can be shown that the debtor paid the debt in the 90 days before the commencement of the insolvency proceedings, such a transfer can be attacked as a preference. If the challenge is successful, the transfers will be recaptured for the benefit of unsecured creditors and the claim of the secured creditor will be postponed to a subsequently registered holder of the international interest. To be able to strike the transfer down as a preference, the insolvency administrator may also need to show that it was a transfer of the debtor's property.[152] If the secured creditor provides a loan to the

[147] Art 30(3) CTC.

[148] R Goode, 'International Interests in Mobile Equipment: A Transnational Juridical Concept' (2003) 15 *Bond L Rev* 9, 17.

[149] Under the US law this period amounts to 90 days before the petition's original filing. See s 547(b) of the Bankruptcy Code.

[150] See *In re Dewey Barefoot*, 952 F 2d 795, 60 USLW 2450, 25 Collier Bankr Cas 2d 1719, 22 Bankr Ct Dec 717, Bankr L Rep P 74, 401, 16 UCC Rep Serv 2d 417, explaining that one of the purposes of statutory power of avoidance is to ensure that all creditors of the same class receive the same pro rata share of the debtor's estate.

[151] See, generally, White and Summers (n 10) Chapter 24.

[152] S 547(b) of the Bankruptcy Code.

debtor to enable it to purchase an aircraft engine and the loan is secured by this object, the transfer may be subject to avoidance as a preference under US law if the secured creditor registers its international interest within the 90-day period prior to the commencement of the insolvency proceedings.[153] This does not necessarily mean that any transfer made within the prescribed period will be set aside as a preference. The international interest can still be saved if one of the exceptions under the applicable law can be invoked.[154] Thus, if the loan was substantially contemporaneous with the perfection of the security interest[155] or the debtor received new value as a result of the transfer to the creditor,[156] then an otherwise preferential transfer can be saved under the applicable insolvency law. Finally, the Convention does not affect any rules of the insolvency procedure relating to the enforcement of rights to property, which is under the control or supervision of the insolvency administrator.[157] These procedures may include rules designed to limit the enforcement of security interests for the benefit of other creditors or in an attempt to affect a reorganisation of the debtor's business.[158]

[153] In contrast, if the loan is secured by a letter of credit, the payment under the letter of credit will not be subject to avoidance as a preference as it will not amount to the payment out of debtor's property. See *In re Leisure Dynamics*, 33 BR 171, Bankr L Rep P 69, 405; *In re Subratek Corporation*, 257 BR 723, Collier Bankr Cas 2d 1223; *In re Clothes*, 35 BR 487; The position is different if the bank takes a security interest to ensure the repayment by the debtor under the letter of credit. See *In re Air Conditioning*, 845 F 2d 293, 18 Collier Bankr Cas 2d 973, 17 Bankr Ct Dec 1385, Bankr L Rep P 72, 302.

[154] J White and D Israel, 'Preference Conundrums' (1993) 98 *Commercial LJ* 98.

[155] *In re David Larry Davis*, 734 F 2d 604, 10 Collier Bankr Cas 2d 1328, 12 Bankr Ct Dec 859, Bankr L Rep P 69, 902; *In re Burton Lewis Arnett*, 732 F 2d 385, 77 ALR Fed 1, 10 Collier Bankr Cas 2d 533, 11 Bankr Ct Dec 1097, Bankr L Rep P 69, 839.

[156] *In the Matter of Oil Fuel Supply*, 827 F 2d 224, 18 Collier Bankr Cas 2d 462, 17 Bankr L Rep P 72, 278, 5 UCC Rep Serv 2d 1446; *In Re Gem Construction Corp of Virginia*, 262 BR 638.

[157] Art 30(3)(b) CTC.

[158] This may include the cases where an automatic stay is imposed to prevent or suspend the security interest's enforcement in a situation where the debtor's business is about to be reorganised. See *In re North Shore & Central Illinois Freight Co*, 30 B 377, 10 Bankr Ct Dec 1003; *In re Delaware River Stevedores, Ins*, 129 BR 38, 21 Bankr Ct Dec 1596. Importantly, the automatic stay may not be available if the Contracting State has made a declaration under Art XI of the Aircraft Protocol, Art IX of the Luxembourg Protocol and Art XLI(4) of the Space Protocol, displacing Art 30(3)(b) CTC.

6

Enforcement of Security Interests under the Convention and the Protocols

I. INTRODUCTION

THE STRENGTH OF security and other international interests held by a creditor in the debtor's asset is truly put to the test when the debtor defaults or becomes insolvent. On the debtor's default, the secured creditor can enforce its international interest by taking possession or control of the object, selling it or leasing it.[1] In addition, the secured creditor can collect or receive any income or profits arising from the management or use of the object to obtain repayment of the debt.[2] For instance, the secured creditor can collect income or profit received by the debtor in the form of payments on the lease of a railway object held by the debtor's lessee. Similarly, in the case of space assets, such as remote sensing satellites, the secured creditor can collect the income generated by the payments received by the debtor from third parties for the data collected by such satellites.[3]

An attempt to take possession of the object may be hindered by various factors, such as the refusal of the State where an aircraft object is registered to allow repossession because it forms part of the fleet of the flag carrier of that State.[4] The State in which the aircraft is registered may also prohibit its de-registration from the national registry system, preventing the secured creditor from registering the aircraft in another State.[5] Repossession and sale or lease of the aircraft object may be delayed or prevented if the jurisdiction, in which the secured creditor seeks to enforce the security interest,

[1] Art 8(1) CTC.

[2] Art 8(1) CTC.

[3] M Sundahl, *The Cape Town Convention: Its Application to Space Assets and Relation to the Law of Outer Space* (Martinus Nijhoff Publishers 2013) 86.

[4] See further P Thorne, 'Aircraft Mortgages' in N Palmer and E McKendrick (eds), *Interests in Goods*, 2nd edn (LLP, London 1998) 717–25.

[5] Art 18 of the Convention on International Civil Aviation 1944, to which many States are parties, precludes dual registration of aircraft objects.

does not allow such actions without obtaining a court order.[6] In addition, some legal systems prohibit the lease of the repossessed aircraft and only permit its sale if conducted by way of a public auction.[7]

Although the agreement giving rise to an international interest will provide the creditor with a variety of remedies exercisable in the case of the debtor's default, its position can change radically on the debtor's insolvency. For example, the filing of a petition for reorganisation under Chapter 11 of the US Bankruptcy Code puts an immediate stay on the enforcement of security interests, which can lead to further delays in obtaining the repayment of the debt.[8] Similarly, the appointment of an administrator under the UK Insolvency Act 1986 automatically stays the enforcement of security interests unless leave of the court or the administrator's permission to enforce is obtained.[9] Often the obstacles in enforcing a security interest are cumulative. Thus, an automatic stay imposed to rescue the debtor's business can coincide with prolonged judicial proceedings required to obtain a court order for a public sale of the object.[10]

Compulsory freezes and other obstacles to enforcement can weaken what was originally granted to the secured creditor by a security agreement and undermine the strength of its international interest. To promote asset-based financing and leasing of the objects covered by the Convention, Chapter III provides the secured creditor and other holders of international interests with a uniform set of clear and robust rules governing their remedies, which are enforceable on the debtor's default and/or insolvency. These rules are testament to and an instance of the Convention's pursuit of legal predictability, one of its key policies and general principles.[11] Predictability gives creditors certainty and a sense of security, facilitating business planning, and confidence that their international interest will be effectively protected. Having that confidence enables creditors to offer financing and to do so on terms favourable to the debtor, thereby promoting accessibility of asset-based financing of high value mobile equipment.

The Convention distinguishes between the remedies available to the secured creditor and those exercisable by a conditional seller and lessor.[12]

[6] G Mauri and B Itterbeek, 'The Cape Town Convention on International Interests in Mobile Equipment and its Protocols on Matters Specific to Aircraft Equipment: A Belgian Perspective' (2004) 9 *Unif L Rev* 547, 553.

[7] This is often the case in civil law jurisdictions, but there are, of course, exceptions. See P Wood, *Comparative Law of Security Interests and Title Finance*, 2nd edn (London, Sweet & Maxwell 2007) 376.

[8] Thorne (n 4) 725.

[9] Para 43, Sch B1, Insolvency Act 1986.

[10] Wood (n 7) 387.

[11] See the Convention's Preamble, para 2.

[12] See, generally, R Goode, *Official Commentary to the Convention on International Interests in Mobile Equipment and Protocol Thereto on Matters Specific to Aircraft Equipment*, 3rd edn (Rome, UNIDROIT 2013) 61–74.

The secured creditor enjoys a greater variety of remedies and, provided that all the necessary prerequisites are met, can: (a) take possession or control of the object; (b) sell or grant a lease of the object; and (c) collect or receive any income or profits arising from the management of such an object.[13] In addition, if at any time after default, the debtor and other interested persons agree, the interest held by the debtor in the object can be vested in the secured creditor in or towards the satisfaction of the debt.[14]

In contrast, the remedies available to the conditional seller and lessor are confined to the power to terminate the agreement and repossess or take control of the object.[15] The conditional seller and lessor do not require more extensive remedies because they retain their ownership of the objects. Once the conditional sale or lease agreement is terminated, the conditional seller/lessor can deal with it as they wish.[16] The creditor can also exercise any additional remedies available under the applicable law, provided that they are not inconsistent with the Convention's mandatory provisions.[17] Such remedies may relate to a right to payment of accrued sums and damages for breach of the agreement.[18]

In some cases, the debtor may challenge the creditor's right to enforce its international interest. Judicial proceedings aimed at resolving the dispute can be lengthy. In the meantime, the physical condition of the object can deteriorate and income which could have been earned from its exploitation may be lost. To address these concerns, the Convention allows the creditor to obtain speedy judicial relief pending final determination of the dispute.[19] Provided that the creditor adduces evidence of the debtor's default, the court should grant the creditor a speedy relief order. Such orders can take several forms, including those allowing the creditor to secure the preservation and value of the object, or to obtain possession, control or immobilisation of the object.[20] In addition, all three Protocols and the draft MAC Protocol state

[13] Art 8(1) CTC.

[14] Art 9(1) CTC.

[15] Art 10 CTC.

[16] Goode (n 12) 288.

[17] Art 12 CTC.

[18] For example, in *Brooks v Beirnstein* [1909] 1 KB 98, following the hirer's failure to punctually pay monthly rent for the hired furniture, the owner was able to terminate the agreement and repossess the goods. In addition, it was held that the owner could also sue for monthly rent which had already accrued and have not been paid by the hirer. See also *Financings Ltd v Baldock* [1963] 2 QB 104; *Brady and Another v St Margaret's Trust Ltd* [1963] 2 QB 494; *Yeoman Credit Ltd v Mclean* [1962] 1 WLR 131. Similarly, following termination of an agreement for the lease of an aircraft and repossession of the object, the lessor may be entitled (under the applicable domestic law) to claim any sums representing accrued and unpaid installments from the lessee. Art 12 allows exercise of additional remedies provided that these remedies are not inconsistent with the Convention's mandatory provisions.

[19] Art 13 CTC.

[20] Art 13(1) CTC.

that sale of the object can be used as the form of the speedy relief, provided that the debtor and the creditor specifically agree to this.[21]

The Convention's remedial scheme is supplemented by the additional remedies provided under the Protocols. These remedies are tailored to the type of the mobile equipment in question and can be exercised by all creditors. Thus, the Aircraft Protocol stipulates that on the debtor's default, the creditor can procure de-registration of the aircraft from the national registry and export or physically transfer it from the territory in which it is situated to another country.[22] This should allow the creditor to move and re-register the aircraft object in a different jurisdiction, where enforcement of remedies may be somewhat easier. Recently, this remedy has been enforced in the decision of the High Court of New Delhi.[23] Importantly, the High Court confirmed that once the requirements for de-registration and export are met, the relevant authority does not have a discretion and must de-register the aircraft from the national registry.

Similarly, the Luxembourg Protocol provides that in the case of the debtor's default, the creditor may procure export and physical transfer of the railway rolling stock from the territory where it is situated to another country.[24] Since repossession of the railway rolling stock may cause disruption to the carriage of passengers and freight, this remedy can only be exercised subject to the public service exemption. If the railway object is habitually used for the purpose of providing a service of public importance it may not be repossessed by the creditor.[25] One question relating to this remedy and considered in this chapter is whether the interest of the creditor can be adequately protected and whether it can still obtain repayment of the debt.

A similar issue arose in the drafting of the Space Protocol as space assets often play a central role in delivering services of public importance in many countries.[26] Article XXVII of the Space Protocol imposes limitations on the creditor's exercise of the remedies in respect of space assets providing public service. Article XXVII becomes operative when the public service provider[27]

[21] Art X(3) of the Aircraft Protocol; Art VIII(3) of the Luxembourg Protocol; Art XX(3) of the Space Protocol; Art IX(3) of the draft MAC Protocol.

[22] Art IX(1) of the Aircraft Protocol.

[23] *Awas 39423 Ireland Ltd & Ors v Directorate General of Civil Aviation & Anr* (WP(C) 871/2015) and *Wilmington Trust SP Services Ltd v Directorate General of Civil Aviation & Anr* (WP(C) 747/2015).

[24] Art XXV of the Luxembourg Protocol. See similarly, Art VIII(1) of the draft MAC Protocol.

[25] Art XXV of the Luxembourg Protocol.

[26] See J Atwood, 'A New International Regime for Railway Rolling Stock Asset-Based Financing' (2008) 40 *UCC LJ* 3 Art 2.

[27] Art XXVII(2)(b) of the Space Protocol defines a public service provider as 'an entity of a Contracting State, another entity situated in that Contracting State and designated by the Contracting State as a provider of a public service or an entity recognised as a provider of a public service under the laws of a Contracting State'.

or the Contracting State registers a public service notice in the International Registry (IR), specifying the nature of the service that will be performed under the public service contract.[28] Once the public service notice is registered, the creditor holding an international interest in the space asset covered by such notice, cannot exercise any of the Convention's or the Protocol's remedies that would make the space asset unavailable for the performance of the relevant service.[29] The Protocol requires Contracting States to make a declaration specifying how long the limitation period is expected to last. The Protocol indicates that the limitation period cannot last less than three months and more than six months.[30] In addition, the creditor needs to register a notice in the IR, stating that it may exercise its remedies if the debtor fails to cure the default within the limitation period.[31] The limitation period begins to run from the date of the registration of the creditor's notice. For this reason, the creditor is required to notify both the debtor and the public service provider of the date of such registration and of the date of expiry of the limitation period.[32] The Protocol envisages that during the limitation period all relevant parties will attempt to find a commercially reasonable solution permitting the continuation of the public service.[33]

One of the most significant provisions of all three Protocols relates to the remedies exercisable by the creditor on the debtor's insolvency.[34] These remedies can only be exercised if the relevant Contracting State has made a declaration to this effect. The Aircraft and Space Protocols offer two alternative sets of rules—Alternative A and Alternative B—governing the creditor's rights in the case of the debtor's insolvency. Once the declaration in favour of either of them is made, the chosen Alternative must be exercised in its entirety. Alternative A, also known as the 'hard option', requires the person in charge of the insolvency, such as an insolvency administrator or the debtor, either: (a) to cure all defaults and agree to perform all future obligations within a specified waiting period; or (b) to give the creditor the opportunity to take possession of the object. Alternative B is the so-called 'soft' option. According to this option the court may permit the creditor

[28] R Goode, *Official Commentary to the Convention on International Interests in Mobile Equipment and Protocol Thereto on Matters Specific to Space Assets* (Rome, UNIDROIT 2013) 473. According to Art XXVII(2)(a) of the Space Protocol a contract will amount to a public service contract if it relates to the provision of a public service, recognised as such under the law of the Contracting State at the time of registration of the public service notice.

[29] Art XXVII(3) of the Space Protocol. The creditor can, of course, still exercise the remedies not rendering the space asset unavailable to the performance of public service, such as collecting payments from leases on space assets.

[30] Art XXVII(4) of the Space Protocol. The declaration must be made under Art XLI(1) of the Space Protocol.

[31] Art XXVII(4) of the Space Protocol.

[32] Art XXVII(4), (5) of the Space Protocol.

[33] Art XXVII(7)(a) of the Space Protocol.

[34] Art XI of the Aircraft Protocol; Art XXI of the Space Protocol; Art IX of the Luxembourg Protocol.

to take possession of the object if the insolvency administrator/debtor fails to present the creditor with the opportunity to repossess it. This may only be accomplished if the insolvency administrator/debtor fails to cure all defaults and agrees to perform all future obligations in accordance with its notice. The Luxembourg Protocol adds to these options a third one, namely Alternative C, which is also present in the draft MAC Protocol.[35] Under this Alternative, the waiting period is referred to as the 'cure period' and the insolvency administrator or the debtor can apply to the court for an order suspending its obligation to return the object.[36] The suspension period commences once the cure period ends and lasts until the expiration of the agreement and on terms considered just by the court.[37]

The Convention's remedies are exercisable either extra-judicially or on application to the court. This will depend on the Contracting State's declaration, which is mandatory and should indicate whether the Convention's remedies enforceable without intervention of the court are to be exercised only on application to the court or whether they can be enforced extra-judicially.[38] This approach of the Convention reflects the fact that not all legal systems encourage self-help remedies. It is up to the Contracting State to choose which of the two approaches it prefers.[39] The declaration indicating its position will clarify this issue for the creditor, who otherwise may not be certain how to proceed with the enforcement.

The availability of self-help remedies means that the time and cost of the enforcement can be reduced. But, even if the declaration allows the secured creditor to repossess, sell or grant a lease without leave of the court, it can still prefer the judicial route in order to avoid being sued for trespass (if it enters the debtor's property when repossessing the aircraft) or damages for wrongful repossession.[40] The enforcement of remedies via the court can also help the creditor resist potential claims that it failed to comply with the requirement of commercial reasonableness. For instance, if the aircraft is sold privately, the debtor may attempt to challenge the sale as being commercially unreasonable if the secured creditor fails to obtain a proper price reflecting the true market value of the object.[41] In addition, the aircraft

[35] Art X, Alternative C of the draft MAC Protocol.

[36] Art IX, Alternative C(4) of the Luxembourg Protocol.

[37] Art IX, Alternative C(4) of the Luxembourg Protocol.

[38] Art 8(1) CTC, Art 54(2) CTC provides that a Contracting State *shall* declare whether or not any remedy available to the creditor under the Convention which is not there expressed to require application to the court may be exercised only with leave of the court. In contrast, the declaration under Art 54(1) CTC in relation to the lease of the charged object is optional.

[39] Goode (n 12) 404–05.

[40] Thorne (n 4) 719.

[41] See, for example, *Cuckmere Brick Co v Mutual Finance Ltd* [1971] Ch 949, where the duty to take reasonable care to obtain true market value of the mortgaged property was breached because the mortgagee failed to advertise planning permission for flats which had already been obtained and this affected the price of the mortgaged land.

authorities may refuse to grant the secured creditor, attempting to enforce the remedies outside of the court, an operating licence or airworthiness certificate for the operation of the aircraft. A court order may help the secured creditor in persuading the relevant authorities to issue these documents.

Finally, the secured creditor does not have to choose between remedies and can enforce any one or more of them.[42] For instance, in many cases, the secured creditor will need to take possession or control of the object before selling or leasing it to another party. If selling the aircraft in a different jurisdiction is likely to increase the sale proceeds, the secured creditor will need to de-register and export the object to such jurisdiction before the sale can be arranged. In certain circumstances, it may be better not to sell the object immediately. On a falling market, the secured creditor can obtain a vesting order transferring the debtor's interest in the object to it in or towards satisfaction of the debt. On a rising market, the creditor can attempt to sell the object at a profit.

This chapter assesses the enforcement of the Convention's and the Protocols' remedies in and out of insolvency and tests their effectiveness. Part II examines the concept of default, entitling the creditor to exercise its remedies. If the parties do not define it, the Convention provides that 'default' amounts to such 'a default which substantially deprives the creditor of what it is entitled to expect under the agreement'.[43] The Convention does not explain what amounts to the creditor's expectation under the agreement and the breach of which terms can lead to its substantial deprivation. Part II proposes and explains the factors that can be relevant when considering these issues. Further, to protect the debtor's interests against the creditor's abuse, the Convention provides that remedies must be exercised in a commercially reasonable manner and that a notice should be sent to the debtor and other interested persons before the object can be sold or leased.[44] However, the effectiveness of these requirements is debatable since there is no intimation as to what consequences should follow if the creditor does not comply with them. Part III examines the scope of application and general considerations relating to the requirement of commercial reasonableness. The defining features and the content of this requirement are extensively

[42] Art 8(1) CTC. The position is, generally, similar in some other jurisdictions. For the position under US law, see *Glamorgan Coal Corporation v Bowen* (1990) 742 F Supp 308, 13 UCC Rep Serv 2d 596; *Ingersoll-Rand Financial Corporation v Atlantic Management and Consulting Corp* (1989) 717 F Supp 1067, 10 UCC Rep Serv 2d 256; *Midlantic Commercial Leasing v Tender Loving Care* (1990) WL 72861(ED Pa), 12 UCC Rep Serv 2d 293; *Vital Basics v Vertrue Incorporated* (2007) 515 F Supp 2d 170; *AVCO Financial Services of Billings One v Christiaens* (1982) 201 Mont 117, 652 P 2d 220, 34 UCC Rep Serv 1445; *In re Adrian Research & Chem Co* (1959) 269 F 2d 734; *Bank One Akron v Nobil* (1992) 80 Ohio App 3d 638, 610 NE 2d 538.

[43] Art 11 CTC.

[44] Art 8(3), (4) CTC.

explored in the sections dedicated to specific remedies. Part IV analyses the remedies available to the secured creditor under Article 8 CTC, namely, possession, control, sale and lease of the object. It also provides detailed treatment of the problem of consequences of a failure to comply with the requirements of commercial reasonableness and notice and develops possible solutions. Part V explores the nature of the remedy of vesting. This remedy allows for the ownership or any other interest held by the debtor in the object to be 'vested' in or transferred to the creditor in or towards satisfaction of the obligation. Part VI examines the remedy of speedy relief pending final determination of the claim. Speedy relief was inspired by the remedy of interim relief, known to many domestic legal systems. At the same time, the Convention's speedy relief has its own distinctive features and, for this reason, is viewed by some commentators as the form of the advance enforcement of default remedies. After testing the nature of speedy relief, this work takes a different view and argues that it cannot be equated with the advance enforcement of default remedies. Although speedy relief is akin to the remedy of interim relief, it has its own unique features and, being the creature of the Convention, must be interpreted according to its principles and policies. Finally, Part VII considers the remedies available to the creditor under the Protocols and exercisable in the debtor's insolvency. The area of remedies is fraught with numerous complications and the scope of this chapter does not permit their detailed examination. For this reason, this chapter only aims to provide a roadmap to the remedies exercisable by the secured creditor. The remedies of the conditional seller and lessor are not addressed.

II. DEFINING 'DEFAULT'

A default by the debtor entitles the creditor to exercise its remedies under the Convention. The Convention provides for two routes of ascertaining the meaning of a default. First, the debtor and the creditor may 'at any time agree in writing as to the events that constitute a default or otherwise give rise to the rights and remedies specified in Articles 8–10 and 13'.[45] Some typical examples of what parties may decide to constitute a default include the non-payment of rentals due under an agreement for the lease of an aircraft,[46] late re-delivery of a leased aircraft,[47] a failure to maintain

[45] Art 11(1) CTC.

[46] *Celestial Aviation Trading 71 Ltd v Paramount Airway Pte Ltd* [2010] EWHC 185 (Comm). See also the decision of High Court of Delhi at New Delhi in *Awas 39423 Ireland Ltd & Ors v Directorate General of Civil Aviation & Anor* (WP(C) 871/2015) and *Wilmington Trust SP Services Ltd v Directorate General of Civil Aviation & Anor* (WP(C) 747/2015) para 16.4.

[47] *Pindell Ltd & Anor v AirAsia Bhd* [2010] EWHC 2516 (Comm).

and repair an aircraft to keep it in an airworthy condition[48] and a failure to procure insurance naming the secured creditor as a loss payee.[49] In addition, the debtor and the creditor can agree in writing that an occurrence of certain events which are not usually considered as a default, but aimed to allocate the risk between the parties, will trigger the exercise of the Convention's remedies.[50] For instance, the changes in taxation legislation, associated with the use of the object or the debtor's insolvency can amount to events entitling the creditor to exercise the Convention's remedies.[51] Secondly, if the parties do not define it, Article 11(2) provides that 'default' amounts to such 'a default which substantially deprives the creditor of what it is entitled to expect under the agreement'.

It is clear that the Convention's standard of substantial deprivation of contractual expectation cannot be applied in relation to the contractually agreed events of default. For instance, the parties can agree that a failure to punctually pay lease rentals amounts to a default allowing the creditor/lessor to terminate the lease and repossess the object.[52] Accordingly, a failure to make a single payment out of, say, 20 rentals will amount to a default. The result is likely to be different if the agreement is silent on this issue and the existence of a default must be ascertained according to the Convention's requirements. Under Article 11(2), not every breach of a term of the agreement will constitute a default. For instance, if the breach of the term is a minor one, such as when the debtor fails to pay one out of 20 rental payments due under the lease, it is unlikely to constitute a default under the Convention. This is because the alleged default must 'substantially' deprive the creditor of its contractual expectation. Consequently, if the parties intend for a particular event to constitute a default, they must clearly state so in their contract. Otherwise, there is no guarantee that this is how the event will be characterised under the substantial deprivation test.

The Convention's definition of a default gives rise to several areas of uncertainty. First, it is not entirely clear what amounts to the creditor's expectation under the agreement. Secondly, it may be difficult to ascertain the breach of which terms will lead to a substantial deprivation of such a contractual expectation. With regard to the first issue, it can be argued that the creditor's expectation should be defined with reference to the obligations stated in the agreement in the sense that the debtor's performance of its obligations can be said to amount to the creditor's expectation. In accordance

[48] *Burton Davis III v American Jet Leasing*, 864 F 2d 612, 27 Fed R Evid Serv 26.

[49] Such an insurance policy will entitle the creditor to claim the amount of covered loss from the insurer which may include the cost of repair and diminution of value of an aircraft following an accident and damage to its parts. See *Center Capital Corporation v National Union Fire Insurance Company of Pittsburgh*, 2010 WL 3941933 (D Idaho).

[50] Goode (n 12) 289.

[51] *Ibid* 290.

[52] This was the position in *Lombard North Central plc v Butterworth* [1987] QB 527. In such a case, the creditor would have to proceed under Art 11(1) CTC.

with this approach, if the agreement states that insurance covering certain political risks, should be provided by the debtor and this has not been put in place, the creditor should be entitled to consider such a breach as a default, depriving it of its contractual expectation.

Alternatively, it can be argued that the creditor's contractual expectation ought to be defined with reference to the purpose for which it entered into the agreement. Once this purpose is established, it may be easier to ascertain whether the breach of a term is likely to substantially deprive the creditor of its contractual expectation. In general terms, the main purpose why the secured creditor enters into a security agreement is to ensure that either the loan will be repaid to it with interest or, if the repayment is no longer possible, that it will have access to the debtor's asset, which serves as security for the performance of the debtor's obligation. The conditional seller intends to sell the object to the buyer and expects that all installments constituting the purchase price will be paid. If the purchase price cannot be obtained, the conditional seller expects that, as the owner of the object, it will be able to take it back. Similarly, when the lessor delivers possession of the equipment to the lessee it expects to receive rental payments for its use or to be able to repossess it. But, the purposes of entering a security, retention of title or a lease agreement, pursued by the creditor, can be defined more broadly. For instance, it can be argued that the creditor's contractual expectation includes the opportunity to earn the interest, associated with the debtor's repayments, which the creditor intends to invest further.

Once the expectations of the creditor under the agreement are ascertained, it becomes clearer that a breach of some terms may interfere with them more than a breach of some other terms. For example, a failure to pay several installments may result in a loss to the creditor, but it is unlikely to substantially deprive it of its contractual expectation, namely that the debt will *eventually* be repaid. But if the debtor indicates that it can no longer pay the installments even if the creditor agrees to reschedule the debt or if it files a petition for reorganisation, the debt may never be fully repaid and the creditor will be substantially deprived of its contractual expectation.

A failure to provide insurance required by the agreement can also amount to a default. For instance, the creditor seeking to sell the repossessed object may find that the proceeds of sale cannot be transferred to the country where the creditor is based or cannot be converted into the currency of its choice. This may mean that the debt cannot be repaid out of such proceeds and the creditor will be substantially deprived of its expectation to obtain repayment. For this reason, a failure to provide insurance covering such loss is likely to amount to a default under the Convention.

Whether the test of a *substantial* deprivation of the creditor's contractual expectation will be satisfied will depend on the circumstances of each case, and future cases decided under the Convention will be vital in drawing its contours. One factor that can help decide whether a breach of a term substantially deprives the creditor of its expectation is to consider the nature and gravity of the negative consequences flowing from it. If the breach of the term goes to the very core of the agreement, such as when it leads to a serious risk of non-repayment of the debt, diminution of the value of the security interest, or destruction or loss of the object, it is likely to amount to a default under Article 11 CTC. In such cases, it can be argued that the term of the agreement is so important to the protection of the creditor's interest and essential to the agreement that its breach is highly likely to lead to a substantial deprivation of the creditor's contractual expectation. For example, if the debtor fails to arrange insurance covering the costs associated with damage, maintenance and repair of the aircraft object, the breach of this term is likely to lead to a substantial deprivation of the creditor's contractual expectation. Should the aircraft object be involved in an accident resulting in damage to its parts, the costs of repair are likely to be significant. This will affect the debtor's financial standing and increase the risk of non-repayment of the debt. This can also diminish the value of the security interest. Instead of having a security interest in an airworthy aircraft which could be repossessed and sold or leased with relative ease, it now has to deal with an object that either needs to be repaired at considerable cost or, potentially, sold in a disassembled condition.

While the factor of the gravity of the potential negative consequences can serve as a starting point in ascertaining the breach of which terms will substantially deprive the creditor of its contractual expectation, it raises the bar too high. It means that only an exceptionally serious breach of a term will entitle the creditor to exercise its remedies, and this could not have been implied by the text of the Convention. In other words, the breach need only satisfy the requirement of a *substantial* and not necessarily *total* deprivation of contractual expectation. While the breach of the term going to the very core of the agreement should undoubtedly amount to a default, the category of the default cannot be restricted to only such breaches.

Another factor which can help to decide whether the breach of a term substantially deprives the creditor of its contractual expectation is to consider whether, despite the breach, a reasonable person in the position of the creditor can still obtain what it is entitled to expect under the agreement. Consider a security agreement containing a restriction on the debtor's leasing or otherwise parting with possession of the aircraft. The reasons why the secured creditor may require such a restriction may include the following.[53] First, the lessee may operate the aircraft in a different country, increasing 'political risks' for the secured creditor. Secondly, the lease of the aircraft object can lead to a change in the registration information relating to it with adverse consequences for the secured creditor whose priority

[53] See Thorne (n 4) 704.

position can be changed or lost. The secured creditor will need to ascertain whether the interest of the lessee will be subordinated to that of the secured creditor. If, in defiance of the restriction, the debtor leases the aircraft, a reasonable person in the position of the creditor may have to consider the circumstances before deciding whether it can still obtain the repayment of the debt. If the secured creditor's international interest is registered in the IR ahead of the lessor's interest, the secured creditor will enjoy priority over the lessee.[54] Conversely, if the lessor registers its international interest ahead of the secured creditor, the interest of the lessee will prevail over that of the secured creditor.[55] Even in this case, the lessee may agree to postpone its interest to the subsequently registered interest of the secured creditor.[56] For this reason, a reasonable person in the position of the creditor may consider that it can still obtain the repayment of the debt. This means that such a breach should not substantially deprive the creditor of its contractual expectation.

In many cases the position will be less clear than in the above examples and issues such as the possibility of cure can be relevant in considering whether the breach should amount to a default. Consider a secured creditor which learns that the insurance covering maintenance and repair of the aircraft has lapsed and the debtor has failed to renew it. This can substantially deprive the creditor of its contractual expectation and amount to a default. But what if the debtor assures the creditor that it will procure a new insurance policy, say, within the next three days? Can the creditor treat the breach as a default and proceed with the repossession and sale of the aircraft or should it refrain from enforcing its remedies and wait until the default is cured? On the one hand, it can be argued that since the secured creditor's remedies are extremely powerful in that they lead to the dispossession of the debtor of a valuable object, a curable breach should not be considered as the type of breach that substantially deprives the creditor of its contractual expectation. On the other hand, if the debtor continues to operate the aircraft (in defiance of the secured creditor's instructions) during the time when it is not insured and the object is damaged during this time, the creditor's security interest will be impaired. Even if the aircraft object is not operated, it can still be damaged or stripped for parts during this short period of time.[57] For this reason, it is suggested that the creditor should be entitled to insist on continuous insurance cover and to treat the breach of the term relating to it as a default.

[54] Art 29(4)(a) CTC.
[55] Art 29(4)(b) CTC.
[56] Art 29(5) CTC.
[57] See *Pindell Ltd & Anor v AirAsia Bhd* [2010] EWHC 2516 (Comm) where an aircraft, parked outside of a hangar, was damaged due to humid weather conditions and stripped for parts.

At the same time, where the debtor's breach can be cured at no inconvenience to the creditor it should not constitute a default. This can be the case where, for example, the debtor's breach consists solely in the failure to place a nameplate on the aircraft engine indicating that the creditor has a security interest in the engine. The purpose of placing a nameplate is to provide an additional safeguard that the security interest in the engine is visible to other persons. The presence of the nameplates does not help the secured creditor to secure a priority position, nor does it serve as a notice to other creditors.[58] To achieve the latter objectives, the secured creditor will have to register its interest in the IR. Consequently, this easily curable breach should not constitute a default under the Convention.

III. THE REQUIREMENT OF COMMERCIAL REASONABLENESS: GENERAL CONSIDERATIONS[59]

Although the Convention does not prescribe the remedies exercisable by the debtor in the case of the creditor's abuse of its powers, it provides several safeguards aimed at protecting its interest. One such safeguard is the requirement that the creditor must procure the debtor's consent in order to exercise its remedies.[60] To enhance the debtor's position, the security agreement can stipulate the extent of the debtor's consent. For instance, a security agreement may provide that repossession or control of the object should be accomplished without breaching the peace or causing interruption to the immediate operation of that object.[61]

In addition, to ensure that the debtor's interests are protected, the Convention requires that the remedies be exercised in a commercially reasonable manner[62] and that a notice be sent to the debtor and other interested

[58] See Thorne (n 4) 705.

[59] The discussion on reasonableness in the context of repossession and sale is based on S Saidova, 'The Cape Town Convention: Repossession and Sale of Charged Aircraft Objects in a Commercially Reasonable Manner' (2013) *LMCLQ* 180.

[60] Alternatively, the secured creditor can apply for a court order authorising or directing exercise of the remedies. See Art 8(2) CTC.

[61] In some jurisdictions, this is one of the preconditions of repossession. For example, §9-609(b)(2) UCC allows repossession without judicial process only if it can be accomplished without breach of the peace. See *General Finance Corporation v Smith* (1987) 505 So 2d 1045, 3 UCC Rep Serv 2d 1278; *Sanchez v Mbank of El Paso* (1990) 792 S W 2d 530, 12 UCC Rep Serv 2d 1169; *King v Citizens Bank of Warrensburg* (1990) WL 154210 (D Kan); *Saice v MidAmerica Bank* (1999) WL 33911356 (D Minn); *Yakity Yaks v Thielen* (2002) WL 31496416 (D Or).

[62] Art IX(3) of the Aircraft Protocol states that Art 8(3) CTC, indicating that only the remedies of the secured creditor provided for in that provision should be exercised in a commercially reasonable manner, should not apply to aircraft objects. Art IX(3) further states that *all* remedies given by the Convention in relation to aircraft objects should be exercised in accordance with this requirement. According to Art IV(3), this provision of the Aircraft Protocol is mandatory and cannot be derogated from by the parties. See Art XVII(1) of the Space Protocol and Art VII(3) of the Luxembourg Protocol for the same effect.

persons before the object is sold or leased.[63] If the secured creditor does not comply with these requirements, the debtor may challenge the manner in which the remedy is enforced. The greater the number of instances where such a challenge can be raised, the weaker the creditor's ability to enforce its remedies effectively will be. In other words, the commercial reasonableness requirement has a direct impact on the strength of the creditor's remedial position. For these reasons, it is important to understand exactly *how* a remedy ought to be exercised to comply with commercial reasonableness.

The examination of the commercial reasonableness requirement makes it necessary to address several questions. First, the scope of the requirement is not defined precisely and it is not entirely clear whether the choice of a remedy must be conducted in a commercially reasonable manner or whether the requirement applies only to the manner in which a specific remedy is enforced. The second issue relates to the content of this requirement. The Convention does not define the commercial reasonableness requirement and merely provides that it is satisfied where the remedy is 'exercised in conformity with a provision of a security agreement except where such a provision is manifestly unreasonable'.[64] This means that the Convention places strong reliance on the security agreement, which should not be easily disturbed.[65] Indeed, a remedy exercised in conformity with the security agreement will, generally, be considered commercially reasonable unless such a provision is *manifestly* unreasonable. But a security agreement cannot cover all possible scenarios and it is not clear what principles and factors are relevant when considering whether the exercise of a remedy complies with the requirement. In addition, it can be difficult to decide whether a provision of the security agreement is *manifestly* unreasonable. Thirdly, the requirements of notice and commercial reasonableness are aimed at protecting the interests of the debtor. However, their effectiveness is debatable since there is no intimation as to what consequences will follow if the secured creditor does not comply with them. These questions are examined in turn.

A. Scope of Application

The first issue that needs to be addressed relates to the scope of application of the standard of commercial reasonableness. The question is whether commercial reasonableness is applicable only to the manner in which a specific remedy is exercised, or whether it is also applicable at the stage when *the choice* of a remedy is made. The decision in *Palk v Mortgage Services*

[63] Art 8(3), (4) CTC.
[64] Art 8(3) CTC.
[65] Goode (n 12) 282.

Funding plc[66] helps to illustrate the point. In this case, the mortgagor was unable to pay the installments due under the mortgage of its house and the mortgagee obtained an order for possession. The sale of the house would enable the mortgagor to repay most of the debt, but the mortgagee refused to sell it. Instead, the mortgagee wanted to let the house and wait until the market improved and a better price could be obtained. The expected annual rent for the house would be considerably less than the interest which could be saved by the sale. The question was whether the mortgagee could take possession and let the house until the market improved, or whether it should have sold the house because the sale would have enabled the debtor to repay most of the debt. It was held that while, when exercising the remedies, the secured creditor was entitled to give preference to its own interest, it ought to keep the mortgagor's interest in mind too. The Court of Appeal directed a sale because the mortgagee's plan of letting the property was too oppressive to the debtor and would lead to a considerable increase of the debt.

Similarly, could it be argued that when market conditions are good, it should not be commercially reasonable to hold on to the repossessed aircraft object and that the secured creditor should be *required* to sell it instead? It is suggested that applying commercial reasonableness at the stage of selecting a remedy is not justified. First, the text of the Convention does not support this view. It expressly provides that 'any remedy ... shall be exercised in a commercially reasonable manner' and it does not require that *the choice* of a remedy should also comply with this test.[67] In addition, the Convention states that the secured creditor can exercise 'any one or more' of the remedies.[68] Accordingly, the secured creditor should be able to decide on its own which remedy would suit its interests best. The Convention's policy of promoting asset-based financing is viable only if creditors are provided with a high level of legal protection and security and, it is suggested, the availability of a wide range of remedies together with a right to choose a remedy play a key role in providing that protection and security to the creditor. From this standpoint, allowing commercial reasonableness to dictate what remedy a creditor is to choose would seem to go against this policy.

Secondly, legal predictability is one of the general principles on which the Convention is based.[69] Applying commercial reasonableness to the stage of selecting a remedy would not sit easily with this principle because that would require a case by case analysis not only of *how* an individual remedy is invoked, but also of *what* remedy should be invoked which, clearly, creates an additional layer of complexity and uncertainty. A final argument

[66] *Palk v Mortgage Services Funding plc* [1993] Ch 330.
[67] Art 8(3) CTC.
[68] Art 8(1) CTC.
[69] Art 5(1) CTC.

concerns a remedy of repossession. Requiring the secured creditor to exercise other remedies once it takes possession of the object may reduce the remedy of repossession to a mere precursor to those other remedies.[70] While in many cases the secured creditor will take possession in order to sell or lease the aircraft, this does not mean that the secured creditor should not be able to repossess the object for other purposes. An aircraft can fly into another jurisdiction in less than an hour and the secured creditor may need to repossess the aircraft to prevent it from moving into a jurisdiction which may be hostile to the secured creditor's interests. In this case, the purpose of repossession may be to freeze the aircraft temporarily and not necessarily to sell it. Thus, it is submitted that commercial reasonableness ought to apply only to the exercise of a specific remedy.

B. Meaning and Content

It is well known that vague standards, such as those based on the notion of reasonableness, cannot be defined in the abstract and acquire specific meaning in the context of the particular facts. This does not mean, however, that it is not possible to identify some general principles, considerations and factors which would shed light on the meaning of such standards and help when applying them in a particular scenario. It is submitted that commercial reasonableness under the Convention comprises the following principles and considerations. First, its very existence, which imposes limitations on a creditor's conduct, reflects a degree of concern for the debtor. Therefore, one aim of this requirement is to ensure that the creditor acts not only in its own interest, but also takes the debtor's interest into account. Secondly, the Convention, like most commercial law regimes, is concerned with promoting economic efficiency.[71] This means that a commercially reasonable conduct is, in principle, one which minimises or avoids economic waste, leads to resources being allocated to where they are valued most, and involves the least costs.[72] At the same time, the creditor's behaviour is only required to be commercially *reasonable* which also means that it must not sacrifice its own interests. While discouraged from being totally passive, a creditor must not be excessively burdened and subjected to adverse economic and commercial consequences. It is in the light of this set of considerations that commercial reasonableness should be applied to the particular facts.

[70] F Adeoye, 'The Anglo-American Law of Mortgagees: A Quagmire for Creditors' (1993) *JBL* 544, 547.

[71] See the Preamble to the Convention.

[72] See, generally, R Posner, *Economic Analysis of Law*, 7th edn (Wolters Kluwer, Law & Business 2007) 9.

IV. DEFAULT REMEDIES OF THE SECURED CREDITOR

A. Taking Possession, Sale or Lease of the Object

i. Taking Possession or Control of the Object

Taking possession or control of high value objects such as aircraft, railway and space assets can be expensive and burdensome. The secured creditor will need to obtain a licence and other necessary certificates enabling it to operate these objects.[73] The costs of storing, preserving, transporting, maintaining and repairing these objects are substantial. In the case of aircraft objects, the secured creditor will also have to pay landing fees as well as navigation, visual and radio charges.[74] When taking possession of an aircraft object is followed by de-registration and transportation to another jurisdiction, the secured creditor will have to obtain approval from the relevant authority in the State where the aircraft object is located. If repossession is challenged as wrongful or premature or where operation of the object causes environmental pollution or other damage, the secured creditor may also have to pay for the resulting damage.[75]

The disadvantages associated with repossession mean that the secured creditor will not always be ready and willing to take possession of the object. But if taking possession and moving the object to a different jurisdiction can help the secured creditor avoid insolvency stays, lengthy court proceedings and increase the likelihood of better sale proceeds, the secured creditor may decide to repossess. Taking possession is a powerful remedy because it divests the debtor of the valuable asset, and in some cases a mere threat of repossession can induce the debtor to cure the default. Once the secured creditor gains physical control over the object, it may find it easier to negotiate with the debtor because the loss or unavailability of even one such object can cause serious disruption to the latter's schedule. Another reason why the secured creditor can take possession of the object is to keep it in operation where the debtor has ceased trading so that profit can still be earned. By taking possession, the secured creditor can also intercept any rentals payable under the leases, provided that they do not terminate once the security interest is enforced. Most importantly, the secured creditor will need to take possession of the object in order to sell it.[76] Since the Convention permits self-help repossession, the secured creditor may be able to seize

[73] Wood (n 7) 370.

[74] See, for instance, *CIT Leasing Corp v Brasmex-Brasil Minas Express LTDA*, No 03 Civ 5077(DAB) (FM), 2007.

[75] Wood (n 7) 369.

[76] Adeoye (n 70) 547.

the object without applying for a court order, saving both time and cost.[77] The availability of the remedy of repossession also means that the secured creditor can be more certain that if the debtor defaults, it can take the object and realise it to obtain repayment of the debt. This will reduce the risk of non-repayment and give the debtor access to credit at lower cost.[78]

When exercising the Convention's remedy of repossession, the secured creditor may be faced with several issues. First, is the secured creditor required to send a notice of intention to repossess to the debtor? Secondly, does the secured creditor owe duties in relation to the preservation, maintenance and insurance of the repossessed object? Thirdly, the Convention and the Protocols stipulate that all remedies of the secured creditor, including the remedy of repossession, should be exercised in a commercially reasonable manner.[79] As noted, since commercial reasonableness is not defined, it may be difficult to ascertain exactly *how* repossession should be handled to comply with this test. The only explanation given in the Convention is that a remedy shall be 'deemed to be exercised in a commercially reasonable manner where it is exercised in conformity with a provision of the security agreement except where such a provision is manifestly unreasonable'.[80]

This guidance is of some help, but it leaves open a number of questions. First, a security agreement, however detailed, cannot be expected to cover all possible aspects of repossession. If a particular aspect of repossession is not dealt with in the security agreement, the question of compliance with commercial reasonableness will have to be examined under the Convention. In this case, it will be necessary to ascertain what principles and factors are relevant in establishing whether this requirement has been met. Secondly, how are the parties to decide whether a provision of the security agreement on repossession is regarded as 'manifestly unreasonable'? It can be argued that if such a provision reflects an accepted international practice on repossession, it is not manifestly unreasonable.[81] One would then have to ascertain what amounts to an international practice and, moreover, how unreasonable the provision of the security agreement has to be before it can be regarded as *manifestly* unreasonable. These issues are dealt with below.

In some cases, taking possession of the charged object may be difficult or impossible to achieve simply because it is not located on Earth. This is particularly relevant in the case of space assets, such as satellites and its component parts. When taking actual possession is not possible, the secured

[77] Although the Convention allows extra-judicial repossession, this right may be varied by a declaration of the Contracting State. See Art 54(2) of the Convention.

[78] For the position in the US law, see T Zinnecker, 'The Default Provisions of Revised Article 9 of the Uniform Commercial Code: Part I' (1998–99) 54 *Bus Law* 1113, 1140.

[79] Art 8(3) CTC and Art IX(3) of the Aircraft Protocol.

[80] Art 8(3) CTC.

[81] Goode (n 12) 282.

creditor's next best option is to take control over the object. To take control over the orbiting satellite, the secured creditor may need to obtain access to the telemetry, tracking and command (TT&C) facility.[82] The code to the TT&C can be changed or caused to be changed at the request of the secured creditor, which should enable it to take control over the space asset. The Space Protocol provides that parties to the security agreement can agree to place codes, giving access to the space asset, with a third party in order to give the secured creditor an opportunity to establish control over it in the case of the debtor's default.[83] However, the right of the parties to enter into such an agreement can be restricted by the applicable domestic law.[84]

a. Notice of the Intention to Take Possession

Once the debtor is in default, the secured creditor can take possession of the object. The Convention does not state whether the secured creditor must notify the debtor of the default and to inform it of its intention to take possession of the object. In contrast, the secured creditor proposing to sell or lease the object must give reasonable prior notice in writing to all interested persons including the debtor, informing them of the proposed disposition.[85] The reason why the secured creditor is required to inform interested persons of the proposed disposition is that the sale or lease of the object can affect the interests of other persons as well as those of the debtor. The sale of the object will also prevent the debtor from discharging the secured obligation and recovering the object from the creditor. The purpose of the reasonable notice, served prior to the proposed disposition, is to warn interested persons that their position will be changed and give them an opportunity to cure the default in order to prevent the loss of the object. But when the secured creditor is merely proposing to take possession of the object, repercussions are less serious and the position is still reversible even after repossession takes place. Thus, if the debtor tenders unpaid interest and agrees to pay all further installments in due course, the aircraft may be returned to it. Another reason why the Convention does not require the secured creditor to send notice of intention to repossess may be that in most cases the debtor will be aware of the default and can expect that the object

[82] D Panahy and R Mittal, 'The Prospective UNIDROIT Convention on International Interests in Mobile Equipment as applied to Space Property' (1999) 4 *Unif L Rev* 303, 309.

[83] Art XIX of the Space Protocol. See M Stanford, 'The Preliminary Draft Protocol to the Convention on International Interests in Mobile Equipment on Matters Specific to Space Assets' (2010) UN/Thailand Workshop on Space Law, 'Activities of States in Outer Space in Lights of New Developments: Meeting International Responsibilities and Establishing National Legal and Policy Frameworks' 1, 15.

[84] Art XIX of the Space Protocol. See also Sundahl (n 3) 99.

[85] Art 8(4) CTC.

will be repossessed. If this is the case, the requirement of notice informing the debtor of intended repossession may be superfluous.

However, the position is less clear when the secured creditor initially refrains from taking possession of the object despite the debtor's default, but later decides to repossess. This can happen if the debtor fails to pay several installments due under the security agreement or if the debtor is consistently late in making the payments. Because of the disadvantages associated with repossession, the secured creditor can agree to reschedule the debt to make repayment easier for the debtor. But if the situation does not improve and the defaults continue to occur, the secured creditor may decide to repossess. If this is the case, should the secured creditor be required to inform the debtor of intended repossession or can it tow the object away without prior notice?

The answer to this question may turn on the interpretation of the security agreement. For example, a security agreement may contain a 'no waiver' clause indicating that acceptance of late payments should not amount to the waiver of the secured creditor's remedies. At the same time, if the debtor fails to pay on time and the secured creditor accepts belated payments, but later (following another default) decides to take possession of the object, the debtor may attempt to challenge repossession. It is possible to argue that earlier acceptances of late payments by the secured creditor established a course of conduct between the parties whereby the debtor could rely on belated payments being accepted. Accordingly, it can be suggested that if the secured creditor decides to break the pattern of accepting the defaults and repossess the object, it should be required to send the debtor a prior notice of its intention, failing which repossession may be held to be wrongful.

This view has received some support in cases decided under US domestic law. For example, in one case the agreement for the lease of a pick-up truck provided that the bank could terminate the lease and repossess the object in case of the debtor's failure to pay rentals or to procure insurance.[86] The bank did not repossess the truck even though the insurance cover was interrupted for 10 months and the debtor was consistently late in paying the rentals. Instead, the bank 'nursed the transaction along' by reminding the debtor about payments and accepting late tenders. Then, without any prior notice, a collecting agent of the bank, which learned about the defaults, repossessed the truck. It was held that the course of dealing established between the parties, whereby the bank accepted late payments, did not result in the waiver of its right to repossess the object following the debtor's default. But a secured creditor who did not insist on strict compliance in the past must, before it can rely on the 'no waiver' clause and repossess the object, notify the debtor that strict compliance with the contract will be

[86] *Nevada National Bank v Huff*, 94 Nev 506, 582 P 2d 364, 24 UCC Rep Serv 1044, 1978.

required to avoid repossession.[87] Since the bank did not notify the debtor of its intention to terminate or take possession of the truck, repossession was held to be wrongful.

At the same time, it can be argued that the secured creditor should not be punished for helping a debtor which is in financial difficulties and that it should be permitted to effect repossession without any prior notice even if it accepted previous defaults of the debtor.[88] This may also benefit the debtor, because if the secured creditor can be certain that it will not be penalised for its forbearance, it may be more willing to accept late payments rather than to declare the default. In addition, requiring the secured creditor to send prior notice of intended repossession where late payments were previously accepted, but not in other cases, can cause confusion and encourage the secured creditor to take possession of the object even in those cases where the default of the debtor would have been condoned if duly cured by the debtor.

With regard to the Convention, it is suggested that the fact that prior notice is expressly required in the cases of proposed sale and lease, but is not mentioned in the case of repossession, means that the secured creditor is not required to send a notice to the debtor before taking possession of the object. However, if repossession is not handled correctly, the secured creditor may face liability for wrongful repossession or trespass under the applicable law.[89] To avoid litigation and possible liability it may be prudent to serve notice of default and intended repossession even if this is not required under the agreement or the Convention.

b. Duties in Relation to the Repossessed Object and the Standard of Commercial Reasonableness

Once the aircraft object is repossessed, the secured creditor will need to arrange for it to be stored, maintained and, possibly, operated. The Convention does not expressly state whether the secured creditor owes to the debtor any duties in relation to preservation of the physical condition of the repossessed object. At the same time, a failure to exercise reasonable care

[87] See further *Cobb v Midwest Recovery Bureau Company*, 295 NW 2d 232, 28 UCC Rep Serv 941, 1980; *Steichen v First Bank Grand*, 372 NW 2d 768, 41 UCC Rev Serv 1866, 1985 and *Slusser v Wyrick*, 28 Ohio App 3d 96, 502 NE 2d 259, 1986.

[88] *Monarch Coaches v ITT Industrial Credit*, 818 F 2d 11, 3 UCC Rep Serv 2d 1274, 1987. See also *KB Oil Company v Ford Motor Credit Company*, 811 F 2d 310, 3 UCC Rev Serv 2d 417; *Lewis v National City Bank*, 814 F Supp 696, 21 UCC Rep Serv 2d 380, 1993.

[89] Some legal systems require the secured creditor/lessor to send notice of default and intended repossession to the debtor/lessee before repossession. See T Rodrigues, 'International Regulation of Interests in Aircraft: the Brazilian Reality and the UNIDROIT Proposal' (2000) 65 *J Air L Com* 279, 298–99.

in its preservation may result in diminution of value, deterioration and loss of the object. It can make the possibility of repayment of the secured debt even fainter and result in unnecessary waste of a valuable asset belonging to the debtor.[90]

Although the Convention is silent on this point, a security agreement can indicate that once the aircraft object is repossessed it will need to be stored, maintained, repaired and insured to preserve its value and safe operation. The provision of the security agreement on preservation of the repossessed object may also warn the secured creditor about possible liability in relation to the object. Should the debtor cure the default before the aircraft object is sold or leased, the secured creditor may have to return the object. If the condition of the aircraft deteriorates because it was not kept in a suitable hangar or its value diminishes because it is involved in an accident, the secured creditor may be held liable for the debtor's loss. Provided that a provision of the security agreement on preservation of the repossessed object reflects an international practice on repossession, it can be considered as commercially reasonable. At the same time, even if the basic duty of preservation of the physical condition of the repossessed object is stipulated in the security agreement, many other situations not dealt with by the agreement may arise. For instance, the secured creditor may defer or outsource the object's maintenance to specialists in another country to reduce the cost of the repossession. While the maintenance is deferred, the repossessed object can be kept in operation and profit can be applied towards the reduction of the secured debt. If maintenance is outsourced to another country where the necessary checks will be performed by unlicenced mechanics and, for this reason, cost less, this too may help the secured creditor to minimise the cost of the repossession. If the security agreement does not address such issues, how can the parties ascertain whether these aspects of repossession comply with the Convention's requirement of commercial reasonableness?

In addition to the duties relating to the preservation of the repossessed object, the security agreement may indicate that it must be operated and all sums received must be applied to the reduction of the debt.[91] If this provision is not manifestly unreasonable, the measures which the secured creditor would have to take to comply with it would, presumably, be regarded as commercially reasonable. In the case of aircraft objects, keeping the aircraft

[90] Similarly, under English law, the mortgagee in possession is under a duty to preserve and take reasonable care in relation to the physical state of the object. See *Palk v Mortgage Services Funding plc* [1993] Ch 330, 338. Cases where the object is repossessed but not exploited are more complicated: the question here is the extent of the mortgagee's duty to make whatever profit could have been made from the collateral. See *White v City of London Brewery* (1889) 42 Ch D 237.

[91] See *White v City of London Brewery* (1889) 42 Ch D 237 which may serve to illustrate the point.

in operation requires purchasing the fuel, paying landing and navigation fees, and incurring other expenses. Since these costs are necessary to operate the aircraft, they are likely to be considered as commercially reasonable. Accordingly, these costs will be deducted from profit made from the operation of the object which would, in general, go towards the discharge of the secured debt. But within these broad contours, there may be situations where some actions of the secured creditor may be challenged as commercially unreasonable.

For example, it can be argued that while the secured creditor undoubtedly needed to purchase fuel, it should have purchased it from the debtor's supplier to take advantage of a considerable discount offered there instead of buying the fuel elsewhere at full price.[92] If the fuel comes in different types, it could be argued that instead of purchasing the best (and most expensive) type of fuel, the secured creditor should have opted for the regular one, usually used in the trade. Finally, it can be argued that while it was necessary to insure the aircraft, there was no need to insure it against war and political risks as it was only intended to be operated in one or two countries which were considered to be politically and economically stable.

If the security agreement does not expressly or implicitly address these issues, then, it is submitted, the meaning of the concept of commercial reasonableness falls to be considered in the light of the Convention's general principles[93] and the broad considerations and ideas, set out earlier, which underlie the notion of commercial reasonableness. One of the main aims of the Convention is to promote economically effective asset-based financing of equipment by ensuring that the cost of borrowing can be reduced to make credit affordable.[94] This can be achieved if unnecessary costs of repossession and waste of valuable resources are avoided. Purchasing the fuel at full price where a discount is available cannot be commercially reasonable because it will increase the cost of repossession and of the overall debt. A secured creditor will repossess an aircraft if the debtor is in default or insolvent, which will usually mean that the debtor is in financial difficulty. The costs of repossession will be added to the amount of the secured obligation. Such costs, if not commercially reasonable, may further aggravate the debtor's financial position and decrease the prospects of repayment, which can hardly benefit the secured creditor. For this reason, it is suggested that commercial reasonableness should mean that a repossessing secured creditor should attempt to deal with an aircraft object in such a way that would enable a debtor to repay the debt. In other words, the secured creditor, while thinking about

[92] See, similarly, on availability of discounts, *Medforth v Blake and Others* [2000] Ch 86. See S Frisby, 'Making a Silk Purse out of Pig's Ear—*Medforth v Blake & Ors*' (2000) 63 *MLR* 413.

[93] Art 5 CTC.

[94] See the Preamble to the Convention.

its own interest, should also have the debtor's interest in mind. This would mean that any unnecessary costs should be avoided.

Another question which may arise is whether the debtor's financial standing should be relevant when deciding whether a remedy is exercised in a commercially reasonable manner. For example, can a defaulting debtor, retaining a relatively strong financial position, claim that a secured creditor, not taking advantage of the discount, does not comply with commercial reasonableness? It would seem that if the cost of paying for the fuel at a full price is easily avoidable, it should not be commercially reasonable to forego such an opportunity even if paying a full price will not greatly aggravate the debtor's financial standing. Paying a full price in these circumstances would amount to a waste of resources, which could be allocated for other purposes. As a matter of principle, therefore, even if the debtor's financial position remains relatively stable the creditor should strive to reduce costs, which are reasonably avoidable.

At the same time, an immediate reduction of the cost of repossession when exercising the remedy should not be the only objective of the secured creditor. For instance, a deferred or outsourced maintenance of repossessed object may reduce the cost of repossession. But, if the necessary checks and repairs are not performed in due course, the condition of the valuable object aircraft may deteriorate leading to its waste. If the object is no longer operational, it will have to be kept on the ground. This may lead to a further increase in the overall debt, which may not be commercially reasonable.

ii. Sale of the Charged Object

a. Sale: Public or Private?

Following the debtor's default, the secured creditor can take possession and sell the object charged to it either in a public or private sale. Not all jurisdictions allow the secured creditor to sell the charged object in a private sale without obtaining a court order.[95] The main purpose of a public auction

[95] This is often the case in civil law jurisdictions. See G Mauri, 'The Cape Town Convention on Interests in Mobile Equipment as Applied to Aircraft: Are Lenders Better off under the Geneva Convention?' (2005) 5 *European Review of Private Law* 641, 649. This is the position in Venezuela, Russia and Croatia. See H Gutierrez-Machado, 'The Personal Property Secured Financing System of Venezuela: A Comparative Study and the Case for Harmonization' (1998) 30 *U Miami Inter-Am L Rev* 343, 367–68; B Bennett, 'Secured Financing in Russia: Risks, Legal Incentives, and Policy Concerns' (1999) 77 *Tex L Rev* 1443, 1460; T Josipovic, 'The Rail Protocol and Croatian Secured Transactions Law' (2007) *Unif L Rev* 489, 506. In Germany, the charged object can be sold at a public auction conducted by a neutral person, but no intervention of the court is generally required. See K Bismarck, 'Secured Transactions in Remedies (Germany)' in I Fletcher and O Swarting (eds), *Remedies Under Security Interests* (London, Kluwer Law International 2002) 125.

conducted under the supervision of the court or a notary is to protect the debtor from the creditor's abuse. It is considered that if the secured creditor is allowed to sell the object without intervention of the court, it may sell at a price sufficient to repay the debt but not representing the true market value of the object. In this case, the holders of subsequent international interests and the debtor will not benefit from the sale.[96] Alternatively, the seller can sell a high value object at a reduced price and claim the remainder of the debt from the debtor.[97] It is also considered that a public sale or auction can attract more bidders, which may increase the selling price of the object.[98] Some jurisdictions have a scaling system of auctions: if the object is not sold at the first public auction at the price set by the court, the price can be reduced for the second auction, and so on until a private sale is ordered. All these measures lead to additional costs and delays for both the secured creditor and the debtor with no guarantees that the object will be sold at a price representing its true market value.[99]

Other jurisdictions allow a private sale of charged objects without court intervention and justify this approach in terms of speed, efficiency and lower costs when repossessing or disposing of the object.[100] Despite these advantages, the secured creditor selling the object at a private sale may face the risk that the sale may not be recognised in another country. This can be particularly relevant in the case of an aircraft sale because some jurisdictions require a certificate of deletion obtained with the court's approval from the State where the aircraft had been registered before it was sold.[101] If some of the aspects of the sale do not comply with the requirement of commercial reasonableness, a private sale can be challenged by the debtor. The secured creditor can also be liable under the sale agreement with the purchaser because a private sale did not extinguish any prior encumbrances, weakening the purchaser's title to the object.[102]

The Convention recognises the differences between the approaches of various jurisdictions towards a private or public sale of the repossessed object, with there being, possibly, no need to reconcile them. To this end, the requirement for the Contracting States to submit a mandatory declaration under Article 54(2) clarifying whether the Convention's remedies, including a sale of the object, could be exercised with or without leave of the court represents a practical solution balancing these different approaches.

[96] Mauri and Itterbeek (n 6) 553.

[97] A Coles-Bjerre, 'Trusting the Process and Mistrusting the Results: A Structural Perspective on Article 9's Law-Price Foreclosure Rule' (2001) 9 *Am Bankr Inst L Rev* 351, 352–54.

[98] Zinnecker (n 78) 1153.

[99] Wood (n 7) 373–74.

[100] H Gabriel, 'The New Zealand Personal Property Securities Act: A Comparison with the North American Model for Personal Property Security' (2000) 34 *Int'l L* 1123, 1130.

[101] Wood (n 7) 374.

[102] *Ibid* 373–74.

b. Sale of the Object in a Commercially Reasonable Manner

Irrespective of whether the repossessed object is sold at a private or public sale, the secured creditor must ensure that this remedy is exercised in a commercially reasonable manner. To this end, the parties to the security agreement can specify how the sale should be handled in order to be commercially reasonable. The sale of the repossessed object is likely to involve many stages and the security agreement may address such issues as a limited clean up and preparation of the object for the sale, content and types of publications where the sale should be advertised, and a time frame within which the secured creditor should be expected to sell the object.[103]

Similar to the Convention, the requirement of a commercially reasonable exercise of remedies can be found in Article 9 of the Uniform Commercial Code (UCC).[104] The cases on a commercially reasonable sale, decided under Article 9, may help elucidate what factors are relevant in deciding whether the disposition complied with this test. In one US case, the secured creditor advertised the sale of the repossessed Sabreliner 60 executive jet in the *Wall Street Journal* 13 days before sale and in a well-known aircraft publication, *Trade-a-Plane*, five days before sale; this was not considered commercially reasonable.[105] The advertisement in the *Wall Street Journal* appeared in a general section as a public notice and not in the aviation section, which was usually used in the trade. The advertisement in *Trade-a-Plane* was considered to be written in terms which were too cautious to encourage any interest from the buyers. But even if both advertisements complied with the stated requirements, this might still not have been adequate, because in accordance with the established practice among aircraft sellers, the secured creditor should have identified individual buyers and aircraft dealers who could potentially be interested in purchasing the aircraft and contacted them by mail or telegram.[106] In this case, the secured creditor had a mailing list of some 5,000 individuals, dealers and companies known to be interested in receiving notices of available jet aircrafts, but failed to contact potential buyers. In addition, the secured creditor took no steps to improve the appearance of the aircraft which could have been done by replacing insured eyebrow windows. The aircraft was kept at a secret location at a small out-of-the-way airport and a dealer seeking to inspect it prior to the sale was refused the opportunity to do so. The secured creditor

[103] Zinnecker (n 78) 1153.

[104] §9-610(b), §9-627 *Uniform Commercial Code: Official Text and Comments*, 2009–2010 edn (Thomson West 2009).

[105] *Connex Press v International Airmotive* (1977) 436 Supp 51, 22 UCC Rep Serv 1310, Civ A No 76-0538.

[106] As was the case in *Cessna Finance Corp v Robert Wall* (1994) 876 F Supp 273, 26 UCC Rep Serv 2d 637, No CA-93-77 ATH(DF).

was the only bidder at the auction and bought the aircraft, worth around $700,000, for $325,000.

This case demonstrates that such factors as advertisement, preparation of the object for sale, an opportunity to inspect and the price at which it is sold may be decisive in determining whether the sale is conducted in a commercially reasonable manner. In relation to advertising the sale, the notice of sale should target a public which is generally expected to be interested in this type of equipment.[107] Thus, in addition to contacting potential buyers via mail, the secured creditor should consider placing a notice in specialist publications and not only in general newspapers.[108] The notice of sale should also be drafted in a way that would create interest among potential buyers to secure the best possible price.[109]

Another relevant factor relates to the preparation of the object for sale by improving its appearance. The Convention does not require the secured creditor to repair or make improvements to the object before it is sold. The question is whether the secured creditor should not only preserve, but also repair or improve the object. For example, if repainting the aircraft would considerably increase its price, should the secured creditor be required to do so to sell the object in a commercially reasonable manner? The answer depends on how the general ideas underlying the notion of commercial reasonableness fare in the context of the particular facts. On the one hand, the experience of different jurisdictions shows that extreme caution is needed before imposing such an obligation on the secured creditor.[110] While repairing the object may increase the likelihood of obtaining a better price, this cannot always be guaranteed and there is a risk that the money put into repairs may not be recovered either from the sale of the object or from the debtor.[111] On the other hand, it is conceivable that it may be commercially reasonable to make improvements, such as repainting the object. This will be so where, among other things, the benefits of such improvements

[107] *Ford & Vlahos v ITT Commercial Finance Corp* (1994) 8 Cal 4th 1220, 885 P 2d 877, 36 Cal Rptr 2d 464.

[108] *Contrail Leasing Partners v Consolidated Airways* (1984) 742 F 2d 1095, 39 UCC Rep Serv 9; R Nowka, 'EBay Auctions of Repossessed Motor Vehicles—A Template for Commercial Reasonableness under Revised Article 9' (2007) 31 *S Ill U LJ* 281, 299.

[109] *Villella Enterprises, Inc v Young* (1998) 108 NM 33, 766 P 2d 293.

[110] English law requires the secured creditor to preserve, but not to improve the object before selling it. See *Garland v Ralph Pay & Ransom* [1984] 2 EGLR 147, 151; *Silven Properties Ltd v Royal Bank of Scotland plc* [2003] EWCA Civ 1409. §9-610(a) UCC states that the secured creditor may dispose of the object in its present condition or following any commercially reasonable preparation or processing. This means that the secured creditor is not obliged to repair or improve the object and can, in principle, dispose of it in its present condition. But if it may be commercially reasonable, some preparation of the object may be undertaken before disposing of it. See Zinnecker (n 78) 1151.

[111] J White and R Summers, *Uniform Commercial Code*, 6th edn (Thomson Reuters 2010) 1346–47.

considerably outweigh the costs and risks associated with them,[112] and where these costs are not unduly burdensome to both the creditor and the debtor, whose debt may increase as a result of such improvements. In fact, the notion of commercial reasonableness is wide enough to include not only improvements and repairs, but a number of other measures such as disassembling the object and selling it in parts. For example, if the secured creditor discovers that the repossessed aircraft is not in a condition to fly, it may be commercially reasonable to disassemble its wings for easier transportation and sell it in parts.[113] Although it may be argued that a disassembled aircraft will raise considerably less than an entire aircraft, the cost of repair may outweigh the potential benefit of its preparation for sale.

Providing potential buyers with an opportunity to inspect the object as well as presenting log books and airworthiness certificates and other documents may also be a relevant consideration when deciding whether the sale is conducted in a commercially reasonable manner.[114] Where the secured creditor refuses to start engines or to present the documents relating to the object,[115] or where it hides the object to prevent its inspection,[116] this may deter potential buyers and adversely affect the price of the object. A sale conducted in such circumstances may not be commercially reasonable.

Another factor relates to the timing of the sale. Selling a repossessed aircraft worth over $2.64m within two weeks of marketing to a purchaser described by the secured creditor's representative as a 'true bottom fisher' for only $2m to prevent a negative impact on the secured creditor's history of loan performance was not be considered as commercially reasonable.[117] At the same time, waiting too long may also be a mistake.[118] The best guide in relation to the time for making a commercially reasonable sale is the nature of the object and the market conditions.[119] Given that objects covered by the Convention are exceptionally expensive, the circle of potential buyers of such objects is likely to be limited. If the industry is going through a recession, this too may affect the purchase capacity of potential buyers. This means that finding a suitable buyer may take time and rushing

[112] See Zinnecker (n 78) 1151. See *Grumman Credit Corporation v Rivair Flying Service* (1992) 845 P 2d 182, 186 18 UCC Rep Serv 2d 978.

[113] *Grumman Credit Corporation v Rivair Flying Service* (1992) 845 P 2d 182, 18 UCC Rep Serv 2d 978.

[114] *Ibid* 186.

[115] *Sunjet Inc v Ford Motor Credit* (1985) 703 SW ad 285.

[116] *Connex Press v International Airmotive* (1977) 436 Supp 51, 22 UCC Rep Serv 1310, Civ A No 76-0538.

[117] *Aviation Finance Group v DUC Housing Pertners* (2010) WL 1576841 (D Idaho) 72 UCC Rep Serv 2d 583.

[118] *Harris v Bower* (1972) 266 Md 579, 295 A 2d 870, 55 ALR 3d 640, 11 UCC Rep Serv 428, where the creditor permitted the repossessed boat to depreciate for two yachting seasons before selling it, which was held not to be commercially reasonable.

[119] *In re Concord Coal Corporation* (1988) 81 BR 863, 6 UCC Rep Serv 2d 1646.

a sale may not be commercially reasonable.[120] Finally, the price at which the object is sold can be another important indicator of a commercially reasonable sale.[121] If the secured creditor is the only bidder and buys the repossessed aircraft for $1m only to resell it later at $1.5m, this is unlikely to amount to a commercially reasonable sale.[122] At the same time, the mere fact that a higher price could have been obtained should not necessarily mean that the sale was not commercially reasonable and other factors discussed earlier should also be taken into account.[123]

While this list of factors is not exhaustive, it helps to shed some light on the standard of commercial reasonableness. For example, the requirement that the sale of the repossessed aircraft should not only be widely advertised, but also that the seller should identify and contact potential buyers, demonstrates that in a commercially reasonable sale the secured creditor should make every reasonable effort to secure the highest possible price for the object. This means that the secured creditor should have the debtor's interests in mind when dealing with the repossessed object since a high purchase price may help the debtor to reduce or extinguish the debt. Looking after the debtor's interests should also mean that a passive attitude in relation to the preservation of the physical condition of the repossessed object should not be encouraged. If the object is not properly stored and any necessary maintenance and repair works are not performed in due course, its physical condition may rapidly deteriorate leading to economic waste of a valuable asset. In contrast, if the object is kept in a good condition, it can be sold or leased to the party who values it most, thereby promoting economic efficiency. In some cases, the interests of the secured creditor and the debtor will coincide. Indeed, if the sale of the object yields high returns enabling the debtor to extinguish the debt, this will benefit the secured creditor as well. At the same time, the Convention does not impose on the secured creditor an obligation to put the debtor's interest before its own and some balance must be struck between the debtor's interest in obtaining the highest

[120] *Nelson v Armstrong* (1978) 99 Idaho 422, 582 P 2d 1100, 24 UCC Rep Serv 1378; *John Deere Leasing Company v Fraker* (1986) 395 NW 2d 885, 2 UCC Rep Serv 2d 1152.

[121] See J Sandrelli, C Ramsay and A Bahadoorsingh, 'Remedies Under Security Interests in Canada: An Overview' in I Fletcher and O Swarting (eds), *Remedies Under Security Interests* (London, Kluwer Law International 2002) 80.

[122] *Ford & Vlahos v ITT Commercial Finance Corp* (1994) 8 Cal 4th 1220, 885 P 2d 877, 36 Cal Rptr 2d 464. The Convention does not preclude the secured creditor from purchasing the collateral provided that the sale is conducted in a commercially reasonable manner. In contrast, English law does not allow the secured creditor to sell the collateral to itself as this may create the conflict of interests. At the same time, the mortgagee may be able to sell the collateral to a company in which it has an interest. In this case the mortgagee or the company has to show that it took reasonable steps to obtain best possible price for the object. See *Martinson v Clowes* (1882) 21 Ch D 857; *Tse Kwong Lam v Wong Chit Sen* [1983] 1 WLR 1349, 1355 per Lord Templeman. See also *Alpstream AG v PK Airfinance Sarl* [2011] EWHC 1002 (Comm).

[123] *Parker-Tweedale v Dunbar Bank plc and Others* [1991] Ch 12.

possible price for the repossessed object and the secured creditor's interest in obtaining a quick repayment of the debt. The secured creditor will, most likely, sell the charged object as a repossessed and used asset. This means that securing the highest price representing its true value may not always be possible. But the secured creditor should seek to obtain the highest *possible* price and, if sale proceeds are not sufficient to extinguish the debt, to claim the remainder from the debtor.

iii. Lease and Management of the Object

Instead of selling the repossessed object, the secured creditor may grant a lease over it and apply rentals to the reduction of the secured debt.[124] Alternatively, the secured creditor can choose to collect or receive income or profit resulting from the management or use of the object to reduce the debt.[125] The exercise of these remedies means that although the debtor may be dispossessed of the object, it will retain its interest in it and, once the debt is repaid, can resume possession. Similar to other remedies of the secured creditor, leasing and collection or receipt or income and profit from management of the object should be exercised in a commercially reasonable manner.[126]

When repossessing the object, the secured creditor may find that it is already leased out by the debtor. If the interest of the secured creditor was registered before that of the debtor/lessor, it will prevail over the interest of the lessee.[127] In this case, the secured creditor may either terminate the existing lease or allow the lease to continue provided that the rental payments are paid to it. In making this decision, the secured creditor will need to exercise commercial reasonableness which may involve the assessment of costs associated with terminating the existing lease and finding a new lessee. Finally, leasing the object may be precluded if the object is situated on the territory of a Contracting State which has made a declaration to this effect.[128]

B. Notice of Proposed Sale or Lease

i. Purpose of Notice

The secured creditor proposing to sell or grant a lease of an object must give a reasonable notice in writing to interested persons informing them

[124] Art 8(1)(b) CTC.
[125] Art 8(1)(c) CTC.
[126] Art 8(3) CTC.
[127] Art 29(4) CTC.
[128] Art 54(1). As at February 2017 only China had made such a declaration.

of the proposed disposition.[129] The Protocols specify a number of working or calendar days within which the written notice should be given by the secured creditor. The Aircraft Protocol states that 10 or more working days written notice of a proposed sale should satisfy the requirement of providing a 'reasonable prior notice'.[130] The Luxembourg Protocol, the Space Protocol and the draft MAC Protocol allow for a longer period and indicate that written notice given to interested persons 14 or more calendar days ahead of the proposed sale or lease should satisfy the requirement of reasonable prior notice.[131] There is no need to send such a notice if the secured creditor proposes to exercise other remedies, such as repossession or collecting or receiving any income or profit arising from the management or use of the object.

The main purpose of the notice is to warn interested persons about the potentially irreversible changes and give them an opportunity to protect their interests in the object. An informed debtor can raise finance to redeem the object to prevent its loss[132] or to purchase the object itself.[133] Alternatively, it can contact other interested persons who may repay the debt. Such interested persons will then be subrogated to the rights of the secured creditor.[134] The notice informing the debtor about the proposed disposition may also provide it with an opportunity to ensure that the sale is conducted in a commercially reasonable manner.[135] This may be beneficial to the secured creditor, as monitoring (or failure to monitor) by the debtor of the commercial reasonableness of the sale may prevent it from challenging a disposition of the object at a later stage.[136]

ii. The Recipients of Notice

The notice of a proposed sale or lease must be given to interested persons,[137] a notion which is only relevant for the Part of the Convention which deals with the creditor's remedies. For instance, Article 9 indicates that unless the secured creditor obtains a court order, it will need the agreement of interested persons to vest in itself the interest held by the debtor in the object in or towards satisfaction of the debt.[138] Similarly, Article 13 provides

[129] Art 8(4) CTC.

[130] Art IX(4) of the Aircraft Protocol.

[131] Art VII(4) of the Luxembourg Protocol; Art XVII(2) of the Space Protocol; Art VIII(4) of the draft MAC Protocol.

[132] *Deere Credit v Lowell Quarries* (2002) F Supp 2d, 2002 WL 1632444 (ND Ill), 48 UCC Rep Serv 2d 40.

[133] *Siemens Credit v Marvik Colour* (1994) 859 F Supp 686, 24 UCC Rep Serv 2d 705 692.

[134] Art 9(4) CTC.

[135] Zinnecker (n 78) 1160.

[136] R Lloyd, 'The Absolute Bar Rule in UCC Foreclosure Sales: A Prescription for Waste' (1993) 40 *UCLAL Rev* 695, 715–20.

[137] See Art 1(m) CTC.

[138] Art 9(1), (2) CTC.

that when granting a speedy relief order, the court may impose such terms as it considers necessary to protect interested persons from the creditor's misbehaviour.[139] The court may also require that a notice is given to interested persons informing them of the request of the speedy relief made by the creditor.[140]

There are three categories of interested persons under the Convention.[141] Some interested persons are entitled to receive the notice of proposed sale or lease; others may only expect such notice if they inform the secured creditor about their rights in the object within a reasonable time prior to the sale or lease.[142] The debtor, ie the chargor under the security agreement, the conditional buyer under the title reservation agreement, and the lessee under the leasing agreement, are in the first category of interested persons.[143] But this category of debtor also includes a person whose interest in the object is burdened by a registrable non-consensual right or interest (NCRI) under Article 40.[144] It may not be immediately clear who this person is. It should be someone who already has an interest in the object and that interest is burdened by the registrable NCRI. Accordingly, it cannot be the holder of the NCRI, but can be either the primary debtor or a holder of another international interest whose interest is subsequent to the registrable NCRI and, for that reason, burdened by it. Since the primary debtor, ie the chargor, conditional buyer and lessee, is defined separately, this means that the person whose interest is burdened by the NCRI may be the holder of a subsequent or subordinated international interest.

For example, if the chargor grants a security interest in a railway object to secured creditor 1 (SC1), a registrable NCRI to creditor 2 (C2) and another security interest to secured creditor 3 (SC3), then the chargor and SC3 will be considered as debtors and will be entitled to receive the notice of the proposed sale or lease as interested persons. In contrast, SC1 will not be considered as the debtor or other interested person falling into the first category. The consequence of the distinction between the holder of the international interest, whose interest is or is not burdened by the registrable NCRI, is that the former (but not the latter) will be among those interested persons who are entitled to receive notice of the proposed disposition. If its interest is not so burdened, the holder of the international interest will fall into the third category of interested persons and will only be entitled to the notice if it informs the secured creditor of its interest in the object.[145]

[139] Art 13(2) CTC.
[140] Art 13(3) CTC.
[141] Art 1(m) CTC.
[142] Art 8(4) CTC.
[143] Art 1(j) CTC.
[144] Art 1(j) CTC.
[145] The purpose of the distinction may be questionable, since in the majority of cases, the holder of the international interest that is not burdened by the registrable non-consensual right

The second category of interested persons includes those persons who, for the purpose of assuring performance of the obligation, give or issue a suretyship or demand guarantee or a standby letter of credit.[146] The third category includes any other persons having rights and interests in the object.[147] This is a wide category and includes senior and junior secured creditors, as well as holders of other interests registerable in the IR. Even the holders of interests which are not so registered may fall into this category. The interested persons in the third category are not automatically entitled to receive the notice of proposed sale or lease from the secured creditor. They can only expect such notice if they themselves notify the secured creditor about their interests in the object within a reasonable time prior to the sale or lease. The registration of such interests in the IR will probably amount to such notice.[148]

Finally, there is no need to use a particular language or include certain information in the notice. The content of the notice is not specified in the Convention and the Protocols. It is suggested that it should include the names of the selling secured creditor and the debtor or other interested persons, to identify the object which is about to be sold or leased as well as the date, the location and manner of the proposed disposition.

iii. Consequences of Not Complying with the Requirements of Commercial Reasonableness and Notice

The main purpose of the requirements of commercial reasonableness and notice of a proposed sale is to protect the debtor from the creditor's misbehaviour. A commercially reasonable sale can reassure the debtor that the secured creditor has put every reasonable effort into obtaining the best possible price for the object. The debtor will primarily be interested in the amount of sale proceeds because these sums will be applied towards discharge of the secured debt. If such sums are not sufficient to extinguish the debt, the debtor will have to pay the deficiency to the secured creditor. If the sale generates a surplus, this may help the debtor extinguish other debts and, possibly, the debtor may even retain the remainder. As noted, the main purpose of the requirement of a prior notice of a proposed sale is to warn the debtor and interested persons that the nature of their interests in the object is about to change.

or interest will register its interest in the IR. This is likely to amount to the notice of the interest which needs to be sent to the selling secured creditor. As a result, the secured creditor will have to send the notice of the proposed disposition to it anyway.

[146] Art 1(m)(ii) CTC.
[147] Art 1(m)(iii) CTC.
[148] Goode (n 12) 64.

The protection of the debtor's interest in the object depends on the secured creditor's compliance with the requirements of commercial reasonableness and notice. But the Convention does not explain what the consequences of non-compliance with them will be. Should the secured creditor exercise a remedy in a way which is manifestly unreasonable or fail to notify the debtor of the proposed sale, the debtor appears not to have any remedy against the secured creditor. It may be argued that the Convention does not govern this issue and that the debtor should proceed against the secured creditor under the applicable law. But if this matter is delegated to the applicable law, the very existence of the requirements of commercial reasonableness and notice under the Convention comes into question. The effect of the Convention and the Protocols is that all remedies of the secured creditor should be exercised in a commercially reasonable manner. If the Convention imposes such an obligation on the secured creditor, it should provide for the consequences of a failure to observe it. Delegating this issue to the applicable domestic law may also lead to non-uniform results because various legal systems may approach the issue of the consequences of non-compliance with the Convention's requirements of commercial reasonableness and notice differently.

If this matter is governed by the Convention, but is not expressly settled in it, it should be settled in conformity with the general principles on which it is based.[149] Before exploring whether there are any general principles capable of resolving this issue and, more broadly, before considering how the problem of the consequences of non-compliance is to be tackled under the Convention, it may be helpful to gain an insight into the experience of some domestic legal systems. For example, under English law, the mortgagee is not required to exercise its remedies in a commercially reasonable manner or, indeed, to exercise them at all. Subject to the duty of good faith, the mortgagee can decide in accordance with its own interest whether and when to sell the object even if its decision has an adverse effect on the position of the mortgagor.[150] But when the mortgagee decides to sell, it owes an equitable duty to the mortgagor and subsequent encumbrancers to take reasonable care in obtaining true market value of the property on the date of sale.[151] What amounts to the exercise of the duty will depend on the circumstances but, generally, the result achieved by this requirement appears to be similar to the one intended under the Convention: to obtain the true market value of the object, the mortgagee should ensure that the sale is advertised in a suitable publication[152] drawing to the attention of potential buyers any

149 Art 5(2) CTC.

150 *Cuckmere Brick Co v Mutual Finance* [1971] Ch 949.

151 *Ibid* 965, 972, 977.

152 *American Express International Banking Corporation v Hurley* [1986] BCLC 52, the case involving the breach of duty where the mortgagee failed to advertise music equipment in a specialist publication.

specific features which may affect the price.[153] Similarly, the mere fact that a higher price could have been obtained does not mean that there is a breach of the duty as long as the price is a 'proper price'.[154]

In one case, the court found that the mortgagee breached its duty to take reasonable care to obtain the true market value of the property because the sale of the building was not adequately advertised and the building was sold to the wife of the mortgagee who was the only bidder at the auction with reserved price.[155] Although there is no fixed rule that the mortgagee cannot sell the mortgaged property to a company in which it has an interest, the close relationship between the mortgagee and the purchaser made it necessary for the mortgagee to show that it had taken reasonable precautions to obtain the best price. The consequence of non-compliance with this duty meant that the sale could be set aside. On the facts of the case, this could not be achieved because of the mortgagor's own failure to bring the action sooner. Some 13 years elapsed before the dispute came for consideration before the Privy Council and it was held that the sale could no longer be set aside. Instead, the mortgagor was entitled to damages, measured as the difference between the best price which could have been obtained at the date of sale and the price paid by the purchaser.

Should a similar approach be adopted when dealing with the consequences of non-compliance with the commercial reasonableness and notice requirements under the Convention? If the secured creditor sells a repossessed aircraft object to a company in which it has an interest for \$1.5m, and that company resells it a week later for \$3m, the sale is unlikely to be held commercially reasonable. Should the debtor be entitled to apply to a court to set the sale aside? The sale could be set aside provided that the debtor is able to redeem the object, in which case the object should be returned to it. Although this approach could work well when applied to these particular facts, it may not be suitable in the context of the Convention. First, as noted, aircraft and aircraft engines are high value objects and the circle of their potential buyers is limited. The prospect of losing the aircraft after great expense may have been incurred to transport it to the jurisdiction of the buyer's choice and to launch it into the sky may deter potential buyers or adversely affect the purchase price. This may run counter to the aim of the Convention to make asset-based financing cheaper because if the secured creditor cannot be certain that the charged aircraft object can be sold relatively quickly, this may affect the cost and availability of credit. Secondly, the purchaser may relocate the aircraft object into a different jurisdiction

[153] *Cuckmere Brick Co v Mutual Finance Ltd* [1971] Ch 949, where a failure to draw to the attention of potential buyers the fact that a planning permission for building of flats was obtained in relation to the mortgaged land, affected the price.

[154] *Parker-Tweedale v Dunbar Bank Plc* [1991] Ch 12.

[155] *Tse Kwong Lam v Wong Chit Sen and Others* [1983] 1 WLR 1349.

where the enforcement of a court order to set the sale aside may be difficult to implement. The decision to set the sale aside may also be subject to various limitation periods under the applicable law. Thirdly, setting the sale aside may be too harsh if non-compliance with the requirements of the Convention is minor. For example, if the secured creditor failed to notify the debtor of the proposed sale, but the price obtained for the object represents its true market value which is sufficient to discharge the debt, disturbing the sale could be unwarranted. This is particularly so where the debtor's financial situation is such that it would not be able to obtain a fresh loan to redeem the object.

In contrast, an approach which does not affect the position of a third party purchaser may be more attractive. For example, if setting the sale aside would be inequitable as between the debtor and the purchaser, the debtor could still be entitled to damages[156] resulting from the loss suffered by it due to the secured creditor's non-compliance with the commercial reasonableness and notice requirements. This could also better reflect the nature of the debtor's loss. In the above example, the debtor may not have suffered *any* loss as a result of the secured creditor's failure to notify it of the proposed sale as it would not have been able to redeem the property in any event. If the view that damages represent a viable and practicable solution to the problem of consequences of non-compliance gains support, the question will arise whether a remedy of damages can be developed within the Convention or whether a damages claim will have to and can be brought under the applicable domestic law. As things stand, there is nothing in the Convention indicating the availability of this remedy.

Similar to the Convention, Article 9 UCC requires that every aspect of the disposition of collateral—including the method, manner, time, place and other terms—must be commercially reasonable.[157] But while Article 9 requires the secured creditor to notify the debtor and dispose of the object in a commercially reasonable manner, its earlier versions did not expressly specify the consequences of its failure to comply with these standards.[158] This resulted in the development of three different approaches, each of which had a varying effect on the secured creditor's right to claim the deficiency.[159] Under the first approach, non-compliance of the secured creditor could preclude it from obtaining the deficiency. If the secured creditor disposed of the object at a significantly lower price (compared to the price at which it has only recently been purchased) at a poorly advertised auction,

[156] *Tse Kwong Lam v Wong Chit Sen and Others* [1983] 1 WLR 1349, 1359–60.

[157] §9-610(b).

[158] *Ruden v Citizens Bank and Trust Company of Maryland* (1994) 99 Md App 605, 638A 2d 1225, 23 UCC Rep Serv 2d 623.

[159] See *Siemens Credit v Marvik Colour* (1994) 859 F Supp 686, 24 UCC Rep Serv 2d 705.

it could be barred from recovering the remainder of the debt.[160] Since this consequence followed regardless of the nature of non-compliance, it was thought to be too harsh on the secured creditor.[161] Debarring the secured creditor from the deficiency payment could also result in a windfall for the debtor. For these reasons, the absolute bar rule was ultimately rejected.

Under the second approach, the secured creditor could obtain the deficiency irrespective of the breach of the requirement of commercial reasonableness, but this was subject to the reduction of damages suffered by the debtor.[162] Finally, the third approach, which is currently accepted under the UCC, is the rule of the rebuttable presumption.[163] According to it, the non-complying secured creditor can still recover a deficiency, but only if it can rebut the presumption that the value of the collateral is equal to the debt. The following example demonstrates how the rule operates.

Assume that the amount of the secured debt is $280m and that the sale of the repossessed aircraft only brought $100m. If the sale is regarded as commercially reasonable and the secured creditor had complied with the requirement of notice, it should recover the remainder of the debt in full ($180m). If the sale is viewed as not complying with the set requirements, the presumption will be that the sum which would have been obtained at a commercially reasonable sale equals the amount of the secured debt ($280m). This means that the secured creditor cannot claim the deficiency from the debtor. The presumption may be rebutted if the secured creditor can show that, even if it had complied with the commercial reasonableness and notice requirements, the sale of the object could not have brought the full amount of the secured debt. For instance, if the secured creditor can show that at a commercially reasonable sale the aircraft could have been sold for $120m, it should be able to claim the remaining $160m from the debtor. By proving the amount which a commercially reasonable sale of the object could have brought, the secured creditor can rectify its own non-compliance. Since the rule places the burden of proof on the secured creditor, it can serve as an adequate deterrent aimed at preventing a commercially unreasonable sale.[164] This means that the debtor's interest can be protected. At the same time, the secured creditor can still claim the remainder of the debt from the debtor.

[160] *Central Budget Corp v Garrett* (1975) 48 AD 2d 825, 368 NYS 2d 268, 17 UCC Rep Serv 327.

[161] See further Lloyd (n 136) 745.

[162] *Associates Capital v Riccardi* (1978) 454 F Supp 832, 24 UCC Rep Serv 1359, 835; *Flickinger Co v 18 Genesee Corporation* (1979) 71 AD 2d 382, 423 NYS 2d 73, 27 UCC Rep Serv 1232.

[163] White and Summers (n 111) 1353–55.

[164] *Ruden v Citizens Bank and Trust Company of Maryland* (1994) 99 Md App 605, 638A 2d 1225, 23 UCC Rep Serv 2d 623, at 1232.

The next question is whether, taking into consideration the Convention's general principles, a similar approach should be developed within its framework. One of the attractions of the rebuttable presumption rule is that the dispute about the consequences of non-compliance with the Convention's requirements is confined to the parties who are immediately affected by them, ie the debtor and the secured creditor. Even if the sale of the aircraft is not commercially reasonable, it is not invalidated and the purchaser can rest assured that once the purchase price is paid, it can safely add the aircraft to its fleet. This means that the price which can be obtained for the repossessed aircraft will not be adversely affected by the prospect that the sale can later be set aside. This, in turn, can assure the secured creditor that it will be able to obtain a proper price for the object and that the debt can be repaid out of sale proceeds which should induce it to lower the interest rate on the loan. This result would accord with one of the Convention's main economic goals of reducing the cost of borrowing against equipment and to make secured financing more readily available. This is also in line with the principle of predictability on which the Convention is based.[165] It is suggested that the rule of rebuttable presumption should be developed under the Convention, because it will clarify what consequences will follow if the secured creditor does not comply with the notice and commercial reasonableness requirements. This approach may also be in line with the Convention's general principle of practicality as it can encourage the secured creditor to put every effort into obtaining the best possible price for the repossessed object to avoid litigation and risk the reduction of the deficiency.

One possible difficulty with the rebuttable presumption rule is that it targets the availability and amount of deficiency—a concept which is not expressly mentioned in the Convention. To prevent the secured creditor from receiving a windfall, as well as to underline the accessory nature of the security interest, any sum collected by it as a result of the exercise of the remedies should be applied to the discharge of the debt.[166] Any surplus which may remain after the discharge of the secured obligation and reasonable costs incurred in the exercise of the remedies should be distributed among holders of subsequent international interests and the debtor.[167]

At the same time, the Convention does not prescribe what the secured creditor should do if the obtained amount is not sufficient to discharge the obligation. First, it is submitted that the secured creditor's deficiency claim should be based on the very notion of the debt: it continues to exist until fully discharged. If the sale proceeds are not sufficient to repay the whole debt, then it is merely reduced by this amount and continues to exist until extinguished. Secondly, some support for the view that the secured creditor

[165] Art 5(1) CTC.
[166] Art 8(5) CTC.
[167] Art 8(6) CTC.

should be able to claim a deficiency can be found in Article 8(5) CTC that provides that 'any sum collected ... as a result of exercise of ... the remedies ... should be applied *towards* discharge' of the debt. This wording suggests that the sum so received should be used as a contribution to the reduction of the amount of the debt. If the sum is enough to extinguish the debt, it should be fully applied for this purpose. The remainder (if any) should be distributed among holders of subsequent international interests and the debtor. If, however, this sum is not sufficient to discharge the obligation, it should still be fully applied to the discharge of the debt, but this does not extinguish the debt. The secured creditor should be able to claim the remaining sum from the debtor.

This analysis can be supported by Article 9(1), which states that, provided that all interested persons agree, the object covered by the security interest can 'vest in the secured creditor *in or towards* satisfaction of the secured obligation' (emphasis added). This means that if the object is transferred to the secured creditor *in* satisfaction of the debt, then the debt is fully discharged. In contrast, if the object is transferred *towards* satisfaction of the debt, the discharge is only partial and the secured creditor should be able to claim the remaining part of the debt. Alternatively, the secured creditor can claim the deficiency from the debtor if this remedy is permitted by the applicable law and is not inconsistent with the Convention.[168]

For these reasons, it is submitted that, first of all, the deficiency can be claimed under the Convention as it naturally flows from the nature of the debt as is supported by the text of the Convention. Secondly, the rebuttable presumption rule which deals with the consequences of non-compliance is an approach which would more effectively (than other considered alternatives) promote and implement the Convention's policies and aims, mentioned above. The Convention's general principles also lend ample support for the development of such a rule. Finally, damages may potentially be an effective and practicable solution along with the rebuttable presumption rule. However, as noted, it is far from clear how and on what basis the remedy of damages could be invoked and applied.

iv. Application of Proceeds and Surplus

Whether the secured creditor takes possession, sells, leases, manages or uses the object, it does not deal with it as its owner. For this reason, any sum received or collected by the secured creditor when exercising its remedies should be applied towards the discharge of the amount of the secured obligation.[169] The sale of the object extinguishes the interest of the debtor

[168] Art 14 CTC.
[169] Art 8(5) CTC.

and any interested persons in it and their only claim is against proceeds of sale. If the sums collected or received by the secured creditor exceed the amount of the secured debt and any reasonable expenses associated with the exercise of remedies, the secured creditor should distribute the surplus among holders of subsequent international interests in order of priority and pay any remainder to the debtor.[170]

V. VESTING OF OBJECT IN SATISFACTION; REDEMPTION

A. Nature of the Remedy

In certain circumstances, a sale of the repossessed object can be financially inexpedient. For instance, when the industry is going through a recession, the sale of the object can bring only a fraction of its value. Similarly, such factors as the availability of a manufacturer's discount and the release on the market of the improved versions of the object covered by the security interest can render its sale financially unattractive. At such times, the amount of debt may exceed the object's value and its sale will not help extinguish the secured obligation.

Instead of selling the repossessed object, the secured creditor can accept it in or towards satisfaction of the secured obligation in the hope that it will be able to sell it (potentially at a profit) when the market improves. To achieve this result, the secured creditor can exercise the remedy of vesting of the object in satisfaction provided by the Convention.[171] The effect of this remedy is that ownership or any other interest of the debtor held in the object will be transferred to the secured creditor in or towards satisfaction of the secured obligation. For example, if an owner/manufacturer grants a security interest in an airframe to the secured creditor in return for a loan and later defaults, the secured creditor can accept this object to discharge the debt. This will 'vest' the ownership of the airframe in the secured creditor. Similarly, possessory interests of a lessee and a conditional buyer or any other interest held by the debtor can be vested in the secured creditor.

The effect of vesting of 'any other interest' and whether it should be different to the vesting of ownership is not explained by the Convention. It is suggested that despite the fact that Article 9(1) distinguishes between 'ownership' and 'any other interest', the effect of vesting of these interests should be the same. This should be the case because Article 9(5) treats both categories of interest in the same manner by providing that ownership or any other interest transferred to the secured creditor should be 'free from any

170 Art 8(6) CTC.
171 Art 9 CTC.

other interest over which the chargee's security interest has priority' under Article 29 CTC. Accordingly, if the lessee grants security interests in the object held by it to the secured creditors 1, 2 and 3 who register their interests in this order, and if SC2 exercises vesting, then it will accept its vested interest free from the subsequently registered interest of SC3, but subject to the previously registered interest of SC1. To obtain an unencumbered title to the object, SC2 would have to pay SC1 a full amount of the debt owed to it by the debtor. Alternatively, SC1 can enforce its own security interest in the object. According to Article 9(5), the same rule would apply to the secured creditor which is vested with the ownership. It seems that the purpose of the distinction between 'ownership' and 'any other interest' in Article 9(1) is simply to recognise that not only ownership, but other interests in the object can be passed to the secured creditor in satisfaction of the secured obligation. In other words, the effect of vesting is to divest the debtor of whatever interest it holds in the object, subject to the possibility of redemption before the object is sold by the secured creditor.[172]

Vesting can be potentially advantageous not only to the secured creditor but also to the debtor. If the secured creditor is not rushed to arrange a sale and sells the object when the market conditions improve, the sale can bring sufficient proceeds to discharge the debt. For instance, selling an aircraft object at the time when major manufacturers offer discounts for similar objects can adversely affect the price. A secured creditor willing to wait until discounted prices are no longer offered and to sell the aircraft object when usual prices return, can yield a higher purchase price. This tactic can be beneficial to both the secured creditor and the debtor as it might help discharge or significantly reduce the debt.

At the same time, the remedy of vesting can be exceptionally disadvantageous to the position of the debtor in a situation where the value of the object significantly exceeds the amount of the secured obligation. Although the sale of the object will undoubtedly discharge the secured obligation, it will result in an unwarranted windfall to the secured creditor because it will be entitled to retain the surplus and disable the debtor from discharging the debts owed by it to its subsequent creditors from the proceeds of sale. Due to the potentially severe effects of vesting on the debtor and other interest holders, some jurisdictions either prohibit this remedy altogether or only allow its exercise under court supervision and provided that all persons who may be affected by it are made parties to the proceedings.[173] In contrast, the Convention permits the exercise of vesting either extra-judicially or on obtaining a court order.[174]

[172] Art 9(4) CTC.

[173] Wood (n 7) 366. For the position of English law, see *Wallace v Evershed* [1899] 1 Ch 891; *In re Continental Oxygen Company* [1897] 1 Ch 511.

[174] Art 9(1), (2) CTC.

Article 9(1) provides for the extra-judicial enforcement of vesting, by stipulating that '[a]t any time after default ... the chargee and all interested persons may agree that ownership of (or any other interest of the chargor in) any object covered by the security interest shall vest in the chargee in or towards satisfaction of the secured obligations'.[175] To protect the debtor from potential abuse by the secured creditor, the Convention provides that even when vesting is exercised extra-judicially, the secured creditor cannot exercise it unilaterally. Extra-judicial vesting under Article 9(1) requires the secured creditor and all the interested persons to reach an agreement that the debtor's interest held by it in the object should be transferred to the secured creditor. As discussed above, the term 'interested person' comprises three categories of interest holders. First, the debtor is clearly an 'interested person' and the secured creditor cannot proceed with the vesting outside the court unless it secures the debtor's agreement.[176]

The second category includes persons who issue suretyship, demand guarantees, standby letters of credit or any other forms of credit insurance for the purpose of assuring performance of the obligations owed to the secured creditor.[177] The third category is very broad and includes all parties having rights in or over the object.[178] This category includes interest holders such as other secured creditors of the debtor (both senior and junior in relation to the secured creditor), conditional and outright buyers, lessees, and holders of a NCRI, as well as holders of non-registered interests in the object.[179] The secured creditor intending to exercise vesting must procure the agreement of all these interested persons. Article 9(1) further provides that the agreement between the secured creditor and all the interested persons may only be reached 'at any time after the default' of the debtor.[180] The aim of this requirement is to offer further protection to the debtor's interest by preventing the secured creditor from including the term permitting vesting at the stage when the security agreement is being concluded and the consequences of vesting may not be fully appreciated by the debtor.[181]

In some cases, the agreement of all interested persons cannot be obtained either because some of them cannot be located or because they refuse to agree. This does not mean that the secured creditor is precluded from exercising vesting. Article 9(2) entitles the secured creditor to apply for a court order permitting the transfer of the debtor's interest in the object in or towards satisfaction of the secured obligation. Provided that the necessary

[175] See Art 9(1) CTC. 'Default' should be defined in accordance with Art 11 CTC.
[176] Art 1(m)(i) CTC.
[177] Art 1(m)(ii) CTC.
[178] Art 1(m)(iii) CTC.
[179] Goode (n 12) 255.
[180] Art 9(1) CTC.
[181] Goode (n 12) 285.

prerequisites are met, the court can grant the order effecting vesting of the debtor's interest in the object to the secured creditor.[182]

B. Exercising Vesting

If the position espoused above in relation to the effect of vesting is correct, in that it results in divesting the debtor of whatever interest it holds in the object, this leads to several consequences. First, since the secured creditor acquires the interest of the debtor to the exclusion of the latter, the secured creditor selling the object at a profit does not have to account for the surplus to the debtor. As the new holder of the debtor's interest, the secured creditor should be entitled to keep the surplus generated by the sale of the object. For the same reason, the secured creditor should not be required to distribute the surplus among the debtor's junior creditors.[183] As mentioned, Article 9(5) provides that '[o]wnership or any other interest of the chargor passing ... under ... this Article is free from any other interest over which the chargee's security interest has priority under the provisions of Article 29'. In other words, the holders of the subsequently registered and unregistered interests cannot apply these proceeds to discharge the obligations owed to them by the debtor.

Secondly, when the secured creditor repossesses and sells the object under Article 8 CTC, it must comply with the requirement of commercial reasonableness and its actions can be challenged by the debtor if the sale is too speedy, or not quick enough, or if the price is not suitably high. Similarly, the secured creditor's failure to notify all eligible persons about the intended disposition in a timely manner can be challenged by the debtor.[184] This is because even though the secured creditor takes possession and sells the debtor's object, it does not become the owner or holder of any other interest held by the debtor in the object and must apply the collected sums towards discharge of the secured obligation.[185] In contrast, Article 9 permits the secured creditor to become the new holder of the interest, previously held by the debtor. Since the debtor is divested of its interest, it is submitted that it should no longer be able to challenge the dispositions as potentially not complying with commercial reasonableness. Accordingly, such aspects of sale as place, time, price or whether an aircraft or rail object should be converted from a passenger to a freight carrier or sold for parts should not be questioned by the debtor as not being commercially reasonable. By the

[182] See Art 9(3) CTC and the discussion below.
[183] This is the effect of Art 9(5) CTC.
[184] Art 8(4) CTC requires the secured creditor to give written reasonable notice of the proposed sale or lease to the interested persons.
[185] Art 8(5) CTC.

same token, once the interest in the object passes to the secured creditor, it should not be obliged to notify the debtor and other interested persons of its intended sale or lease.[186]

The ability to deal with the repossessed object free from the requirement of commercial reasonableness and to keep any surplus generated by the proceeds of sale can, without a doubt, render the remedy of vesting attractive to the secured creditor. It can give it a degree of flexibility and potentially result in a greater yield. A secured creditor not pressed to sell the object in a speedy manner in adverse market conditions can wait until the market improves and sell the object at a higher price even if the consummation of the sale takes longer than a commercially reasonable sale would permit.

At the same time, the absence of the commercial reasonableness requirement may provide an opportunity for abuse. The availability of vesting may encourage the secured creditor to sell the repossessed object at an undervalue and claim the remainder of the secured debt from the debtor. The secured creditor can sell the object to a company in which it holds an interest, in order to resell the same object again at a later time and at the price representing its true value. In this way, the secured creditor can both make a profit from the sale of the object and claim the remainder of the secured debt from the debtor. In addition, as noted above, vesting can be particularly disadvantageous to the debtor if it is exercised in circumstances where the value of the object significantly exceeds the amount of the secured obligation because by retaining the surplus the secured creditor will not only receive a windfall, but will cut the debtor out of proceeds which could have been used to discharge the obligations owed by it to other interest holders.

That said, it must be noted that, in practical terms, a surplus resulting from the sale of the repossessed object is often nothing but a 'shimmering mirage' and it is a deficiency that is usually the 'grim reality' facing the secured creditor after the disposition.[187] For instance, if a 10-year-old aircraft object is repossessed during a recession and the secured creditor has to wait to sell until the market improves, it may be difficult to sell this aircraft object at a profit or at all. The object's age will have an impact on its productivity and increase its maintenance costs and the secured creditor may be forced to sell it at a much reduced price or for parts. Even in these circumstances, however, if the sale proceeds are not sufficient to discharge the secured obligation, the secured creditor may be able to claim the deficiency from the debtor. Thus, the deficiency claim can further weaken the position of the debtor, which is already divested of its interest in what may well have been one of its most valuable assets.

[186] Indeed, Art 9 CTC does not require the secured creditor to notify the debtor or other interested persons about the impending disposition.

[187] See White and Summers (n 111) 1353, citing Professor Gilmore.

As noted, the Convention does not expressly state whether the secured creditor can claim the deficiency from the debtor. However, Article 9(1) does indicate that the object covered by the security shall be vested in the secured creditor 'in or towards' satisfaction of the secured obligation. Accordingly, the availability of the deficiency claim may depend on whether the secured creditor agrees to accept the debtor's interest in the object in full or partial satisfaction of the secured obligation. If the secured creditor accepts the debtor's interest *in* satisfaction of the secured obligation, it will be extinguished regardless of whether the sale proceeds are sufficient to discharge it. In this case, the secured creditor should not be able to claim the deficiency. In contrast, the position of the secured creditor agreeing to accept the debtor's interest in the object *towards* satisfaction of the debt may be different. In this case, Article 9(1) admits the possibility that, if the proceeds of sale applied towards the discharge of the secured obligation are not sufficient, the secured creditor should be able to claim the remainder of the debt from the debtor.[188]

Does transfer of the debtor's interest to the secured creditor by means of vesting mean that the latter is fully absolved from the test of commercial reasonableness? Although the Convention does not require vesting to be exercised in a commercially reasonable manner,[189] all three Protocols state that the Convention's remedies should be exercised in accordance with this requirement.[190] This means that vesting, similar to other remedies of the Convention, should be exercised in a commercially reasonable manner. However, it is submitted that in the context of this remedy, the requirement of commercial reasonableness should not relate to the aspects of the object's disposition. As the new holder of the debtor's interest in the object, the secured creditor should be entitled to decide for itself how to best deal with it.

What then should commercial reasonableness mean in the context of vesting? Article IX(3) of the Aircraft Protocol provides that any remedy provided by the Convention 'shall be exercised' in a commercially reasonable manner.[191] Clearly, the sale or other dealings with the interest held in the object by the secured creditor will only occur *after* the vesting remedy has been exercised. This must mean that it is the process of vesting itself and the considerations relevant to deciding whether the debtor's interest in the object should be transferred to the secured creditor that need to be accomplished in a commercially reasonable manner.

[188] Goode (n 12) 286.

[189] See Art 9 CTC.

[190] Art IX(3) of the Aircraft Protocol; Art XVII(1) of the Space Protocol and Art VII(3) of the Luxembourg Protocol.

[191] See Art XVII(1) of the Space Protocol and Art VII(3) of the Luxembourg Protocol for the same effect.

The Convention does not explain what factors need to be taken into account in order to comply with commercial reasonableness in exercising extra-judicial vesting. At the same time, Article 9(3) does provide for a mechanism that should be employed by the courts when determining whether to grant an order permitting vesting. The court should only grant an order allowing vesting provided that the amount of the secured obligation to be satisfied by such vesting is 'commensurate with the value of the object after taking account of any payment to be made by the chargee to any of the interested persons'.[192] In other words, in assessing whether to grant a vesting order, the court ought to proceed in three stages.

First, the court must ascertain the value of the object and the amount of the secured obligation. The Convention is silent as to the time of valuation, but it seems that the value of the object and the amount of the remaining indebtedness should be assessed at the time of default. Such valuation can help the court paint a more realistic picture as to the relative value of the object at the time of the proposed vesting compared to the remaining indebtedness. Secondly, the court should assess whether the proposed vesting will be commensurate with the value of the object. If the object's value greatly exceeds the amount of the secured obligation, the court should refuse vesting.[193] For example, the secured creditor may have a security interest in an aircraft object worth $150m to secure the repayment of a loan of $100m. If the secured creditor applies for a court order to vest the object in satisfaction of the debt, the order should be refused since the value of the object greatly exceeds the amount of the debt. Vesting, granted in such circumstances, would not be commensurate with the value of the object and would confer a windfall on the secured creditor at the expense of the debtor and its other creditors.

Thirdly, the court must consider whether the secured creditor will have to make payments to other interested persons before applying the remaining sum to discharge the debt and ascertain the amount of such payments. For instance, if, in the above scenario, the amount of the debt is $100m and it would cost the secured creditor $45m to repay an additional debt owed by the debtor to its prior creditor, the court should agree to grant a vesting order to the enforcing secured creditor.[194] This is because the amount of the debt coupled with the payment which the secured creditor will have to make to the prior creditor is 'commensurate' with the value of the object.

All these measures, ie ascertaining the object's value and comparing it with the amount of the secured obligation as well as enquiring whether the secured creditor would have to make payments to other interested persons

[192] Art 9(3) CTC.
[193] See Goode (n 12) 289, Illustration 8.
[194] Based on Illustration 9 in Goode (n 12) 289.

before applying the remaining sum to the discharge of the obligation, demonstrate that the Convention aims to find a commercially reasonable and balanced solution that would allow the secured creditor to discharge at least a greater part of the secured obligation and ensure that the debtor is not unnecessarily deprived of a valuable asset where it could have been used more efficiently. In other words, the process through which the court is required to go in order to decide whether to allow vesting is aimed at ensuring that this remedy is exercised in a commercially reasonable manner.

If this view is correct, it gives rise to the question whether similar considerations that must be taken into account by the court when deciding whether to grant a vesting order should be considered when the secured creditor and all the interested persons are attempting to reach an extra-judicial agreement permitting vesting. It is clear that vesting must be exercised in a commercially reasonable manner regardless of whether the secured creditor enforces it extra-judicially or via the court. It also seems clear that commercial reasonableness should apply to the process of vesting itself and the considerations to be taken into account when deciding whether the debtor's interest in the object should be transferred to the secured creditor and not to the manner in which the secured creditor disposes of its interest in the object. This is precisely what the court-based Article 9(3) mechanism aims to achieve. Its purpose is to ensure that the court only permits vesting if the object's value is commensurate with the amount of the secured obligation, in order to prevent an unwarranted windfall for the creditor and unnecessary aggravation of the debtor's position. This objective demonstrates the Convention's concern for the position of the debtor and other interested persons, but also helps to ensure that if the value of the object is comparable with the amount of the obligation, the secured creditor is able to exercise vesting.

It is submitted that similar considerations should be taken into account by the secured creditor and all the interested persons when deciding whether the secured creditor should be permitted to enforce vesting extra-judicially. This should be the case because the Convention's aims are the same in relation to both extra-judicial and court-based vesting. First, Article 9(1) clearly seeks to protect the position of the debtor by specifying that the agreement to vest its interest in the secured creditor can only be achieved *after* the default, when the consequences of vesting can be clearly appreciated by it. If vesting is discussed by the relevant parties after the default and not at the time of the conclusion of the security agreement, it will allow the parties to ascertain the object's value and the amount of the remaining indebtedness, both of which are likely to change from the moment of the conclusion of the security agreement, with greater precision. This should help the parties to establish whether the value of the object and the amount of the secured obligation are commensurate.

Secondly, Article 9(1) requires the secured creditor to ensure that not only the debtor, but all other interested persons agree to vesting. The Convention thus recognises that the position of interested persons may be adversely affected if vesting is exercised where the value of the object greatly exceeds the amount of the secured obligation. In this situation, the secured creditor will be entitled to retain the surplus and can disable the debtor from discharging the obligations owed by it to the interested persons. This means that, similar to the court-based Article 9(3) regime, extra-judicial vesting exercised in a commercially reasonable manner must take into account the need to protect the position of all the interested persons. If the parties agree that the value of the object and the amount of the debt are commensurate and if the secured creditor would have been entitled to repossess and sell the object in priority to the interested persons, there seems to be no reason why the interested persons would not agree to vesting.

In contrast, where the value of the object greatly exceeds the amount of the secured obligation, it seems unlikely that the interested persons would agree to vesting as this could decrease their chances of obtaining the discharge from the debtor. On the basis of these considerations, it is suggested that while the ability of the secured creditor to enforce vesting will ultimately depend on reaching the agreement with all relevant parties, in order to comply with commercial reasonableness, the parties will have to take into account similar considerations as the ones that the court would have to examine under Article 9(3) CTC. In other words, after the default, it will be necessary to ascertain the value of the object and the amount of the secured obligation still owed by the debtor to the secured creditor. It will also be necessary to clarify whether the secured creditor will have to discharge obligations owed by the debtor to its senior creditors who have priority over the secured creditor. If the value of the object is commensurate with the amount of the remaining secured obligation together with the sum that the secured creditor will have to pay to the senior creditor, and provided that all interested persons agree to vesting, the exercise of vesting should be considered as commercially reasonable.

Finally, even though vesting transfers to the enforcing secured creditor the debtor's interest in the object, all is not lost for the debtor. At any moment before the object is sold by the secured creditor or before the court grants an order allowing the vesting, either the debtor or any other interested person may discharge the security interest by paying in full the amount secured by it.[195] If the debtor discharges the security interest, its interest in the object will be redeemed and returned to it.[196] If the discharge occurs with the help

[195] Art 9(4) CTC.

[196] This contrasts with the approach of some other jurisdictions where foreclosure, a remedy similar to vesting, has the effect of extinguishing the opportunity of redemption. For the position under English law, see *Heath and Another v Pugh* (1880–81) LR 6 QBD 345; *Sadler v Worley* [1894] 2 Ch 170.

of another interested person, this person is subrogated to the rights of the secured creditor.[197]

VI. SPEEDY RELIEF PENDING FINAL DETERMINATION

A. Purpose and Economic Significance

When the debtor opposes the creditor's right to enforce a remedy, the latter can start court proceedings against it to resolve the dispute. The trial and, potentially, the appeals can take considerable time, sometimes years. During this period, the creditor's position can be exposed to many risks. The objects covered by the Convention can be moved to a different jurisdiction by the debtor, preventing their repossession by the creditor. In addition, delays in court proceedings can deprive the creditor of the opportunity to earn income from the object's use or management.[198] Another risk associated with lengthy court proceedings is that, while the trial lasts, the object may be abandoned, stripped for parts or not properly maintained by the debtor and its condition may rapidly deteriorate both physically and commercially.[199] Although objects covered by the Convention have a long economic life, they can depreciate very quickly if not properly maintained. For instance, the cost of putting an aircraft back into service can rocket in a matter of days if it is not properly maintained for more than a week.[200] Lengthy court proceedings in relation to an object of an advanced age may mean that by the time the dispute is resolved, its commercial value and prospects of a profitable sale or lease will decrease to a vanishing point. In other words, high mobility of the objects covered by the Convention and rapid depreciation

[197] Art 9(4) CTC.

[198] See *Shilmore Enterprise Corporation v Phoenix 1 Aviation Ltd* [2008] EWHC 169, a case decided under English law before the Convention was ratified by the United Kingdom. In this case, the aircraft lease agreement contained an option to purchase the aircraft exercisable by the lessee within 45 days of the lessor's notice that the latter started negotiations with a third party about the sale of the object. On receiving the lessor's notice, the lessee purported to exercise the option to purchase but failed to complete the sale within the required timeframe. Resolution of the dispute as to whether the lessee correctly exercised its option to purchase would take considerable time and as soon as the lessor threatened to start court proceedings, the lessee flew the aircraft to the Seychelles and refused to return it. As a result, the lessor could not repossess and lease or sell the aircraft and lost income that could have been generated while the standoff between the parties continued. After considering which course of action would involve least risk of injustice, the court granted a mandatory interim injunction against the lessee ordering it to return the aircraft to the lessor.

[199] See, for example, *Pindell Ltd & Anor v AirAsia Bhd* [2012] 2 CLC 1 where an aircraft, the parts of which were wrongfully removed, was parked outside of the hangar and left in humid conditions which led to its physical and commercial deterioration.

[200] D Gray, J MacIntyre and J Wool, 'The Interaction Between Cape Town Convention Repossession Remedies and Local Procedural Law: A Civil Law Case Study' (2015) *Cape Town Convention Journal* 17, 22–23.

of their physical and commercial value coupled with the high cost of putting these objects back into service mean that lengthy court proceedings are likely to expose the creditor's position to considerable financial risks. These risks reduce the value of the creditor's international interest. They will have to be taken into account when the creditor determines whether to provide a loan for the debtor and at what cost.

To address these concerns, Article 13 CTC allows the creditor, who 'adduces evidence'[201] of the debtor's default and 'to the extent that the debtor has at any time so agreed',[202] to seek from the court a speedy relief order which can be obtained in advance of final determination of the dispute.[203] Provided that a Contracting State does not disapply Article 13 by means of a declaration under Article 55 CTC[204] and all necessary prerequisites are met, the creditor can obtain from the court a speedy relief order which can take the form or forms of: (a) preservation of the object and its value; (b) possession, control or custody; (c) immobilisation; and (d) lease or (where not covered by the above options) management of the object and the income therefrom.[205] All three Protocols[206] provide that apart from these forms of relief, speedy relief can also take the form of sale and application of proceeds to the dispute, but this can only be achieved if both the debtor and the creditor specifically agree to this option. A sale as a form of speedy relief proved to be contentious for the Convention's drafters. Some legal regimes recognise a sale as a form of interim relief and maintain that sale can be beneficial to both the creditor and the debtor in the case of perishable

[201] Art 13(1) CTC.

[202] Art 13(1) CTC.

[203] Art 13 CTC must be examined together with Art 55 CTC, regulating the declarations which may be made by Contracting States in relation to the applicability of Art 13, and Art 43, dealing with the jurisdiction of the courts considering whether to grant the relief to the creditor. Art 43 operates on the premise that some forms of speedy relief, such as preservation of the object, possession and immobilisation relate to the object and are *in rem* in nature. In relation to these forms of relief, the court has jurisdiction either if it is the court of a Contracting State chosen by the parties or if it is the court of a Contracting State on the territory of which the object is situated. Other forms of speedy relief, such as lease, are considered to be *in personam* in nature. In relation to such forms of relief, jurisdiction may be exercised either by the courts chosen by the parties or by the courts of a Contracting State on the territory of which the debtor is situated. In addition, Art 13 must be considered together with Art X of the Aircraft Protocol, Art VIII of the Luxembourg Protocol and Art XX of the Space Protocol.

[204] Where a Contracting State makes a declaration excluding the applicability of Art 13 CTC, it will also have to exclude the applicability of Art 43 CTC regulating the jurisdiction of the courts dealing with the grant of relief. Similarly, where the Contracting State declares that Art 13 is excluded in part, the corresponding declaration must be made in relation to Art 43. On the origins of Art 55, see Goode (n 12) 405. On the relationship between Art 13 CTC and Art 31 of the Brussels Regulation, see A McCarthy and M O'Brien, 'Article 13 of the Cape Town Convention and Article 31 of Regulation No. 44/2001—An EU Law Perspective' (2014) *Cape Town Convention Journal* 33–47.

[205] Art 13(1) CTC.

[206] See Art XX(3) of the Aircraft Protocol; Art VIII(3) of the Luxembourg Protocol and Art XX(3) of the Space Protocol.

or rapidly depreciating objects.[207] Other legal systems regard the sale as incompatible with the idea of relief pending final determination of the claim because it bears 'the element of finality' and cannot be reversed.[208] To reconcile these views, it was decided not to include sale as one of the forms of relief available under Article 13 CTC. Instead, the sale was added as a form of speedy relief under all three Protocols and it can only be invoked if a Contracting State makes a declaration to this effect. This approach allowed to alleviate some of the concerns of the Contracting States opposing to a sale as a form of relief,[209] but retained the opportunity to use the sale as such for the Contracting States regarding it as a chance of obtaining better financial benefits under the Convention and the Protocols.[210]

The Convention is silent as to how speedy the relief ought to be. The Aircraft Protocol[211] specifies that 'speedy' means 'such number of working days from the date of filing of the application for relief as is specified in a declaration made by the Contracting State in which the application is made'.[212] This language indicates that, once the creditor makes the application, speedy relief should be granted in a matter of days rather than months. Indeed, many Contracting States declared that various types of relief should be granted within 10 or 30 days from the day of filing of the application.[213]

[207] See, for example, comment of the Delegation of the United Kingdom at the Diplomatic Conference, Commission of the Whole, 10th Meeting, 6th November in *Convention on International Interests in Mobile Equipment and Protocol Thereto on Matters Specific to Aircraft Equipment: Diplomatic Conference to Adopt a Mobile Equipment Convention and an Aircraft Protocol—Acts and Proceedings* (Rome, UNIDROIT 2006), 825.

[208] See comment of the Delegation of France in the *Diplomatic Conference* (n 207) 824.

[209] In particular, the Delegation of France noted that the approach requiring a Contracting State to make an opt in declaration did not alleviate all of its concerns because it was still possible to envisage a situation where a French national (debtor) had to deal with an object registered in a Contracting State who made the declaration and that such a debtor would have to comply with provision regarding sale of the object. It was suggested that the draft Art X of the Aircraft Protocol adding sale as a form of relief had to be amended to state that the parties should specifically agree to the sale. See *Diplomatic Conference* (n 207) 825–26. The final version of Art X(3) of the Aircraft Protocol and similar provisions of the Luxembourg and Space Protocols state that sale and application of proceeds can only be used as a form of relief 'if at any time the debtor and the creditor specifically agree'.

[210] The comments of the Chairman, *Diplomatic Conference* (n 207) 824.

[211] Art X(2) of the Aircraft Protocol.

[212] Art X of the Aircraft Protocol becomes applicable only if the Contracting State has made the declaration under Art XXX(2). Art VIII of the Luxembourg Protocol provides that 'speedy' in the context of obtaining relief means 'such number of *calendar* days from the date of filing of the application for relief as is specified in a declaration made by the Contracting State in which the application is made'. See also Art XX of the Space Protocol which replicates Art VIII of the Luxembourg Protocol.

[213] Many Contracting States, making the declaration under Art XXX(2) of the Aircraft Protocol in relation to the applicability of Art X of this Protocol, stated that 'speedy' for the purposes of obtaining the relief should mean a period of 10 working/calendar days in relation to the forms of relief available under Art 13(1)(a), (b), (c) CTC and 30 working/calendar days in relation to the forms of relief available under Art 13(1)(d) and (e) of the Convention. See the list of the declarations at www.unidroit.org/depositary-2001capetown-aircraft?id=450 (last visited March 2017).

Relief pending final determination can prove to be of significant economic importance. It can help protect the creditor's financial position in circumstances requiring urgent intervention. For example, if there is a danger that the object is about to be moved to a different jurisdiction, the creditor can request a court to issue an immobilisation order. In addition, a speedy relief order can help avoid unnecessary waste of valuable objects. If the debtor allows the object to depreciate during the standoff or if it is unable to maintain and manage the object due to financial difficulties, a relief order giving the creditor speedy access to the object can help ensure that it will continue to generate profit. Finally, the availability of speedy relief provides assurance to the creditor that it can protect its position prior to the final determination of the dispute. This can encourage the creditor to extend finance and to do so on terms favourable to the debtor.

At the same time, speedy relief can lead to harsh results for the debtor. First, since the relief must be 'speedy' the debtor's position may change very quickly, yet the debtor may not even know that the creditor applied to the court to obtain it. This is because the Convention provides that before granting relief, the court 'may' require the creditor to notify interested persons, including the debtor about its request.[214] In the absence of this nudge from the court, the Convention does not require the creditor to notify the debtor about its request for the relief. Accordingly, the debtor may find itself in a situation where it learns about the creditor's application after the court grants the speedy relief order.

Secondly, the relief can take drastic forms and deprive the debtor of the opportunity to generate profit from the object's use. While some forms of relief, such as the preservation of the object, can be invoked to restrain the debtor from doing something, such as to prevent it from disassembling the aircraft or from removing its engines, other forms of relief can be more intrusive and require the debtor to take certain positive actions, such as to surrender possession of the object to the creditor. Once these positive actions are taken, it may be impracticable, time consuming, expensive or impossible to reverse them. Consequently, while the relief is only granted 'pending final determination' of the claim, in practice its effect may be irreversible. Thus, if the debtor/lessee is required to surrender possession of the aircraft object to the creditor/lessor, it may be impracticable to expect that the lessor will return the object to the debtor in the case that its default is not established at the final hearing.[215] For instance, it may well be that by the time the

[214] Art 13(3) CTC.

[215] See G Cuniberti, 'Advance Relief under the Cape Town Convention' (2012) *Cape Town Convention Journal* 79, 84, making a similar point in relation to the position of the conditional seller and suggesting that this feature of the relief implies that it is in fact not an advance relief but an early enforcement of the creditor's remedies.

trial closes, a lease would have terminated because its term would have run out.[216] Similarly, speedy relief allowing the creditor to sell the object will most likely be irreversible.[217] In these circumstances, the debtor's compensation will lie in damages but the object itself will be lost to it. Finally, speedy relief should be granted before the hearing of the merits begins and the debtor's default is unequivocally established. This can have the effect of curtailing the debtor's right to use the object prematurely in circumstances where, absent default, it should not have been interfered with. This can be particularly harsh on the debtor if at the actual trial it is found that it was not in default after all.[218]

In order to alleviate the concerns of the creditor and the debtor in circumstances where, on the one hand, the creditor's position requires urgent protection and, on the other hand, the debtor's interest can be wrongly interfered with, Article 13 provides that while the creditor can obtain speedy relief order, it will only be able to do so if it 'adduces evidence' of the debtor's default. The difficulty with this requirement is that it is not clear what the standard of proof is required for the requisite evidence. In addition, Article 13 seeks to protect the debtor's position by stating that speedy relief should be available to the creditor 'to the extent that the debtor has at any time so agreed'.[219] The efficacy of this safeguard is questionable. If the parties are in dispute, the creditor may find it difficult to secure the debtor's agreement enabling it to apply for speedy relief. It seems unlikely that the debtor, challenging the creditor's right to enforce its remedies, would voluntarily agree to let it take possession or lease the object before the final determination of the dispute. In other words, an attempt to seek the debtor's agreement in the midst of the dispute can prove futile and stifle the operation of Article 13. This is probably why the Convention states that the debtor's agreement can be obtained 'at any time' and a prudent creditor would want to secure it when the agreement, giving rise to its international interest, is entered into. However, at this stage, the debtor may not fully appreciate the consequences of giving its consent enabling the creditor to avail of the machinery of speedy relief. If this is the case, then while the formal requirement of agreement will be satisfied, its purpose, ie protection of the debtor's interest, may not be met.

[216] This was the position in the *Shilmore* case discussed above.

[217] A Veneziano, 'Advance Relief under the Cape Town Convention and its Aircraft Protocol: A Comment on Gilles Cuniberti's Interpretative Proposal' (2013) *Cape Town Convention Journal* 185, 188.

[218] Art 13(2) CTC aims to protect the debtor's position by stating that the court may impose such terms as it considers necessary to protect the interested persons in such circumstances, but the application of this provision can be excluded by the parties.

[219] Art 13(1) CTC.

Once the creditor obtains speedy relief, it may fail to perform the obligations owed by it to the debtor under the Convention. For example, the creditor may sell the object at undervalue contrary to the commercial reasonableness requirement. Alternatively, the creditor may fail to establish its claim in the final determination of the dispute and it may be found that the debtor was not in default after all. To protect the debtor and other interested persons in these circumstances, Article 13(2) provides that the court may 'impose such terms as it considers necessary' in return for granting the speedy relief. These terms may include the requirement that the creditor should provide a demand guarantee or an undertaking to pay damages to the debtor should it fail to establish its claim on the final hearing. However, the protection offered by Article 13(2) is fragile because its application can be excluded by the parties under the relevant Protocol.[220] The agreement excluding Article 13(2) must be made in writing and it is hoped that compliance with this requirement will bring home to the debtor that, once the Convention's protection is removed, it can only rely on the applicable domestic law.

B. Nature and Exercise of the Remedy

The availability of speedy relief depends on the compliance with a number of the Convention's requirements. First, the creditor will not be able to apply for a speedy relief if the Contracting State where the court, having the jurisdiction to grant the relief is located, has made a declaration under Article 55, excluding Article 13's application. Secondly, to secure speedy relief order from the court, the creditor must 'adduce evidence' of the debtor's default. Thirdly, speedy relief can only be granted by the court 'to the extent that the debtor has at any time so agreed'. The court can further grant speedy relief in the form of a sale and application of proceeds to the dispute provided that the Contracting State has made the required declaration under the relevant Protocol and the debtor and the creditor specifically agree to it. Provided that these requirements are met, the court does not have discretion and must grant speedy relief order requested by the creditor.[221]

The remedy of speedy relief presents several difficulties of interpretation. First, the nature of this remedy is not entirely clear. On the one hand, the Convention's speedy relief may seem similar to the remedy of interim relief available in some domestic legal systems. If this is the case, it is important to appreciate that speedy relief is the legal construct created by the Convention and should be interpreted in line with its principles and policies and not by reference to domestic legal systems. On the other hand, it can be argued

[220] See, for instance, Art X(5) of the Aircraft Protocol.
[221] Goode (n 12) 71.

that speedy relief is, in effect, 'an advance enforcement remedy' entitling the creditor to speedily enforce the Convention's default remedies.[222] This view may seem persuasive because some forms of speedy relief, such as the surrender of possession and sale of the object, can have an irreversible effect which does not sit easily with the temporary nature of interim relief. In addition, most forms of speedy relief are identical to default remedies available under Articles 8 and 10 CTC. It can be argued that the only difference between relief pending final determination and default remedies is that the former must be granted by the court in a speedy manner.[223] Nevertheless, it is submitted that speedy relief should not be equated with the advance enforcement remedy because it could, among other things, render the default remedies under the Convention superfluous. Secondly, the requirement of 'adduced evidence' of the debtor's default presents a difficulty because the Convention does not explain what the standard of proof of the evidence presented by the creditor must be. In particular, the Convention does not state whether the standard of proof should be the same as at the actual trial or whether it may be lower than at the hearing of the merits. These issues will be considered in turn.

i. The Nature of Speedy Relief

When examining the nature of speedy relief it may be helpful to look at Article 13(4) CTC, providing that '[n]othing in this Article ... limits the availability of forms of interim relief other than those set out in paragraph 1'. The main purpose of this provision is to expressly indicate that the availability of the Convention's speedy relief does not preclude the creditor from invoking the forms of interim relief available under domestic law. In addition, Article 13(4) can impliedly suggest that the Convention's speedy relief is a similar legal construct to interim relief known to many legal systems. The language of Art 13(4) equates the notion of 'forms of interim relief' available under domestic law with 'those set out in paragraph 1', namely preservation, possession, immobilisation and lease or management of the object, known as forms of speedy relief under the Convention. This approach is repeated in Article 43(2) espousing which courts may exercise '[j]urisdiction to grant relief ... or other interim relief by virtue of article 13(4)'. So too, Article 55 CTC, stating that a Contracting State may declare that it will not apply Articles 13 and 43 wholly or in part, provides that if the Contracting States choses to apply Articles 13 and 43 in part, it should indicate under which conditions these provisions will continue to apply 'or otherwise which other forms of interim relief' will be available.

[222] Cuniberti (n 215) 86.
[223] See Veneziano (n 217) 186.

These provisions seem to indicate that the nature of the remedy of speedy relief is similar to that of interim relief known to domestic legal systems. Indeed, the Official Commentary states that Article 13 'builds on forms of relief pending final determination ... commonly available in national legal systems'.[224] At the same time, while the Convention's speedy relief is similar in its nature to the remedy of interim relief, it is in truth the creature of the Convention and should be interpreted in line with its policies and principles and not by reference to domestic legal systems. It is for this reason that the description of speedy relief as the remedy of 'interim relief' was deliberately avoided in the heading of Article 13.[225]

The purpose of the remedy of interim relief found in domestic legal systems is, broadly speaking, similar to the objective of the Convention's speedy relief and shares some of its features. Interim relief is usually granted before the actual hearing of the trial, where the position of the party seeking it requires urgent protection. Interim relief can take many forms depending on the circumstances in which it is sought. For example, an order can be granted to restrain a party from removing an object from the jurisdiction,[226] to prevent it from destroying the documents and to require it to deliver them to the other party[227] or to require the lessee to return the object before the start of the hearing.[228] Since interim relief is usually granted when the party's position needs to be urgently protected, there is often little time to consider complex facts and evidence in detail. Once the facts and evidence are given the benefit of full consideration at the actual trail, it may be found that relief should not have been granted because the alleged default could not be established. For this reason, at the interim stage, the court may condition the grant of relief on provision of some guarantee or another undertaking on the part of the party seeking relief for the benefit of the other party.

The proposition that the Convention's speedy relief is inspired by the remedy of interim relief can be supported by Article 13(1), providing that it should be granted 'pending final determination' of the claim. This wording clearly indicates that speedy relief should be granted before the actual hearing of the claim. Similarly, Article 13(4)(b) recognises the possibility that the creditor can eventually 'fail to establish its claim ... on the final determination of that claim'. These provisions not only make it clear that speedy relief is obtainable before the hearing of the merits, but also that the Convention

[224] Goode (n 12) 292.

[225] *Ibid* 70. This would mean that the requirements established in *American Cyanamid Co v Ethicon Ltd* [1975] 2 WLR 316 should not be applicable under the Convention, namely, first, the evidence of the merits showing that the claim is not frivolous or vexatious and that there is a serious issue to be tried, secondly, the adequacy of damages as an alternative remedy and, thirdly, the overall balance of convenience.

[226] *Allen v Jumbo Holdings Ltd* [1980] 1 WLR 1252.

[227] *Thunder Air Ltd v Mr Hilmar Hilmarsson* [2008] EWHC 355.

[228] *Shilmore Enterprise Corporation v Phoenix 1 Aviation Ltd* [2008] EWHC 169.

recognises that due to time constrains in which relief should be granted, it is possible that it may later be found that the debtor was not in default after all. To protect the debtor's position, the court may impose 'such terms as it considers necessary', such as requiring the creditor to provide an undertaking to pay damages to the debtor if default is not eventually established.[229] These features of the Convention's speedy relief render it similar to the interim relief known to domestic legal systems. However, since speedy relief is the creation of the Convention, its features must be defined with reference to the principles and policies on which the Convention is based. Doing so will accord with the need to have regard to the Convention's international character and the need to promote uniformity and predictability in its application.[230] It would be impossible to achieve a uniform exercise of the remedy of speedy relief, if its features were to be interpreted by reference to domestic legal regimes. This is due to the plethora of forms of interim relief and their treatment available in various legal systems and the difficulty of deciding whether the remedy of interim relief is of procedural or substantive nature.[231] For these reasons, the nature and features as well as such questions as the determination of how high or low should be the standard of proving the evidence adduced by the creditor must be decided in accordance with the principles and policies underpinning the Convention.

Alternatively, it has been argued that the Convention's speedy relief lacks the essential characteristics of interim relief present in 'virtually all legal systems'.[232] Instead, it is argued that the effect of speedy relief is to provide the creditor with an 'advance enforcement remedy', entitling it to exercise default remedies under the Convention at an earlier stage. While this view may seem plausible, it is difficult to agree with it. First, it is indeed true that, unlike the remedy of interim relief found in some domestic legal systems, the Convention does not require the creditor to demonstrate the existence of the alleged rights and that it has a significant chance to win on the merits.[233] There is no requirement of an imminent danger that judgment recongising the creditor's rights will not be enforced.[234] However, since the remedy of speedy relief was created under the Convention, there seems to be no reason why it should reflect the requirements present in some domestic legal systems. It is perfectly possibly to create a new legal construct, inspired by some domestic legal systems but not sharing some of its requirements.

[229] Goode (n 12) 239.

[230] Art 5(1) CTC.

[231] See B Crans and R Nath (eds), *Aircraft Repossession and Enforcement: Practical Aspects* (Wolters Kluwer Law & Business 2009) for the general overview of the remedy of interim relieve in the context of different jurisdictions.

[232] Cuniberti (n 215) 82.

[233] *Ibid* 82.

[234] *Ibid* 83.

While the idea that speedy relief should be obtainable prior to the final determination of the claim may be inspired by the remedy of interim relief, its salient features should be interpreted and developed in line with the Convention's policies and principles.

Another reason why the Convention's speedy relief can be viewed as a mechanism for an early enforcement of the creditor's default remedies is that some forms of relief, such as possession and sale, can have an irreversible effect. It is difficult to reconcile the temporary effect that speedy relief should have on protecting the creditor's position until the actual trial occurs, and the irreversible nature of some forms of speedy relief. However, it is submitted that this feature does not render speedy relief an advance enforcement remedy. Speedy relief is aimed at providing urgent protection of the creditor's position. For example, if the lessor learns that, following the onset of the dispute over the rental payments, the lessee has removed the aircraft object to another jurisdiction, it may need to urgently return the aircraft and, for this reason, require the court to grant the relief in the form of a possession order. Similarly, if the creditor leans that the aircraft held by the debtor is not properly maintained and its value is depreciating at an alarming speed, the creditor may need to quickly sell it before it becomes worthless.

It is true that if at the trial it is found that the debtor was not in default, its compensation is likely to be monetary and the object itself will not be returned to it. But not allowing the creditor to take possession and sell the object may lead to unnecessary and avoidable waste of a valuable object. Although not all domestic legal systems consider such irreversible acts as forms of interim relief, there is no reason why the Convention should not treat them as such. The availability of possession and sale as forms of speedy relief can help ensure that a valuable asset is not wasted and continues to generate profit even when the parties find themselves in dispute. This can help secure the creditor's position because these forms of relief can increase its chances of obtaining repayment of the debt. The possession and sale of the object prior to the actual trial can also be beneficial to the debtor because the profit generated by sale will be applied towards the discharge of the debt. So, it is the need to urgently protect the creditor's position, coupled with the speed with which the objects governed by the Convention can depreciate or be relocated, that justifies the grant of forms of speedy relief which may prove to be irreversible. It is submitted that for these reasons, the irreversible nature of some forms of relief and the fact that they can amount to the enforcement and not merely protection of the creditor's remedies, do not turn the remedy of speedy relief as a whole into an advance enforcement remedy.

Further, the forms of speedy relief—namely possession, lease, management of the object and its income, and sale of the object—are identical to default remedies available under Article 8 and Article 10 CTC. This may mean that the only difference between relief pending final determination and default remedies under the Convention is that relief must be 'speedy'. Therefore, it can be argued that the nature of relief pending final determination is different to interim relief and that it is, in effect, 'an advance enforcement remedy'.[235] While this argument has some force, it is difficult to agree with it. First, if the view that speedy relief should be considered as an advance enforcement remedy is correct, it can make default remedies under Article 8 and 10 CTC superfluous. In this case, the only potential advantage of default remedies would be their extra-judicial enforcement. This advantage can be further curtailed either because a Contracting State declares that remedies should be exercised via the court or because the creditor chooses to enforce default remedies via the court to ensure that it is not later accused of breaching its obligations under the Convention. It is hard to envisage that this could have been the intention of the Convention's drafters.

Secondly, although there is a clear overlap between some forms of relief and remedies under Article 8 and 10, speedy relief can take other forms, such as immobilisation and preservation of the object. These forms of relief are likely to have temporary and passing effect. The immobilisation and preservation of the object can be invoked when the creditor seeks to retain the existing state of affairs between the parties until full hearing of the merits starts. Inclusion of these forms of relief can be indicative of the drafters' intention to provide a transitional remedy to help the creditor secure its position until the dispute is resolved. Accordingly, speedy relief should not be equated with an early enforcement of default remedies.

Thirdly, if the view that speedy relief is in effect an advance enforcement remedy were correct, this would mean that court's decision to grant the relief would be equated with its judgment following the actual trial. Indeed, in practice, the effect of granting speedy relief may be that parties refrain from initiating the actual trial. Speedy relief can provide the creditor with the means of protecting its position and the debtor may realise that its chances of winning at the full trial are negligible.[236] Nevertheless, even though in practical terms, it may well be that the grant of speedy relief dispenses with the need to initiate full court proceedings, it is important that the possibility of such proceedings should still be open to both parties. The decision to grant the relief must be reached by the court in a short space of time and in circumstances requiring urgent actions. Complex facts and evidence of the debtor's default cannot be examined by the court in detail.

For these reasons, the risk that the court can be wrong in granting speedy relief cannot be excluded. Allowing the creditor to enforce its default remedies at the stage when the debtor's default is not unequivocally established without the possibility of full trial would go beyond relieving the

[235] See Veneziano (n 217) 189, supporting this view.
[236] See Cuniberti (n 215) 87.

creditor's position at the time when it needs urgent intervention. It would have the effect of not simply protecting, but also cementing the creditor's position. It is submitted that this would go against the spirit of Article 13 as it expressly states that speedy relief should be granted 'pending final determination' of the claim and because it clearly admits the possibility of a wrongly granted relief. Equating the court's decision to grant speedy relief with advance enforcement of default remedies could also be inequitable to the debtor. Speedy relief can have drastic consequences on the debtor's position because it may require it to relinquish the possession of a valuable object and lose an opportunity to earn profit from its use. In these circumstances, it would be inequitable to deny the debtor even the prospect of full hearing of the merits where all facts and evidence of the debtor's default can be assessed. Moreover, while in certain circumstances the parties may regard it impracticable to initiate a full trial following the grant of the speedy relief order, there will be situations where a full trial may be considered feasible and practicable and the parties should have the possibility to employ this route.

ii. Standard of Proof

Obtaining a speedy relief order from the court requires the creditor to 'adduce evidence' of the debtor's default. Article 13 does not provide what the standard of proof of the debtor's default should be. Similarly, the preparatory history sheds little light on the meaning of the requirement of adduced evidence. Clearly, much will depend on the particular facts of the case and it is difficult to formulate a fixed standard of proof of default. However, some indicators as to the meaning of the requirement of adduced evidence can be found in Article 13 and its preliminary draft.

At the third Plenary Session of the Joint Session of the UNIDROIT Committee of governmental experts for the preparation of the Convention's draft, it was agreed that the reference to '*prima facia* evidence in the chapeau of the Article was not a sufficiently high standard considering the effects of the remedies envisaged'.[237] It was also agreed to delete the words '*prima facia*' in Article 13(1).[238] Furthermore, a number of delegates indicated that the word 'clear' instead of '*prima facia*' could be acceptable, but, in the end, it was decided not to include it at all. This drafting history may suggest, and it has been argued that, the standard of proof of default should not be lower than in the actual trial and that the creditor must 'actually demonstrate that a default occurred'.[239] Indeed, the forms of speedy relief

[237] See *Diplomatic Conference* (n 207) 593.
[238] *Ibid* 594.
[239] Cuniberti (n 215) 85.

under Article 13 and the Protocols, such as surrender of possession and sale, provide the creditor with powerful remedies that can significantly change the debtor's position. A low standard of proving the debtor's default leading to such changes in its position is difficult to justify.

At the same time, this does not mean that the standard of proof should be as high as that applicable at the actual trial. Clearly, the relief is granted 'pending final determination' and even if, in practice, the parties choose not to initiate the full trial, the possibility of a substantive hearing of the merits should continue to exist. For this reason, it can be argued that the standard of proof cannot be the same as that at the actual trial since it would render the trial unnecessary.[240] Another reason for this suggestion is that the court granting relief must reach its decision quickly and, therefore, cannot be expected to examine the complex facts and evidence gathered by the creditor in detail. However, taking into account the potency of forms of speedy relief and their effect on the debtor, it seems that while the standard of proof should be lower than that at the actual trial, it must still be reasonably high in order to protect the debtor's position.

VII. REMEDIES AVAILABLE UNDER THE PROTOCOLS

In addition to the Convention's remedies, each Protocol provides the creditor with the equipment-specific remedies to further enhance and strengthen its international interest in the case of the debtor's default and insolvency. The following sections examine the remedies of de-registration and export of aircraft objects and export and physical transfer of railway objects, and consider the issues of the public service exemptions relating to railway objects and space assets. The chapter also examines alternative sets of remedial rules exercisable by the creditor in the case of the debtor's insolvency.

A. Equipment-specific Remedies

i. Aircraft Protocol: De-Registration; Export and Physical Transfer of the Aircraft Object from the Territory in Which It is Situated

Once an aircraft is repossessed, a creditor[241] may wish to move it to another country if, for example, it considers that the sale of the object in that country is likely to generate greater proceeds and help reduce or discharge

[240] Goode (n 12) 71.

[241] The remedies under the Protocols are not confined to secured creditors and can be exercised by all creditors, eg conditional sellers and lessors.

the debt. To achieve this objective, the creditor will have to ensure that a purchaser is able to register as the new owner of the aircraft in the country of the aircraft's new nationality. This registration, however, will not be possible until the aircraft is de-registered or deleted from the register where it is currently registered because the Chicago Convention, to which many countries are Contracting Parties, prohibits dual registration of aircraft nationality.[242] To assist the creditor, the Aircraft Protocol equips it with two separate remedies exercisable in addition to the Convention's remedies.[243] Article IX(1) of the Protocol stipulates that the creditor may: (a) procure the de-registration of the aircraft from the nationality register; and (b) procure the export and physical transfer of the aircraft object from the territory in which it is situated to another country.[244] This process does not involve de-registration of the aircraft from the records of the IR where the interests held in it are registered. The process of de-registration is primarily concerned with the deletion of the aircraft from the records of a national registry authority maintaining an aircraft registry in a Contracting State.[245] Once the aircraft is de-registered from the current records of the registry authority, its new nationality can be re-registered in the registry authority of another country.[246]

The remedies of de-registration and export of the aircraft object cannot be exercised without the debtor's consent but there is no need to stipulate for this consent in the international interest agreement because it can be obtained at any time.[247] De-registration and export can affect the position of other creditors holding interests in the aircraft object. For this reason, Article IX(2) of the Protocol requires the enforcing creditor to obtain prior written consent of the holder of any registered interest ranking in priority to that of the de-registering creditor. Similar to other remedies, de-registration

[242] Art 18 of the Convention on International Civil Aviation, adopted at Chicago on 7 December 1944. The Chicago Convention came into force on 4 April 1947. There are currently 190 Contracting States to the Chicago Convention. The list of Contracting States is available at www.icao.int/publications/Pages/doc7300.aspx (last visited April 2017).

[243] For a detailed analysis of the remedies of de-registration and export, see D Gerber and D Walton, 'De-registration and Export Remedies under the Cape Town Convention' (2014) *Cape Town Convention Journal* 49.

[244] De-registration can only be exercised in relation to an aircraft as a whole because it is registered for the purposes of nationality as such and there is no need to employ de-registration in relation to aircraft engines. In contrast, the remedy of export can be exercised in relation to aircraft and its engines which explains the reference to 'aircraft objects' in Art IX(1)(b) of the Protocol. See Goode (n 12) 181.

[245] Art (2)(o) of the Protocol defines 'registry authority' as the national authority of the Contracting State maintaining an aircraft register and responsible for the registration and de-registration of aircraft in accordance with the Chicago Convention.

[246] Art 18 of the Chicago Convention.

[247] Art IX(1) of the Aircraft Protocol.

and export must be exercised in a commercially reasonable manner.[248] As noted, the remedy shall be deemed to be exercised in a commercially reasonable manner if it is exercised in conformity with a provision of the agreement unless it is manifestly unreasonable.[249] The provision is likely to be considered manifestly unreasonable if it contradicts an established international commercial practice.

The Protocol provides for two alternative routes which can be utilised to procure de-registration and export of the aircraft object from the territory in which it is situated. These routes can only be used by the creditor if the Contracting State, ie the State of the aircraft registration, has made the relevant declaration under the Protocol. First, to achieve de-registration and export of the aircraft, the creditor can employ the 'court route' under Article X(6) of the Protocol.[250] This route obliges the registry authority and other administrative authorities in the Contracting State to make de-registration and export available to the creditor provided that it obtains speedy relief under Article 13 CTC.[251] Speedy relief must be obtained from the court in the State of the aircraft registration or from a foreign court whose jurisdiction is recognised by the court where de-registration and export are sought.

Once speedy relief is obtained, the creditor must notify the relevant authorities of: (a) the grant of speedy relief and (b) that the creditor is entitled to procure these remedies in accordance with the Convention.[252] De-registration and export must be made available to the creditor 'no later than five working days' after the authorities are notified.[253] The creditor will be 'entitled to procure' de-registration and export in accordance with the Convention when the 'circumstances specified' in Chapter III CTC, dealing

[248] Art IX(3) of the Aircraft Protocol disapplies Art 8(3) CTC in relation to aircraft objects and provides that 'any remedy given by the Convention in relation to an aircraft object shall be exercised in a commercially reasonable manner'. On the one hand, it can be argued that since the remedies of de-registration and export are not 'given by the Convention' in that they are available under the Protocol, the requirement of commercial reasonableness should not apply to them. On the other hand, if Art IX(3) is interpreted broadly in that it imposes the requirement of commercial reasonableness to the exercise of all remedies 'in relation to an aircraft object', this would suggest that the remedies of de-registration and export should be exercised in accordance with this requirement. This view seems preferable because the Convention's remedies are not equipment specific and the reference to the remedies 'in relation to an aircraft object' in Art IX(3) of the Protocol must support the broader view.

[249] Art IX(3) of the Aircraft Protocol.

[250] Although the exercise of Art IX of the Aircraft Protocol is not predetermined on a declaration, the enforcement of Art X, providing for the court route to de-registration and export, is premised on the declaration under Art XXX(2) of the Protocol.

[251] Due to a drafting error, Art X(6)(a) of the Aircraft Protocol mistakenly refers to Art IX(1) instead of Art 13 CTC. The confusion is clarified by the Official Commentary. See Goode (n 12) 184. For the discussion on speedy relief see the discussion above.

[252] Art X(6)(a) of the Aircraft Protocol.

[253] Art X(6)(a) of the Aircraft Protocol.

with default remedies, are satisfied.[254] This means, among other things, that the creditor must demonstrate that the debtor is in default in accordance with Article 11 CTC.[255] The Protocol further buttresses the obligation of the authority to make the remedies available to the creditor by requiring it to 'expeditiously co-operate' and 'assist' the creditor in the exercise of such remedies. The co-operation and assistance, however, should not affect any applicable aviation safety laws and regulations.[256]

The second route, also known as the 'IDERA route' can be invoked under Articles IX(5), (6) and XIII of the Protocol. Provided that a Contracting State has made a declaration that it will apply Article XIII of the Protocol,[257] the debtor can issue an irrevocable de-registration and export request authorisation (IDERA) and submit it for recording by the relevant registry authority.[258] The IDERA should indicate the sole person in whose favour the authorisation has been issued or name its certified designee.[259] Only the authorised party or its certified designee should be able to procure de-registration and export of the aircraft object, which should be done in accordance with the authorisation and applicable aviation safety laws and regulations.[260] Once the IDERA is issued, it cannot be revoked by the debtor without the written consent of the authorised party.

Finally, if the Contracting State has not made the required declaration, the creditor cannot rely on either of these routes, but it can still submit the IDERA to the registry authority.[261] In this case, the registry authority will be bound to honour its request provided that the authorised party complies with three requirements. First, it should observe any applicable safety laws and regulations.[262] Secondly, the IDERA should be properly submitted by the authorised party.[263] There is no indication what should amount to a proper submission, but the form of the IDERA annexed to the Protocol can probably be used as an example. According to this form, the IDERA should name the issuer of the request and the authorised party; identify the aircraft object by the manufacturer's name, serial number and registration mark or number; and indicate that the authorised party is entitled to procure de-registration and export without the issuer's consent. Thirdly, the registry authority may require the authorised party to certify that all registered

[254] Art IX(1) of the Aircraft Protocol.

[255] Goode (n 12) 183.

[256] Art X(6)(b), (7) of the Aircraft Protocol.

[257] Art XIII(1), Art XXX(1) of the Aircraft Protocol.

[258] Art XIII(2) of the Aircraft Protocol.

[259] Art XIII(3) of the Aircraft Protocol.

[260] Art XIII(3) of the Aircraft Protocol.

[261] Art IX(5) of the Aircraft Protocol. This is because the availability of these remedies under Art IX(1) is not conditioned on any declaration.

[262] Art IX(5) of the Aircraft Protocol.

[263] Art IX(5)(a) of the Aircraft Protocol.

interests ranking in priority to that of the creditor, in whose favour the authorisation has been issued, have been discharged or that the holders of such interests have consented to the de-registration and export.[264] If the secured creditor proposes to de-register and export the aircraft without leave of the court, it should give reasonable prior notice in writing to the interested persons[265] about the proposed de-registration and export.[266]

The IDERA route has recently been used in the *Spicejet* case where the debtor/lessee executed the IDERA in favour of the creditor/lessor in relation to several aircraft registered in the Indian Civil Aviation Register (ICAR).[267] Following the lessee's default (failure to pay rentals), the lessor terminated the lease and requested the Director General of Civil Aviation (DGCA) to de-register the aircraft from ICAR and to issue an export certificate of airworthiness enabling the lessor to export the aircraft. In accordance with the requirements of Article IX(5) and Article XIII(3) of the Aircraft Protocol, the lessor informed the DGCA that it had acted as the sole authorised person entitled to invoke de-registration and export and that the holders of prior ranking registered interests had provided their consent. The lessee refused to surrender the certificate of registration and the DGCA failed to de-register the aircraft. In addition, the lessee claimed that the lessor had failed to obtain the consent of all prior ranking interests because it had not provided evidence that the holders of non-registrable rights and interests arising under Article 39 CTC had agreed to the de-registration and export.

It was correctly held by the High Court in New Delhi that Article IX(5)(b) of the Protocol only required the consent of prior ranking *registered* interests and this excluded *non-registrable* rights and interests. Crucially, the court held that once the requirements for the IDERA route were met, the relevant authority did not have the discretion and ought to de-register the aircraft from the national registry.[268]

ii. The Luxembourg Protocol: Export and Physical Transfer of Railway Objects and the Public Service Exemption

Similar to the Aircraft Protocol, Article VII of the Luxembourg Protocol provides for the remedy of export and physical transfer of railway rolling stock exercisable by all creditors in addition to the Convention's remedies.[269]

[264] Art IX(5) of the Aircraft Protocol.

[265] See Art 1(m) CTC for the definition of 'interested person' and the discussion above.

[266] Art IX(6) of the Aircraft Protocol. The requirement of notice follows that of Art 8(4) CTC.

[267] *Awas 39423 Ireland Ltd & Ors v Directorate General of Civil Aviation & Anr* (WP(C) 871/2015) and *Wilmington Trust SP Services Limited v Directorate General of Civil Aviation & Anr* (WP(C) 747/2015).

[268] *Ibid* para 23.3.

[269] Art VII(1) of the Luxembourg Protocol.

The creditor can transport the railway rolling stock from the territory in which it is situated if the debtor and any holder of a registered interest ranking in priority to that of the creditor consent to the exercise of this remedy.[270] In addition, the secured creditor, intending to exercise this remedy extra-judicially, must send notice of the proposed export to interested persons.[271] The Protocol requires a Contracting State to ensure that the relevant administrative authority expeditiously cooperates and assists the creditor in exercising this remedy, but this obligation is subject to the applicable safely laws and regulations.[272]

One of the most difficult issues which had to be resolved by the Protocol's drafters relates to the fact that besides being valuable assets against which finance can be raised, railway objects are exceptionally important in the transportation of passengers and freight.[273] The repossession of a railway object can cause great disruption to the carriage of passengers and goods, which may have negative economic and political consequences for the Contracting States.[274] Some balance had to be struck between the interests of the creditor and the interests of the general public and Contracting States. The discussions on the conflict between the necessity to keep trains running irrespective of the debtor's default and the availability of adequate remedies for the creditor resulted in the 'public service exemption'—an unusual solution, but not unknown to some jurisdictions.[275] Under the public service exemption, a Contracting State can declare that it will continue to apply the rules of its domestic law which preclude, suspend or govern the exercise of the Convention's and the Protocol's remedies relating to the railway rolling stock habitually used for the purpose of providing a service of public importance.[276] In effect, this may mean that the creditor may be deprived of all the Convention's and the Protocol's remedies. Clearly, this can hinder the availability and the cost of credit, unless the interest of the creditor is adequately protected.

It can be argued that since the Contracting State will have to submit such a declaration, the creditor will be aware that its interest in the railway object

[270] Art VII(1), (2) of the Luxembourg Protocol.

[271] Art VII(6) of the Luxembourg Protocol. See Art 1(m) CTC for the definition of 'interested persons'.

[272] Art VII(5) of the Luxembourg Protocol.

[273] B Bodungen and K Schott, 'The Public Service Exemption under the Luxembourg Rail Protocol: A German Perspective' (2007) *Unif L Rev* 573, 577.

[274] Bodungen and Schott (n 273) 577.

[275] H Rosen, 'The Luxembourg Rail Protocol: A Major Advance for the Railway Industry' (2007) *Unif L Rev* 427, 441 referring to the UK Railway Act 1993, s 30.

[276] Art XXV(I) of the Luxembourg Protocol. For an insightful discussion see R Goode, *Official Commentary to the Convention on International Interests in Mobile Equipment and Luxembourg Protocol Thereto on Matters Specific to Railway Rolling Stock* (Rome, UNIDROIT 2008) 108–12.

may not be adequately protected in this State. The creditor will then be able to assess the financing risks and either increase the interest rate or refuse to provide a loan altogether.[277] Furthermore, the declaration can only be made in relation to railway rolling stock habitually used to provide a service of public importance. Whether the object is used habitually (or occasionally) and whether it provides a service of public importance (and not merely interest) is a question of fact and must be decided by the Contracting State. When considering these questions, factors such as the volume of traffic, perception of public importance of the service in the Contracting State, availability of other services or means of transport and, in the case of carriage of freight, the nature of transported goods, can be relevant.[278]

The Protocol provides for a solution which can help adequately protect the creditor's interest while keeping the railway object in operation. Under this scheme, once the debtor is in default, any person, including a governmental or other public authority, can take possession or control of, or use, the railway object.[279] This person should preserve and maintain the railway object until the time when its possession, control or use can be restored to the creditor.[280] This means that if the object deteriorates or is left uninsured, the person responsible for its preservation and maintenance will be held liable for the creditor's loss. Most importantly, even though the creditor cannot take possession and dispose of the railway object, the said person should pay to the creditor either: (a) such amount as that person would pay under the rules of the law of the Contracting State or (b) the market lease rental in respect of such railway rolling stock, whichever is the greater.[281]

This arrangement can adequately protect the creditor's interest because it enables the creditor to receive the payment to which it would have been entitled under the agreement with the debtor even though it cannot take possession and dispose of the object.[282] If the creditor is paid the amount of lease rentals, it should be calculated based on what would be available to the creditor in the current market, which may differ from the amount agreed in the contract between the creditor and the debtor. This way, the creditor is placed in the position in which it would have been had it repossessed and leased the object itself.[283] The creditor's interest is further protected by the requirement that the first payment must be made within 10 calendar days of the date on which such power is exercised by the authorised person and that

[277] Rosen (n 275) 439.
[278] Goode (n 276) 109.
[279] Art XXV(2) of the Luxembourg Protocol.
[280] Art XXV(2) of the Luxembourg Protocol.
[281] Art XXV(3) of the Luxembourg Protocol.
[282] H Rosen, 'Public Service and the Cape Town Convention' (2013) *Cape Town Convention Journal* 131, 142.
[283] Rosen (n 282) 142.

all subsequent payments must be made on the first day of each month.[284] If the sum paid to the creditor exceeds the amount owed to it, the surplus should be distributed among holders of subsequent interests in the order of priority.[285]

Although this scheme can provide a much needed balance between the interests of the creditor and that of the general public, some Contracting States were not ready to accept it.[286] To allow a Contracting State to block repossession without compensating the creditor, the Protocol permits it to declare that it will not apply the rules on payment to the creditor in those cases where it may be precluded from exercising the remedies in relation to the railway objects.[287] But in making such a declaration, the Contracting State is required to take into consideration the interests of the creditor and the effect of the declaration on the availability of the credit.[288] Finally, even if the Contracting State makes such a declaration, the authorised person may still agree with the creditor to utilise the scheme designed under the Protocol.[289]

iii. The Space Protocol: Limitations on Remedies and Public Service Exemption

The Space Protocol modifies the Convention's remedies to reflect the needs of the space industry in a number of ways. For instance, Article XIX of the Protocol stipulates that parties can contractually agree to place command codes and related data and materials with another person to afford the creditor an opportunity to take possession, establish control over or operate the space asset.[290] This provision limits the enforcement of remedies because it will not be possible for the creditor to take control or sell an orbiting space asset unless the necessary command codes and materials are made available to it.[291] Article XVII(3) also provides for a situation where the effect of enforcing the creditor's international interest in a space asset would be to damage the international interest of another creditor held in a separate but physically linked space asset.[292] This provision reflects the nature of certain space assets, such as modular space stations comprising several separately

[284] Art XXV(3) of the Luxembourg Protocol.
[285] Art XXV(3) of the Luxembourg Protocol.
[286] Bodungen and Schott (n 273) 580.
[287] Art XXV(4) of the Luxembourg Protocol.
[288] Art XXV(6) of the Luxembourg Protocol.
[289] Art XXV(4) of the Luxembourg Protocol.
[290] This provision takes effect subject to Art XXVI of the Luxembourg Protocol according to which a Contracting State may apply its own laws regulating the placement of command codes. See M Sundahl (n 3) 99.
[291] Sundahl (n 3) 99.
[292] Art XVII(3) of the Space Protocol.

financed modules, which cannot be easily disassembled.[293] To this end, the Protocol provides that, unless parties agree otherwise, the creditor cannot enforce its international interest in a space asset that is physically linked with another space asset if this will harm or interfere with the operation of that other space asset. In order for this limitation on the enforceability of the creditor's remedies to apply, the international interest held in or sale in relation to that other space asset will have to be registered in the IR prior to the international interest being enforced.[294]

Finally, similar to the Luxembourg Protocol,[295] Article XXVII of the Space Protocol establishes certain remedial limitations in respect of the provision of public service. The enforcement of the creditor's remedies might lead to a significant disruption of public services, such as air traffic control, navigation and communications. To strike a balance between the need to protect the public interest and the creditor's interest, Article XXVII provides that if a public service provider[296] or the Contracting State register a public service notice[297] in the IR, the creditor will be precluded from exercising the Convention's and the Protocol's remedies that would make the space asset unavailable for providing the relevant public service.[298]

To overcome this limitation, the creditor will have to register a default notice in the IR, stating that the creditor may exercise its remedies if the debtor fails to cure the default within the suspension period.[299] The creditor must notify the debtor and the public service provider of the date of the registration of its default notice and the date of expiry of the suspension period.[300] The suspension period should last not less than three months and no more than six months from the date of the registration of the default notice by the creditor.[301] During the suspension period, the creditor, the debtor and the public service provider shall co-operate in good faith in order to find a 'commercially reasonable solution' that would permit the public service to continue.[302] If the default is not cured upon the end of the

[293] For a more detailed discussion see Sundahl (n 3) 100–02.

[294] Art XVII(3) of the Space Protocol. See Goode (n 28) 450–52.

[295] See, generally, H Rosen, 'Public Service and the Cape Town Convention' (2013) *Cape Town Convention Journal* 131.

[296] For the definition of a 'public service provider', see Art XXVII(2)(b) of the Space Protocol.

[297] 'Public service notice' means a notice, registrable in the IR, describing the services, which under the contract are intended to support the provision of public service. The notion of 'public service' must be interpreted in accordance with the law of the Contracting State. See Art XXVII(2)(a), the Protocol.

[298] Art XXVII(3) of the Space Protocol.

[299] Art XVII(3), (4) of the Space Protocol.

[300] Art XVII(6) of the Space Protocol.

[301] Art XVII(4) of the Space Protocol. The Contracting State must make the declaration under Art XLI(I) of the Space Protocol at the time of ratification, acceptance, approval or accession to the Protocol specifying the duration of the suspension period.

[302] Art XVII(7)(a) of the Space Protocol.

suspension period, the creditor will be able to exercise its remedies under the Convention and the Protocol.[303]

B. Remedies on Insolvency

i. General

In some cases, the creditor will need to enforce its remedies when the debtor becomes insolvent. This may be difficult because domestic legal systems tend to impose restrictions and compulsory freezes on the enforcement of the creditors' remedies in such circumstances.[304] The ability to exercise a remedy may depend on the type of the insolvency proceeding involving the debtor. For example, under English law, one of the purposes of administration is to rescue the company.[305] This may require the administrator to dispose of charged objects and their repossession by the chargee may prevent it from achieving its objective.[306] For this reason, the chargee may not be able to exercise its remedies unless leave of the court or the administrator's permission is obtained.[307]

In some legal systems, the insolvency legislation freezes the insolvent debtor's assets and automatically stays all actions against the debtor's objects.[308] The obstacles created by insolvency laws of various domestic legal systems are often underpinned by policies such as the need to promote equality for creditors during the debtor's insolvency, rescue the company as a going concern,[309] and protect the economy and jobs.[310] These restrictions

303 Art XVII(8) of the Space Protocol.

304 Wood (n 7) 385.

305 Para 3(1), Sch B1, Insolvency Act 1986 indicates that the administrator's main objectives are: (a) to rescue the company as a going concern; or (b) to achieve a better result for the company's creditors as a whole than would be likely if the company were wound up; or (c) to realise property to make a distribution to one or more secured or preferential creditors. See also *In re Atlantic Computer Systems plc* [1990] BCC 859; P Fidler, 'Administration: Leave to Enforce Security on Property Rights' (1991) *JIBL* 78, 79.

306 M Elland-Goldsmith, 'Real Security Over Personal Property in English Law' (1995) *IBLJ* 145, 167.

307 Para 43, Sch B1, Insolvency Act 1986. For example, leave is likely to be refused if enforcement of secured creditor's interest is likely to cause a disruption that would be out of proportion to the loss which it would suffer if the leave were not granted. See Wood (n 7) 404; *Innovate Logistics Ltd (In admin) v Sunberry Properties Ltd* [2009] BCC 164.

308 This is the position under the US Bankruptcy Code. See M Edelman in Crans and Nath (n 231) 1073–82. For a suggestion that collective exercise of the exception to this rule by aircraft financiers under s 1110 of the Bankruptcy Code may help such creditors to eliminate market competition and force the debtor to pay higher-than-market-rate rental payments under leases, see J Janaitis, 'Bankruptcy Collides with Antitrust: The Need for a Prohibition Against Using S. 1110 Protections Collectively' (2008) 25 *Emory Bankr Dev* J 197.

309 See, generally, V Finch, 'Re-Invigorating Corporate Rescue' (2003) *JBL* 572.

310 See, generally, Wood (n 7) 363.

significantly impair the strength of the security interest. It is clear that if the remedies are not available to the secured creditor in the debtor's insolvency, they are not available when they are most needed.[311]

The need for clear rules and assurance of protection of the creditor's rights in the debtor's insolvency is particularly acute when the type of equipment governed by the Convention is taken into account. First, the level of financing of aircraft, railway and space objects is exceptionally high and debtors usually rely on secured borrowing or leasing to acquire these types of equipment. Secondly, such objects have a long economic life requiring long term financing. Thirdly, despite a long economic life expectancy, these objects are susceptible to rapid deterioration if not maintained regularly. This feature can be particularly relevant if the debtor is involved in lengthy reorganisation proceedings. During this period, the debtor may not be able to properly maintain the object and the creditor may be precluded from repossessing it. Finally, such objects can move across the borders or leave the Earth altogether, complicating their location and repossession.[312] For these reasons, uncertainty with respect to the remedies exercisable in the debtor's insolvency can significantly impede the availability and cost of the credit.

The aims and policies underpinning the domestic insolvency laws and the need to protect the creditors' interests can often clash, making the degree of protection afforded by an insolvency regime to the creditor and the debtor a sensitive issue for domestic jurisdictions.[313] This is why the Protocols' insolvency provisions come in several alternative sets of rules and a Contracting State may adopt any of these alternatives. Whichever alternative the Contracting State selects, it must be adopted in its entirety.[314] The Contracting State may choose to apply separate alternatives to different types of insolvency proceedings. However, the parties can exclude the application of the chosen alternative by a written agreement.[315] All three Protocols and the draft MAC Protocol provide for Alternative A, the 'hard' or rule-based version, and Alternative B, the 'soft' or discretion-based version.[316] In addition, the Luxembourg Protocol adds Alternative C to

[311] Goode (n 12) 458.

[312] A Sabino, 'Flying the Unfriendly Skies: A Year of Reorganizing Airlines, Aircraft Lessors, and the Bankruptcy Code' (1992) 57 *J Air L Com* 841, 843–44.

[313] For an insightful discussion of the goals of insolvency law and the need to maintain the balance between the interests of secured creditors and other stakeholders at the international level, see I Mevorach, *Insolvency within Multinational Enterprise Groups* (Oxford, OUP 2009) 111–12, 120–23.

[314] Goode (n 12) 459.

[315] Art IV(3) of the Aircraft Protocol.

[316] See, generally, Goode (n 12) 458–63. See also K van Zwieten, 'The Insolvency Provisions of the Cape Town Convention and Protocols: Historical and Economic Perspectives' (2012) *Cape Town Convention Journal* 53.

these options.[317] Alternative C is also present in the draft MAC Protocol.[318] The aim of these rules is, generally, to ensure that if the insolvency-related event occurs,[319] the creditor can either: (a) repossess the object or (b) ensure that the insolvency administrator or the debtor, as the case may be, cures all past defaults and undertakes to perform its future obligations.[320] The insolvency regime under the Protocols will only apply if the Contracting State, that is a primary insolvency jurisdiction,[321] makes a declaration to this effect.[322] Alternatively, the Contracting State may choose not to make a declaration and to apply its own insolvency law instead.

ii. Alternative A

Alternative A establishes a strong creditor-protective legal regime exercisable in the debtor's insolvency. It constitutes a major inroad into policies of domestic insolvency laws such as company rescue, equal treatment of creditors and protection of jobs. The Protocols recognise that the creditor-orientated insolvency scheme may be a sensitive issue for domestic legal systems and do not require the Contracting States to subscribe to it. Nevertheless, most declaring Contracting States so far, with the exception of Mexico, have chosen Alternative A as the relevant insolvency regime under the Aircraft Protocol.[323] This can be explained on the following grounds, which are also relevant in the context of other types of equipment covered by the Convention.

First, the aircraft, railroad and space industries are widely considered by States as strategically important economy sectors and their development

[317] Art XI of the Aircraft Protocol; Art IX of the Luxembourg Protocol; Art XXI of the Space Protocol; Art X of the draft MAC Protocol. See also R Goode, 'International Interests in Mobile Equipment: A Transnational Juridical Concept' (2003) 15 *Bond L Rev* 9, 18.

[318] Art X of the draft MAC Protocol.

[319] Art I(m) of the Aircraft Protocol defines an insolvency-related event as: (i) the commencement of the insolvency proceedings; or (ii) the declared intention to suspend or actual suspension of payments by the debtor where the creditor's right to institute insolvency proceedings or to exercise Convention's remedies is prevented or suspended.

[320] Insolvency administrator means a person authorised to administer the reorganisation or liquidation, including one authorised on an interim basis, and includes a debtor in possession if permitted by the applicable insolvency law. See Art 1(k) CTC.

[321] This would be a Contracting State in which the center of the debtor's main interests (COMI) is situated. See Art I(n) of the Aircraft Protocol. The term COMI follows the same concept used in European insolvency law. See The Legal Advisory Panel of the Aviation Working Group: Practitioners' Guide to the Cape Town Convention and the Aircraft Protocol (Aviation Working Group 2015) 128–29.

[322] Art XI(1), Art XXX(3) of the Aircraft Protocol. See also R Goode, 'The Cape Town Convention on International Interests in Mobile Equipment: A Driving Force for International Asset-Based Financing' (2003) 36 *UCC LJ* 2 Art 1.

[323] The full list of declaring Contracting States is available at http://www.unidroit.org/depositary-2001capetown-aircraft?id=450 (last visited April 2017).

is critical to the economic growth of nations. This is particularly true in the context of developing countries, where the growth of these industries depends on the existence of a clear legal framework and considerable injections of finance. But this issue is equally topical in developed economies, which are experiencing ever-increasing volumes of passenger and freight transportation. This is why it is vital to encourage financing and ensure that these industries are supplied with up-to-date equipment.

Secondly, because these industries require continuous inflows of very high levels of financing, they rely on external secured borrowing and leasing, and the role of State financing gradually decreases. It is clear that to ensure that creditors continue to finance the acquisition of equipment, they must have confidence in their ability to quickly repossess it and/or obtain repayment in the case of the debtor's insolvency. This is why a strong creditor-protective insolvency regime is indispensable in securing financial support from creditors.

Finally, the creditor-orientated Alternative A can help prevent the debtor's insolvency. This is because the creditor, confident in its ability to effectively enforce its remedies in the debtor's insolvency, will be more likely to provide the debtor with finance on favourable terms. The availability of affordable finance can reduce instances of the debtor's insolvency and promote industry growth. For these reasons, a Contracting State, opting for Alternative A under the Aircraft Protocol, is considered to have made one of the most important 'qualifying' declarations[324] entitling it to obtain significant financial incentives, such as export credit fee discounts, provided under the Organisation for Economic Co-operation and Development Aircraft Sector Understanding (OECD ASU).[325]

Alternative A allows the creditor to enforce its remedies, out of court, on the expiration of either: (a) the end of the waiting period; or (b) the date on which the creditor would be entitled to possession of the object if this provision of the Protocol did not apply, whichever of these dates is earlier. The Protocol refers to these mutually exclusive periods as the 'specified time'.[326] Provided that within this specified time the debtor: (i) cures all defaults; and (ii) agrees to perform its future obligations under the agreement,[327]

[324] *Practitioners' Guide* (n 321) 129–30.

[325] OECD ASU document is available at www.oecd.org/officialdocuments/publicdisplaydocumentpdf/?cote=tad/asu(2011)1&doclanguage=en. Last viewed April 2017. Most declaring Contracting States, with the exception of Mexico, chose Alternative A as the governing insolvency regime under the Aircraft Protocol. The full list of declaring Contracting States can be viewed at http://www.unidroit.org/depositary-2001capetown-aircraft?id=450 (last visited April 2017).

[326] Art XI, Alternative A(7) of the Aircraft Protocol.

[327] Art XI, Alternative A(2) and (7) of the Protocol; Art IX, Alternative A(3), of the Luxembourg Protocol and Art XXI, Alternative A(2), of the Space Protocol are drafted in similar terms.

it can retain the possession of the object. Accordingly, this rule puts the creditor in the position where it can either obtain the benefit of the agreement in that the defaults are cured and contractual obligations continue to be performed *or* enforce its remedies without the intervention of the domestic insolvency law restrictions and without the need to apply to court. In this regard, Alternative A has the effect of displacing Article 30(3)(b) CTC because it precludes the applicable insolvency law from imposing automatic stays or freezes aimed at stopping the creditor from exercising the remedies available to it under the Convention and the Protocols after the expiration of the specified period.

The duration of the waiting period, during which the creditor's enforcement rights are effectively stayed, must be indicated in the Contracting State's declaration, stating its choice of the relevant Alternative.[328] For example, China, Jordan and New Zealand, among other countries, have declared that they will apply Alternative A to all types of insolvency proceedings and that the waiting period will be 60 days. The waiting period in Nigeria is 30 days and in Malaysia it is 40 days.[329] The meaning of the second option, ie the date on which the creditor would be entitled to possession, is not quite clear. Under this option, the enforcement of the creditor's right can be stayed until 'the date on which the creditor would be entitled to possession of the aircraft object if this provision of the Protocol did not apply'.[330] It seems that in this situation, recourse must be made to the applicable insolvency law in order to ascertain the waiting period or any other date on which the creditor would be entitled to possession under that applicable law. For instance, if the Contracting State made a declaration, specifying that the length of the waiting period will be 60 days, but under its applicable insolvency law the aircraft financier is entitled to a shorter waiting period of 30 days, the creditor may be entitled to enforce its remedies on the expiration of the shorter period. This should be the case, because the effect of this rule is that the earlier of the two options should prevail.

During the specified period, the enforcement of the creditor's remedies is stayed and the insolvency administrator or the debtor is given breathing space to assess its position, cure past defaults,[331] and agree to perform future contractual obligations or give possession of the object to the creditor.[332]

[328] The declarations must be made under Art XXX(3) of the Aircraft Protocol, Art XXVII of the Luxembourg Protocol and Art XLI(4) of the Space Protocol.

[329] The list of countries opting for Alternative A is available at www.unidroit.org/depositary-2001capetown-aircraft?id=454 (last visited April 2017).

[330] Art XI, Alternative A(2)(b) of the Aircraft Protocol.

[331] This does not include default relating to the opening of the insolvency proceedings, because this type of default cannot be cured. Art XI, Alternative A(7) of the Aircraft Protocol.

[332] Art XI, Alternative A(2), (7) of the Aircraft Protocol, Art IX, Alternative A(7) of the Luxembourg Protocol is drafted in similar terms. Since it may be impossible to take possession of space assets, Art XXI, Alternative A(8) of the Space Protocol adds that not only possession,

At the same time, even if the lessor regains its possession of the object, it cannot be prevented from exercising any other remedies against the debtor. For instance, the lessor can still demand payment of unpaid rentals accrued at least up to the moment when the lease was rejected by the debtor.[333]

If the debtor retains the object, cures past defaults, and agrees to perform future obligations under the agreement, but then later defaults, the question can arise as to whether the debtor is entitled to a new waiting period allowing it to cure the default. The Aircraft Protocol states that no second waiting period is allowed in respect of a default in the performance of future obligations under the agreement.[334] It is submitted that this rule should apply irrespective of whether the fresh default occurs during the original waiting period or after its expiration. This must be the case because allowing the debtor to invoke a second waiting period in relation to a fresh default occurring *during* the original waiting period, will have the effect of extending the waiting period without the creditor's consent. Similarly, a second waiting period in relation to the default, occurring *after* the original waiting period expires, will have the effect of granting the debtor a virtually continuous waiting period for each fresh default. This can prevent the creditor from repossessing the object and contravene the purpose of the creditor-protective regime of Alternative A.

What is less clear is whether the debtor, who cures the defaults, agrees to perform its future obligations under the agreement and commits a fresh default during the specified period, should be given an opportunity to cure this new default for as long as this period continues. In other words, should the debtor have the benefit of full duration of the specified period to cure any subsequent defaults? Alternatively, once a fresh default occurs, can the creditor cut short the specified period and repossess the object? Alternative A does not expressly address this situation. However, Alternative A(7) indicates that the insolvency administrator or the debtor may retain possession of the aircraft object where it has cured all defaults and agreed to perform its future obligations 'by the time specified',[335] that is, either by the end of the declared waiting period or the relevant date under

but also control over space assets can be retained by the insolvency administrator or the debtor provided that it cures all defaults and agrees to perform all future obligations by the end of the specified period.

[333] Alternative A(9) states that no exercise of remedies permitted by the Convention or the Aircraft Protocol may be prevented or delayed after the expiration of the waiting period. Art 12 CTC states that the creditor may exercise any additional remedies permitted by the applicable law as long as they are not inconsistent with its requirements. Accordingly, if the applicable law allows the lessor to claim payment of the unpaid rental payments, accruing before termination of the lease, the lessor should be able to claim such amounts under Alternative A of the Aircraft Protocol.

[334] Art XI, Alternative A(7) of the Aircraft Protocol.

[335] Art XI, Alternative A(7) of the Aircraft Protocol.

the applicable law, whichever is the earlier. In addition, Alternative A(7) provides that within this specified period, the insolvency administrator or the debtor must cure 'all defaults'.[336] There is no indication that all such defaults must have occurred around the same time, namely the time when the insolvency-related event happened and the waiting period or the relevant period under the applicable law started to run. Accordingly, these defaults may include subsequent defaults which occurred later but still within the waiting period. This wording of Alternative A(7) seems to indicate that the debtor should be entitled to retain the opportunity to cure the original and any subsequent defaults provided that this is accomplished before the expiration of the specified time.

It is suggested that this approach will also better reflect the principle of predictability underpinning the Convention. Since the duration of the specified time will be ascertained by the creditor at the time of the occurrence of insolvency-related event, it will be clear how long it will have to wait before enforcing its remedies. This means that subsequent defaults, which can be cured by the end of the specified time, should not unduly jeopardise the creditor's position. At the same time, allowing the debtor to continue curing all defaults until the specified time expires, will lead to clearer and predictable results because there will be no danger to the debtor that this period can be prematurely shortened. This should give the debtor confidence that provided all defaults are cured by the end of the specified time and future obligations continue to be performed, it can still retain the object.

Finally, the Protocol provides that although parties can derogate from or vary its selected provisions, this is not permitted in relation to Article XI(2)–(4),[337] which states, among other things, that the insolvency administrator or the debtor is required to return the possession of the object either by the end of the waiting period or in accordance with the relevant period under the applicable law. The express prohibition to derogate or vary these rules also seems to indicate that the length of the specified time, whether it is the waiting period or the period under the applicable law, should not be shortened or lifted by the creditor.[338] At the same time, while the Contracting States' declarations impose a clearly specified period, the position relating to the period under the applicable law may be more complicated. For instance, it may well be that the applicable law, whilst setting a certain period of time on the expiration of which the creditor is entitled to enforce its remedies, allows the creditor to lift or shorten this period on the

[336] Apart from the default constituted by the opening of the insolvency proceedings because it cannot be cured.

[337] Art IV(3) of the Aircraft Protocol.

[338] Art IV(3) of the Aircraft Protocol.

occurrence of specified events taking place within that period. This position under the applicable domestic law can have the result of entitling the creditor to cut the duration of that period under the Protocol.

Therefore, it is tentatively suggested that, in relation to the waiting period, the duration of which is stipulated in the Contracting State's declaration, the creditor should not be permitted to shorten such waiting period if the debtor commits new defaults, provided that all such defaults are cured and the debtor undertakes to continue to perform its future obligations under the agreement by the end of this period. However, it is also suggested that the result may be different if the 'specified time' has to be ascertained under the applicable domestic law. If the applicable domestic law permits the creditor to lift or shorten the duration of this specified period (for instance, due to the occurrence of fresh defaults), this may have the effect of cutting the originally set period and enabling the creditor to repossess the object sooner.

The equipment governed by the CTC is susceptible to rapid physical and commercial depreciation in the absence of adequate maintenance. For this reason, Alternative A expressly indicates that until the creditor is given an opportunity to take possession of the object, the insolvency administrator or the debtor must preserve and maintain the object and its value in accordance with the agreement.[339] Thus, the insolvency administrator or the debtor must ensure that the aircraft object remains in an airworthy condition, well maintained, repaired and insured and, possibly, kept in operation in order to preserve its value.[340] If the object's value diminishes, its condition deteriorates or the creditor's interest becomes otherwise unprotected, the creditor can apply for interim relief available under the applicable domestic law.[341] In this case, the Aircraft Protocol does not require the creditor to wait until the waiting period expires and it should be able to apply and, potentially, obtain an interim relief during such period. This can have the effect of shortening or lifting the waiting period or the relevant time under the applicable domestic law. This outcome can be justified on the ground that interim relief is normally granted when the circumstances require urgent intervention, and if the waiting period (or the period under the applicable law) could not be lifted, the interim relief might fail to protect the creditor's interest effectively.

Finally, Alternative A provides that de-registration and export of the aircraft object must be made available to it by the registry authority no later than five working days after the date on which the creditor notifies such

339 Art XI, Alternative A(5)(a) of the Aircraft Protocol.
340 Art XI, Alternative A(6) of the Aircraft Protocol.
341 Art XI, Alternative A(5)(b) of the Aircraft Protocol.

authorities that it is entitled to procure those remedies in accordance with the Convention.[342] The registry authority is also required to expeditiously co-operate with and assist the creditor in the exercise of these remedies in accordance with the applicable safety laws and regulations.[343]

iii. Alternative B

Instead of the creditor-protective, 'hard' or rule-based Alternative A, a declaring Contracting State may choose to apply a 'softer' or more debtor-protective Alternative B to the insolvency proceedings. Under Alternative B, upon the occurrence of an insolvency-related event, the debtor is required to give notice to the creditor indicating whether it will: (a) cure all defaults[344] and undertake to perform its future obligations under the agreement and related transaction documents or (b) give the creditor the opportunity to take possession of the object in accordance with the applicable law.[345] The debtor's notice should only be given upon the creditor's request and within the time specified in the Contracting State's declaration.[346] To this date, only one Contracting State has selected Alternative B and declared that the debtor's notice must be given to the creditor within contractually agreed time period.[347] Accordingly, the notification period may only start to run from the date of the creditor's request.[348] If the insolvency administrator or the debtor fails to notify the creditor about its decision, or if it notifies the creditor that it will give it the opportunity to take possession of the object but fails to do so, the creditor cannot repossess the object extra-judicially.[349]

In contrast with Alternative A, under Alternative B the creditor must proceed via the court and rely on its discretion to allow the repossession of the object. Moreover, the court can require the creditor to provide additional guarantees or comply with any terms imposed by it.[350] Since Alternative B involves a court application, the creditor has to provide evidence of its claims and proof that its international interest has been registered.[351] Accordingly,

[342] Art XI, Alternative A(8) of the Aircraft Protocol.

[343] Art XI, Alternative A(8) of the Aircraft Protocol.

[344] Similar to the position under Alternative A, 'all defaults' under Alternative B do not include a default constituted by the opening of insolvency proceedings. See Art XI, Alternative B(2)(a), of the Aircraft Protocol.

[345] Art XI, Alternative B(2) of the Aircraft Protocol.

[346] Art XI, Alternative B(2). The declaration should be made under Art XXX(3) of the Aircraft Protocol.

[347] See declaration by Mexico available at www.unidroit.org/depositary-2001capetown-aircraft?id=454 (last visited April 2017).

[348] Goode (n 12) 462.

[349] Art XI, Alternative B(5) of the Aircraft Protocol.

[350] Art XI, Alternative B(5) of the Aircraft Protocol.

[351] Art XI, Alternative B(4) of the Aircraft Protocol

although the registration of the international interest in the IR is not, generally, required for the purpose of the enforcement of remedies, it is essential if the creditor is required to proceed under Alternative B in the debtor's insolvency. Finally, Alternative B protects the debtor's position by precluding the creditor from taking possession and selling the object until the court reaches a decision concerning its claim and international interest.[352]

iv. Alternative C

In addition to Alternatives A and B available under all three Protocols, the Luxembourg Protocol adds Alternative C, drafted in terms similar to Alternative A.[353] Alternative C aims to achieve the same result, ie upon the occurrence of an insolvency-related event, to give the creditor the opportunity to either: (a) ensure that the debtor cures all defaults other than a default constituted by the opening of insolvency proceedings and promises to perform all future obligations under the agreement and related transaction documents; or (b) take possession of the railway rolling stock in accordance with the applicable laws.[354] But, under Alternative C, the waiting period is referred to as the 'cure period' and is specified to start on the date of the insolvency-related event.[355] The Protocol does not indicate the length of the cure period and delegates this issue to the Contracting States.[356]

In contrast to Alternative A, which does not envisage a court application, and Alternative B, which allows the creditor to apply to the court, Alternative C permits the insolvency administrator or the debtor to apply to the court for an order suspending its obligation to return the railway object.[357] The suspension period commences once the cure period ends and lasts until the expiration of the agreement or its renewal and on terms considered just by the court.[358] This means that in order to be eligible for the suspension period, the insolvency administrator or the debtor should apply to the court before the cure period expires.[359] The effect of the suspension order is that the creditor is precluded from repossessing the object during the suspension period. Moreover, once the insolvency administrator or the debtor makes the application, the creditor cannot take possession of the object, pending the court's decision.[360] To protect the creditor's interest,

[352] Art XI, Alternative B(6) of the Aircraft Protocol.

[353] Art IX, Alternative C of the Luxembourg Protocol.

[354] Alternative C(3) of the Luxembourg Protocol. Art X, Alternative C of the draft MAC Protocol is drafted in similar terms.

[355] Alternative C(3), (15), of the Luxembourg Protocol.

[356] Alternative C(15) of the Luxembourg Protocol.

[357] Alternative C(4) of the Luxembourg Protocol.

[358] Alternative C(4) of the Luxembourg Protocol.

[359] Alternative C(4) of the Luxembourg Protocol.

[360] Alternative C(5) of the Luxembourg Protocol.

the court order must provide that all sums, accruing to the creditor during the suspension period must be paid to it from the insolvency estate as they become due and that the insolvency administrator or the debtor must perform all other obligations arising during such period.[361] Accordingly, the insolvency administrator or the debtor will have to take measures to preserve and maintain the railway rolling stock and its value. In other respects Alternative C appears to follow Alternative A. Thus, during the cure period, the creditor is entitled to apply for interim relief available under the applicable law. Once the cure period expires, a second cure period cannot be imposed and the creditor cannot be precluded from exercising the remedies under the Convention and the Protocols.[362]

361 Alternative C(4) of the Luxembourg Protocol.
362 Alternative C(6), (8) of the Luxembourg Protocol.

Index

www.ingramcontent.com/pod-product-compliance
Lightning Source LLC
LaVergne TN
LVHW052301200926
848481LV00002B/430